SIR ROGUE

Books by Leslie Turner White

Me, Detective (*an autobiography*)

NOVELS:

Harness Bull
Homicide
River of No Return
Six Weeks South of Texas
Five Thousand Trojan Horses
Look Away, Look Away
Lord Johnnie
Magnus the Magnificent
The Highland Hawk
Sir Rogue

LESLIE TURNER WHITE

SIR ROGUE

CROWN PUBLISHERS, INC. NEW YORK

Copyright, 1954, by Leslie Turner White
Library of Congress Catalog Card Number: 54-6639

To
L. T. W., Jr.

MY DEAR SKIPPER:

It seems peculiarly fitting that I should dedicate this tale of high adventure to you, for as I watched you swagger across the lawn towards the bull pens, a few minutes ago, you seemed the very incarnation of the true Elizabethan adventurer.

I particularly admired your dogged but unhurried progress, laced with just the proper dash of swagger; I imagine Francis Drake walked like that when he sauntered from his game of bowls to "singe King Philip's beard." I noticed, too, the respectful way the great black bulls backed from the fence as you drew nigh, manifestly awed by your boldness and singleness of purpose. The Spaniards used to bow so before the approach of Captain Hawkins. Like those great men, you know no fear.

Aye, son, you belong to that peerless company of Gentleman Adventurers, and at the gallant age of eighteen months, you stand on the threshold of the Unknown. What wonderful worlds are yours to conquer! You're going to have a busy year! The hobby-horse is yet to be "broken," and you must swim this year. The "brooding forest" beyond the pastures harbors a host of mysteries, and the river beckons temptingly. The herons and the swans fill you with wonder; the scurrying little crabs, with delight.

With so much to explore, it will be a long time before you have interest in lesser heroes. But, alas, the years eventually slow us down and the horizons move closer, and our brave ship gathers barnacles in the lost lagoon of dreams. 'Tis then we turn to tales such as these. May that day be long in coming, but when as must it does, you will find this story fashioned especially for you by . . .

Your affectionate father,
LESLIE T. WHITE

At the White Anchors,
Virginia

SIR ROGUE

For the benefit of those readers who may have an interest in, or a curiosity about, the period covered by this novel, a few historical notes pertaining to some of the incidents herein will be found at the end of this volume.

1

It was back in the golden, boisterous days of good Queen Bess, towards the close of the year 1576, that five worried gentlemen, furtively masked and muffled, slipped singly through the darkened, fog-infested streets and into a clandestine little tavern on London's waterfront. Because their very lives and fortunes teetered in the balance, they had come to learn their fate from the lips of their agent, Captain Caleb Lymeburner, but it was a gratuitous coincidence that the dive in which they met so stealthily was named the Handcuff Inn, since the wily shipmaster was, technically, a fugitive from justice.

Howbeit, if this trifling happenstance troubled the five investors, legally (and now regretfully) welded into *The Honorable Companie of Merchant-Adventurers Trading into Unknown Northern Islands*, it bothered Master Lymeburner no whit, for he had spent most of his predatory life beyond the law. What did concern him at this juncture was that his timorous backers might abandon him just when he had a fabulous fortune at stake, for six more variegated characters could hardly have been assembled under one roof. Yet there *was* a common denominator—though admittedly in varying degree—and that was avarice. It was on this tenuous foundation that Master Lymeburner built his hopes. At the moment, however, these hopes were in jeopardy, for the meeting threatened to dissolve in recrimination.

"Me lords, me lords!" pleaded the captain anxiously. It was characteristic of the sly old rascal that he use the titled form of address, even though there was not a nobleman in the room. "Me lords, wi' a million guineas worth o' furs an' precious stones in our possession 'tis no time to abandon ship!"

This proved to be an unfortunate choice of words.

"*Possession?*" shrilled a rotund little goldsmith. "Whose possession? The bloody Tatars? The English Muscovy Company's?[1] Curse me, not ours, 'tis certain. Sir, you are an unregenerate scoundrel! You were engaged to voyage into northern waters in search of unknown islands, not—I repeat, sir!—*not* to poach on the preserves of a rival

[11]

English company! At least not a company in which Her Gracious Majesty is privately interested, you dull-witted oaf! You should be..."

"Gently, friend Yancy, gently!" placated the philosophical old gentleman in the scholar's robe. "Let us not lose our course in a storm of invective. Granted the good mariner erred when he trespassed into Muscovy, yet..."

This brought the Reverend Belcher (an unfrocked and indigent vicar who had been promised financial backing in his battle for ecclesiastic reinstatement if the venture prospered) roaring to his feet. "And, prithee, sir, why should the honest mariner *not* go into Muscovy? Certes, it is vast enough for all, and hath not the Almighty shown how He doth favor the English peoples? Dare thou deny that Muscovites are naught but vile pagans and heretics? I summon the Lord Jehovah..."

"Tut, tut, man, spare us another oration!" cut in Mr. Paxton, the scholar. "You strain the patience of the Lord, to say nothing of the rest of us! I can recall that when you were in your twenties, you were but a humble servitor of God, then somewhere in your thirties, you began to consider it an equal partnership. Yet methinks when you presume to order the Lord about, you go too far!" He held up a restraining hand for silence, and continued.

"Gentlemen, let us review the facts objectively! First, being caught up in the prevailing madness for exploration and quick profits in trade, we hastily formed this little company for that purpose and engaged Master Lymeburner to act for us and operate the vessel, *The Dainty Virgin*, in our behalf. Rightly or wrongly, yet undeniably acting in our name and as our representative, he did wilfully sail into Russian territory which is the monopoly of the English Muscovy Company. There, he loaded his ship..."

"*Our* ship, damn it!" grumbled a burly ship chandler named Bendix, who had made a fortune supplying rotten stores to the navy.

"Very well—*our* ship, if it please you," went on Mr. Paxton. "Having trespassed, in violation not only of the monopoly and the Queen's command, but of Russian law as well, Master Lymeburner, by means which, perchance, we had best not examine too closely, managed to garner a cargo which he estimates to be worth several thousand pounds."

"Yer pardon, yer Honor!" interposed the worthy in question. "May God keel'aul me if the value be a farthin' less than *a million guineas!*"

The old scholar smiled wryly. "Alack, I fear it makes little difference, sir, since it is most unlikely we shall ever see any of it, as the Muscovites have seized both ship *and* cargo. You, Captain, are to be congratulated in that you, at least, escaped with your life and were able to reach London."

The grizzled mariner contrived to look suitably humble. "Thankee, m'lud! 'Twas but the will o' the Almighty, 'oo was me constant companion."

"Oh, come, come, man!" chided Mr. Paxton. "You strain our credulity with a statement like that, for we all know that our good Reverend has kept the Lord occupied right here in London Town!"

The parson flushed and the captain's features, pitted and weathered to the texture of a crocodile's hide, darkened perceptibly, but the old philosopher gave them no opportunity to retort.

"Permit me, please, to conclude my summary, for we now come to the crux of this unfortunate affair, and the purpose of this meeting. Obviously, we can have scant hope now of any of those vast profits which lured us into his scheme, like a carrot dangled before the nose of another form of jackass; nor do I need to remind you gentlemen that we stand to lose every farthing already invested, which to many of us spells disaster! Alack, an even worse fate stares us in the face—*imprisonment*, and, possibly, *execution!*" He paused to let them absorb the implications, then continued calmly.

"Although allegedly a court secret, it is fairly well known that our beloved Queen—may God bless and cherish her!—has a strong extra-legal interest in the English Muscovy Company, hence we can expect scant leniency when she learns that we have violated, however unwittingly, her express decree. That she will learn of it, of course, is inevitable." He spread his hands in a gesture of resignation.

"Personally, I see no way out of our dilemma, but Master Lymeburner, being made of sterner stuff, claims to have a plan which may save us. It is to consider this scheme that we have placed ourselves in jeopardy by assembly here tonight." He turned his clear eyes on the doughty sea-rover. "Very well, Captain, the floor is yours!"

Master Lymeburner, who had been seated at the head of the long table, took one hasty glance at the clock above the hearth, then rose to his feet. In appearance, he was a bundle of contradictions. On the surface, he was a jolly-looking, elflike creature with dainty feet, slim ankles, ponderous thighs and an enormous belly which made him resemble a spinning-top such as urchins play with. His face was a ruddy moon which appeared to radiate warmth, but which in point of fact held no warmth at all. His eyes, pale and restless, seemed to vanish in creases of joviality when he smiled, yet a closer inspection would have revealed shuttered lids through which he peered calculatingly. Under a full, sensuous mouth, he carried two chins, with a spare tucked under them, like a reef in a mains'l. Viewing him thus, it was difficult to believe, as reported, that this merry hulk could move with the speed of light.

"Me lords," he cajoled them, "all the illustrious gentleman ha' told ye be the gospel! God love ye, had I the benefit o' such august counsel w'en I was a-gropin' through strange seas, belike we'd not now be scrapin' keel to reef, as the sayin' is. Yet, me masters, may God witness . . ." He let his eyes swivel ceilingward in a pious arc before proceeding. "I done what seemed best, at the time, that is, fer your interests, knowin' ye'd invested to the gunn'ls, so to speak! There I was, gentlemen, wi' empty 'olds an' no 'eart to come 'ome an' break the bad news! So I risked me ship, aye, an' the very lives o' me poor lads to try an' win ye a fortune! May God gi' me the cat, gentlemen, if I didn't nigh succeed, an' 'ere's me oath on 't! Think o' it, me masters—*better'n a million quid to divvy amongst ye!*"

The astronomical sum dizzied most of the audience, yet Mr. Paxton only chuckled.

"Alas, Captain, we have thought of that phase too much! We came to hear a tangible suggestion—*if* you have one."

Master Lymeburner stifled his irritation and stole another surreptitious glance at the clock. It still lacked a quarter of an hour until eight, which meant he had but fifteen minutes to whip them into line. This would be ample if he could but counteract the cool logic of the venerable Paxton.

"Aye, sir, aye. That I have!" he went on when the suspense had formed sufficient vacuum to suck up his every word. "I reckon we be all agreed we've sort o' drifted o'er our depth, to turn a phrase."

"Ah, into the hands of the Almighty!" brayed Belcher, looking hopefully towards the burly Bendix, who was his patron.

The ship chandler said nothing, and only a faint coloring of impatience momentarily marred the serenity of Master Lymeburner's face, to vanish quickly.

"True, your Reverence, true!" he conceded. "Yet, 'twas not preecisely me meanin', fer as matters stand, this affair has gone where God seldom goes—into political circles!" This was plain treason, if not actual heresy, but no one noticed. The speaker shrugged. "Now, bones o' me, gentlemen, I'm naught but a rough, blunt-spoke ol' sea-dog, and you're all good, honest, God-fearin' Christians! So 'tis plain none o' us be capable o' wadin' through the quicksands o' diplomacy!"

Mr. Paxton touched the tips of his long fingers together and suppressed a smile. "Just exactly what are you getting at, Captain?" he demanded.

"Only this, m'lud—*every cobbler to 'is last,* as the sayin' is!" retorted the mariner. "W'at we needs is a courtier who can slip up the backstairs, so to speak, an' whisper a kindly word to our gracious sovereign, Lord love 'er! A knave who knows who to"—he was about to say *bribe,* but restrained himself in time—"to get a hearing with the right ministers."

Bendix snorted. "Bah! Where can we find such a paragon of duplicity?"

And Belcher echoed the ship chandler faithfully. "Aye, tell us where?"

Master Lymeburner had waited for this invitation; more, he had maneuvered the talk until it was inevitable. He looked openly at the clock: it lacked ten minutes of the hour.

"Gentlemen, we have such a rogue right here in London!" he announced, with the air of a juggler conjuring a rabbit out of a hat. "A schemer eminently fitted for the chore!" He seemed about to name his man, but instead shied skittishly away.

"Me masters, this be no time for squeamishness! To speak plain, we be on the rocks an' makin' water fast, as the sayin' is! The only thing w'at can save us—an' may God keel'aul me if else!—is a competent pilot what can con us through the shoals!"

As the investors leaned forward in unison to catch his words, the little goldsmith burst out: "And this veritable prince of rogues is . . . ?"

The doughty captain braced himself and figuratively shortened sail against the squall he was about to bring down around his ears. *Six minutes more to go!* He kept his voice steady when he said: "Sir Guy Spangler!"

This engendered a moment of terrible silence. Belcher, being the most vociferous, loosed the first blast.

"*Guy Spangler!* That Godless knave, that drunken reveller, that worshipper of the Golden Calf! *Sirrah,* how dare thou breathe his vile name in the presence of Christian gentlemen?"

Being a seasoned mariner, the captain offered no resistance; he merely hove-to and waited for the gusts to pass over.

The second squall came from the direction of Yancy, the goldsmith. "'Od's fish! Are you mad, sir, to think we'd truckle with a crafty, unprincipled scoundrel who blatantly makes his livelihood preying off honest men?"

"You're a damn scoundrel yourself, sir, if you think we would!" thundered Bendix, the patron of Belcher and the supplier of rotten food to sailors.

Now spoke for the first time an overserious young man named Tutweiller, who had come to the meeting in place of his father who, in turn, had suffered a stroke on learning of their plight.

" 'Twould be rank folly, gentlemen!" piped this youth of nineteen. "Why, I've heard the pater say that others who have turned to this dastard in an extremity have lost everything, for he invariably demands the lion's share!"

Captain Lymeburner stood as resolutely as if on the poop of his own brig, his head drawn into his soiled ruff, a frozen smile on his storm-chipped face. He knew the squall was almost over.

The parson had retained a gust in reserve. "A damned heretic, a blackmailer, a duellist, a creeper-up-backstairs! May the Almighty spare me long enough to see him hanged, drawn and quartered! Say you not so, Master Bendix?"

"Eh? Oh, aye, aye!" fulminated the ship chandler. "All that, and more!"

Old Paxton's sudden laughter was like sunshine bursting through the clouds. " 'Pon my soul, I have never heard so many heartfelt tributes paid to one solitary rogue!" he chortled. "For in truth, gentlemen, your very accusations are but sincere recommendations for the task our good mariner would assign him!"

Belcher bounced to his feet. "Sirrah! Wouldst thou enlist the services of the devil's chief deputy?"

Mr. Paxton sniffed. "Pshaw, man, I'd enlist the devil himself if he could extricate us from this most untoward predicament." He ignored the parson to address the group as a whole. "Consider, I beg you! We stand under the very shadow of the gallows! I know not this Sir Guy, save as almost everyone knows him by notoriety, who, though admittedly a rogue, appears to be a most efficient one. And if he is the only individual who can disentangle us, then I declare we should examine the possibilities."

"We would rather hang!" bawled the Reverend Belcher, glancing obliquely at Bendix.

"H'mnn! Speak for yourself, man!" rumbled the ship chandler. "You're in charge o' my soul, *not* my neck!"

Paxton laughed. "If you hang, Parson, you won't see Sir Guy drawn and quartered!" he pointed out. "For heaven's sake, gentlemen, let us be realistic! None of us were concerned too deeply with ethics when we snatched at the bait of exorbitant returns, so it seems a trifle ludicrous to adopt a holier-than-thou attitude at this juncture. As Lymeburner has observed—every cobbler to his last. Obviously, no one of us is qualified to handle the situation, and as morals have no relation to political acumen, save possibly as a handicap, it now appears a rogue is required to manage the business. If this be true, then it behooves us to get a competent rogue. Granted I have not met this fantastic Sir Guy, yet rumor has it he is close to the Queen." Mr. Paxton smiled when he said *close*. "Perchance he can borrow her ear."

Bendix snorted. "Hey-day! 'Tis hinted he's had more'n her ear!"

The scholar shrugged. "So much the better," he conceded. "It is axiomatic that many a momentous problem has been resolved on the pillow." He turned to the mariner. "Well, Captain, what is your plan?"

Master Lymeburner beamed, "Why, God love ye, me masters, I have no plan; I'd prefer to sound out Sir Guy, since he's had more experience in skulduggery than me." He acknowledged this with becoming modesty. "Need I remind ye all o' the time he slipped into Spain an' snatched a score o' good Devon lads from the very bowels o' the Holy Office? Or when he journeyed into Italy, incognito, so to speak, and rescued the Earl o' Dunstable from a Florentine dungeon?"

Mr. Yancy neighed like a restless colt. "And need *I* remind *you*, sir, that it cost the City of Plymouth a year's taxes to recompense this adventurer, and that the Earl of Dunstable had to sell most of his estates to pay for *his* salvation!"

Master Lymeburner laid a stubby finger alongside his nose and winked knowingly.

"Tut, tut, me masters, Sir Guy'll not get the best o' Caleb Lymeburner," he vowed. "May God gi' me the cat, if else! Mebbe a paltry four or five percent o' the profits on a *no prey, no pay* basis. Not a farthin' more!"

"Damme, he'll not do it for that!" snorted the worldly Mr. Bendix.

"Nay, not for that!" chorused the Reverend Belcher.

The old clock's striking mechanism gave a warning click. Captain Lymeburner offered up a silent prayer and touched off another storm.

"Gentlemen," he said crisply, "we will soon know whether anything can be salvaged or not! I took the liberty o' outlinin' our plight to Sir Guy—without, o' course, mentionin' a single one of your names—an' he agreed to come here tonight an' . . ."

The Reverend Belcher howled as if someone had built a fire under him, and shot to his feet.

"Come *here?* In the very presence of honest Mr. Bendix and Mr. Yancy and . . ." Those two were his patrons, so he stopped at that. "We'll not be seen in the same chamber with that dastard!"

"Eh? Quite right, Belcher, quite right!" harrumphed Bendix. "We'll leave, by God!"

The goldsmith was equally emphatic. "You treacherous scoundrel!"

he shouted at Lymeburner. "First you ruin us, then attempt to compromise us as well! Blast you, sir, I'll not remain to be insulted by a rogue!" He, too, was on his feet.

Young Tutweiller slapped his sword-hilt with gusto. "By the Mass, gentlemen, there shall be no insults bandied while Philip Tutweiller..."

The clock began to strike! *One ... two ... three ...*

Master Lymeburner discovered he was holding his breath. The others, all save the aged scholar, were milling about preparatory to leaving. Yancy was shaking so he couldn't pick up his cloak; the parson was unctuously trying to assist the truculent ship chandler, while Tutweiller was jerking his sword partially out of the scabbard, then banging it back in place.

As the clock struck eight, the mariner's heart sank. His stratagem had failed! Yet the chime still echoed through the old tavern when there came a sharp, imperious rap on the door!

The inmates went rigid. The rap was repeated.

Master Lymeburner exhaled a relieved sigh. "Me lords!" he hissed, *sotto voce*. "Put on your masks so that ye cannot be identified! Comes now the greatest rogue in England!"

As they hastily covered their faces, he crossed the chamber and yanked open the door.

"Gentlemen! Sir Guy Spangler!"

2

GUY SPANGLER was one of those rare individuals who really look the part assigned to them by Destiny. And while externals admittedly have little to do with character, in Sir Guy's case they had what might be termed a metaphorical connotation. His silky blond hair, worn shoulder-length, combined with sea-green eyes, brought to mind the ruthless and marauding Viking of old. His carriage had a certain esprit which testified to gentle breeding, yet over it was superimposed a supple, leggy litheness of motion that suggested the swashbuckling *condottiere*. He seemed to walk to dance-time. His features, though finely sculptured, were large, which on occasion gave him a faunlike expression; this was further aggravated by a quizzical cast of eye. His mouth was a trifle difficult to define: it was large and flexible—plainly the mouth of a hedonist—yet it held none of the thick-lipped grossness of Master Lymeburner, for example, nor, at the other extremity, the thin, starved barrenness of Belcher. In fine, it was evident that when Sir Guy entered the lists of gallantry, it would require from his tilting partner not only beauty, but also exquisite artistry. He was a perfectionist.

With an innate sense of drama which characterized his every move, he was, of course, dressed for his role as he sauntered elegantly into the hushed chamber. His long, shapely legs were sheathed in silk, with extravagant trunk-hose, paned and slashed, and above that he wore a peasecod-bellied doublet of gold stuff, ornamented with costly lace, and topped by an enormous ruff—of the kind known significantly enough as the "three-steps-and-a-half-to-the-gallows' ruff" because this type was so expensive many men committed crimes to possess them.

If Sir Guy was conscious of the tension his entry had engendered, he gave no sign; he seemed to accept their strained postures as his due. He strode to the head of the table, settled himself in the chair lately vacated by Master Lymeburner, arranged his long rapier comfortably between his legs, then with the air of a prince of the blood, gestured the very dazed *Companie of Merchant-Adventurers* towards their respective places.

For an agonized moment, no one budged. At last the old scholar sank into his chair.

Sir Guy nodded graciously. "Thank you, Master Paxton," he drawled, and as the old man stiffened, he eyed the others. "Come, gentlemen, please be seated! You, Reverend Belcher, be good enough to sit opposite me; a hungry vicar is like a hungry fox, and I prefer to keep an eye on you." He ignored the strangled gasp brought on by this remark, and shifted his gaze to the goldsmith and the ship chandler.

"Surely, my dear Yancy, you're too shrewd a money-lender to abandon your share of the loot at this juncture," he went on teasingly. "Or you, Master Bendix! Why, I understand you won't part with food until it can perambulate under its own power! Sit you down beside your ecclesiastical lackey, my jolly profiteer!"

The Reverend found his voice; a not too difficult task for him. "You lying knave!" he shrilled at the stupefied Lymeburner. "You swore you had not divulged our identities! Perfidious wretch that thou art!"

"I ... I ... I ... !" stammered the mariner, as if his jaw were swung on a loose hinge, but Sir Guy cut him off with a merry laugh.

"Nor did he," he assured the company. "In point of fact, gentlemen, our worthy mariner was excessively coy about the whole affair. Yet you'll grant I'd have been a simple fool, fit only for gallows' bait, if

I would walk into a conclave of other rogues without knowing *who* they were!"

Young Tutweiller, balanced on the meridian between youth and manhood, threateningly rattled his sword.

"'Sdeath, sir! You dare call us rogues?" he challenged.

The knight cocked one eye. "Aye, my pretty 'Titwillow,' I *dare!* Now be a nice boy and sit down before you get spanked!"

Once again it was the elderly scholar who brought reason to the fore. Chuckling ruefully, he gestured for Lymeburner to close the door, then he jerked off his own mask and tossed it on the table.

"Alack, gentlemen, we have been outmaneuvered, yet we may as well concede it in comfort. Pray be seated! I shall not ask Sir Guy by what legerdemain he discovered who we are, yet from the apoplectic expression of our good agent, 'tis plain *he* had naught to do with it." He chuckled again. "At least, not directly." Sobering quickly, he leaned across the table.

"Sir Knight," he asked earnestly, "will you tell us what else you know about this unfortunate business?"

As the others were still on their feet, Sir Guy did not reply at once, but tilting back, glanced at each man in turn. It was almost as if his eyes had physical powers, for as they focused on a man, that individual sank into the most convenient chair. Thus, in a matter of seconds, all were seated, albeit a trifle stiffly. The visitor smiled.

"I know only that your redoubtable agent, acting in your names, poached on the preserves of the English Muscovy Company," acknowledged Sir Guy in a tone that intimated he knew a great deal more. "This particular offense, I might add parenthetically, is a tender spot with Her Majesty. I've been given to understand that the Muscovites have seized both ship and cargo. From our jolly mariner's coquettish advances, I presume you wish me to pluck your chestnuts out of the fire. Is that correct?"

The clergyman opened his mouth to say something, but for once Bendix got ahead of him.

"Damme, sir, let us have no misunderstanding!" he bumbled aggressively. "No misunderstanding, I say! We must know: first, whether you think you can do it, and, second, what it will cost us? Eh? I'll speak plain: it must be on a *no prey, no pay* basis!"

"Aye! No prey, no pay!" responded Belcher dutifully.

The knightly rogue chuckled softly. "Alas, my dear tradesmen, that basis is the standard operating procedure amongst all thieves and pirates, hence it is meet that we adopt it here. As for your other queries, why, I have no doubt I can manage the affair, badly bungled as it now is. In speaking of cost—do you refer to the cost of salvaging ship and cargo, or of saving you from the hangman?"

His very calmness wilted them. Master Lymeburner, having regained something of his equilibrium, decided it was time for him to take over.

"To speak true, m'lud, we'd like to save both the loot *an'* our necks!"

Sir Guy's eyes twinkled. "A laudable ambition, my good fellow! Howbeit, it might be advisable to suppress the crime of poaching before we attempt to retrieve the game." He let his glance make another circuit of the board. "Even a million guineas would hardly repay you worthy gentlemen for a series of stretched necks, now would it?"

"Ain't that the God's trufe!" conceded Master Lymeburner, running a finger around the inside of his ruff.

"Has the Queen learned of this as yet?" inquired the knight.

Master Lymeburner could not suppress a shudder. "Lor' love a duck, sir—I hopes not!"

Sir Guy nodded. "Aye, in all truth it would be a most inauspicious moment! Fortunately, the Queen is a woman, and women change their minds! It is merely a matter of finding the propitious instant when they cross the emotional zenith, if you follow me, my dear mariner."

This left Master Lymeburner so completely befuddled, Mr. Paxton picked up the gage.

"You emphasized that this was a *most inauspicious moment*, Sir Guy. Precisely what did you mean?"

The knight seemed almost reluctant to reply, as he sat absently tracing with his finger the gold inlay of his sword hilt. But finally he answered.

"Only that two days past a personal envoy of the Tsar arrived in London from Moscow!"

Little Mr. Yancy staggered to his feet, bawling tearfully: "All is lost! All is lost!"

Sir Guy smiled. "Not necessarily, my little blood-sucker! He comes in search of beauty, being here on behalf of Ivan Fourth to solicit a kinswoman of Her Majesty for ... ah ... well, shall we call it *marriage*, if you ken my meaning?" He winked broadly at the Reverend Belcher.

The latter gulped down the bait, then yelped as if stabbed in the vitals: "Oh, those vile and lecherous Muscovites!"

His tormentor laughed delightedly. "Lecherous, you say, Parson! Ah-h, perhaps, yet what voluptuous, rapturous, delectable lechery!" He let his glance play over Belcher's flaming features. "Has your Reverence ever ... ah ... visited a harem?"

"*Sirrah!*" choked the victim.

"'Ere, 'ere!" growled Bendix. "That ain't no way to talk to a brother o' the cloth! No way, I say! Eh?"

Mr. Paxton smothered a chuckle. "I have little doubt, Sir Guy, that at a later date, our worthy vicar would be most interested in an academic discourse on harem life. At the moment, however, those of us beyond the age of desire are primarily concerned with preserving what few years the Lord has left us. Therefore, will you kindly shape your advice towards that end."

The notorious visitor bowed. "Your pardon, Ancient," he said without malice. "I was carried away by the parson's enthusiasm. Well, back to business. By a fortuitous coincidence, I shall be with the Queen shortly. We are ... ah ... going hawking very early in the morning." It was astonishing how he could say one thing while so obviously meaning another. "This may be a never to be repeated opportunity to present your case to Her Majesty when she is in an ... ah ... *relaxed* mood." He chuckled softly to himself, then added casually: "I shall, of course, require a petition for pardon signed by each of you."

His offhand tone did not lull them, and consternation was general.

"A *petition?*" trumpeted Bendix. "'Twould be a *confession,* egad! Damme, sir, do you ask us to sign our own death warrants?"

"Preposterous!" shrilled the parson.

"Impossible!" piped the goldsmith.

"*Absolutely* impossible!" chimed Tutweiller.

Without seeming to move so much as a muscle, Sir Guy contrived to turn from silk to steel.

"The only thing *impossible,*" he said icily, "is that you can save your drab little lives without a petition. Posture all you please before others, but do not blind yourselves to realities. If Her Majesty does not already know of this misadventure, she soon will—have no doubt on *that* score! And if I have learned one thing in this life, it is this: it is better to nip a fire whilst it is small than wait until it is a conflagration before attempting to extinguish it!" He paused, then when no one challenged his assertion, he went on.

"After I have secured Her Majesty's pardon for you, I doubt not I can smooth matters with the Emperor of the Russians. His Imperial Envoy, Count Nikita, is under some slight obligation to me. Thus, in addition to being on very friendly terms, the Count and I"—Sir Guy permitted himself a sly, meaningful smile—"share, shall I say, a *common philosophy* of life."

The suggestive leer was more than Belcher could stomach. He lurched to his feet, overturning his chair.

"A pair of unsaved and unregenerate heretics?" he burst forth. "Gentlemen, do not place your trust in these confessed dealers in chaste womanhood! Nay, nay! Rather put your faith in the Almighty! Pray for guidance . . ."

He stopped short in terror, mouth still open, as there came an ominous pounding on the door. Then, from beyond the panel, a harsh voice bellowed:

"*H'open up! H'open up in the Queen's nyme!*"

There was no escape! The chamber had but the one door, and the leaded windows opened onto the dark, unfriendly river. For a portentous moment the company waited in soundless horror, then the stillness was broken by the lazy drawl of Sir Guy.

"Your advice was opportune, Reverend. This is an excellent time for prayer."

The thumps on the door were repeated, this time with a cudgel or stave.

"H'open! H'open!" roared the man in the hallway. "H'open in 'Er Marjesty's nyme afore we rips the bleedin' 'ouse down!"

Master Lymeburner turned frantically towards Sir Guy, but that worthy had slumped in his chair and rested his head on his arms as if in sleep. Desperate, the mariner looked to Mr. Paxton, who shrugged resignedly and nodded towards the door. Master Lymeburner sighed sorrowfully and drew the bolt.

The door crashed inward as two men gripping bailiffs' staves lunged into the chamber.

They made a terrifying tableau! One was short, with a set smile that somehow resembled an old battle-scar, whereas his companion was excessively tall and gaunt and wore the expression of a man who had never smiled. It was the latter who spoke first.

"Caught 'em red-'anded!" he intoned dolefully. "Unlawful assembly an' consortin' in an 'ouse o' ill-repute."

The men at the table exchanged agonized glances. Mr. Paxton acted as spokesman.

"I believe you men have made a mistake," he said quietly. "We were merely discussing personal matters."

"W'at-'o!" jeered the merry bailiff. "A likely tale! W'y, wi' our own eyes we seen ye gents come a-sneakin' down the streets, duckin' an' connivin'. Sergeant Pistol 'ere, 'e s'ys to me, 'e s'ys: 'Affable Jones (which, gents, be me!) I swear them knaves be a-plottin' ag'in 'Er Marjesty!' So we follows ye 'ere an' lissens at the door! An' w'at does

[23]

we 'ear?" He fair howled with glee. "A-plottin' to cheat 'Er Marjesty, hang me if else!"

The lank bailiff, obviously growing impatient, prodded Belcher with his stave.

"Move to the 'ead o' the line," he barked. "The rest o' ye fall in be'ind! Lively now! We'll march ye to the Tower instead o' Newgate, considerin' yer crimes o' treason an' w'at not!" As the terrified clergyman shrank against the wall, the sergeant circled the table, prodding the others to their feet. Mr. Yancy kept bawling: "All is lost! All is lost!"

Up to this point, Sir Guy had remained inert, his head pillowed on his arm, but at the touch of the stave, he reared back in his chair and turned the full power of his eyes on the startled bailiff. The latter leaped backwards as though he had turned up a bear.

"*Sir Guy*, sir!" he bleated in fright. "Afore God, yer Gryce, I tyke oath I didn't know 'twas ye, sir!"

The knight stared about him with the air of a man just awakened. "What goes on here?" he demanded.

The bailiff trembled as with the palsy. "I cry ye mercy, m'lud!" he stammered. "I knows better'n to lay finger on 'Er blessed Marjesty's favorite! Ye can leave, yer 'Ighness, leave scot-free. 'Tis plain ye was asleep w'ilest these knaves was a-schemin' to poach on the preserves o' the Queen—God bless 'er!"

Sir Guy yawned languidly and pushed to his feet. A golden coin appeared as if by magic in his right hand. He juggled it a couple of times whereupon it seemed to slip out of his fingers. Quite by chance, Sergeant Pistol caught it before it could hit the floor. The sergeant made no immediate effort to return the coin, nor did Sir Guy seem conscious of the oversight.

He merely asked: "Isn't it barely possible you might have been mistaken in what you thought you overheard, Sergeant?"

The bailiff knuckled his forehead. "W'y, to speak true, yer Excellency, nothin' be impossible," he conceded. "Yet 'tis me employment to round up all traitors an' such scum."

Sir Guy nodded sympathetically. "Zeal is always commendable. What is your name, my brave fellow?"

"Sergeant Pistol, yer Imminence!"

"A likely name for a likely rogue!" approved the knight. "Yet are you content with trailing your betters and eavesdropping at tavern doors for a paltry bailiff's stipend?"

Sergeant Pistol fingered the wattles on his neck. "W'y, as to that, yer Honor, 'tis a sorry livin', I own. Yet a man 'as to feed 'is dependents."

"So? You have a wife?"

"Nay, but I do 'ave a belly!"

Sir Guy's smile seemed a trifle strained. "And pray who is this jubilant cutthroat with you, Sergeant?"

"'Im? Oh, 'e's just Affable Jones!"

"The pride of Newgate, I'll wager!" observed the knight.

Affable Jones accepted the compliment. "On an' off, yer 'Oliness!" he confessed cheerfully. "Though I don't get there so oft as o' yore."

Sir Guy laughed heartily. "An indication of progress!" He produced another coin which by sleight-of-hand found its way into the second bailiff's grubby paw. "'Pon my honor, I do believe I could advantageously use two such ambitious rascals in my own service! What say you, merry gentlemen?"

Affable Jones swept off his hat and made an extravagant bow—which revealed a gleaming pate, like the tonsure of a monk. "Yer 'umble servant, m'lud!" he chortled. "So soon's we lock up these ruddy conspirators, an' collecks our blood money, we be at yer service, hang me if else! W'at-'o, Sergeant?"

"W'y, to that I'll not say nay," temporized the sergeant. "'Owbeit, I'd prefer to wait fer the 'angin' o' these desperadoes! A gawky lout like him there"—he nodded towards the cringing clergyman—"does a right merry dance on a rope's end."

Sir Guy dismissed the matter with a shrug. "As you wish," he said indifferently. "In any event, I should appreciate it if both of you will just step out into the hall for a moment or two. I desire a final word with these gentlemen before we part company."

Sergeant Pistol tugged his wattle and looked doubtful, but Affable Jones chuckled happily.

"'Ell, Sergeant, w'y not? They can't go no plyce!"

The sergeant allowed himself to be persuaded, and so in due time the pair backed into the corridor and closed the door.

As the company of *Merchant-Adventurers* collapsed shakily into their chairs, Sir Guy appraised them closely.

"As this may well be our last meeting this side of hell," he needled them, "kindly state your pleasure."

Mr. Paxton leaned forward and fixed the knight with a half-amused, half-accusing stare.

"That little exhibition had the air of being rehearsed, sir!" he said pointedly.

Sir Guy grinned. "I confess, Ancient, that I have bribed my way out of similar scrapes before."

"It was not that to which I had reference, as you very well know," the old man retorted dryly. "Howbeit, let it pass." He surveyed his quaking companions. "I presume, gentlemen, that by now you are almost eager to sign the petition?"

Mr. Yancy ran a nervous finger around the inner band of his ruff, as if it had suddenly become too tight for him.

"Oh, aye, aye!" he agreed hastily. "It seems pointless to quibble further!"

Young Tutweiller raised an issue. "But . . . but, gentlemen! Will not this document irrevocably place us in this man's power?"

"Bones o' me, lad!" gasped Lymeburner. "Would ye rather 'ang?"

"Eh? *Hang*, you say?" snorted the ship chandler. "Hey-dey, what's to prevent it with those accursed bailiffs . . ."

"I feel reasonably confident I can handle them," Sir Guy said with a smile.

Mr. Paxton nodded. "I am quite sure of it," he remarked acidly.

It being now agreed, parchment and quill were produced, and after the venerable scholar had inscribed the body, as dictated by Sir Guy himself, each member of that brave *Companie of Merchant-Adventurers* affixed his signature. Lacking sand, Sir Guy waved it until the ink was dry, then folded it carefully and slipped it into his doublet. As he rose, the ship chandler groaned.

"Curse me, we still have not agreed on terms!" he complained. "Lymeburner suggested five percent of . . ."

Sir Guy's words were like a whiplash. "It is ridiculous to haggle over terms until I find out what *has* to be done, or what *can* be done for you!" He sauntered around the table to the door. "All of you remain where you are while I attempt to deal with these minions of the law. If I succeed in purchasing your freedom, meet me here at this same hour tomorrow night!" He glanced at Mr. Paxton and there was a perceptible twinkle in his eye when he added: "Try not to lead any more pursuivants to our rendezvous, however!"

On that note, he left them.

"Eh? Egad, I reckon we were clumsy!" rumbled Bendix.

"Think you he'll be able to pacify those bailiffs?" whimpered Yancy distractedly.

Old Mr. Paxton looked around at his companions as if seeing them for the first time. Then he exhaled a long, disillusioned sigh.

"He will, Yancy, he will! Depend on it!"

3

BEING SOMETHING of a migratory bird of prey, Sir Guy Spangler had no *home* in the customary sense of the word, yet at this particular time, he dwelt in an old house canted perilously over the Thames within bow-shot of The Strand. Judged by externals, it in no wise resembled the popular conception of the residence of a sometime-favorite of the Queen, hence Dame Gossip was hard put to explain its singular location. Two cynical versions were currently in circulation: that Sir Guy had chosen the site because, due to a fortuitous bend in the river at this point, he could view Her Majesty's bedchamber from his own windows; that Elizabeth herself had selected the ancient structure on the waterfront so that her royal barge could dock at the handsome courtier's very door, day or night.

Though Sir Guy was much too shrewd to deny these rumors, the real truth was much less romantic. He had carefully handpicked the place, to be sure, but not because of any potential *affaire d'amour;* his sole reason was that the old house offered an unrivaled avenue of escape by water, *if,* or *when,* the pendulum of his fortunes swung the other way.

Due to his picaresque mode of livelihood and other circumstances peculiar to his existence, this possibility, like a sword of Damocles, hung tenuously above his head. Nay, it was more than a possibility; it was a probability. Inevitably, his fantastic luck must change, for he who would make a profession of danger needs reckon with the law of averages. Sir Guy had ignored these natural laws as he had ignored man-made ones, and though academically he knew he was operating on borrowed time, emotionally he thumbed his nose at Fate and went his jaunty way as if life would always remain a perpetual summertime.

And now, an hour after he had left the cowed *Companie of Merchant-Adventurers* quaking in the Handcuff Inn, Sir Guy stood in his own seraglio-like chamber and stared musefully out of the window. The fog had lifted, and as the tide was at full flood, the river ran high and broad between her banks. Despite the hour, boats of varying descriptions dotted the surface, and here and there a stately swan drifted in lazy circles with the current. As the courtier gazed on the scene, a great barge, all gilt and glamor, floated past, and under its ornate awnings, he could distinguish lovely ladies singing to the muted music of guitars. There were a few little cockleshells of the humbler folk, and an occasional wherry bearing a merchant and his family. Dimly in the background, dignified as dowager duchesses, reared the big deep-

[27]

water ships, each surrounded by a personal court of barges and lighters.

Once, in the not-so-long-ago, such a scene as this would have fascinated and stimulated Sir Guy, but now, somehow, it depressed him. Those stately ships, he had come to know, had wormy bottoms; those beautiful, chaste-looking maidens could be easily purchased for a pouch of gold. Some wit had lately remarked of Guy Spangler that he knew the price of everything, but the value of nothing. Tonight, soured in part by the picayunish business at the Handcuff Inn, he was nearly ready to concede the point.

Yet it was more than a mere indisposition. Sir Guy had been playing a role so long he had come to accept the image as himself, like a player who confuses the stage with reality; he had, in a perverse manner, lost contact with the man he was behind the mask. And of more pressing moment, in following this self-created Pied Piper, he had blithely danced up a blind alley of financial disaster. If he could still toss golden coins to every jackanapes who did him a penny-worth of service, or purchase all rights to every lovely jade who quickened his pulse, he owed a prince's ransom to an ever-widening circle of usurious leeches who were draining the very life's blood out of him, yet clamored for more, more, always more!

His reverie was interrupted by a discreet cough, and he turned, welcoming the diversion, to find Sergeant Pistol standing in the entry. The sight of the funereal horselike features revived Sir Guy's good humor.

"By my troth! The Queen's bailiff, no less!" he hooted. "Where is that other buffoon?"

Sergeant Pistol shrugged and managed to look even gloomier, but before he could open his mouth, there came a happy cackle from the stairwell, and a moment later Affable Jones himself bounced into the room.

"That's me, yer Honor!" he caroled. "'Ow'd we do as bailiffs, sir?"

Sir Guy wagged his head. "Terrible! If you two louts would spend more time observing your betters, you might give a better performance. As it was, had I not softened them to a point of near-submission, they would have seen through the farce." He clucked tongue to teeth. "The old man saw through it in spite of me!" He backed into a chair.

"Well, did you get the information you were sent after? How about you, Pistol?"

"'Tweren't easy," grumbled the sergeant. "Them Muscovites be a suspicious lot, an' nobody could speak English. Howbeit, wi' me expert knowledge o' French . . ."

"For the love of God, stop bragging!" snapped Sir Guy. "Give me your report, sans verbiage!"

The tall man sighed. "Aye, aye, sir! Well, it seems the Tsar o' Muscovy seen an ivory miniature paintin' o' Lady Mary Hastin's, 'Er Marjesty's kinswoman. Ivan got o'er-'eated about 'er an' wants to add 'er to 'is collection so 'e sent over 'ere to Lunnon this Count Nik . . . Nikilitch, er Nikovitch . . ." As the sergeant began to flounder, Sir Guy helped him over the difficulty.[2]

"I know all that, man! The question is—has Count Nikita interviewed the Hastings woman?"

Pistol shook his head. "'E ayant located 'er, sir! The bitch—beggin' yer pardon, sir!—flounced out of Lunnon an' 'as gone into 'idin'. The Count's most un'appy, so I 'ears."

Sir Guy rubbed his hands delightedly. "Excellent, Pistol, excellent!" he gloated. "Now I have a more difficult assignment for you—I want to *borrow* that miniature, if you comprehend?"

Sergeant Pistol grew increasingly morose. Affable Jones nudged him with a chubby elbow.

"'Is Worship means 'e wants ye to *steal* it, ye goat!" he hissed.

The other, meanwhile, had been groping around inside his jerkin, and at this point withdrew his hand, which held a small leather case. He proffered it to Sir Guy.

"I figgered it might come in 'andy, sir," said Pistol sadly.

Sir Guy opened the case and whistled admiringly, for in a nest of purple velvet lay an exquisite painting of a girl's face.

"'Pon my soul, you are a treasure, Sergeant!" exclaimed Sir Guy. "This will save us better than a full round of the clock." He sobered abruptly. "Did you accomplish it quietly and without . . . er . . . bloodshed?"

The sergeant appeared most unhappy. "Only a few giggles an' no blood, sir," he confessed. "'Twon't be missed for several days."

"Topping! We'll have it back within four-and-twenty hours!" He studied the portrait a moment longer, then swung on the fat man. "Did you fare as well, Affable?"

Mr. Jones tilted back his head like a cock about to crow. "Well, I went to dear ol' Newgate as ye ordered, yer 'Oliness," he explained in his rollicking fashion. "Oh, 'twas a reg'lar 'omecomin', so it was, wi' ol' Alexander all set to pitch me in a dungeon until 'e learned I'd come from yer Gryce. Then 'e chynged 'is tune, 'e did—the slimy son-o'-a-bitch!"

"A concise summarization of the creature, to be sure," agreed the knight. "Yet my interest lies, not in the Keeper of Newgate Prison, but in its feminine inmates. How is the supply?"

"Terrificable, m'lud, terrificable!" swore Affable Jones, making ribald gestures with his hands. "The bloody gaol o'erflows wi' pulchritude—succulent female debtors, one lydy poisoner, an' fair scads o' luscious bawds! W'at-'o! Alexander said 'e 'oped ye'd find summat to please yer fawncy amongst the debtors. As for the lydy poisoner, 'e s'ys she's ugly an' 'twould be chancy to disappoint the Saturday crowd w'at's countin' on seein' 'er tortured at Tyburn."

Sir Guy sniffed ironically. "Far be it from me to disappoint the gentle citizenry, so they shall have their victim for all of me." He shook his head. "Is Master Alexander readying the beauty parade?"

Affable hooted with laughter. " 'E is that, sir, an' wi' bad gryce, fer 'is gout be torturin' im—thank God. They'll be ready as soon's we arrive. Shall I summon yer chair, sir?"

Sir Guy nodded, and when Jones waddled off, Pistol asked gloomily: "D'ye want I should accompany ye, sir?"

"No. I have a more important task for you. Do you remember James Ashby, the Earl of Carver?"

Sergeant Pistol screwed up his nose in concentration. "Ye means that gent ye sneaked out o' Lord Mayor Robertson's wife's bedchamber w'ilest 'is ruddy ludship was a-tryin' to chop down the door?"

"That's the one," agreed Sir Guy. "After that escapade, he temporarily stopped bedding other men's wives and got himself a mistress, for whom he lavishly fitted out a house on The Strand. In due time, he kicked her out, locked up the house, and returned to his wife."

"Wery, wery logical," approved Sergeant Pistol.

"Typical, rather than logical, my dear Pistol," jeered the knight. "Howbeit, what concerns us for the nonce is the unused house on The Strand. Go to friend Ashby, and with your inimitable subtlety, remind him of his indebtedness, and tell him I wish to borrow his ex-seraglio for a few days. Do not take no for an answer; I'll leave the tactics to you. In brief, I require the key by the time I return from Newgate."

"Aye, aye, sir!" Sergeant Pistol said drearily and went out—just as Affable Jones bounced in to report the chair was waiting.

4

Sir Guy's imperishable *bon mot* to the effect that Master Alexander, the infamous Chief Gaoler of Newgate Prison, resembled a "corpse which had floated for two midsummer weeks in the Thames with the little fishes nibbling it" may have been inelegant, but it was not inapt. The gaoler was a prodigious man, with a monstrous bloated belly which seemed to roll over the rim of his belt. As if designed by nature to support this excrescence, his legs were spaced abnormally far apart. These repulsive appendages were encased in tight-fitting hose, and the stinking, half-cured leather jerkin Master Alexander favored also added nothing to his personal charm.

His head was merely a slightly smaller version of his body: a small crown pasturing lank straight hair, protruding, baggy eyes, a bulbous nose many times broken, and ponderous dewlaps which obliterated any evidence of neck. Sir Guy's reference to the nibbling of fishes was prompted by the sordid pox marks which pitted his face and hands and harbored grime like ruts in a muddy street.

A gross, brutal man when aroused, he was even more offensive when attempting to please. With no more physical movement than a rubbing of hands and a slight bending of paunch, he gave the impression of groveling. At such times, his voice took on a fawning lisp and he drooled from both floppy nether lip and rheumy eye. Yet, withal, Master Alexander had one priceless talent—he knew *when* to fawn, and when to play the beast. He might flay the hide of a hapless urchin, but now that he was in the presence of the notorious Sir Guy, he literally dripped to curry favor. Had he so much as dreamed that if Sir Guy's current enterprise should fail that worthy knight might well be numbered among his "guests," Master Alexander's attitude would have been somewhat less effusive.

The three men—Sir Guy, Master Alexander, and the irrepressible Affable Jones—sat side by side under an open window in the visitors' hall and appraised the procession of female offenders being herded before them. Despite Affable Jones's extravagant rhapsody about "pulchritude, succulent female debtors and luscious bawds," Sir Guy found them a sorry lot. Water being one of the rarest of prison commodities, their skins had an almost uniform griminess. The debtors, for whose support the law allowed no funds, were emaciated and listless, with the exception of a brazen few who knew how to "utilize the talents the good Lord gave 'em"—to borrow a favorite quote from the practical Master Alexander.

But if his companions were enchanted by the hidden promise of lowered lid and twitchy hip, Sir Guy was not. And so the debtors filed past without his finding what he sought. Then came the thieves and bawds. These frowzy wenches put on an exhibition which nearly unseated the susceptible Mr. Jones, who began breaking out in a veritable rash of ribald ejaculations.

"Lor' love a gallopin' goose, yer 'Oliness!" he'd gasp. "Pipe the revolvin' stern o' that neat little craft—third from the end! Won't *she* do, sir?" Or, a moment later: "W'at-'o! 'Tis Venus 'er ownself, sir! That's the one ye want!"

To all this, and more, Sir Guy wagged his head. Then Master Alexander leaned close and pointed to a huge painted strumpet.

"Ha! Look there, m'lud!" he slobbered. " 'Ow'd ye like 'er?"

Sir Guy pushed him away and waved a perfumed handkerchief under his nose.

"Stop breathing in my face, you lout!" he snapped. "That sewer gas is enough to strangle me! Is this shoddy collection the best you can offer?"

Master Alexander knew when *not* to be offended. "Alack, 'tis every last dove in the covey, sir!" he admitted reluctantly, for he could plainly envision a sack of gold slipping away from his avid clutches.

As Sir Guy started to rise, Affable Jones, momentarily forgetting his station in his overenthusiasm, stabbed him with an elbow.

"There be the one fer ye, master!" he panted. "I swear ye ne'er seen such pulchritude, such dazzlin' lamps, such bussable lips, such curves . . ." Affable had to pause for breath.

Sir Guy chuckled. "Why, man, you have the soul of a poet, if the judgment of a vulture! Where is this incomparable Aphrodite?"

Affable was only too eager to point her out, but as Sir Guy expected, the wench was just another buxom *cocotte*, albeit a most provocative one. She had curly blonde tresses, a saucy face with stubby nose, impish eyes, and cherry-colored lips. She stood slightly apart from the others, her hands on her hips and her breast thrust hard against her bodice. Being much too obvious for Sir Guy's own taste, he was about to shake his head when Affable Jones added: "Wouldn't that little sugar-tart melt in this Count Nikelitch's mouth? *H'mnn-mmn!*"

Sir Guy pursed his lips, then burst into laughter. "By my troth, my friend, though 'twas not my original intent, you've given me an idea." He turned to the gaoler. "What is that busty minx charged with?"

Master Alexander grimaced. "Lip, m'lud, just plain *lip!*" he grumbled, expectorating as if to show his disapproval.

The knight arched a brow. "A new crime," he observed sarcastically. "I own I never heard of it before. Enlighten me, please?"

"W'y, sir, she lipped the bailiff w'at was a-doin' 'is Christian dooty, she lipped the Lord Justice, an' tolt 'im if 'e'd step into 'is chymbers wi' 'er in private, she'd myke a man o' 'im, an' . . ."

"Did the Lord Justice comply?" interrupted Sir Guy, smiling.

The gaoler snorted. "No, but 'e give 'er three years an' a whippin' at a cart's tyle-gate to learn to keep a civil tongue in 'er saucy 'ead, 'e did!" Master Alexander made an expansive gesture with a grimy paw to dismiss the subject. "By the bye, sir, I jes' recolleck I got a tidy morsel tucked aw'y in durance vile, as they s'y!" He winked broadly, and lowered his voice. "A bigamous bitch!"

"Then why in God's name have you kept me staring at this offensive rabble when you have something better in reserve?" Sir Guy demanded irritably.

Master Alexander began to slobber. "Curse me, yer Honor, but I was ordered—oh, I'll not mention by 'oo!—to *sink 'er deep an' ferget 'er!* I almost did, bleed me, if else!"

"There are no charges against her?"

The gaoler smiled his jackal smile. "W'y, sir, I can't rightly s'y there is, since the gent'man in question was married at the time 'e wedded 'er."

"H'mnn! In which event he may be a *bigamous bastard,* to paraphrase your witticism, but she can hardly be held responsible."

Master Alexander pouted his cheeks and looked foggy. "Damme, I ain't no ruddy chief justice, I ain't!" he retorted. "The gent 'as influence, an' she 'asn't, so it's no skin off my 'ide. W'en I'm tolt to drop 'em down an 'ole, I drops 'em—wi' nary a question." He sighed. "But the bloody h'injustice of it is that I don't get no *per diem* fer 'er substance! A shyme, I s'y!" He hesitated and looked questioningly at his visitor. "If I could be certain she'd never be 'eard of again . . . ?" he suggested.

"Trot her up for inspection," countered Sir Guy.

Affable Jones groaned audibly. "Beggin' yer pardon, sir!" he cajoled. "Fer the love o' 'eaven, don't let this 'ere blonde bit o' paradise hescape us, sir!"

The knight laughed. "Very well, we shall hold her in reserve. Gaoler, remove these other unfortunates before my heart bleeds, then produce your tid-bit. But don't keep me waiting longer than necessary! This pesthouse gags me!"

"Aye, aye, sir!" gloated the gaoler. "Stryngely enough, many folks feel the syme w'y!" He came to his feet. "I'll be briefer'n a ha'p'ny upright!" And off he padded, bawling at the guards to clear the room of prisoners.

Within minutes, Sir Guy found himself alone in the cavernous chamber, save for the little *grisette*, incarcerated for "lip," and Affable Jones who remained panting at his side. Sir Guy appraised the girl with the objectivity of a diamond merchant appraising a stone.

Obviously she had not long been imprisoned, since her skin lacked the overlayers of grime which blighted the others. Her eyes, like Sir Guy's own, were green, and unusually alert. She, too, seemed to be making an appraisal.

"What is your name, girl?"

"W'at's yours, sir?"

Affable Jones gasped. " 'Ere, 'ere, ye saucy baggage!" he scolded. "Ye don't know 'oo ye address!"

She wrinkled her stubby nose at him. "That, ye goat, is w'at I be tryin' to find out!"

Sir Guy grinned. "Suppose I told you I was *Master Gold-giver*," he said. "Would that satisfy you?"

She smiled—a most genuine smile. "W'y, sir, if ye proved ye was, I'd do me best to *satisfy* ye!"

"Now, may I have your name?"

"Moll Lane, sir."

Sir Guy winced. "Good Lord, methinks all the bawds in London must be named Moll," he reflected. "For an extra quid, may I have the privilege of renaming you for the . . . ah . . . duration of your service?"

She giggled. "Me lud, fer a quid ye can do wi' me as ye wish!"

"W'at-'o! W'at-'o!" yelped Affable Jones, literally pawing at the air. "Can I 'ave an advance on me next year's wages, yer Worship?"

The knight ignored him. "Very well, young woman. Henceforth you shall be known by, and only answer to, the name of *Charity . . . Charity Lane!* Agreed?"

Her eyes danced mischievously. "Bless ye, sir, o' course! Yet, 'tis a misnomer, for though 'tis said that 'charity begins at 'ome,' I cannot afford to gi' . . ."

Sir Guy silenced her with an imperious hand. "Hold!" he warned sternly. "Else I cannot be responsible for the conduct of this spaniel I have at my side! Rest assured that, though you shall be known as Charity, you will be paid handsomely in the coin of the realm for *all* services performed in the line of duty!"

She was making him a deep, acknowledging curtsy when the door at the far end of the hall opened, and Master Alexander ushered in another prisoner.

This one stumbled into the room with a kind of terrified eagerness, and for a passing instant, her eyes shimmered with anticipation, as if expecting to find someone she knew. However, when her gaze settled on Sir Guy, the light died, and her whole body appeared to sag, until she looked like a half-drowned gray cat the brawny gaoler might have picked out of a kennel.

Affable Jones groaned aloud, and even Sir Guy's sigh was audible. Alexander gave the girl a shove that sent her reeling towards the other two men, then spread his hamlike hands in a gesture of resignation.

"Curse me, if she ain't thinned out considerable since I last seen 'er!" he apologized in disgust.

The gray drab would have toppled to the floor had not Charity run forward and supported her.

"Aye, an' is it any wonder she's thinned, ye pot-bellied wart 'og!" hissed the buxom blonde. "Certes, the poor lambkin be no thinner than that swillish water-soup ye slop out to 'em as cannot p'y."

Master Alexander began to swell up like a toad, but before he could explode, Sir Guy barked an order.

"Gaoler, fetch a chair for the lass! Then all of you will leave except the prisoner. I wish a word with her in private."

Master Alexander was not accustomed to waiting on his charges, particularly the non-paying ones, hence he complied with bad grace. Yet the chair was brought, and as he beckoned Charity and Affable to accompany him out of the chamber, the blonde patted the other girl encouragingly on the shoulder.

"Chin up, dearie!" she said earnestly. "Don't let this 'andsome rake tyke advantage o' yer condition to buy ye too cheap. 'E's got the gold, an' if 'e wants ye bad enough, 'e'll p'y fer't!" Then she looked directly at Sir Guy, wrinkled her nose in friendly fashion, then twitched out of the chamber in the wake of the others.

The newcomer hung her head and shuddered. "Merciful God!" she whispered to herself. "Has it come to this?"

Sir Guy felt a tinge of irritation. He was one of those who made a cult of *savoir faire*, and while he could tolerate jesting and banter, to exhibit an adverse emotion was, to him, a form of weakness. He lived within a steel shell, polished and tempered to a diamond hardness.

"Come now," he said. "Let me look at you!"

The suave coolness of his tone acted like a dash of cold water thrown in her face. She sat up straight, and his sharp eyes noted the genteel way her hands fell into place on her lap—a mark of the well-born. He chuckled inwardly, for it tended to confirm the first impression he had formed when she entered the chamber. He leaned back and studied her with brutal candor.

In a sense, it was like trying to identify a person through a dirty windowpane. Her hair was a tangle of dark and muddy strands; her skin, as brittle as gray parchment. To the casual eye, she was anything but attractive. Yet Sir Guy was making no casual inspection. He noted that her features were finely sculptured, and that if her pride was not immediately evident, it lurked not far beneath the surface. Her eyes bothered him; they had a lackluster that he sensed was neither characteristic nor brought on by physical weariness. Doubtless, it reflected a weariness of the spirit. He shrugged the thought aside. He could manage such minor difficulties in their proper sequence.

Her body remained, at the moment, a mystery, for it was encased in a shapeless, sacklike garment which obliterated all trace of line or form. Plainly, the rag was not hers; she had probably sold her own gown to pay for survival. Yet even this hideous garb did not hide the straight spine, nor the careful placement of her legs.

Sir Guy pondered. Certainly this drab slattern, well-born or no, was a long cry from the scintillating creature he had envisioned for his fantastical scheme, yet as time was of the essence, he could delay no longer. Perhaps, if she could be induced to cooperate, it was possible he might succeed. He leaned towards her.

"Who are you?" he asked.

She stiffened with a touch of hauteur. "I cannot see where that concerns you, sir!" she retorted.

He smiled. "How shall I address you then?" he parried disarmingly.

"I care naught how nor whether."

He smothered his irritation. "I have a predilection for apt names," he said. "So we shall call you Ellen—Lady Ellen, since you are obviously gentle-born."

She colored faintly, but said nothing, so he decided to bear down.

"I am going to be quite candid with you," he told her bluntly. "You know, of course, the fate that awaits you here: death by slow starvation, possibly rape and murder, or the lash and execution!" He saw her flinch, then he added: "On the other hand, if you obey me implicitly, I can offer you luxury beyond your wildest dreams!"

She made a grimace of distaste. "Why do you come here to torture a sorry creature like me?" she cried angrily. "Since I am not a whore, I am not for sale!"

He nodded approvingly, not at her words, but at the flash of spirit.

"My dear Ellen," he drawled, "everyone is *for sale* in his life. It is merely a matter of finding a mutually agreeable medium of exchange."

"La! I loathe cynics!"

Sir Guy laughed. "A good many cynics have been developed in this edifice of learning, my dear! Now—if I offered you a position as Lady-in-Waiting to Her Majesty, what would you say?"

"That you were a liar!"

H'mnn! A vein of wit beneath the grime, he thought.

"*Touché!*" he conceded with a smile. "Yet the . . . ah . . . position I do offer you was first proposed to an actual lady-in-waiting!" He saw her face cloud with puzzlement. "Weigh *that* against the gentle ministrations of Master Alexander and the ultimate dance at Tyburn, to say nothing of the lashing you will . . ."

She had closed her eyes, then suddenly her body went rigid. She shoved a knuckle into her mouth as if to stifle a scream . . . and before Sir Guy realized what was happening, she slipped to the floor with a crash! By the time he reached her side, Affable Jones came charging into the hall, followed closely by Charity and the gaoler.

"W'at the bloody 'ell 'appened?" bellowed Master Alexander.

When Sir Guy did not answer, Affable Jones elucidated the obvious. "She fynted!"

Charity, meanwhile, elbowed the knight out of her way and dropped beside the inert figure. Cradling Ellen's head in her arm, she glared defiantly at the male trio.

"*Fynted*, me butt-end!" she snarled. "Weak wi' starvation, so she is, the poor mite! For shyme! W'y don't ye feed 'er afore ye lead 'er to slaughter? Ye'd do as much to cattle, so ye would!"

Master Alexander had suffered enough insults for one evening, so he reached a horny talon towards the mass of blonde curls. Charity, in a rush of maternal ferocity, bared her own claws. To Affable Jones's keen disappointment, Sir Guy prevented a battle.

"The minx speaks true," he conceded. "I shall take them both and see if a bit of decent food won't melt resistance."

Master Alexander concealed his delight behind a commercial-wise mask. "Curse me, yer Honor, much as I'd like to oblige ye—as I've allus done in the past—on second thought, I dunno as I dast let this bigamist go. Me orders came from a mighty 'igh source, an' if she was found loose in London, it 'ud go 'ard wi' me!"

Sir Guy fished a small leather pouch out of his doublet. He waggled it until it tinkled like tiny bells, then without even looking at the gaoler, tossed it in his general direction. Deft from long practice, Master Alexander plucked the golden harvest out of the air.

"She shall not be found loose in London," promised the knight. "Either she goes to the Continent, or I shall have her returned to your tender hands."

Discovering the pouch was slightly heavier than usual, Master Alexander bowed until it seemed almost as if his belly sloshed on the floor.

"God bless ye, me lud, God bless ye!" he blubbered, jingling his reward like a child with a rattle. "Anythin' else I can do fer yer Worship?"

"Aye, summon me a conveyance to take my sorry prizes home!" snapped Sir Guy.

Charity gave a derisive snort. "*Sorry?* Glory be, w'at d'ye expect fer a couple of quid?" she jeered. "To bed the Queen?"

Affable Jones shouldered her aside. "'Old yer tongue, me saucy baggage! If ye want to know some'at, 'tis said 'is Honor *as* bedded the Queen!"

The little bawd whistled softly and reappraised her new master.

"Aye, I can well believe it!" she breathed admiringly.

Sir Guy was already stalking out of the chamber. Affable scooped up the limp figure from the floor, and with a beckoning jerk of his head to Charity, followed.

5

THE TRIP WAS a bleak ordeal. Not trusting his beloved master to the tender mercies of a strange coachman, Affable Jones had roughly shouldered that worthy out of his box and taken over the reins. Adding insult to injury, he forced the dispossessed driver to wallow through the mud and filth ahead of the coach, carrying a torch like a common link-boy.

Nor was it much more comfortable inside the lumbering vehicle, which seemed to drop from one deep rut to another with spine-jarring jolts. Conversation was, therefore, impractical, if not impossible.

Sir Guy, braced on the after-seat, was just as well pleased. The two women sat facing him. Charity seemed to be enjoying herself, despite the rough handling and the clammy fog which had again settled over the scene. She was wedged into a corner, a sisterly arm around the shoulder of the other girl to steady her. Although by law every householder was supposed to hang out a lantern at nightfall for the benefit of passers-by, this ordinance was seldom strictly obeyed. But when the coach did flounder within the radius of one of these primitive lights, the sallow glow afforded Sir Guy a glimpse of his charges.

However, when they clumped onto The Strand, lately paved, the going was vastly better. Affable Jones bellowed at the disconsolate coachman to jump on behind, then without bothering to ascertain whether or not he complied, lashed the horses into a gallop. Within a short time they pulled up before the domicile of Sir Guy.

Almost immediately thereon, a loud and profane altercation was joined between the coachman and Affable Jones. The former insisted on double pay, arguing that his chances of picking up a fare at this time of night and in this district were remote. On Mr. Jones's definitive refusal, the coachman cursed him for a faun's hind-end, and swore that he would remain in front of the residence until better paid. Affable assured him he was welcome to remain until his nags' manure reached the housetops. The coachman was hard-put to better that insult, so leaving the two flunkys to their talented obscenities, Sir Guy ushered the women into the house.

If the externals of the aged structure were disappointing, the interior most certainly was not. There was little that was English in the place; it was, rather, a visual record of Sir Guy's wanderings around the then-known world. The great central chamber was on the second floor; a difficult room to classify, for it was neither parlor, dining room, nor bedchamber, but rather a combination of all three. There was but one chair; an exquisite example of Florentine craftsmanship and reputedly used only by the Queen herself. However, there were myriad downy cushions strewn about the thick Persian carpets, and nestled in a partially screened alcove was a tremendous piece, half-bed, half-divan. The south end of the chamber was taken up largely with windows which overlooked the Thames.

Charity was enchanted. "Oh, sir, 'tis lovely!" she cried in starry-eyed rapture. She made a run for the sumptuous divan in the alcove, but came to a breathless pause when, on rounding the edge of the tapestried screen, she spotted a low, round table laden with viands.

"Food!" she squealed hysterically. She dashed back for the other girl who had entered the room with the vagueness of a somnambulist. "Look, dearie . . . *food!*" When Ellen continued apathetic, Charity shook her by the shoulders.

"Don't ye unnerstan', honey? 'Tis the cure for all w'at ails ye!" A sudden doubt flashed across her mind, for she glanced over her shoulder at their host. " 'Tis for us, ayant it, sir?"

Sir Guy laughed. "Every morsel of it, Charity!" he assured her.

"Howbeit, unless you are accustomed to Rhenish wines, I'd not imbibe too freely."

Charity tossed her head and sent a peal of laughter tinkling through the house.

"Aye, I'll line me belly first, then I care naught w'at the wine does to me, nor ye either, see—God love ye!" She tugged the other girl towards the table. "Come on, Duchess, let's stuff our gullets afore the dream vanishes!"

Ellen hesitated and looked down at her grimy hands and soiled garb. Sir Guy saw this, and pointed to a curtained archway.

"There's a dressing room where you can tidy up," he told them. "In the morning, I'll have baths prepared. In the meantime, you'll find sundry articles in there for your convenience." He bowed and opened the door. "And now, if you will excuse me, I'll bid you both adieu until tomorrow." Then he was gone.

Left to themselves, the two girls stared at each other in bewilderment.

"Well, I never! If 'e ayant the damndest rake'ell I ever seen!" marveled Charity. "See ye termorrow, 'e s'ys! W'at's 'e doin' *ternight*, I arsks ye?"

"It is doubtless a trick," cautioned Ellen. "You heard him say that a little food would melt resistance."

"*Resistance?*" gasped Charity. "'Oo'd resist an 'andsome rogue like 'em? Ho, not me, m'girl!" Her eyes narrowed and she tapped the other with an emphatic forefinger. "Nor ye either, if ye're 'arf smart, me 'aughty miss! I knows not w'at ye m'y *'ave* been, but I 'eard 'em s'y w'at ye *are*—a *bigamist!*"

Ellen turned away. "It was unintentional!" she choked. "I never dreamed he was already married!"

Charity sniggered. "W'ich be neither 'ere nor there! They'll flay the 'ide off'n ye, jes' the syme, an' w'en ye're danglin' in chynes, the 'ungry crows won't care w'ether ye was guilty or innercent!"

Ellen closed her eyes tight as she fought for control. "God in heaven, it is hard to believe men can be so bestial! Oh, I loathe them!"

Charity laughed outright, and gave the other an impulsive hug. "Lor' love ye, lamby, 'twould be a dreary life if they didn't 'ave a bit o' the ol' Nick in 'em! W'y, I don't know 'ow a poor girl 'ud get along; I swear I don't!" She giggled.

Ellen shuddered and moving towards the arch, half fearfully pushed the curtains aside. Finding the little chamber untenanted, she took heart and stepped inside. Charity hurried in behind her.

Manifestly the chamber was maintained for the exclusive use of feminine guests. The place was walled with French mirrors and dreamily illuminated with flattering candlelight. On an inlaid table stood a silver basin, supported by tiny silver cupids, and an urn of scented water. There were perfumed soaps and towels of caressing softness; there was a priceless collection of jeweled combs and a variety of brushes. But what wafted Charity into a seventh-heaven of ecstasy was a closetful of exotic negligees, ranging from sheer décolleté to regal fur-trimmed velvet.

"Glory be!" she chirruped, holding up a gown of black transparent silk. "Tyke a gander at this, will ye! Wouldn't 'ide no more'n would a puff o' smoke, I trow. Heigh-ho, 'e don't miss a trick, not 'im!" She displayed two or three others for her companion's inspection. "W'ich'll ye wear, dearie?"

But Ellen was not listening, for in lifting a folded towel, she had uncovered a cache of five gold coins! She stood staring at them in disbelief.

Charity, on peering over her shoulder, saw the gold and guessed what was in the other's mind.

"Ah-ah! Don't fall fer that ol' gyme, me girl!" she cautioned. "Doubtless 'e left 'em there to tempt ye! Tyke 'em, an' ye'll get no more! I knows that from h'experience, 'avin' myde the mistake onc't!"

"I don't want any *more!*" Ellen said grimly. "I just want to get out of this trap!"

Charity heaved a discouraged sigh as she returned the wispy garment to its rack.

"Ye're balmy in the crumpet, that's w'at!" she snorted.

Ellen slipped the coins in her bodice, then hastily washed her face and hands. She tried to comb out her long tresses, but they were so tangled from weeks of inattention, the teeth of the comb broke. Brushing it as best she could, she did her hair up in a bun on her nape. Charity, having completed her own brief toilette, nodded approvingly.

"Bless ye, sugar!" she observed with disarming candor. "Ye ayant 'arf so ugly as I thought!" She put a friendly arm about Ellen's waist and drew her gently towards the other chamber. "Let's eat, dearie! Ye'll feel friskier on a full belly!"

The table was low and intimate, so they sat opposite one another, cross-legged on little individual nests of cushions. Colored candles, cleverly aided by tiny mirrors, warmed the setting with a dancing light that seemed almost to whisper. It was a touch of fairyland! A scene from the Arabian Nights!

There were over a score of dishes, ranging from the familiar to exotic concoctions from the mysterious East. Charity was enthralled and clapped her hands in rapture, then she stuck an explorative forefinger into each strange dish in turn and tentatively sampled them.

"Lor' love ye!" she cried. "I 'ardly knows w'ere to begin!"

Ellen picked up a bottle of wine, and after sniffing it suspiciously, poured a little into each of their goblets.

"I know not how long you have been hungry," she murmured, "but for myself, I dare not eat more than a mouthful." She lifted her glass with quaking hands, and as the wine passed her lips, she closed her eyes tightly, as if, perhaps, to stifle a remembrance. Two tears escaped down her pale cheeks.

Charity observed this, but with native tact, said nothing.

There was a haunch of venison directly in front of Ellen, so after she had sampled her wine, she offered to carve a portion for Charity, but Charity scorned anything so commonplace and heaped her plate with exotic dishes. Between mouthfuls, she maintained an almost unbroken and cheerful prattle.

Ellen, on the contrary, said little. She carved herself a thin slice of meat. Then, as she started to lay down the blade, she became suddenly aware it was not an orthodox carving knife at all, but a magnificent dagger of Damascus steel.

When this knowledge entered her consciousness, her ravishing hunger went out. She stared at it for a long time in a terrible fascination, after which she seemed suffused with a deadly calm.

Though Charity did not comprehend the reason, she sensed something peculiar had happened.

"Ye act like ye'd got yer strength all o' a sudden!" she observed.

"I have, Charity, oh, I have!" breathed Ellen, and smiled.

However, it was not a smile to inspire confidence, and Charity was concerned.

"Tyke it easy, sugar!" she cautioned. "Ye'd better not eat too much!"

Ellen smiled again, and tilted her head, as if listening. Puzzled, Charity followed suit. From somewhere in the house below came the murmur of masculine voices; the jolly twang of Affable Jones and, less often, the disciplined steeliness of their host. Drowning these out, with persistent regularity, was the rumble of coach-wheels, noisy testimony that the disgruntled coachman was carrying out his vow.

Peculiarly enough, these unrelated sounds seemed to please the woman known as Ellen. She pushed her plate away, refilled her goblet, then settling back into her nest of cushions, studied her companion over the rim of her glass.

This continued until Charity could stand it no longer.

"'Ere now, 'ere now, m'girl!" she protested. "W'y d'ye stare at me so, like ye be givin' me the evil-eye? Be'n't I yer friend?"

"Are you truly?" asked Ellen softly. "Will you prove it, Charity?"

The latter shivered. "Well, lack-a-day! I'll not say nay until I 'ears w'at ye want o' me."

"Help me get out of this hell-hole!"

Charity's eyes widened. "Ye're daft!" she cried. "'Ow'd we get out? W'ere'd we go? An' w'y, I arsk ye, *w'y?* Surely, even 'Er Synted Marjesty couldn't arsk fer more'n we got now!"

Ellen drained her glass, bringing a flood of color to her cheeks. Then she leaned forward and her voice, though softer, had the ring of sword steel.

"Harken to me, Charity! I have here five pieces of gold! Do you hear the coach outside? Well, for one piece of gold, the driver will take us anywhere in London! When that is done, you can have the other four!"

"I never!" gasped Charity. "What about ye, ma'am?"

Ellen's eyes and mouth had narrowed until her face took on a feline expression.

"I shall go to a certain address," she explained in a tone of awesome finality. "I shall leave it with my name cleared, or . . . *or I will not leave it!*"

Charity glanced longingly around the room. "Ah me, I'd 'ate to abandon this 'ere bit o' 'eaven, dearie!" she argued. "W'y not jes' ferget this other gent w'at done ye wrong? Men will be men, ye know, an' there's naught a gal kin . . ."

"*Please,* Charity! I cannot stand this!" Her jaw tightened. "If you refuse to aid me, I shall tell this . . . this fiend to take us back to Newgate!"

"Heigh-ho, ye *are* balmy!" deplored Charity. She turned her head to look at the door, thus she did not see Ellen snatch up the knife and slip it between the folds of her dress.

"Alas," continued Charity with a sigh, "since 'twas plainly ye 'e wanted instead o' me—though God knows w'y, I declare!—if we're determined to pull out, w'y, there's naught for it, I suppose. Howbeit, there's no need to gi' me all the gold. Share an' share alike, I allus . . ."

Ellen darted around the table and gave her a quick hug.

"No, no—you shall have all four!" she insisted warmly. "I shall have no need for gold, that is sure!"

Having made the decision, Charity assumed leadership. Purloining a long-necked, unopened bottle of Rhenish wine to serve the double duty of weapon and future provender, she tiptoed to the door at the head of the stairs. As she opened it, the sound of voices grew clearer. She laid an admonishing finger across her lips, then beckoning the other girl to follow, slipped onto the landing.

Step by step, keeping close against the wall to avoid making the stairs squeak, they ghosted down the long flight. They had a bad moment on reaching the ground floor when they discovered that the door leading into the chamber where the men were chatting was ajar. The rectangular patch of light projected on the floor of the hallway was a hazardous obstacle to be hurdled.

Scarcely daring to breathe, the two girls crouched in the shadows at the foot of the stairs until an uproarious burst of laughter from the other room suggested the men were occupied. Charity hissed, *"Now!"* and they flitted across the danger patch into the haven of darkness beyond.

After that, it was but the work of an instant to draw the bolt, ease open the heavy planked door and glide swiftly into the fog-infested night.

Ellen sobbed in relief. "We made it, thank God!" .

"Aye," conceded Charity wistfully, "we myde it. Yet, damme, I'd 'ave rather known 'is ludship better! D'ye believe 'e truly bedded the Queen?"

Ellen raised her chin a notch. "I cannot say! Yet I would prefer to believe Her Majesty above such debauchery!"

Charity hooted derisively. "Well, she ayant—God love 'er! Our Good Bess be 'ooman an' earthy, an' the people love 'er fer it! She ayant no femyle monk, she ayant. Not 'er!"

Out of the cloying mist came the rumble of wheels to ease their tension.

"It is our coach!" breathed Ellen relievedly. "For the love of heaven, do not let it elude us!" She stepped into the roadway.

When appealed to, the voluble coachman was not only willing, he was delighted. He swore he'd take them any place within five-and-twenty miles of London for a quid; he was so elated, he wanted to pound on Sir Guy's door and boast to that gentleman's face that he had found a fare, but Ellen forbade it.

"Whither art bound, *m'lydy?*" he asked in mock humility.

Ellen hesitated. "Do you happen to know the residence of Lord Darlington?" she inquired.

"Ho, that . . . ?" The driver pulled up short with a suggestive leer. "Aye, ma'am, I knows the gay dog! 'E lives on The Strand near . . ."

Ellen cut him short. "Take us there at once!" she said with such icy authority that both Charity and the coachman gaped in astonishment.

"Aye, m'lydy, aye!" muttered the coachman civilly, and knuckled his forelock as the girls climbed into his conveyance.

"Glory be!" marveled Charity as she settled on the hard seat. "Ye truly does sound like a duchess, I trow!"

The coachman was as good as his boast; he eventually located the house he sought along The Strand—but not until he had lost his way in a fog-infested labyrinth of alleys and by-ways for the better part of two hours. By the time he brought his clumsy vehicle to a halt, the two girls were shaken and exhausted. Ellen urged Charity to retain the coach to carry her to whatever destination she should choose, but Charity swore she would rather crawl all over London on her hands and knees than longer risk her poor bones in that brutal conveyance. So with no lost love, they bade the coachman farewell, and appraised the house before them.

It was small but extremely fashionable, and what interested them the more, it was the only house on the street with lights still burning.

"So this be the 'ome o' yer lover, eh?" admired Charity, gesturing with the long-necked bottle. "Not bad, dearie, not 'arf bad!"

Ellen bit her lip. "You must leave now, Charity!" she said tautly.

Charity stole a sidelong glance at her. In the sallow glow of the doorlamps, Ellen's features looked gray and strained.

"Ashamed o' me, 'oney?"

"Dear Lord, no!" Ellen assured her. "You have proven yourself a true friend! It is only I do not want you jeopardized by . . ."

Charity interrupted with a mischievous giggle. "Saints o' glory, sweetie, so much 'as 'appened to me, I can't rightly recall w'ether I been *jeopardized* or no, but I'm willin' to gi' it a whirl! One thing I do know—ye ain't a-goin' into this 'ouse wi'out me, myke up yer mind to that!"

Ellen seemed to have lapsed into a trance. Shrugging absently, she walked up to the ornate door. She knocked, and in the heavy stillness of the night, the sound seemed to spread in all directions. After a long pause, a wooden-faced lackey opened the door and bowed them inside. If he was surprised by the lateness of their visit, he gave no sign.

[45]

"Take me to your master at once!" Ellen said in a tone that brooked no opposition.

"Aye, m'lady. His lordship is waiting in the game room," murmured the lackey, and ushered them down the hall.

Charity giggled softly and whispered in Ellen's ear. "'Is ludship m'y be wytin', but I'll wyger it ayant fer us! Eh, dearie?"

Ellen made no reply.

The servant led them into a room at the far end of the hall, and backing out, softly closed the door. Thus they found themselves in a long chamber, hauntingly illumined by candles set in niches around the wainscotted walls. At the far end, opposite the entry, was a massive fireplace with great logs burning cheerily.

A man was standing just to one side of the hearth so that the blaze projected his shadow on the southern wall. His back was towards the door, and from the way he leaned against the mantel, he seemed oblivious of the arrival of his guests. He was gorgeously arrayed in padded trunk-hose and a doublet of silver cloth.

The two girls stood silent for a moment in a little well of shadow. Still the man did not turn, and the only sound was the crackle of burning logs. Charity began to squirm restlessly. Then Ellen slipped her hand into the bodice of her prison dress and took a step forward.

"*My lord!*" she challenged, in a voice as clear as a trumpet call.

The man jerked convulsively, like an awakened sleeper, then turned slowly.

"No doubt you thought you were easily rid of me, my lord!" Ellen went on. "Yet the evil thing you did . . ." She came to a choking pause as the man's features came within the radius of light. "Oh, God help me—*you!*"

The man was Sir Guy Spangler!

Charity's nimble mind first grasped the situation. "Saints o' glory!" she cried. "'E foxed us, so 'e did! Law me, I should 'ave suspicioned 'twas a trick w'en that broad-butted knave bounced us all o'er Lunnon Town!"

Sir Guy laughed heartily, and sauntered towards them. "Bless you, Charity, I'm glad you did not! Howbeit, my pets, it was not so much a trick as an expedient device to transport you to these quarters, which I am sure you will find suitable."

Ellen appeared stunned. "Then this is not the home of . . . ?" she began, then stopped abruptly.

"*Darlington?*" Sir Guy finished for her, with a short chuckle. "No, I'm thankful to say, it is not. Did you have something for that elusive seducer? A message, perhaps? A gift?" He moved in front of her.

Ellen drew herself up to her full height until she seemed balanced on the balls of her feet. For an instant she closed her eyes, as if in mute prayer, then suddenly throwing up her right arm, she cried: "Aye! I had *this* for him!" and drove the blade at the knight.

At the first glimpse of bared steel, Charity bleated in alarm and tried to grab the arm of the hysterical girl. But she was too late! The blow took Sir Guy full in the chest! He had time for but one startled grunt of astonishment before he sank backwards against a table.

"God syve us!" shrieked Charity. "Ye've kilt 'im dead!"

6

PECULIARLY ENOUGH, Sir Guy did not appear either dead, or seriously wounded; in point of fact, he was grinning crookedly.

"You exaggerate, Charity," he remarked whimsically, "though I confess the chit has more strength than I anticipated." He straightened coolly, glanced down at the ruinous slash of his doublet—through which could be seen a section of the chain mail which had saved his life, then reaching forward, removed the dagger from Ellen's nerveless fingers.

"You will have no further need for this," he assured her. "I merely loaned it to you to learn whether you were weak enough to take your own life, or spirited enough to attempt mine."

"You know now!" grated Ellen.

"Ayant it the ruddy trufe!" sighed Charity. "Though to speak free, m'lud, 'twas a scummy trick to pl'y on a lydy, I declare! Be ye tryin' to get us 'ung?"

A ghost of a smile flitted over the man's face, then his manner underwent one of those mercurial changes for which he was notorious.

"Hold your tongue!" he barked at Charity so suddenly he left her gasping, then fixed his now cold gaze on Ellen.

"As for you, madame, I demand an instant and unequivocal answer: do you agree to do my bidding, or do you start back for Newgate and whatever fate awaits you?"

Ellen's spine went rigid, and she met his steel with flint of equal temper. It was Charity who broke the deadlock.

"Saints o' glory, m'lud, the gaoler said 'e didn't want 'er back!"

Sir Guy raised one eyebrow, then clapped his hands smartly. Almost simultaneously, the door opened and three men shoved into the long room—Sergeant Pistol, Affable Jones, and their late coachman (whose presence elicited a strangled oath from Charity). In this luxuriant setting, their obvious villainy was accentuated.

"I said *start back for Newgate!*" the knight corrected the bawd. "Alas, I know not what orders good Master Alexander may have given this cutthroat lackey of his, in the untoward event our haughty miss be returned to his loving care." Sir Guy indicated the coachman, who bowed as if flattered. "Nor can I guarantee the treatment you might receive from these faithful spaniels of mine, who are, on occasion, overzealous in my interest." He shrugged in resignation. "So make up your mind, madame, but make it up quick!"

Ellen's cold stare never wavered. "Turn your curs loose!" she dared him. "Vile as they are, nothing they could do would be half so loathsome as an affair with you!"

"Oh, dear Jesus!" gasped Charity unbelievingly.

Sir Guy laughed mockingly. "By my troth, madame, I do admire your spirit, e'en though in all fairness to myself, I cannot respect your judgment! Be that as it may, let me assure you in the utmost sincerity, you are not the type to arouse me. So, in that at least, we meet on common ground."

"God, 'e's blunt!" marveled Charity.

Ellen, too, was a trifle nonplused. "Then, dear Lord in heaven, what *do* you want?" she burst out distractedly.

"Complete compliance!" snapped Sir Guy. "Nay, more—your cooperation in a venture which, if it succeeds, will make you the envy of every woman on the Continent!"

"You are insane!"

Their host chuckled without mirth. "Desperate, perchance, but not insane." His voice resumed its cutting edge. "Believe me, madame, if another wench would do—Charity here, for instance—you would now be safely returned to your dungeon in Newgate or"—he nodded towards the three knaves—"floating in the Thames."

Ellen wasn't intimidated by the threat of either death or prison, but the reference to Charity startled her. She looked into the flushed face of the little blonde, then swung back to her tormentor.

"What happens to . . . to Charity?" she asked, her defiance slightly moderated.

Sir Guy spread his hands. "That depends entirely on you! Should you accept my offer, she shall remain as your personal maid."

"If I refuse . . . ?"

The man sighed. "Alas, in that unpleasant event, she must, perforce, share your fate."

"Your beast!" Ellen rasped between clenched teeth. "You inhuman beast! You leave me no alternative!"

"Then you agree to obey me implicitly?"

The girl hesitated a long time before nodding. "I agree—on two conditions," she said with careful deliberation. "First, that no harm befalls Charity, since she is, in effect, an innocent bystander, and, second—and in this, sir, I am adamant!—that *you* will not touch me! Whatever other fate may befall me matters little, but on those two points I must have your solemn oath before witnesses!"

Sir Guy laughed. "'Pon my soul, I can agree to those stipulations readily enough. And as for witnesses, why, we have them here at hand!" He glanced over his shoulder at the villainous trio. "Attend, you knaves! Mark well my vow! I hereby solemnly swear that by no act nor order of mine shall harm come to a certain saucy bawd, known to us here as Charity Lane; I further take oath with equal solemnity that I, personally, will not now, or ever, touch, fondle or defile, for purposes of romantic or carnal pleasure or pursuit, the person of this woman, to be known henceforth as 'Lady Ellen' . . ." He heard Charity's audible sigh, and added mischievously, "Unless the said Lady Ellen should herself beseech it. Amen!"

"*That*," cried Ellen feelingly, "will never happen!"

The man bowed mockingly. "Thank you, madame! I shall regard that as a promise."

Her face flamed red. "Enough of your ill-bred sneering!" she cried. "What is this venture in which I am to *cooperate?*"

His smile was tantalizing. "Ah, my lady, that is a delicate matter which you and I will discuss under more auspicious circumstances. In the meantime, consider this house your own. You will find it competently and discreetly staffed, and everything supplied for your comfort. Charity, here, shall remain in your service, and my peerless henchman, the inimitable Affable Jones"—Sir Guy couldn't repress a chuckle at the expression on Ellen's face—"will be practically at your elbow at all times to see that your slightest whim is gratified. Just command him, but—a word of caution!—Do not permit him to inveigle you in any games of chance. He is an inveterate gambler."

Ellen shut her eyes tightly as she fought for self-control. "I do not understand it!" she whispered, more to herself than to anyone else.

"Don't try," advised Sir Guy. "I shall see you anon and coach you in the first phase of our operation. Meanwhile, may I suggest a good night's rest?" With a brief nod, he left them.

When the men were gone, Ellen collapsed shakily into a chair. Charity exhaled a long bewildered sigh.

"Well, I never!" she muttered. "'E's a character, that one! Yet I do declare, m'lydy, methinks ye done sore wrong to myke the deal ye did!"

Ellen heaved her shoulders. "What else *could* I do? It was death, or worse, for . . . well, for both of us!"

"Lor' love ye, dearie, 'twasn't *that* deal I meant!" snorted the other. "'Twas in makin' 'im swear 'e'd ne'er touch ye! Ye may live to regret that, me girl!"

Ellen went white, and her glance cut like a bull-whip.

"*Charity!* Never, *never* suggest such an offensive thing to me again!"

Charity made a deep curtsy, more to hide a smile than anything.

"As ye will, m'lydy!" she agreed demurely.

Despite her predicament, Ellen slept soundly. She had gone to bed too exhausted to undress, and it was with the leaden sensation of coming out of an opiate that she opened her eyes in response to the pummeling of the anxious Charity.

"Lor' love ye, ma'am, wyke up!" pleaded the latter. "'Tis four hours since cockcrow, an' 'is nibs promised 'e'd . . ."

Ellen had begun a yawning smile, but at the reminder of her host, the smile vanished.

"What a ghastly thing to awaken to!" she said bitterly. She started to throw back the covers, but Charity stopped her. "Tarry, m'lydy! Breakfast be comin' up, so ye kin eat in bed, like a ruddy princess! I also ordered a tub o' warm water an' a good stiff scrubbin' brush brought in arter ye've et!"

Ellen had to smile. "Charity, you *are* a treasure!" she said with sudden warmth. "How did you happen to know the one thing I wanted most in this world was just that—a hot bath?"

Charity giggled behind her hand. "W'y, to speak true, ma'am, 'twas Affable thought o' it, not me."

Ellen frowned in puzzlement. "Affable . . . ? Who . . . ?" Her mouth flattened. "Oh! You refer to that revolting wretch who cuts throats or something for . . ." She stopped, as if gagging on the name of him whom she loathed so intensely.

"Aye, that's Affable!" rattled the other. "Jolly bastard, so 'e is! Kept me in stitches 'til I thought I'd bust a . . ."

"*Please!*"

"Yes 'mmnn!" muttered Charity.

A servant brought in a tray of food, and while Ellen was eating, two sturdy lackeys placed a wooden tub in the center of the spacious bedroom, and partially filled it with steamy hot water. Charity promptly began scenting it with various perfumes chosen from the fascinating array of bottles on the dressing table. In her lavish enthusiasm, she soon had the chamber smelling like a tropical swamp.

"Merciful heavens, child! You're strangling me!" gasped Ellen, hopping out of bed. "Open the windows, I beg you!"

Charity reluctantly interrupted her experiments to throw back the shutters, whereupon a shaft of sunlight splashed a pool of glory on the carpet.

Ellen stretched luxuriously, and crossing to the window, looked down into the private garden behind the mansion. It was magnificently, if seductively, laid out, with charming footpaths and enticing arbors, the whole completely enclosed by a serpentine brick wall. Yet it was not the beauty Ellen saw; it was the bars on the window and the formidable height of the garden wall.

"Ah, I am still in prison!" she mused sadly.

Charity hooted. "Ho, if this be prison, ma'am, I 'opes nobody ever turns me out!" Apparently the hideous garb Ellen was wearing reminded her of Newgate, for she added feelingly: "'Ere, sugar! Let me dig ye out o' that stinkin' sack!"

With a rueful smile, Ellen moved into the patch of sunlight and stood still while the other went to work on the objectionable dress. Whether the cloth was actually rotted, or whether Charity shredded it wilfully, Ellen could not be certain, but in any event, the garment was ruined beyond all hope of repair by the time Charity tossed it into a corner—out of sight.

During the whole act of denudation, Charity maintained an unbroken flow of surprised ejaculations, shrill squeals of delight, and ribald commentary that had Ellen in a veritable ferment of embarrassment. The bawd had an earthy simile for almost every anatomical feature her divestment bared. She went into raptures over Ellen's high, firm breasts, the slimness of her waist, and the balanced perfection of her thighs and graceful legs.

"Saints o' glory, honeybun!" she cried ecstatically. "If I 'ad a body like that to work wi', w'y, I'd be the richest woman in England, I trow!"

Ellen giggled in spite of herself, then said as sternly as she could: "Charity, you must not say such things!"

Charity, down on her knees peeling off the last stocking, reared back on her haunches in astonishment.

"Lor' love ye, ma'am, I didn't mean no 'arm! 'Twas from the 'eart I spoke!"

Ellen sighed, and leaning over, patted the girl on the cheek.

"I know you meant it as a kindness," she said gently. "But a lady does not say such things."

The mischief kindled in the other's eyes. "Aye, but I ayant no lydy, ma'am; I'm a bawd, an' a ruddy good one, if I do 'ave to s'y so me ownself!"

Ellen shrugged and turned towards the tub. "Charity, I'm afraid you are incorrigible! Yet . . ." She glanced over her shoulder with a sad smile. "I love you in spite of it!" She sampled the water with an explorative toe, then finding the temperature to her liking, stepped daintily into the vessel and sat down. As the scented water enveloped her body, she relaxed sensuously.

"Oh, dear Lord, this is heavenly!"

Charity scrambled to her feet. "Ye jes' lie there an' soak, dearie, w'ilest I chyce the mice out o' yer 'air!"

Ellen needed no urging. The size of the wooden tub was such that by clasping her upraised knees with her hands, and settling a trifle, she could rest the back of her neck on the curved rim. Thus, when she tilted her head, her long tresses trailed on the carpet. Charity, meanwhile, had armed herself with a comb and brush, and, seated on the floor behind Ellen, began to brush the tangled mess.

It was a difficult chore that brought forth impatient oaths from Charity and wails of protest from Ellen. When the worst of the task was over, Charity went to work with the comb, while Ellen closed her eyes and settled deeper in the water.

Under the repetitious ministrations of Charity, the lackluster mousiness of the hair was transmuted to a rich wine-redness, with an iridescence, stolen from the shaft of sunlight, which made it appear flecked with gold dust.

"May God strike me dead if I lie!" Charity breathed fervently. "Ye're almost bootiful, m'lydy!"

From behind Charity, a mocking voice responded: "Why, Charity—she *is* beautiful!"

With a bleat of surprise, the little bawd toppled over backwards to lie gaping up at the sardonic face of Sir Guy. Ellen gasped in dismay and started to rise, then abruptly reminded of her nudity and conscious that the soapy water offered the only chance of concealment, she shrank down until the water was level with her chin. Of her body, all that was visible were her knees—two dimpled islands in a sudsy sea.

"How dare you, sir!" she fumed at him. "Leave this room instanter!"

Sir Guy chuckled heartily, then hooking a chair with his boot, hauled it into position between window and tub.

"And not only beautiful, but high-spirited as well!" he applauded, sprawling in the chair, his long legs stretched before him. "Charity, go below until I summon you."

The blonde hastily scrambled erect. "Aye, sir!" She started for the door, only to stop short at a sharp cry from Ellen.

"Charity! Don't you *dare* leave me like this!"

Charity turned back. "If ye s'y so, m'lydy," she sighed. Then she encountered Sir Guy's unwavering stare, and fled the room.

"*Charity* . . . !" wailed Ellen frantically. But Charity was gone.

Then followed a painful silence. Under the cool derisive gaze of the courtier, Ellen shrank even lower, but her eyes blazed with such fury, he was moved to remark: " 'Pon my soul, you can look poisonous as a viper!" He chuckled to take the sting out of his words. "I'm sure you must be beastly uncomfortable! May I hand you a gown?"

"And rise before you?" she lashed back. "Thank you! I prefer to remain where I am!"

He shrugged, patting back a yawn. "Aye, I suppose it is preferable to the gaol. By the way—did Alexander make his usual advances?"

"You evil-minded beast!"

"I was merely curious. Doubtless the brute first wanted to be sure you would not be pardoned."

Ellen's cramped position was fast becoming unbearable. She pressed her hands against the bottom of the tub in an effort to support her bowed back. The movement brought her shoulders above the surface.

"In God's name!" she fulminated. "Say what you have to say and get out!"

He nodded. "In due time, my dear. You recall, I presume, our little agreement?"

"Yes, yes! I am not in the habit of breaking my promises!" she cried impatiently. "What disgusting thing is expected of me?"

Sir Guy glanced over his shoulder to make certain they could not be overheard, then he leaned forward and rested his elbows on his knees. When he spoke, he fitted each word to the next with careful deliberation.

"Ellen, I am going to be completely candid with you because I would prefer to have you as a partner in this venture, rather than as a pawn—so to speak! That choice will be yours, but it must be one or the other, because too much is at stake for me to temporize!"

"Get on with your story!" she urged desperately.

"Well, this is the background: the Tsar of Muscovy—potentially one of the richest monarchs in the world!—saw in the possession of a traveler an ivory miniature of a titled English woman, a certain Mary Hastings, a kinswoman of Her Majesty. The Tsar was smitten, so he obtained the painting and dispatched an envoy to England to bring Lady Mary back to Muscovy to be his wife." Sir Guy cocked his head. "Do you follow me thus far?"

In her anguish, Ellen had straightened a trifle until the upper halves of her breasts showed like twin headlands jutting into the sea.

"I fail to see what any of this has to do with me?"

He grinned. "Patience, child, patience!" He sobered as he paused to pick up the threads of his discourse.

"The Imperial Envoy, a Count Nikita, landed in London, armed with the potent ivory miniature so that there could be no mistake in his selection. That was ten days ago, to be exact. Meanwhile, in some fashion not yet clear, Lady Mary discovered the purpose of his mission before the envoy could interview her and"—Sir Guy spread his hands in an eloquent gesture—"*vanished!*

"The Count, naturally enough, is in a fine lather! It appears that the Muscovite Emperor, known to those he has befriended as 'Ivan the Severe,' and to those who have incurred his enmity as 'the Terrible,' is not a prince to disappoint with impunity. In a word, the envoy is desperate, and to anyone lifting him down from the horns of his dilemma, his gratitude would be boundless!"

"*Please!*" whimpered Ellen. "I can't stand this!" She shifted her position, no longer caring how much of her body was exposed.

"I'm fast approaching the climax," he assured her.

"Not half fast enough!"

He chuckled. "Well, this is the crux: by happy coincidence, I discovered that Lady Mary has a twin sister, heretofore unknown, who is even more alluring than Mary. Within an hour or two, I am going to introduce this twin to Count Nikita. If she looks sufficiently like the miniature to pass inspection—and I have sound reason to believe she will—the Count will engage to escort her to Muscovy, there to wed the Tsar of All the Russias! Think of it, my dear! A virtual queen, with the fabulous wealth of the East at her feet!"

Ellen stared at him in bewilderment. "In God's name, what has all this intrigue to do with me?"

Sir Guy rose and bowed. "It has everything to do with you, my lucky lady!" he said softly. "For that twin sister is—*you.*"

Ellen sat bolt upright. "*Me?* Father in heaven—have you lost your mind?"

"I hope not," he said with a grin, "else I'll lose my head!" His smile soured. "What ails you, madame? Are you so enamored of the coziness of Newgate's dungeon that you prefer it to palaces of Muscovy? Or can it be that you are not willing to trade the odoriferous charms of Master Alexander to be the consort of the Tsar of All the Russias?"

The girl was wild-eyed. "The scheme is utter madness!" she cried. "I happen to know that Mary Hastings has no sister!"

"Ah—but I happen to know she has! I just gave her one!"

Ellen gave a distraught sob. "What happens when this Muscovite envoy learns the truth?"

"Nothing, my dear, nothing! Count Nikita has long since learned what all men of the world eventually learn—to hold his tongue!" Sir Guy chuckled. "A laudable accomplishment that need not be limited to the male sex, my lady!"

"Dear Lord, I cannot agree to this hellish plot! It is doomed to . . ."

The steely claws cut through the velvet gloves. "You have already agreed!" he cut her off. "I am *commanding*, not *requesting!*" He let his glance sweep her half-bared torso until she shrank down into the water. After that, he gave her a warped smile.

"You must hurry! I have arranged for a hairdresser, who is already on his way here. He will be followed by a costumier, after which you will sit briefly for your portrait, or, rather, shall we say—an *alteration* of your portrait." He laughed softly. "By four of the clock this afternoon, you should be sufficiently impressive to be interviewed by the Emperor's personal envoy!"

"*Inspected*, not interviewed!" sobbed Ellen. "God in heaven! If I am to be sold into slavery, why waste time with costumiers and hairdressers? Why not just stand me on the auction block and complete my degradation?"

"Well, by my troth!" he marveled mockingly. "What a miraculous change a little food and a night's sleep hath wrought! Yet, I'll wager that when you lay starving in Newgate gaol, tortured by rats and lice, and haunted by your coming fate, what I now offer would have seemed a gift from paradise!"

She seemed not to hear him. "*Slavery!*" she muttered in revulsion.

He jeered at her. "Methinks you should not object to slavery, my lady, since you've just come from something perhaps even worse!"

Her chin snapped up and she glared at him through her tears.

"*Get out!*" she rasped between clenched teeth. "Get out of my sight!"

At the door, Sir Guy paused to give her a courtly bow.

"Until four, my lady!" he murmured, and backed out of the chamber.

7

AT EXACTLY half after three of the clock, Sir Guy's coach-and-four clattered noisily up to the front of the temporary abode of the Muscovite envoy, while simultaneously Sergeant Pistol, with all the considerable furtiveness at his command, slithered into the same edifice from the rear. Precise timing was essential, since Sir Guy had come to discuss the miniature, whereas Sergeant Pistol had come to return it.

With due ceremony, Sir Guy was ushered into the great hall. If he felt the slightest perturbation, it was not reflected in his demeanor. Gorgeously arrayed in white satin, ornamented with silver and Flanders lace, he seemed the very epitome of the Elizabethan courtier as he sauntered into the presence of the Imperial Envoy of the Tsar.

Count Nikita Alexanderovitch Prokoff was a *boyar*, a member of the nobility, and he looked the part. It was said the Muscovites "esteemed great beards and great bellies," and the Count was well endowed with both. Yet his corpulence was not indicative of softness, for his very carriage suggested great power and endurance. This burly Muscovite was dressed in an exotic garment the like of which, in richness and beauty, the Englishman had never seen before. It was a long, flowing coat of rich purple damask, heavily embroidered and decorated with gold thread and precious stones. The luxurious collar of white fur V-ed at the throat, then straightened upright until it touched the lobes of the ears, thus forming a kind of heart-shaped setting for the envoy's striking head.

It was that head which commanded the visitor's minute attention. The shaved pate was concealed beneath a close-fitting cap, at least half an ell in height, fashioned of sable and studded with pearls. A broad forehead rested on a base of craggy brows which, in turn, shaded the most piercing eyes Sir Guy had yet encountered. A long curved nose, with prominent nostrils that seemed to quiver with suppressed excitement, gave the face a hawkish cast. The upper lip supported a ferocious-looking mustache that arced out on either side to merge finally with the great beard cascading down to his chest. The nether lip was clean-shaven, revealing a mouth peculiarly like the Englishman's; a mouth suggestive of a wide range of emotion.

After an exchange of formalized civilities, conducted in Latin, since the envoy spoke no English, the latter flipped his hand, and as if by magic, his fierce-looking attendants vanished. Only then did he deign to smile.

"Ah, my friend!" he boomed in a throaty growl. "Your communication raised my hopes. Am I to understand you have located the elusive damsel?"

The Englishman's shrug would have done justice to a Frenchman for its eloquent ambiguity. The Muscovite's eyes grew a shade brighter, but his fixed smile remained unchanged.

"In any event, let us discuss the matter in comfort," he suggested heartily, and steered Sir Guy into a small anteroom. Obviously this chamber had been prearranged for the purpose, since a low table containing liquor and two golden goblets stood in the center with two richly carved chairs on either side. A fitting stage for a game in which the stakes were so high, Sir Guy conceded to himself as he sat down.

There was nothing subtle about Count Nikita's gambit. He poured two gigantic potions of the liquor—which the wily Englishman identified as *Tzarkowino,* a paralyzing Russian libation—and offered a toast to Elizabeth. Sir Guy was, of course, obligated to toast the Emperor of Muscovy. The Count filled the goblets a third time, and countered with a toast to England, following which the fiery pendulum swung to the Land of Muscovy. When they finally got down to toasting each other, Sir Guy decided it was time to break the sequence.

"And now," he suggested with a significant smile, "a toast to the enchanting playmate for your imperial master!"

Count Nikita emptied his goblet in one swallow and shoved it aside. He leaned across the table.

"Ah-h! Then you *have* found her?"

Sir Guy pursed his lips. "That depends on varying factors."

Without shifting his gaze from the Englishman's face, the Count reached under the folds of his coat and produced a heavy leather sack of gold which he plumped on the table. Sir Guy's pulse quickened, for there was plainly a fortune in the bag, yet he contrived to shake his head. The other blinked in surprise.

"You misinterpret my meaning, Niki," Sir Guy began with easy familiarity. "And in any event, you and I should not be bargaining like Syrians, since we are in somewhat similar straits. Look now—we both know that if you return to your Grand Prince empty-handed, you are doomed; only my cooperation can save you! By the same token, I am also involved in a delicate predicament from which, perhaps, only you can extricate me." He smiled a conspiratorial smile. "There are some things gold alone cannot accomplish."

The envoy's blazing eyes probed like scalpels. "You have only to command me, my friend!" he boomed.

Sir Guy absently revolved his goblet stem between his finger and thumb. "A ship, in which I have a major financial interest, wandered into the northern domain of your master," he explained slowly. "It was seized by the Tsar's officers."

"Ah-ha! I take it your ship was not under the protection of the English Muscovy Company?"

"Unfortunately," Guy confessed, "it was not."

Count Nikita ripped the seal off another bottle and poured another lethal round.

"Disastrous!" he murmured regretfully. "There is an ironclad treaty covering that point!"

Sir Guy managed a long, discouraged sigh. "Alas, then we must both concede defeat!"

The Count shrugged, but his eyes were watchful. "The day of the miracle is not past," he said. "For example, if I could be certain you have this woman, this Lady Mary . . . ?"

Sir Guy stared moodily into his glass. "To speak true—I do not have Mary Hastings."

Temper snapping, the Muscovite lurched angrily to his feet. "By the bones of my grandmother!" he exploded. "If you do not have her, come you here to mock me?"

"Softly, softly!" placated Sir Guy. "Are we men of the world capable of diplomacy, or are we common fishwives?"

The Count dropped heavily into his chair and gulped down his drink.

"Bah! My ears weary of meaningless words! You English talk, talk, talk . . . yet say *nothing!* Since you do not know the whereabouts of this Hastings woman, what call is there for diplomacy?"

The other man grinned. "Ah, but if I did have her, simple barter would suffice! Hark you, my friend, I have something as good, perchance even better because more compliant—*Lady Mary's twin!*"

The Muscovite glowered. "What trick is this? I myself have examined the Hastings' pedigree. Lady Mary has no sister!"

"I said *twin*, not sister!" Sir Guy said slyly. When he saw the thunderheads begin to form on the Russian's swarthy brow, he added: "Do you not have a miniature of the Hastings' wench?"

"I have, thanks be to God!" stormed the Count. "I shall not be hoodwinked!"

"Splendid! I'll make you a sporting wager: bring this miniature with you, and we shall visit this damsel this afternoon. Compare her in person with your painting, and if she does not look more like the portrait of Mary Hastings than Mary herself would look, then on my oath, I'll don harness and haul your coach down The Strand!"

The envoy rose and stomped restlessly around the room. "It is sheer lunacy to discuss it!" he fumed. "You must be mad! I was assured you were a courtier, instead I find you prattling the nonsense of a pot-boy! We waste time!"

Sir Guy chuckled softly. "Aye, precious time! Yet you would make a mountain out of a molehill, when the problem is so simple; ergo: your master sent you after an English woman. I have the woman."

The Count raised his arms above his head as if summoning the Almighty to witness his travail.

"*Hospodi Buchmilo!* Lord be merciful to me!" he trumpeted. "Crazy you are! My Prince desires one certain noblewoman—not just any old slut in England! Cannot you comprehend?"

Sir Guy sniffed. "After some not inconsiderable experience, I have been forced to the unromantic conclusion that there is remarkably little difference in females."

"Bah! The words of a callow schoolboy! No, no! No, it cannot be considered! If it was discovered . . ."

Sir Guy knew he had him on the hook. Suppressing a smile, he leaned forward and his voice became cajoling.

"How could it be discovered, if you and I don't talk? God knows, the maid wouldn't dare! There is relatively no intercourse between our respective courts, and few travelers." He spread his hands. "By the time it did come out, if ever, your master would doubtless have wearied of her anyway."

Count Nikita exhaled noisily through his mustache and increased his pace.

"You do not know the Grand Prince! To us *boyars* he is well named Ivan the Terrible, for to cross him is to invite unspeakable tortures! Out of sheer caprice, he murdered a cousin of mine by forcing him to drink scalding soup. What he would do to me if he learned I had deceived him, I shudder to imagine!"[3]

"What happens if you return without the woman?"

The envoy winced. "I prefer not to think about that, either!"

"Well, I suggest you *do* think about it," suggested Sir Guy, "whereupon it will be evident that by returning empty-handed, you have no chance, whereas if you bring him an enchanting damsel, even though not the one expected, you are almost certain to be rewarded. It doesn't take much of a gambler to appreciate those odds."

The Count paused, and gripped the back of a chair. "I take it you wish to share my reward?"

"Not at all! I ask only that our ship be released with cargo intact. If you petition the Tsar in his first flush of ecstasy, such as the sight of this dainty lass is sure to engender, it should be a simple matter to get his concurrence."

Count Nikita pouted out his lips and made a thoughtful sucking noise. "This woman—is she well-born?"

"She is," Sir Guy said without hesitation.

"You will personally vouch for her?"

"Why, yes, certainly!"

The Count pushed away from the chair and took another slow turn about the room. When he again faced the Englishman, his eyes held a glint of cunning.

"My artful friend, I shall bow to your politic judgment," he said with undisguised cynicism. "What you have said is only too true—that to return empty-handed would be fatal, whereas to please my Prince will mean riches. It is fitting, therefore, that as instigator of this little stratagem, you should share my largess."

Sir Guy could feel the axe coming, but he could not tell from which direction.

"I ask only for my ship," he sparred.

His opponent smiled without mirth. "Ah, you are overmodest! Why, my friend, I would not even consider the proposition unless you agreed to share the rewards . . . *whatever they are!*"

Sir Guy braced himself against the blow. "Go on," he said dryly.

This time it was the envoy who measured out his words. "I will inspect this mysterious female. If she is satisfactory, *you* will accompany our entourage to Moscow, where you can vouch for this woman to my Prince in person!" He chuckled sardonically at the expression on the Englishman's face. "Since you are so certain the deception will succeed, there will be scant risk, and Ivan can be extravagantly lavish when well pleased. Your ship will doubtless be but a small portion of your reward!" His voice turned truculent. "Those are my only terms!"

Sir Guy deliberated briefly. True, this was far more than he had bargained for when he opened the game, yet the stakes had multiplied, and it would be folly to withdraw at this juncture.

"Let us be quite certain we understand each other," he cautioned. "If I accompany you and the girl to Moscow, and vouch for her to the Emperor, you will undertake to have my impounded vessel released and, in addition, share your reward equally with me? Is that what you mean?"

"Precisely!" agreed the Muscovite. "Howbeit, Ivan's *reward* may not turn out to be what you expect!"

The Englishman shrugged. "That's a chance we'll have to take." He came erect. "Very well, I accept those terms."

They sealed the pact with another draught.

"Now, if you will wait one moment until I get the miniature," boomed the Count, "we will go and visit this beautiful impostor!"

8

LONG BEFORE THE APPOINTED HOUR, the quaking *Merchant-Adventurers* had again met in the backroom of the Handcuff Inn. Their collective mood, with one notable exception, was sullen and defiant, and they wore the bleak determination of men who, having been bested in one encounter, intend to see it does not happen a second time. While awaiting their formidable opponent, they whetted their barbs on the rhinoceros-hided Master Lymeburner.

"You should have forewarned us, sir!" Yancy stormed at the doughty mariner. "Curse me, he'd not have bullied *me* into putting my name to that hellish petition if I'd known what to expect!"

Lymeburner shrugged. "Ye'd 'ave slipped yer hawser, so to speak, an' drifted aw'y if I'd tolt ye 'e was comin', gentlemen!"

"Aye, thou Judas!" hissed the Reverend Belcher. "Thou betrayer!"

"Bones o' me! W'at's eatin' ye gents?" growled the old sea-dog. "Afore Sir Guy come in, ye'd conceded defeat an' was a-moanin' about yer necks! Now there's 'ope!"

"Hey-day, but at what price?" snorted Bendix, the ship chandler. "Egad, gentlemen, I declare we should agree on a maximum amongst ourselves before he gets here!"

"Excellent, brother, excellent!" chirped the parson. "Shoulder to shoulder we will stand like the kine! Truly, the wages of sin are death!"

Old Paxton laughed heartily. "Hardly an attractive medium of exchange, Reverend," he observed. "Gentlemen, are you seeking Sir Guy's help, or are you trying to avoid it? Certainly, you should decide *that* question before you haggle about the cost."

"Sir!" cried young Tutweiller. "I did not come here to cast away my father's fortune!" He looked towards Mr. Bendix. "Did we not agree on five percent of the gross?"

"Eh? Oh, aye—five percent it was!" harrumphed the ship chandler, looking, in turn, to the agent. "Right-o, Lymeburner? Eh, w'at?"

[61]

"Aye, aye, sir, an' a ruddy 'andsome sum 'twill be, may God keel'aul me if else!"

Mentally calculating five percent of "over a million quid," the little goldsmith declared the fee exorbitant. "Curse me, gentlemen, I doubt not we could shave it down to *two* percent, or even less, if we hold a united front!"

Paxton tushed them. "*Hold* as you did when it came to signing the petition?"

"Egad, sir, that remark was unfair!" rumbled Bendix. "We were trapped into signing!"

"Tricked, perchance, but not trapped!" snorted the old philosopher. "Gentlemen, why not be honest with yourselves, at least! We do not . . ."

"Yes, with God's help we shall triumph!" brayed Belcher, pounding the table to drown the solitary voice of reason. "Let us all take a holy vow to pay two percent or nothing?"

"Splendid notion, Reverend, perfectly corking, damme if else!" applauded Bendix. "To give the devil his due, Sir Guy's a suave rascal! He'll come prancin' in here oozin' with cocky confidence, as he did last time, an' if we're not careful, egad, we'll agree to more! As the vicar suggests—let's take an oath! Eh?"

All agreed—that is, all but Mr. Paxton.

"You remind me of a pack of jackals deciding on the portion to be allowed a lion, provided *he* makes the kill," he told them candidly. "My sense of humor precludes my taking part in such a farce."

They were just concluding their solemn vows when he spoke again.

"You had best hurry with your oath-taking, gentlemen," he chuckled. "Methinks the *lion* draws nigh!"

After a curt knock, Sir Guy stalked into the chamber. He seemed hardly aware of the tense group, and with a terse nod of acknowledgment, threw himself wearily into a vacant chair and stared at the ceiling. The company, braced against an overdose of charm and optimism, was completely nonplused. There was little about this wearied and discouraged-looking man to remind them of the mocking courtier they had interviewed just twenty-four hours before.

"My God, what a day!" groaned the knight. "Will someone order me a drink?"

The investors gaped at one another in dismay. Finally, at a nod from Bendix, young Tutweiller fled the room in search of wine. The little goldsmith was the first to succumb to the suspense.

"Zounds, sir!" he choked anxiously. "You have failed to save us?"

Their tired guest took an almost unbearably long time to reply.

"On the contrary, gentlemen, I have succeeded!" he said at last. "Though only at the cost of implicating my own neck in your collective noose."

Bendix's eyes brightened, and flashing a message around the board which plainly said *leave this to me, gents, for, being business, it is right in my line,* he impaled the knight on a frosty stare.

"Ha, speakin' of costs," he bumbled aggressively, "we have, ah, we have decided the five percent figure we discussed yestereve . . ."

Sir Guy cocked his head after the fashion of a rooster eyeing a worm. "*We* discussed? I told you last night it was pointless to quibble about terms until we knew what had to be done!"

"Egad, sir, we do not intend to quibble!" growled the ship chandler, trying to maintain his forward momentum. "We have sworn . . ."

"By my troth, I'm delighted to hear it!" cut in the courtier with a flash of his old mockery. "I loathe quibblers. Ill-bred haggling over a few paltry guineas when human lives are at stake infuriates me out of all reason!" He leveled his head so his eyes could rake them at will. "And speaking of lives—I was unable to present your petition to Her Majesty. You sought my help a trifle tardily."

By this time, Master Bendix had come to a verbal standstill, so the Reverend, rarely afflicted in that fashion, seized the gage.

"You assured us you had succeeded!" he shrilled.

"Aye, your Holiness, but I had reference to your ship and cargo, knowing that your prime interest lay in the material rather than the spiritual."

The clergyman popped to his feet. "*Sirrah!* Dost mock me?"

Sir Guy laughed at him. "Perish the thought!"

Old Paxton reached over and pulled the irate parson into his seat. Fortunately, young Tutweiller arrived just at that moment followed by a serving-wench bearing mugs and wine. By the time the wine was broached, tempers had somewhat cooled. Mr. Paxton tried again to inject a little reason.

"Manifestly, sir," he addressed the knight, "you have either arranged for the release of our property, or at least have a plan in mind. Be so good as to relieve our anxiety on this score."

Sir Guy nodded. "I have not closed my eyes since we met here last night," he told them. "Howbeit, I have contrived a personal treaty with the Muscovite envoy by which, for certain arrangements made by me, he will undertake the release of both ship and cargo. And while nothing in this life is sure, I believe you may count on a complete recovery. That, gentlemen, is the story in a nutshell!"

Yancy, the goldsmith, sniffed. "Certes, but you accomplished that without too much difficulty," he said pettishly. "We are appreciative, nevertheless, and will assign a committee to iron out the details."

The knight made a gesture of indifference. "As you wish," he drawled.

Mr. Bendix, having recovered his second wind, figuratively made another assault on the problem closest to his mercantile heart.

"In which case, sir, there remains naught but the matter of terms, eh? We have concluded . . ."

Sir Guy met the charge with a steely stare that brought the ship chandler to a stammering halt.

"One moment, my avaricious little tradesman, I am not interested in what you may or may not have concluded," the courtier said coldly. "I price my own services, which, in this particular instance, is . . . fifty percent of the gross!"

There was a vacuous moment of shocked silence. Mr. Bendix reacted as if pole-axed.

"Oh, aye," he mumbled confusedly. "Fifty per . . ." He floundered out of his mental fog. "Great God in heaven! What, sir, what did you say? Eh?"

"I said fifty percent," reiterated Sir Guy.

"*Fifty* percent? *Half?*" trumpeted the ship chandler, windmilling his arms. "Egad, sir, 'tis ridiculous! Ridiculous, I say!"

"'Tis robbery!" shrilled Yancy.

"Sheer piracy!" screamed Belcher.

"We shall not be plundered so!" yelped Tutweiller.

"May God keel-'aul me, if else!" concurred the mariner, drifting with the tide of emotion.

Mr. Paxton merely looked thoughtful.

Sir Guy appraised them with a hangman's smile. "By my oath, what a congress of grubby little woodpeckers!" he jeered, his glance searing them individually as he described each in turn. "How you bluster when selling rotten food to poor seamen (Mr. Bendix), or bully when cheating a widow of her mite (Mr. Yancy), or collapse when your miser's hoard be threatened and need be represented by a beardless stripling (Philip Tutweiller), or vociferously pretend to serve God while fawning at the feet of Mammon (Reverend Belcher). . . . Bah! the odor of you would sicken a vulture!" The knight pushed disgustedly to his feet.

"There is nothing further to discuss. I cannot journey to far-off Muscovy and appear before the Tsar of All the Russias without being assured . . ."

Master Lymeburner popped out of his chair. "God's life, sir! Was it your thought to go to Muscovy in person?"

Sir Guy elevated one eyebrow. "Naturally! You didn't think I'd trust you gold-worshippers to divide the loot, did you?"

"Of course not, of course not!" babbled the mariner. "Yet, blow me down, sir, I swear this puts a different cloud in the sky! Methinks ye'd earn the fifty percent . . ." As this heresy was greeted with lowering scowls, he hastily amended it: "Not that it ben't too high a price, as the sayin' is!"

"Egad, sir!" raged Bendix. "Who asked for your opinion?"

"You took a sacred oath!" hissed the clergyman.

Master Lymeburner, however, had recovered his aplomb. To these and other epithets, he merely beamed.

"Me lords! I did not understand Sir Guy meant to go to Muscovy wi' us," he argued persuasively. "W'y, it raises me 'opes, for I swear if he chats w' the Tsar, we'll get our ship! An', gentlemen, a 'arf cargo be better'n no cargo at all!"

"Trite but true!" sniffed Sir Guy, resuming his seat.

Then followed a verbal free-for-all in which the knightly subject took no part. But it was sound without substance, since having already signed what was tantamount to a confession, there was little else they could do save acquiesce. In the end it was decided to accept the harsh terms with the proviso that a committee of the investors accompany the expedition. This august body was to be comprised of the venerable Paxton, Philip Tutweiller, and the Reverend Horace Belcher. In the case of the last named, who was chaplain of the *Honorable Companie*, rather than an investor, a special dispensation was necessary to induce him to abandon the Lord's work in England, to wit: it was agreed that if the gamble succeeded, sufficient funds would be allocated out of the profits to establish him for life in an ecclesiastic sinecure.

This accomplished, Sir Guy rose once more and bowed to them collectively.

"Now, gentlemen, I shall make arrangements for sailing as soon as possible," he said, smiling. "Meanwhile, I leave you to your recriminations! Good night!"

Hardly had the door closed behind him, however, before Messers Yancy, Bendix and the good Reverend fell upon their agent.

"Traitor!" . . . "Dastard turncoat!" . . . "Violator of oaths!"

Master Lymeburner received this hail of vituperation with a beatific, cat-that-ate-the-canary smile. When the tirade had expended itself for very lack of fresh invective, he leaned towards them.

"Me lords, give it nary another thought!" he told them in a conspiratorial whisper. "If ye recollect, I made sure 'twas agreed to pay the knave *only when we got safely 'ome to England!*" He gave them a

[65]

prodigious wink. "If Sir Guy goes into Muscovy, 'e'll not return—trust Caleb Lymeburner fer that!"

There was a shocked pause, in which Mr. Paxton's voice cracked like a whip.

"I have tolerated a maximum of chicanery in these conferences," he said sternly. "But as God is my witness, gentlemen, I draw the line at murder."

"Certes, it would be risky!" murmured Yancy nervously.

Master Lymeburner's little rat eyes twinkled. "There's more'n one way to catch a fish, as the sayin' is," he chortled. "Me lords, I wean we've made a shrewd deal!"

Old Mr. Paxton sighed softly. "Too shrewd, methinks," he prophesied.

9

ON THE TWELFTH DAY of May, 1577, the *Sea Sprite*, fifty tunnes, commanded by Caleb Lymeburner, "Master under God," departed Gravesend, England, for the Land of Muscovy. She was not a happy choice, being old and far too small for so large a company, but at that particular time bottoms were scarce, and in this particular case, time was precious, and the *Sea Sprite*, for all her age and lack of spaciousness, was swift.

And she had good reason to fly. Queen Elizabeth, learning of the disappearance of Mary Hastings, and concerned lest the implied rebuff anger the Tsar and cause him to sever the lucrative treaty with the English Muscovy Company, was of a mind to send an embassy of her own to conciliate the Muscovite monarch. The very possibility of this was sufficient to make the sweat break out on Count Nikita. Furthermore, a suspicion was current that the news of Master Lymeburner's poaching had already reached the jealous ears of the London office of the English Muscovy Company, and that the latter was taking steps to claim *The Dainty Virgin* for its own profit. The prospect of this calamity was like the rack and the screw to Master Lymeburner and his backers.

Count Nikita marched on board with a formidable retinue: a baker's dozen arrogant henchmen, the majority of whom were volatile Tatars. Sir Guy, on the contrary, had pared his staff to an irreducible minimum, to wit: Affable Jones and Sergeant Pistol. These two worthies doubled in whatever capacities were needed. Sir Guy at first considered Ellen and Charity as part and parcel of his own contingent, but Ellen's cold hauteur and disdain set up, in effect, a standard of her own. Yet she, in her turn, likewise erred in deeming Charity of her camp, for little Charity displayed a disconcerting universality, and though loyal to Ellen, was at the same time everybody's friend.

Under the circumstances, trouble was inevitable, yet when it first appeared, it came disguised. At the time Sir Guy was playing chess with Count Nikita in the cramped quarters of the after-cabin; he was less interested in the game as such than in the insight it afforded into the mental and emotional processes of the burly Muscovite, who in his maneuvers swarmed across the board in the brutal, aggressive fashion of a Tatar horde. Then, just at a crucial point in the game, young Tutweiller burst in on them, big-eyed with excitement.

"Sir Guy! Sir Guy! I think the Lady Ellen intends to leap into the sea!"

At that precise moment, Sir Guy was jockeying to strangle the envoy's bishop, so he was loath to desist.

"If she leaps, toss her a line," he advised Philip. "I'm busy."

The young man, however, was too distraught to be rebuffed. "God's death, sir!" he cried. "You cannot mean it! 'Twill spell disaster for us all if she jumps!"

Sir Guy frowned in attempted concentration. "She won't, Titwillow, she won't!" he assured the lad.

This exchange, of course, was carried on in English, which Count Nikita did not understand. But as it was obvious something was amiss, he demanded to know what it was, and on learning what Philip had reported, he sprang to his feet in a great passion, overturning the chess board.

"*Hospodi Buchmilo!*" he roared. "We must put her in irons!"

Sir Guy stared glumly at the wreckage of his game, then rose with a sigh. "You fools!" he growled. "She is already in irons!"

Philip stared in open-mouthed amazement. "Why, Sir Guy, I just this moment saw her walking aft and there was no iron . . ."

"The irons are verbal, you imbecile! She gave her word!"

When this was translated to the Count, he threw up his hands in disgust.

"By the bones of my father, thou art a fool!" he stormed. "With so much dependent on this woman—our very lives, in fact—you trust her . . ."

Sir Guy laughed at him. "Not her, Niki," he interrupted. "It is my own judgment I trust."

But the Muscovite was not so easily pacified. "Bah! We will see!" he insisted, and stooping to miss the low-hanging crossbeams, headed for the ladder. With mounting impatience, Sir Guy followed.

When they debouched on deck, there was Ellen leaning on the taffrail abaft the steersman, staring westward where long since the shores of England had disappeared into the mists.

"See!" hissed Philip. "She means to jump!"

"H'mnn! So you read minds, do you?" jeered Sir Guy.

Young Tutweiller reddened to the lobes of his ears. "Why is she gazing at the water so?"

"We will talk to her!" declared the Count roughly. He started to stalk aft, but Sir Guy stopped him.

"Hold, Niki! Converging on her en masse would really give her cause to jump from sheer terror," he continued.

The Muscovite struck down the restraining arm and his great beard jutted out at an aggressive angle.

"How dare you!" he blustered, his eyes flashing dangerously. "I do as I please . . ."

Sir Guy stepped directly in front of him to block his passage. "Not on board this vessel, you don't!" he cut in. "You will abide by my instructions the same as the others, else I'll clap you in irons, or worse! Take your choice!"

The Count began to swell until his eyes bugged out and his puffed cheeks resembled those of a foraging squirrel. But just when an explosion seemed inevitable, he pivoted on his heel and stomped forward in high dudgeon.

Young Tutweiller apparently wanted to argue further, but though his mouth went through the motions, under the cold stare of Sir Guy no words were audible. Spangler snorted and sauntered aft.

If Ellen was conscious of his presence, she gave no sign of it. Half amused, half piqued, Spangler rested one hip against the taffrail and studied her.

"How now, mistress?" he began. "Your most ardent admirer, the handsome-if-callow Philip, informs me you mean to leap overboard!"

She turned her head no more than was necessary to give him a glance of disdain.

"Were you concerned, sir?"

He chuckled. "Concerned, but not worried, though I'm naturally loath to lose you at this juncture."

A faint flush heightened her coloring. *"Naturally,"* she mocked in a voice that dripped scorn. "While I had not heretofore regarded a rogue as a merchant, I presume, like any other tradesman, he must protect his investment."

Sir Guy laughed, albeit a trifle mirthlessly, for in that era, a courtier would rather be called a pimp than a tradesman. "Alas, mistress, I own there's a kernel of truth in what you say," he retorted. "Peradventure I should take the Count's advice and clap you in chains?"

"Why don't you?" she dared him. "It would be in perfect keeping with my fate! Are not slaves always led about in chains?"

"*Slaves?* Why, bless you, my dear, you go as a *bride!*"

Her eyes blazed. "You lying cur! This prince to whom you barter me is a monster who has hundreds, nay, it is *thousands*, of virgins paraded before him every year so he can choose those to slake his lusts!" [4]

Sir Guy whistled in mock admiration. " 'Pon my soul, in addition to your multiple accomplishments, I now discover you a student of Muscovite customs!" He chuckled wickedly. "Howbeit, my lady, to speak true, you would hardly be eligible for the parade of virgins."

She went white. "That was contemptible, sir! Is it absolutely necessary that you degrade and abuse me so?"

He shrugged. "I came here merely to see if you were all right," he reminded her. "You rebuffed my concern with ill-temper."

"Have I not a right to be bitter?"

"A *right*, perchance, but certainly no justification. You choose to forget that I saved your life, in effect, when I fished you out of that slimy kennel known as Newgate. Or did I wrong?"

She ignored the attempted logic. "So now it is gratitude you expect!"

He wagged his head. "We had a definite agreement."

She held up an imperious hand. "Spare me a reiteration! Aye, Sir Rogue, I acquiesced to your terms, since I could not do otherwise, and I shall keep my word. But let there be no misunderstanding between us: I loathe and despise you. You almost make me ashamed of being an Englishwoman, when I see *you* regarded as an Englishman. Why, even your Russian confederate, for all his gross swinishness, is at least consistent, and true to his breed. But *you*—" She fairly choked. "Ah-h— I cannot find words to describe you!"

"By the gods, my lady, it is quite a portrait you painted with the words you did find!" Sir Guy feigned an exaggerated sigh of discouragement. "Ah me, 'tis axiomatic we resent those to whom we are most indebted, so I shall endeavor to bear your lack of grace as best I can! Yet, I must confess I envy the Tsar the delights such innate fire and passion will engender!" Leaving her to recover from that thrust, he walked away.

Somewhat to his chagrin, he discovered he was trembling slightly from the encounter—a most abnormal experience for Sir Guy!—and he was provoked that he had permitted himself to have been inveigled into two such senseless tiffs. Quarrels like these were ofttimes malignant, in that they festered and grew into major brawls which could well endanger the whole enterprise. He warned himself that he had to tread warily henceforth.

The difficulty, as he saw it, was a matter of propinquity. On land he had studiously and deliberately created a role for himself from which he rarely deviated: the dashing and mysterious cavalier, the notorious rogue. His appearances and disappearances were dramatic and spectacular, and always he did the unexpected. All these were his stock in trade.

Here on shipboard the conditions were almost exactly reversed. It was impossible to maintain a pose when you were rarely out of sight of the entire company. To have attempted it would have been to make himself ridiculous. Yet to lose face would be disastrous. It was going to call for a new strategy.

He was about to descend to the cabin when he spotted young Tutweiller lurking behind the foremast. Sir Guy strode forward, and steering the lad out of sight of the taffrail, demanded: "Philip, have you been filling that chit's head full of nonsense about the Tsar and his concubines?"

The sudden rush of color to the other's cheeks was sufficient affirmation, even though Philip evaded a direct reply.

"I felt sorry for her," he muttered lamely.

"*Sorry?*" scoffed Spangler. "Why, you bloody fool—if that wench doesn't go through with the deal she made, you'll lose more than your investment, I can promise you!"

Philip's jaw tightened. "Sir! An English gentleman doesn't profit from the sacred bodies of his countrywomen, like a common whoremaster!"

"God give me patience with you!" groaned Sir Guy. "Now I could simply order you to stay away from her and have you ironed if you disobeyed, yet because of your extreme youth and innocence I am going to reason with you—*just once!* So attend me carefully: this adventure could well have international repercussions if it misfires, and having committed ourselves, there can be no backing out or welching; it is a case of sink or swim. Hence, not only our fortunes, but our very lives depend on the compliance of that lone woman! Can you not understand that, lad?"

"And I say again that it is immoral, dishonorable and degrading to sell a pure young English female—"

The courtier's cynical laughter brought him up short. "Lancelot on a white charger! *Pure young English female?* Oh, you fool, you pathetic fool!" Sir Guy stopped smiling and his eyes sparked like struck flint. "Heed me! That 'pure young English female' is a confessed bigamist I dug out of a stinking dungeon in Newgate!"

"That's a lie!" cried Philip, white-faced.

Sir Guy arched his brows. "Is it so?" he asked mildly. "Then we shall go aft together—you and I—and ask her *ladyship*. She shall also tell you of the unspeakable degradation and death that awaits her if she should be found loose in London." He took the younger man by the elbow. "Come, my pretty skeptic!"

Philip pulled away, but made no move to go aft. He drew the back of his hand across his forehead in a dazed fashion.

"Can it be? Can it be?" he muttered.

The other snorted. "Ask her if doubts again assail you," he taunted. "She'll concede the fact that never again can she rightfully march in a 'parade of virgins,' as you so dramatically phrased it!" And leaving Philip pale and shaken, Sir Guy sauntered below.

The next link in the chain of trouble was reported to Sir Guy by the Reverend Belcher. On that unhappy occasion Sir Guy was reclining as comfortably as the swooping motion of the *Sea Sprite* would permit, being shaved by his jack-of-all-trades, Affable Jones, when the clergyman sidled into the cabin.

Affable Jones paused with his razor in mid-air. "Don't apologize," he chuckled. "We be gettin' accustomed to ye, Parson."

Sir Guy gave his facetious barber a warning dig with his elbow and raised his head sufficiently to peer over the lather.

"Woe is unto us!" bleated Belcher. "The serpent hath entered into Eden. I saw it with mine own eyes!"

Affable scratched the tip of his nose with the back of his razor. "D'ye suppose 'e could 'ave mistook a weevil fer a serpent?" he asked Sir Guy in great seriousness. "God knows, this tub's full o' 'em!"

"Jest not, ye sinful man!" thundered the visitor. "I speak of fornication!"

Affable howled delightedly, clapped shut his razor and sank onto a bunk. "W'at-'o, Parson, 'tis me favorite subject. Tell me more!"

Sir Guy chuckled. "Pay him no heed, Parson," he urged kindly. "What has happened to disconcert you?"

Belcher covered his eyes with his hand as if to blot out some terrible scene he had witnessed.

"I was seated in the shade of the forecastle, reading the Scriptures," he went on in the manner of a confessional, "when I noticed that wanton, that minx, that Jezebel—"

"'E must mean little Charity!" marveled Affable Jones.

"Aye, I refer to that strumpet!" snapped Belcher. "She went below into the darkened bowels of the vessel and crawled away aft. Then—oh, the horror of it!—shortly thereafter that rakehell, that vile deceiver—"

"Pistol, none other!" conjectured Affable.

"The same. He followed the slut."

"I take it you followed them closely?" broke in Sir Guy.

But Affable cursed bitterly and thumped his head with the heel of his palm. Belcher looked vaguely mollified.

"Ah! I am glad to see you so displeased, my good man!" he approved.

"*Displeased?*" snarled Affable unaffably. "That ayant the word fer 't! W'y, damme, I aimed to get 'er afore Pistol did, the treacherous 'ound!"

Before the indignant clergyman could recover from this unexpected admission, Sir Guy took command of the situation.

"Your zeal is remarkable," he said dryly. "Have you any other revelations of like character?"

Belcher nodded. "Aye! Even as I was coming hence, one of the seamen—a good, God-fearing Christian lad—told me he saw this trollop with one of those pagan wretches from Tatary."

Affable's affability returned. "'Eaven 'elp us poor seamen at a time like this, w'en we got a bloody shipload o' spies aboard!" he chortled. "A man ain't got no privacy at all!"

"I demand you do something about this dissolute jade!" thundered the Reverend.

"Damme, I intend to!" vowed Affable.

He was ignored. "I shall talk to Charity," Sir Guy promised. "She will have to be more circumspect."

Belcher gasped in disbelief. "More *circumspect!* Sirrah! Do my ears deceive me! Can it be you are not going to have her whipped?"

Sir Guy's lip curled. "Did not your ogling satisfy you? No, I am not going to have her stripped and lashed for your edification."

For a moment it looked as if Belcher was going to leap at Sir Guy's throat, but judgment, or cowardice, as the case might be, gained the ascendance, and he staggered back, clutching at his doublet.

"Never have I been spoken to in that manner!" he panted.

Sir Guy sniffed. "Which only goes to prove you should fraternize more often with honest men," he observed, then amended with a smile: "Or at least, *candid* men. It is no wonder the church found you too rich for its blood."

Quaking as with the palsy, the parson leaned forward and aimed a bony finger at Sir Guy.

"Thou fiend! Thou deputy of hell!" he sputtered. "I swear before Almighty God that you shall have cause to repent what you said to me!"

Affable Jones opened his razor and began to strop it noisily on a horny palm.

"Damme, yer ludship!" he addressed himself to Sir Guy. "I declare the parson needs a shave—especially across the gullet! W'at s'y I gi' . . ."

By that time the indignant parson had taken his gullet out of the cabin.

Despite his seeming levity and his contempt for the snooping proclivities of the Reverend Belcher, Sir Guy was only too well aware of the explosive potentials of a promiscuous wanton inflaming the lusts of men concentrated in the too close confines of a vessel at sea. So he sent for Charity Lane.

She made a disconcertingly attractive picture as she came breathlessly into the cabin, her hair windblown into golden sheaves, her cheeks rouged by the sun and her green eyes a-sparkle. She wore a simple gown, the very simplicity of which tended to accentuate the voluptuous charms it so rigidly imprisoned. After his first all-encompassing glance, Sir Guy had to remind himself that his was the role of a jurist.

Charity made him a low curtsy that partly revealed her lovely breasts, after which she gave him a look from under her long lashes that tingled along his spine like a jolt of chain-lightning.

"Ye want me, sir?" she asked softly.

Her ingenuous phrasing shattered Sir Guy's solemn resolve and set him laughing in spite of himself.

" 'Pon my soul, Charity!" he chuckled, albeit a trifle ruefully. "You are a veritable Aphrodite, I swear!"

"Be that good or bad, sir?"

He sighed. "She was the goddess of love, Charity!"

"Oh, then it's good!" laughed the girl.

"Not always," he retorted, sobering. "There have been some very serious charges leveled against you, my girl!"

Her eyes grew big. "Ye mean—I've done sum'at wrong, sir?"

"It is stated you committed a cardinal sin with one of the Muscovites!"

Charity exhaled relievedly. "Oh, *that!* Glory be, I feared maybe I'd done sum'at serious!"

Sir Guy scowled judiciously. "*Serious?* Good Lord, haven't you the wit to know that is wrong, and hence forbidden?"

She wrinkled her snub nose. "Aye, m'lud, I know it be forbidden by such as ol' Belch, but as to w'ether it be *wrong* or no, is a matter o' opinion."

Such disarming candor put Sir Guy on the defensive, and he began to regret he had not summoned some oldster, such as the venerable Mr. Paxton, to share the responsibility of judgment. Then, paradoxically, because this very wish was an alien sensation, it irritated him.

"Watch your saucy tongue, you brazen hussy!" he growled. "By the laws of both land and sea, I should have you whipped!"

"Well, I 'opes ye won't, m'lud!" Charity said, unabashed. "I 'ave a very soft an' tender 'ide, as ye're welcome to see."

Sir Guy bit his nether lip. "Did you, or did you not, commit . . . er . . . a sin with the Muscovite in question?"

"W'y, of course, sir!"

"Knowing you should not have so done?"

Charity sighed at the memory. "To speak true, sir, I tolt him no, but 'e couldn't speak h'English an' I could speak no Musky, so"—she shrugged her shapely shoulders to indicate the utter inevitability of the situation—"there was naught fer it but to agree. 'Twas the on'y thing we both unnerstood!"

Sir Guy hid a smile behind his hand. "You entertained Sergeant Pistol in the same . . . ah . . . fashion," he continued sternly. "I happen to be aware that he understands the English tongue tolerably well. How do you explain that lapse?"

A gentle smile spread over Charity's features. "Poor Pistol," she breathed with almost maternal tenderness. " 'E was so lonely an' wistful-like—"

"God grant me patience!" growled Sir Guy, then suddenly, at this description of his henchman, his powers of restraint snapped and he exploded into laughter.

10

FOR CERTAIN POLITICAL REASONS, their entry into Muscovy had to be made by the circuitous northern route around the Land of Lappia and thence into the White Sea. This inaccessibility was in part responsible for the Russias' uncompromising aloofness towards the Western peoples, but it was not from choice, nor was it geographical; it was a political isolation cunningly fostered by such self-seeking neighbors as Poland, Lithuania, and the Baltic provinces, all of whom were in league to form a barrier between Muscovy and the other nations of Europe. Hence, as no Muscovite was permitted to pass through this conspiratorial wall, Archangel was the only gateway to the Western world, a misfortune which made foreign intercourse both arduous and hazardous.[5]

Had it not been for the presence of Count Nikita and his staff, the Englishmen might have debarked at Riga, off the Baltic, and thence made their way overland through the Baltic provinces into Muscovy, but as the envoy was indispensable to Sir Guy's scheme, there was naught for it but to brave the dangers of the Arctic passage. Thus it came about that on the twenty-third of June, after a tortuous voyage of seven hundred and fifty leagues, the battered little *Sea Sprite* curtsied into the Bay of St. Nicholas, slipped through a narrow, clawlike gut which was guarded on the south by a long spit of sand and on the north by a saw-edged reef, and two leagues up the River Dwina, came at twilight to anchor in the fabulous Land of Muscovy.

The hook had barely set before Count Nikita dispatched a messenger ashore to announce his presence to the Governor of Dwina, who, by way of acknowledgment, caused the great guns of the fort to be discharged in salute. And since it was obviously too late an hour for a proper reception, his Excellency sent out a cask of *Berozevites* for the well-born, a delicate drink made from the root of the birch tree, and a hogshead of throat-burning *mead* for the common people. Both factions fell to with a will.

For some reason not clear even to himself, Sir Guy felt in no mood to celebrate, so as the casks were broached, he slipped away and climbed the mast to the highest yard to be alone. He was not prone to introspection, and customarily preferred gayety and conviviality to solitude. Yet tonight, despite his satisfaction at successfully completing the difficult passage, he felt not elation but depression.

He sat with his back braced against the topmast and stared broodingly at the rude collection of wooden buildings, dominated by the fortress on the hill, and tried to recapture some of his earlier enthusiasm for the venture. Meanwhile, the loudening sounds of revelry wafted aloft to his perch. The twilight lingered until well past midnight, bathing the whole panorama in a bluish afterglow. Once a fight broke out in the waist, but even as Sir Guy glanced downward, he saw Master Lymeburner fell both brawlers, then toss them into an open hold.

As the rotund little mariner swayed aft, Sir Guy sighed and went back to his speculations. It was said the sea changed men, he reflected, but he was beginning to question whether it was a *change* so much as a *disclosure*. Perchance that was it: the sea and the confines of a small vessel rubbed away the veneer men wore on land; you saw them temperamentally and morally naked, stripped of the fripperies of class society. But now that the *Sea Sprite* had anchored, the great deception would commence anew and all the characters on shipboard would once more don their ostentatious masks and resume their self-appointed roles. Even he, Sir Guy conceded wryly, would do likewise. Yet he doubted, after such a bald unveiling, if the illusion could be recaptured.

One by one, he ticked off his companions: Lymeburner, a fawning, unctuous knave. Yet a capable mariner, and if devoid of scruples and treacherous, he could be counted on not to endanger his own interests. Tutweiller, wallowing in the conflict between idealism and money-grubbing, was hence unpredictable and not to be trusted. Mr. Paxton, like little Charity, exhibited his true self whether ashore or afloat, hence was a mature, steadying balance-wheel to offset the impetuosity of his younger companions. Belcher was an obsessed prude who would betray anyone for a so-called moral reason. Ellen he dismissed without a reappraisal; in terms of power, he deemed her less a person than a pawn. The individual who gave him the most concern at the moment was Count Nikita Alexanderovitch Prokoff.

The transient glimpse he had obtained behind the brittle mask of that worthy was somewhat hair-raising, for it had revealed a species of primitive aristocrat, ruthless, selfish and absolutely fearless; a creature half barbarous, yet with a civilized self-control and a predatory ability to await the most auspicious moment to pounce. He would be a deadly enemy, yet not without a certain rude honor; if he would give no quarter, he would not expect it from others. For what he was, he warranted respect. He was, Sir Guy concluded, the sort of man you could kill willingly, yet at the same time feel constrained to salute in death.

Ever since their set-to, early in the voyage, Count Nikita had studiously avoided a second quarrel. His manner towards Sir Guy had been smilingly courteous and deliberate; so much so, it put the Englishman in mind of a great tiger playing the kitten. Sir Guy had no illusions: the burly Muscovite would cooperate just so long as cooperation was advantageous or necessary; after that . . . ?

Sir Guy shrugged the problem aside and decided to go below, for the yelps of revelry had diminished with the darkening twilight. Then as he turned to descend, he glimpsed a white-clad figure glide out of the companionway and flit across the afterdeck. It was Ellen.

On reaching the taffrail, she halted, her hands gripping the rail, her head bent forward as in dejection. After a long pause, she straightened in seeming resolution and spread her arms wide, as if drawing into her lungs the land-scented air.

Sir Guy decided not to go down immediately, being in no mood to face her biting contempt. Then while he hesitated, he saw Count Nikita emerge on deck and hurry aft. Half amused at this, Sir Guy leaned forward, the better to witness the rebuff he was certain would come when the Muscovite thrust his presence on the Englishwoman.

To Sir Guy's surprise, and somewhat to his chagrin, Ellen did not dismiss the Count. On the contrary, they remained side by side, apparently chatting cozily, for what seemed to the watcher the better part of an hour—in reality about ten minutes. What they discussed, Sir Guy had no way of knowing; nor did he understand his own reaction, which was one of mounting fury. Just when he was certain he could stand it no longer, Ellen turned abruptly and hurried below decks. The Count stared off towards the shadowy outlines of the fort for a few moments longer, then raising his hand in what could have been either a signal or a salute, he, too, went to his cuddy.

Sir Guy waited until he was certain the deck was cleared, then he reached for a halyard and slid soundlessly to the deck.

Early the following morning, the Governor's equerry was ferried out to the *Sea Sprite* with a blanket invitation for all persons of quality on board to be his guests at a banquet to be held that afternoon in honor of their arrival. Reasonably enough, the equerry desired an immediate answer.

Sir Guy would have preferred to discuss the matter with Count Nikita, since there might well be political aspects to consider, not to mention various questions of protocol, but the Muscovite could not be aroused, having spent the latter half of the night consuming copious quantities of the potent birch wine. So in the end, Sir Guy accepted the invitation for all, and sent the equerry away happy, and richer by a pouch of English gold.

As was to have been expected after the dreary weeks of confinement, nearly everyone on board was only too eager to attend. The exception was Ellen. She pleaded an indisposition and begged to be excused. Nor did she take the trouble to address her refusal in person; she sent the message through Charity.

Sir Guy was highly provoked. It was one thing, he told himself, for him to palm her off as a "lady of quality," but quite another for her to adopt such high-flown arrogance in her dealings with him. Thus his first reaction was to insist she attend, not only as a matter of discipline, but also because he did not want to risk offending Colonel Karamsin, the Governor. He had learned already how susceptible to slight these Muscovites could be.

However, after due deliberation, he decided to let her refusal stand —not for her sake, but because, as she herself had so bitterly phrased it, she was a valuable piece of merchandise, and it would not be wise to have her "shopworn" prior to her unveiling before the Tsar. And as he meditated these matters, he made a mental note to inquire into the status of females in the vast Muscovite domain. Someone on board, other than the Russian contingent, must know the answers, for he was certain that Philip Tutweiller had not gleaned from the Count that ridiculous story about naked virgins being paraded before Ivan IV, and he was equally sure the dolt hadn't the wit to make it up out of whole cloth.

In the meantime, if he was going to leave Ellen on board, it might be advisable to have Charity remain with her. True, Charity—along with Affable Jones and Sergeant Pistol—had been temporarily elevated to the status of "quality" for the duration of the venture. Nevertheless, there was sound reason to doubt her ability to undergo the metamorphosis on such short notice.

When he notified Charity of this decision, she was audibly disappointed.

"Oh, m'lud, but w'y? Be ye ashymed o' me manners?"

Not wanting to hurt her, Sir Guy tried to dissemble But he should have known better, for she stopped him halfway through his ambiguous speech.

"Ye've said enough, sir," she cut him short. "I ken the meanin' be'ind yer words, if not the words themselves."

"I hoped you'd understand," he said lamely. She had the most disconcerting way of making him feel like a perfect liar.

She gave a barklike laugh. "Glory be, I unnerstands on'y too well, m'lud! I ayant wanted, that's w'at!" She gave a mighty sniffle, then rubbed her stubby nose with the back of her hand. "Oh, don't look so pyned, sir; I ayant a-goin' to blubber; I ayant the blubberin' kind!

W'at I *don't* unnerstan' is men!" This called forth another momentous sigh. "Aye, I thought I did, fer I assumed men was at least as intelligent as a common little street mongrel. But they *ayant*—may God strike me dead if I lie! Be nice to even the mangiest cur dog, an' 'twill show its appreciation, be ye beggarman or prince. But *man?* Not im! Nay, 'e'll tyke yer fyvers an' yer *dearie* this an' 'oney that—until 'e's 'ad 'is w'y wi' ye, *then* 'tis 'Out o' the w'y, me bitch! We carn't 'ave common sluts eatin' at the syme board wi' us 'igh-an'-mighty gentle folks! No, sir!' "

Sir Guy frowned. "You know that is not true, Charity!" he said sharply.

She planted her knuckles on her ample hips and stood with arms akimbo.

"Ayant it so, m'lud? Every man on board this wormy tub 'as tried to lay wi' me, yet now . . ."

Sir Guy repressed a smile. "Easy, girl, easy! I haven't, for one, and . . ."

"More's the wonder o' it, too!" she snorted. "Nay, ye'd rather mope about 'ungerin' fer that frigid 'aughty wench wi' the . . ."

"*Silence!*" thundered Sir Guy, crashing his fist on the table. "How dare you talk to me like that, you . . . you . . . !"

". . . 'ore's the word ye mean, ayant it?" she asked imperturbably.

Ashamed of his outburst, Sir Guy tried to pull himself under control, although badly shaken inwardly.

"Charity, don't ever speak so to me again!" he said with measured grimness. "*Ever!*"

The girl shrugged. "As ye wish it, m'lud! Yet I own I had a sort o' dream that w'en we left England, we also left be'ind all that mummery about quality an' gentry, about well-born an' base-born, about rich an' poor, an' good an' bad!"

"Those things are deep within us, Charity," he explained, not unkindly. "They are the very foundations of society, hence we can do nothing about them."

She wagged her head stubbornly. "Beggin' yer pardon, sir, I won't believe it! I carn't 'elp but feel, an' me 'eart assures me 'tis so, that somew'ere . . . *somew'ere* in this big world be a plyce w'ere those empty things don't matter; w'ere kindness an' . . ."

Sir Guy cut her off with an impatient gesture. He knew she was talking utter nonsense, of course, yet he didn't quite know how to convince her of that obvious fact.

"Perchance on some barbaric isle such a Utopia exists, Charity, but certainly not in Muscovy."

[79]

"Ye mean—Muscovy be as bad as England?"

"Worse, very much worse!" he assured her with conviction. "'Pon my honor, Charity, I've heard it said the Grand Prince annually lines up thousands of virgins to choose those to slake his lusts!"

To his vexation, the little bawd burst into gales of merriment. "Saints o' glory, m'lud, if that be true, then it goes to prove the Muscovites ha' more sense than the English, for at least they *examines* w'at they want an' get someone w'at suits 'em best, rather 'an do like the English 'oo choose a bed-fellow by 'oo's got the longest line o' corpses in the family gryveyard!" She clapped her hands at his evident discomfiture. "Well, I never! *Thousands,* eh? These Muskies must be real men!" Without giving him an opportunity to reply, she skipped out of the cabin.

He was glad enough to see her go, for of late she seemed to best him on nearly every encounter. He cursed softly, and turned to other matters. There was the question of what to do about Captain Lymeburner. This posed a delicate problem, for though the seizure of *The Dainty Virgin* had been made in territory under the jurisdiction of the Governor of Dwina, the order had not been signed by Colonel Karamsin, but by his predecessor. Nevertheless, there was quite likely to be some subordinate officers present who might recognize the slippery little English mariner—a disastrous possibility. Be that as it may, the master of a visiting foreign vessel could hardly refuse the Governor's invitation, however hazardous attendance might be. So Sir Guy willed that the captain accompany the party, and his only concession to the danger was to change the master's name from Lymeburner to "Lemonsqueeze," a jest the elflike mariner failed to appreciate.

Sergeant Pistol, to his abject disappointment, was detailed to remain aboard in charge of the crew. As a counterirritant, and also to get him safely out of the way, the Reverend Horace Belcher was left to care for both the souls and bodies of Ellen and Charity. At the appointed time, all the others went ashore.

The Governor's palace was a vast, chilly structure of timber and stone, very crude by English standards. The banquet hall was a barnlike cavern draped with a patchwork of tapestries that resembled great sooty webs; at each end of the hall was a niche occupied by a sacred image, badly made. The tables, laid out in the form of a giant "T," and bowed under a profusion of unfamiliar viands, were fashioned of rough planks rubbed to a wavy smoothness by the elbows of uncounted guests. The earthen floor was covered with a mulch of rushes generously interlaced with old bones in varying stages of decay, all of which produced a pungent bouquet sufficient to smart the eye. A score of tawny wolfhounds lolled about, waiting for scraps to be either dropped or tossed by the revelers.

Though long inured to the vicissitudes of foreign travel, even Sir Guy was a trifle nonplused by the squalor, but after a few drinks of a small-beer the Muscovites called *quas*, he became somewhat less critical. Before long, in his expanding mellowness, he was able to discover heretofore latent charms in the setting: a certain rustic quality which brought to mind the romantic legends of ancient Britain in the days of Hereward the Wake.

And the food, if a mite too ripe and perhaps not *all* palatable to English tastes, was invariably interesting. For themselves, the Muscovites did not care particularly for beef or mutton, although the district abounded in both; they preferred seafood and vegetables. However, in honor of their guests, they had thoughtfully made huge quantities of small pies filled with minced meat and chibols, and highly seasoned with pepper. These were about the size of a tuppn'y loaf, and called *piroguen*. In addition, of course, was the seemingly endless supply of sturgeon and caviar, flanked by innumerable varieties of wild-fowl. If there were no such good old familiar wines as Rhenish and Madeira—since the Muscovites deemed them too weak and insipid—there were more than enough volcanic Russian substitutes.

But inevitably the spiritous glow, like a brief sunset, was followed by gloom. Sir Guy found it increasingly difficult to maintain the role of guest of honor. He felt tired and resentful, and, worst of all, he did not know why. That in itself disturbed him, since these moods of sinking depression were beginning to recur with disturbing frequency. He attempted to lose himself in conviviality, yet even in this he was defeated, for in all that concourse of Muscovites, there was none (save Count Nikita, of course) with whom he could converse in a common tongue.

Paradoxically, the Count seemed less sure of himself, now that he was in his own country, than he had been in England. Whether this was engendered by fear or by impatience, Sir Guy could not tell, but the envoy's manner was marked by an increased intensity of emotion and a growing truculence which the Englishman found both suspicious and difficult to stomach.

Sensing that he might need an influential friend in Muscovy, Sir Guy concentrated all his charm on Governor Karamsin, who tried equally hard to be the jovial host. Typically, the colonel was squat and corpulent, and in keeping with his caste wore a massive beard and shaved pate, which latter he kept covered with a tall velvet cap.

Unfortunately, he seemed to hold to the belief that if he bellowed loudly enough in Sir Guy's ear, the latter would be able to comprehend him, as if he were deaf, not English. When this skull-shattering procedure failed, he resentfully summoned an interpreter, though his manner plainly indicated he considered his guest uncooperative. But the interpreter had also imbibed too freely, hence conversation through that fuzzy medium soon lost its zest. So by mutual if unspoken accord, Sir Guy and the colonel settled down to silent eating and drinking.

Viewing the scene, Sir Guy was thankful he had not included Ellen and Charity in his party, since no other women were present. However, the rest of the English contingent seemed to be making out in one way or another. Master Lymeburner, ensconced far down the board, seemed to have found a kindred Russian soul—a grizzled mariner, from the looks of him. They were boisterously sailing on a sea of alcohol, and their efforts to understand each other kept them in a veritable paroxysm of mirth. Young Tutweiller, appalled by the diet and the confusion, had sat self-consciously alone, but this time when Sir Guy looked for him, the young man was not in evidence. The courtier shrugged, and glanced across the board to where Mr. Paxton was deep in conversation with a scholarly-looking Muscovite priest. Sir Guy was slightly puzzled, for he was under the impression that the old man did not speak the Russian language, but as he watched their lips, he concluded that it was not Russian they were speaking, but rather some strange Eastern tongue. At the extreme end of the table, Affable Jones was holding court with his treasured gambling equipment. It was plain that the irrepressible Mr. Jones needed no language to bolster him just so long as he had the use of his dexterous hands.

Thus the banquet progressed. Enormous quantities of both solids and liquids were consumed—by the Muscovites through habit, and by the English who were starved for a change from the limited diet of shipboard. It seemed endless, and though the feast had begun shortly after the noon hour, they were still hard at it six hours later. Moreover, the Muscovites were habituated to cat-napping during the meal, a minor social grace with which Sir Guy was unacquainted. Thus he was somewhat startled when his host, seated on his immediate left, began to snore in a flutey tremolo. Yet by seven of the clock, Sir Guy was only too willing to succumb to local custom and seek relief in slumber. So as he felt the leaden drowsiness steal over him, he tossed the goose-leg on which he had been nibbling to a watchful wolfhound and closed his heavy lids. The buzz of conversation faded. . . .

He awakened to find Sergeant Pistol vigorously shaking him by the shoulder. Still befuddled, he failed at first to grasp the significance of the henchman's presence, so he merely grinned at the somber, taut expression on the equine face and glanced sleepily at the rest of his party distributed around the board. The Count was tilted back in his chair, making barklike noises in his sleep; Master Lymeburner lay slumped over the table, his melon head pillowed on the tangled luxuriance of his fellow-mariner's beard; Mr. Paxton and his theological friend continued their scholarly discourse, while at the opposite end of the hall, Affable Jones, by now red-eyed from his endeavors, was seated on the floor, still merrily fleecing a circle of bewildered Muscovites.

Sir Guy chuckled softly. "Apparently I surrendered into the arms of Morpheus, Pistol!" he remarked.

The sergeant snorted. "If so, sir, then the slut must o' sneaked aw'y w'ilest ye snoozed! Howbeit, that ben't all w'at sneaked aw'y—Titwillow's made off!"

Sir Guy gave a bored yawn. "Aye, I hadn't seen him around. I trust you bade him God-speed?"

"Burn me, 'tain't likely," growled the sergeant, "seein' as 'ow everythin' I owned was aboard!"

The amused smile half formed on the knight's face warped into a puzzled frown.

"What did you say?"

"Ye must be drunk, sir!" snapped Pistol disrespectfully. "I be tryin' to tell ye—*Tutweiller's run off wi' the Sea Sprite!*"

Sir Guy came to his feet so abruptly he overturned his chair.

"That's impossible!"

Pistol inclined his head in the general direction of the door. "Say ye so? If ye'll step onto the ramparts, yer Gryce, perchance ye kin still glimpse 'er stern as she 'eads fer England!"

"And the girl—what of her?"

"W'ich girl?"

"The Lady Ellen, of course, you dull-witted oaf!"

Pistol's horsy face lengthened. "Oh, 'er? W'y, nacherly she went along wi' 'im, o' course!"

By this time, every wakeful eye in the hall was focused on them, but Sir Guy was too perturbed to care. He tore across the room and through an arch which led onto the battlements, high above the bay. The view was spectacular. For miles in every direction the countryside spread out like a huge relief map, illumined by a mysteriously indirect lighting that was neither of the day nor yet of the night, but rather

[83]

an awesome gloaming, for in these northern latitudes the sun never quite relinquished its authority.

From the snug little harbor nestled below under the protective guns of the fort, the river wended its way to the delta like a pewter-colored artery, thence through the claw-shaped gut into the great bay beyond. Now halfway along the liquid highway, between the fort and the maw of the sea, moved a black shadow, like a beetle crawling along the back of a serpent.

"That's 'er!" observed Pistol, who had followed the courtier onto the ramparts—as had practically everyone able to move.

"That's *'oo?*" demanded Affable, showing up beside them. "W'at's 'appened?"

"*'Appened?*" grumbled Pistol. "We be marooned."

Sir Guy spun around, and palming a handful of the man's doublet, lifted him clear of the flagging.

"You damned scoundrel!" he raged. "I left you in charge! Why did you let him take it?"

The sergeant seemed unruffled; he merely looked a trifle more morose.

"W'y, m'lud, yer message plainly st'yted that . . ." he began, but Spangler cut him short with a shake that made his very teeth rattle.

"*Message?* What are you talking about, you lying knave?"

In this wise, the scheme cunningly nurtured in the adolescent brain of Philip Tutweiller, was brought to light. Recounted for the most part by the dour sergeant, it was substantiated and corroborated by Charity and the Reverend Belcher, who had by this time pushed to the fore of the crowd milling about the ramparts.

It developed that shortly before sunset, young Tutweiller had returned to the *Sea Sprite,* and with a convincing display of reluctance, had announced that Governor Karamsin had insisted that all passengers on board be presented to him forthwith. Tutweiller claimed, however, that Sir Guy had given confidential orders to the effect that Ellen was to remain on board, but be kept carefully out of sight, in the unhappy event the Governor, in a drunken mood, should decide to visit the ship in person. In the meantime, while Charity, Sergeant Pistol, and Belcher went ashore for their command appearance, he, Philip Tutweiller, was to remain in charge of the vessel. The trio were instructed to wait at a certain tavern on shore until his Excellency should send the proper official to escort them into his exalted presence. Tutweiller had even had the wit to warn Charity, in the name of Sir Guy, to try to conduct herself as a lady should.

"An' so we w'yted at the ruddy tavern until I 'appened to see the ol' tub under weigh," concluded Pistol. "I thought ye'd want to know."

Count Nikita shouldered the sergeant roughly aside and glared stormily at the Englishman.

"Mother of God!" he exploded in Latin. "Did I correctly interpret the foreign gibberish of this dog? Did he say the woman had gone back to England?"

The envoy looked so much like a balloon about to burst that Sir Guy could not repress a dry chuckle.

"He said *going*, not *gone*, although, as you can see for yourself, Count, the distinction is largely academic!"

Count Nikita's eyes blazed dangerously. "You laugh? So—it was your judgment you trusted, eh? *Hospodi Buchmilo!*" He thumped his chest until it resounded like a drum. "Gone! Gone! And I will be put to the torture!" He jackknifed forward and thrust his face close to Sir Guy's own. "But you will precede me, Englishman! By the bones of my blessed mother, I swear it!"

They might well have drawn swords had not the Governor, at that instant, demanded an explanation of the disturbance from Count Nikita. As the latter moved to obey, Sir Guy turned back to the embrasure and stared bitterly at the black speck which was at once his ship and his hope. It was evident that most of the crowd considered Tutweiller's stratagem a *fait accompli*, yet Sir Guy refused to concede it.

Meanwhile, the Governor began to bawl like a freshly weaned calf. His horrendous wails continued unabated until the courtyard of the castle overflowed with soldiery, including a wild-looking company of mounted Tatars. These latter galloped up and down the enclosure in a veritable frenzy of swirling swords and pounding hooves.

"W'at bellers!" marveled Affable Jones, referring to the caterwauling Governor. "Lumme, but I'd like to 'ave that bastard along in a fog!"

"W'y don't 'e beller up a bloody nyvy?" grumbled Pistol.

"'Cause 'e ayant got no bloody nyvy, 'at's w'y!" snorted Affable. "W'at these Muskies carn't do wi' an 'orse, they don't do!"

"Well, 'tis a cinch ye carn't chyce a ship wi' an 'orse! Burn me, look—they even got a ruddy cannon mounted on a nag! Ayant 'at ridickerless?"

"Absolutely balmy!" agreed Affable Jones.

Sir Guy was not consciously listening to this trivial interchange. Yet Sergeant Pistol's sarcastic rejoinder whetted the edge of his mind.

"*Ye carn't chyce a ship wi' an 'orse!*"

Even as he stared, the little *Sea Sprite* stood around a bend and passed from his vision. But there was, he noted, a road that paralleled the river from the harbor to the bay, where on a long, scythelike spit of sand brooded the ruins of a tiny fort. Time and tide had wrought their work and the shifting sands had inched the channel out of range, so now the fort stood, gutted and abandoned. Only the road remained serviceable.

"*Ye carn't chyce a ship wi' an 'orse!*"

A grim smile twisted the corners of Sir Guy's mouth as he shouldered his way through the crowd in search of Count Nikita.

11

Despite his hysterical outburst, Count Nikita grasped at the slim straw Sir Guy held out. He spoke to the Governor, and when that dignitary seemed inclined to argue, the Count imperiously commandeered the whole mounted squadron in the name of the Grand Prince. Horses were quickly obtained for the Englishmen, and in a matter of moments, the howling cavalcade swept through the castle gates and went plunging down the steep hillside.

It had not been Sir Guy's intention to include any of his companions in the chase, save, of course, Affable Jones and Sergeant Pistol. Yet as they galloped through the gates, he saw by the light of torches that old Paxton, Lymeburner, and Charity were in the train. Even the Reverend Belcher had taken horse. By that time, it was too late to object, for Sir Guy's own nag, vying for the lead with a wiry jennet superbly ridden by Count Nikita, was soaring through the night.

Since the beast was better qualified than he to find her way through the darkness, Sir Guy gave her her head and contented himself with staying in the saddle—a handsome contrivance of wood and sinews. The tree was gilded with damask work, and the seat padded with cloth of gold, the rest being made of Saphian leather exquisitely stitched. Instead of spurs, each rider had a little drum attached to his saddle bow, which he thumped to urge the wiry nags to even greater speed. There was no opportunity for conversation, nor was there any need for it. The thunder of hooves, booming of drums, and clank of scimitars—all overlaid with a crescendo of piercing shrieks from the wild Tatar horsemen—left little room for talk.

Sir Guy was just as well pleased that this was so. He had no specific plan, or, rather, the half-formed scheme he did have needed to be weighed against the actual setting before he was ready to broach it. As he recalled the gut, on the advent of their entry the previous night, it had seemed dangerously narrow; barely wide enough for the *Sea Sprite* to squeeze through between the groping finger of the sandspit on one hand and the hungry teeth of the rocks on the other. So he had conceived the reckless notion that by urging the horses into the water, enough men might be able to claw their way aboard the passing ship to retake her.

By the time they reached the point where the river widened into the delta, they had passed the *Sea Sprite*, and any hopes Sir Guy had of taking the vessel by surprise were dashed when the Tatars set up such an unholy clamor of triumph that it nearly terrified their own mounts. The only acknowledgment from the *Sea Sprite* was the prompt addition of more canvas until she seemed likely to fly out of the very water.

Sir Guy soon learned another bitter lesson—that in this land of midnight twilights, distances were deceptive. As the road to the bay was much longer than he had anticipated, when they finally guided their lathered nags onto the bar, he found to his dismay that the gut was a great deal wider than it had appeared. Furthermore, the combination of current and ebb tide created a seething race which would have made any attempt to stem it by man or beast a form of suicide.

They brought the company to a halt, whereupon Sir Guy dismounted and strode to the water's edge, to be joined immediately by the Count and others of his party. There they watched the *Sea Sprite* come ploughing toward them on the bias, her cutwater foaming like an angry charger, and her longboat bobbing astern. From the castle tower she might have resembled a tiny beetle, but viewed from sea level she looked as impregnable as a rogue elephant.

Master Lymeburner fair quivered for the safety of his vessel. "Bones o' me! The man's daft to drive 'er like that!" he moaned. "There ben't a fathom to spare on either board."

As Sir Guy bit his lip in vexation, Belcher let go a wail that made them all jump.

"*Silence!*" raged Sir Guy. "I'll pistol the next knave who . . ." He paused and shot another look at the onrushing ship.

"By the gods, I have it!" he roared in better humor. "Bring up all the firearms! A hundred guineas to the lad who can pick off the steersman and bring the *Sea Sprite* up into the wind!" This offer was volubly relayed to the Tatars.

"God love ye, sir!" protested Lymeburner. "That'd ground her on this sand-bar!"

"Better that than she escape us!" reasoned Sir Guy. "Anyway, a flood-tide will float her without harm. Affable, you dog—my pistols!"

Affable Jones vanished, and Sir Guy strode restlessly up and down the strand. He wore only his dress sword, which had never seemed more useless than at this moment. Some of the others in the party had already opened fire on the ship, but by this time, she was so close aboard that her high bulwarks and generous tumble-home completely protected her company. For the second time within the hour, Sir Guy had erred.

Then just as the *Sea Sprite* came about for her final dash through the gut, Sir Guy remembered something.

"The *cannon!*" he bellowed suddenly. "Where is that mounted cannon?"

Behind the other horses, the nag burdened with the little gun lashed to a special saddle was just coming onto the spit. Sir Guy nodded to Affable Jones, who hastily procured a linstock.

"D'ye s'y an *'undred quid*, m'lud?" he asked, grinning.

"*Two* hundred, if you stop her!" swore Sir Guy. When Count Nikita moved to interfere, the English knight held him back.

"Tarry, Count!" he cautioned. "Jones was one of the best gunners in Her Majesty's service!"

And indeed the versatile Mr. Jones gave a most encouraging display of competence. He looked to the loading and the priming, placed himself behind the primitive little weapon, and while sighting along the badly cast barrel, began cooing to the bronze gun.

Because of the plunging speed of the target, and the lack of maneuverability of the weapon, Affable Jones had set his sights on a pre-estimated spot where he expected the vessel would be, rather than where she was. And so it was a breathless group who waited in silence for the target to come within range, and every eye was riveted on the upraised hand of Mr. Jones as he poised the smouldering linstock above the touch-hole.

"The bowsprit it'll be, gents!" he boasted cockily.

Swiftly she came! Now the *swish-swish* of her stem through the water was audible! Faster, faster! Two lengths . . . one length . . . a half . . . ! Affable Jones sucked in his breath, and lowered the linstock . . . !

"*Oh, Lord God—favor our unworthy efforts!*" yowled the Reverend Belcher just as the match touched the powder.

It may well be doubted that in all his martial experience had that

Tatar pony ever heard a more discordant wail, or else, as Belcher afterwards insisted, the beast was but a pagan nag. In any event, the nerve-shattering screech startled the jennet out of its well-trained calm, so that at the precise moment of discharge, he shied sideways. Thus the carefully laid calculations of Her Majesty's ex-gunner were irrevocably ruined.

Though customarily good-humored to a fault, Mr. Jones was basically an artist, with an artist's temperament. Finding his aim spoiled, with the accompanying loss of the two hundred guineas prize-money, Affable belied his name by flinging himself on the parson.

"Ye gospel-'owlin' screech-owl!" he shrilled, in a tone closely approximating the parson's own. "I'll larn ye . . ." He punctuated this with a clout that sent the startled Belcher swapping ends across the sand. Affable followed with the avowed intention of continuing this form of education, when a mighty roar gave him pause. He gaped about him in bewilderment as Sergeant Pistol bellowed: *"A direct 'it! She's our'n! She's our'n!"*

Such appeared to be the case. True, the ball had not severed the bowsprit, as promised, but it *had* shattered the whipstaff where it joined the rudder-post. Thus the little *Sea Sprite,* suddenly deprived of human guidance, strove automatically to come up into the wind, a natural maneuver now prevented by the force of the tide. Unable either to turn or go forward, she slewed sideways uncertainly, like a terrified doe unable to choose between the precipice or the hounds.

"She's comin' ashore right 'ere!" shouted Pistol.

Indeed, this seemed probable, for the sandy arm reached into the gut as if to pluck any helpless vessel out of the race. Yet the *Sea Sprite* veered skittishly towards the opposite shore. The audience gasped, while some impulsively cried out advice, as if in some miraculous fashion the little ship could help herself. Strangely enough, she did seem to react, as when Master Lymeburner sobbed: *"Larbu'd! Larbu'd! Fer the love o' God, lass, come about!"*

She turned her head towards him, but she had neither the help nor the strength to withstand the brutal elements which, in a hissing fury, lifted her high on a wave and crashed her broadside on a spear-headed rock. Her vitals pierced, she shuddered out the last of her life, and came at last to rest with her proud little forecastle buried in the swirling waters.

Mute and shaken, the company on the beach remained where they were. Then, anticlimactically, the longboat, which had been set adrift when the ball shattered the whipstaff, came drifting forlornly towards the bar, for all the world like a bewildered fawn which may run towards the very hunter who has slain its dam. Sergeant Pistol waded waist-deep into the race and snatched the end of the painter. Others helped him haul it inshore.

Sir Guy climbed grimly aboard, followed by the Count and as many of the company as could crowd into her. Somehow, in the darkness and confusion, Charity and Belcher also managed to squeeze in. If Sir Guy noticed their presence, he said nothing; he had troubles of vaster import. Plainly, the *Sea Sprite* was done for, but he could still reckon with Ellen and Philip Tutweiller.

To the intense disappointment of the boarders, there was no resistance. There was considerable grumbling and resentment that Philip Tutweiller was taken alive, and even he himself appeared somewhat bewildered by this. But Sir Guy had long since learned the value of ritual and example. Before he would even deign to glance at his prisoners, he convened a drumhead court-martial on the sloping, wind-lashed afterdeck of the wrecked *Sea Sprite*.

It was typical of Sir Guy that when others gave way to their emotions, he seemed best able to keep his own under control, and by so doing, even extend his control to theirs. Thus he had the ship's bell tolled solemnly, and taking his place with the cool deliberation of a justice, invited counsel of those around him as to the most fitting punishment for the deserter Tutweiller.

Most of the party argued that a trial, even a mock trial, was a waste of time. Affable Jones recalled to his master's attention that he had spent several enforced years among the Moors of Barbary and pleaded to be allowed to demonstrate his skill with a special improvisation of the garrote, which he promised was a most entertaining method of strangulation.

The Reverend Belcher vociferously denounced this mode of execution as barbaric and unchristian. He demanded instead that Tutweiller be burned in the ecclesiastically approved manner so that Philip would have ample time, during the slow roasting, to meditate and confess his sins.

Count Nikita impatiently brushed aside these suggestions as childish and, even worse, dull spectacles. If the lad was doomed, certainly the others might as well get some fun out of it. No, they should toss Tutweiller in with a maddened bear. As a matter of fact, Governor Karamsin maintained a bear and a pit especially for this edifying pastime.

Master Lymeburner, though considering himself the one most sinned against by Philip's gross violation, pronounced these penalties unreasonably harsh, lubberly, and not tailored to the crime of piracy which, he argued, belonged within the sacred orbit of admiralty law. Therefore, as Master under God, he insisted on his right to administer a fair and humane punishment, in this case a thorough keel-hauling after which, if the defendant still breathed, he be mercifully flogged to death.

"M'luds!" he pleaded in conclusion. "Remember, ye be Christian gentlemen!"

Sir Guy smiled cynically and turned to Mr. Paxton who sat quietly in the lee of the bulwark.

"We haven't heard from you, Ancient! Cannot you suggest some unusual punishment?"

The old gentleman shrugged. "Possibly, yet it matters little what mode you choose, for eventually you will repent it! What distinguishes torture is not so much that a human being is slain, but that he is slain by the cruelty, the fiendish ingenuity and the murderous hand of his fellow-man."

Belcher threw up his hands in pious horror. "*What!* Dost deny the very word of the Lord, to extract an eye for an eye?"

Mr. Paxton looked at him with something akin to pity. "Aye, Parson, I unequivocally deny and decry your interpretation of the Lord's word," he said. "And as for the law . . ." He chuckled reflectively. "I am inclined to agree with Attic Solon who once said that laws are like cobwebs, in that when any trifling and powerless thing falls into them, they hold fast, whereas if the object be weightier, it breaks through and is off."

The clergyman mumbled something about "accursed heretics" under his breath, but Sir Guy broke in with a hearty laugh.

"'Pon my soul, comrades, you've heard the plea for the defense, now . . ." He sobered quickly. "Ah! Here come the prisoners . . . !"

The mood changed. Smiles became scowls. In a portentous silence, broken only by the hissing of angry waters, Tutweiller and Ellen were marched aft through a waist lined with sullen seamen. Philip had maneuvered a pace or two ahead of the girl, as if to shield her with his body. It was not his fault he was alive, and he still seemed a trifle dazed to find it so. Yet if his face was pale, he seemed sustained by the self-hypnosis of the martyr.

Ellen, on the contrary, wore an air of active defiance, not unmixed with scorn. She moved proudly, with an unhurried step. A shrewd observer (and there were several) could sense her impatience with Philip's protective gesture. Her contempt for the whole affair was obvious.

Sir Guy shifted in his chair and appraised the pinioned man with cold eyes. Roles such as this were his forte, and he knew how to squeeze the very essence of drama out of them. The silence became so uncomfortable that when a block swung against a spar, the crash made everyone jump.

Philip's poise began to crumble. "Why do you drag me here like this?" he cried. "Why didn't you kill me in the taking?"

"And afford you a soldier's death?" jeered Sir Guy. "You, a cowardly thief and deserter who would wilfully abandon your comrades in a foreign land? Bah, such a spineless cur does not deserve a trial, yet, by the gods, you shall have one, if only for example!"

The prisoner loosed a high-pitched laugh, like the neigh of a nervous mare.

"A *trial!* God's love, what mockery is this? And I presume you . . . *you*, a professional rogue and a hired mercenary, will sit in judgment?"

"One moment, if you please!" Ellen cut in sharply. "If Philip is to be 'tried,' I demand the right to be tried with him."

Sir Guy's lip curled. "Your crimes, madame, are not the same," he told her. "Now, be so good as . . ."

"How do you know what my crime is?" she challenged.

Philip turned distractedly. "God's life, my lady, you had naught to do . . ."

"Hold your tongue, Philip!" she snapped. "I have no fear of this conniving rogue!"

"He will execute you, too!"

"Saints o' glory!" cried out Charity. "The poor loon's in love wi' 'er lydyship!"

All of this was translated to the Tatar mob and received with brandished torches and howls of glee.

Sir Guy regarded Ellen sternly. "Madame, we will deal with you in our own good time! You have broken your oath to plot with this treacherous hound, yet much as you may merit an identical fate, for obvious reasons we must break up any suicidal love-pact between you."

She tossed her head in disdain. "Passing over your filthy innuendoes," she retorted, "I demand a straightforward answer to one simple question."

"Granted—if you can limit yourself to *one*."

"Do you intend bodily harm to Philip?"

Most of those who understood English laughed heartily, but when the question was translated to the Tatars, they seemed puzzled by its very naïveté. The Count thereupon added some gratuitous fillip which drew gales of merriment.

Ellen stood tight-mouthed until the bellows of mirth subsided, continued in a voice which, though pitched very low, came plainly to all.

"Because, if that is your plan, I wish you to hear this oath, which I now make in the presence of God and these witnesses: *That I, the woman known to you as Ellen, now swear before the Almighty God, that if any physical harm, either by accident or by design, should befall Philip Tutweiller before he safely returns to England, I, the woman known as Ellen, will acquaint Ivan the Fourth, Grand Prince of Muscovy and Emperor of All the Russias, with the sordid facts surrounding this deception which you and your confreres mean to perpetrate upon him . . . so help me, God!*"

There followed a stunned silence. Count Nikita, who had been tumultuously interpreting her words as she went along, had stopped abruptly in mid-sentence when he caught her drift. Now he stood gaping at her, his mouth still open.

She gave him a contemptuous glance. "You pause, Count? Did I speak too rapidly for your limited understanding of my language? Shall I repeat my vow? In Latin, perchance?"

The Muscovite hastily shook his head. Sir Guy grunted. "You spoke plainly enough, my lady!" he remarked dryly. He stroked his chin meditatively. For all the garrulity of his companions, not one of them came to his assistance now. He decided to use his heretofore almost infallible tactic—the counterattack.

"What good are your oaths or vows?" he accused her. "You broke your last vow!"

"You are a damnable liar!" rasped Ellen, with a candor that made even Affable Jones and Sergeant Pistol redden. "I did *not* break my vow! I had nothing to do with the . . ." She stopped short, realizing abruptly that she was in fact confirming the charges against Philip. With her face aflame, she cried out in tortured confusion: "You disregard my oath at your peril!"

"The child is accursed!" babbled Belcher. "Let me guide her footsteps in the path of . . ."

"*Silence!*" thundered Sir Guy, grateful for a vulnerable target for his wrath. Then leaving the clergyman wheezing, he blundered into the breach opened by the girl.

"I shall require time to study this peculiar request."

His choice of words was unfortunate, as she promptly let him know.

"So, *Sir Rogue*, you plead for time to study?" she word-lashed him. "Did you give me time for study when you browbeat the first promise out of me? Did you give me time for study before you brought me to this spot to be pilloried, mocked and degraded? The answer to those questions is my answer to yours . . . *no!* You shall swear before this assemblage what I have asked . . . nay, *demanded!* For my own part, I would not trust a word that passed your lying lips. It is for the effect upon the others that I insist on your oath."

The stillness was acute. Every eye turned on Sir Guy. Better perhaps than anyone present, he realized his predicament. The canted deck underfoot, which might at any instant slide into the snarling, unswimmable waters, was symbolic of his whole plight. The Muscovite soldiers, suspicious of the cessation of hostilities, were clamoring for action. If they grasped so much as a hint of what Ellen had said, Sir Guy knew it would inevitably reach the ears of the Grand Prince—for Muscovy was notoriously a land of spies. To be bested by this chit, his prisoner and his prize, was to lose face so thoroughly with his own contingent that surrendering to her would be practically to abdicate his command.

In his dilemma, and with more intent to gain time than be witty, he turned to Mr. Paxton.

"What was that quip you made about cobwebs, Ancient?"

The old man sighed. "I declare it was more apropos than I anticipated," he confessed. "And I feel certain that if Attic Solon could have witnessed this coup, he would have amended his original epigram to add that once the cobweb is broken, the lighter creatures on occasion may wiggle out in the wake of the weightier."

Sir Guy chuckled, though there was scant mirth in it.

"There is a potency to your plea that cannot be ignored," he told Ellen, keeping his voice calm and judicial. He looked at the astounded Tutweiller.

"Well, Philip—if it should be our pleasure to spare your miserable life, will you give your parole, as a gentleman, that you will make no more attempts of this kind, and recompense us for . . ."

"Oh, of course he will give his parole!" Ellen interrupted impatiently.

"May the devil seize me if I do!" the young man exploded. "Not even to save my life will I be a party to the enslaving of this . . ."

"*Philip!*"

Philip thrust out his jaw, albeit a bit tremulously. "No, never, never shall a Tutweiller give his parole to a whore-master!"

Ellen turned so pale that Charity moved forward to support her, but Ellen waved her back.

"O-o-oh, you impossible fool!" Then she swung on Sir Guy. "Regardless of whether he gives his parole or not!" she insisted defiantly. "My vow stands!"

Sir Guy tried again to save face with his audience. "Touched as I am by this exhibition of sacrificial love and devotion emanating from both you and Titwillow," he taunted her, "I cannot liberate this rodent without his parole. Even you, my lady, should be able to understand *that*."

Ellen flashed her co-defendant a look that blistered his features a bright scarlet.

"I cannot make him do something he . . ." she began, but Sir Guy was ruthless.

"You made him steal this ship without too much difficulty!"

"That's a lie!" shouted Tutweiller. "She urged me not . . ."

"Hold your foolish tongue, Philip!" Ellen snapped. Then to Sir Guy: "Keep him under surveillance, if it please you, since he refuses to help himself, but—and mark this well, Sir Rogue!—he is not to be hurt! From that position I will not budge, if you expect me to go through with my bargain!"

Both Belcher and Lymeburner vociferously decried this arrangement, and Count Nikita added his clamor to theirs, but Sir Guy impatiently silenced them, then turned to his two henchmen.

"Attend what I say with care, my faithful spaniels!" he warned them. "I am turning his jackanapes over to your tender care. You have heard the terms imposed by her Grace, so be guided by them. Precisely how long we shall remain in Muscovy is now a moot question, thanks to the imbecile under discussion. Be that as it may, you are to stay with him night and day and I shall hold you responsible for his conduct. If he causes me any further trouble—may God have mercy on you both, for I shall not! Do I make myself clear?"

"Clear as a Lunnon fog, sir!" grumbled Sergeant Pistol. "W'at if the bloke gets rambunctious?"

With the receding tide, the ship was rocking dangerously, and Sir Guy was growing weary of the farce.

"Damn it, you've had your orders!" he cut Pistol off. "Now get him out of my sight!"

As the appointed keepers moved up on either side of him, Philip threw himself on his knee before Ellen.

"My lady, my lady!" he cried. "I would ten thousand times suffer the worst tortures these hell-hounds could devise than see you sell yourself . . ."

But Ellen wearily gestured him away. "For the love of heaven, leave, Philip! You are embarrassing me!" She fixed her gaze on Spangler.

"I await your oath, Sir Rogue!"

To the surprise of the assemblage—who until this moment expected to see the wily Sir Guy wriggle out of the trap—that worthy gentleman took solemn oath to see that, save for causes patently beyond human control, Philip Tutweiller would be safely returned to England and suffer no bodily harm; this oath to be predicated on the strict compliance by Ellen of her own vows.

And thus the incident ended. The English seamen under Master Lymeburner turned to in an effort to salvage what they could from the doomed vessel, and all but a corporal's guard of the Tatar cavalry was detailed to remain with them.

The others mounted horse for the return.

12

To PROVIDE A MEANS OF retreat is an elemental law among both generals and thieves. Even the commonest houseprowler leaves a rear door unlocked by which he can make his escape in the unhappy event of discovery. In the current enterprise, Sir Guy had deemed the *Sea Sprite* his mode of emergency exit. Now she was gone, and with her his only means of retreat. It was, therefore, a sobering experience to find himself marooned, as Sergeant Pistol had phrased it, in a hostile foreign land, surrounded by stupidity, bigotry, treachery, and hatred even in his own party, and all this within the orbit of a despot so ruthless that even in an age of cruelty and lust, he had won for himself world-wide infamy and the appellation of "the Terrible."

And it was this tyrant, Ivan the Terrible, Grand Prince of Muscovy and Tsar of All the Russias, whom Sir Guy had come to gull! Small wonder, then, that the ride back to the village was made in somber silence.

It had been decided not to return to the castle, as the Governor's natural curiosity might lead to serious complications, but to repair to the tavern in the village. As the Count explained, every good town in Muscovy had such a convenient establishment, known as a *cursemay,* which though the actual property of the Emperor, was farmed out to, or in certain instances bestowed upon, some noble in recompense for his services. So long as his tenure lasted, the noble thus favored is lord of the community, robbing and despoiling at his pleasure, until in a short time he amasses a fortune. Then the Emperor honors him again, this time with a high commission in the army, and sends him off to the wars, where, it being mandatory he maintain his command at his own expense, he spends all the riches gleaned from the hostelry. By this ingenious system, the nobleman is afforded an idyllic interlude and the Emperor wages war at little personal cost to himself.

"In fine," observed Mr. Paxton, who had listened with interest to the recital, "the common people pay for it."

Count Nikita turned in surprise. "Who else would pay for it, old one? Has anyone ever paid for war, save the vulgar poor?"

"Hardly," agreed the aged scholar, "else it would cease to exist."

The Muscovite snorted in disgust. "Bah! Thou art either a dangerous free-thinker, or a simple fool! Without war, what would a gentleman do with himself?"

Sir Guy frowned warningly at the old man. They could not afford to quarrel with the envoy at this juncture.

As soon as they were lodged in the *cursemay*, with Ellen locked in a suite with Charity, and the still incorrigible Philip in the protective custody of Sergeant Pistol, Sir Guy convoked a council of what he pointedly termed his "fellow-conspirators"—a designation which made them wince. Convened ostensibly to plot their future course, the meeting was in reality called to impress on each the precariousness of their situation, for like the suave politician he was, Sir Guy was well aware that fear, more than any other human emotion, will hold a group together.

Master Lymeburner wanted to reopen the charges against Philip.

"Aye!" cried the Reverend Belcher. "Thou hast jeopardized our lives and our fortunes by releasing that godless traitor!"

Sir Guy had been on edge up to this point, but a full look at the parson restored his saving sense of humor. If he was a fanatic, he was also painfully sincere; yet since his very livelihood depended on such avaricious tradesmen as Mr. Bendix, *et al*, he had the almost impossible chore of trying to reconcile the tenets of religion with the precepts of business; a task which has defeated cannier men than Horace Belcher.

Sir Guy turned back to the others. "I did not summon you here to reopen the past, but to discuss the future. Nor is it my custom to explain my actions. It should be obvious to you all—even to *you*, Parson

—that the woman would have betrayed us had I executed the lovesick idiot."

Count Nikita nodded in approval. "By the forked tail of my mother-in-law, I swear that is so! Sir Guy is shrewd like the weasel! Humor her now, then after she is safely delivered to the Kremlin, why then we have some fun with this Titwillow? Maybe we throw him to the bear, eh?"

Sir Guy grinned. "It is the delivering which concerns us at the moment," he countered. "How far are we from Moscow?"

The Count stared meditatively at the ceiling while he ticked off the distances on his fingers.

"Let us see," he mused. "It is something under a hundred *versts* from here to Colmogro, about one thousand *versts* from Colmogro to Vologhda, and then another five hundred to Moscow. Roughly, the journey will cover about sixteen hundred *versts*."

"Which, in English means . . . ?"

"Approximately one hundred and fifty French leagues."

Belcher winced and swiveled his eyes. "Peradventure it would be more sensible that I remain here," he suggested. "It will lessen the number traveling and at the same time afford an opportunity for spreading the Word."

"It would ha' been more sensible 'ad ye st'yed in Lunnon!" remarked Affable Jones.

"And you must be extremely careful about this spreading of words," warned the Count, not comprehending the Scriptural connotation. "We have here in Muscovy the terrible *Opritchnina*, Ivan's own secret police!" [6]

Sir Guy arched his brows. He had long heard of this fabulous spy organization, but it had seemed as unreal as most of the tales emanating from the mysterious East. The story was that because of his tragic youth, suspicion of treason had become an obsession with Ivan the Fourth. To protect himself, he had established the infamous spy system, formed of the worst dregs of society, which scoured the country seeking out traitors or reasonable facsimiles thereof. Evidence as such was not required of these minions, for Ivan himself was the judge and, very often, the executioner.

"Does the *Opritchnina* reach into these remote hinterlands?" Sir Guy asked.

The Count nodded grimly. "The *Opritchnina* is everywhere! It has a million eyes and ears! In Muscovy, one dare not trust his own brother!"

Master Lymeburner shuddered. "The devil's own truth!" he agreed.

"It was a ragged 'ungry-lookin' beggar we took to feed aboard *The Dainty Virgin* w'at betrayed us! 'E was naught but a ruddy spy!"

Nikita leaned forward. "By the way, Captain, exactly *where* did you leave this vessel of yours?"

Master Lymeburner bit his lip in hesitation and glanced sideways at Sir Guy, but there was precious little the latter could do save acquiesce.

"Count Nikita is one of us," Sir Guy said, albeit a trifle lamely.

The mariner bowed his head. "W'y, m'lud, last I saw o' 'er, she lay snug an' sound in a little cove wi'in cannon shot o' a village called Slabotta."

The Count nodded as if pleased. "A clever cache, my Captain! You were smart, like a shark!"

"Thankee, sir, but I weren't smart enough to get 'er out—more's the pity!" He sighed deeply. "I 'opes the lads 'ave kept 'er seaworthy."

Plainly, the Reverend Belcher had lost his zest for the journey. "Would it not be wisdom to have the Count take this . . . these, er, female *creatures* to the Emperor, while the rest of us remain here?"

Sir Guy started to laugh, expecting the others to do likewise. But to his sobering surprise, Count Nikita snatched at the suggestion with alacrity.

"Excellent, Father! I can . . ."

Belcher could not let that pass. "Sirrah!" he interrupted indignantly. "I am no *priest*, but a . . ."

The Count brushed the objection aside with a hearty laugh. "Your secret is safe with me, little Father!" he chortled. "By the Seven Masses, you have spoken wise words! I will take this woman to my imperial master and . . ."

Sir Guy held up a restraining hand. "Not so fast, gentlemen!" he cut them off. "We will follow our original plan and travel together to Moscow." He glanced at the flushed, half-angry features of the envoy. "You will make the necessary arrangements for the journey, as agreed, Count?" This last was more of a statement than a query.

The Muscovite rose and covered his obvious chagrin with a booming guffaw.

"I bow to your wisdom, my friends. Karamsin has already been advised to ready a caravan so that we shall leave with the dawn!" He raised a massive hand in a gesture of salutation. "Ah, my comrades, now that we are in Muscovy, I shall have an opportunity to repay the many courtesies I received when you were my hosts! So, until the break of day . . . !" He bowed from the waist and backed out of the room.

"For a pagan, he means well," observed the Reverend Belcher, as the door closed. "His offer of kindness shows the wisdom of God's Word when He sayeth: 'Cast thy bread upon the waters . . .'"

Sir Guy sighed. "Oh, that for just once you were right, Parson. Howbeit, I greatly fear the courtesies to which he referred are not the coin you'd care to be paid in."

"You intimate he lied?" gasped Belcher, bobbing to his feet.

Affable and Lymeburner both rose. "I reckon I'd better cast me ownself in bed," yawned Mr. Jones.

The mariner hesitated. "Bones o' me, I wish't 'is 'Ighness 'adn't arsked fer the position o' *The Dainty Virgin*," he grumbled.

"I wouldn't 'a tolt 'im at all," observed Affable Jones.

"In which event," put in Mr. Paxton, "he would have made other inquiries from the local officials."

"Pree-cisely me own thought," said Master Lymeburner, "w'ich was w'y I tolt him w'at I did, fer the *Virgin* ben't at *Slabotta* but at *Slobitia*."

Affable snorted. "Ye mean there's a difference?" he asked sarcastically.

"About ninety leagues," grinned Lymeburner.

Sir Guy laughed. "Excellent, Captain, excellent! Instead of proceeding with us to Moscow, you will quietly slip away and head for *Slobitia*. There you will doubtless be interned with the rest of the crew, but at least you can have things ready for a quick get-away in the event we should have to leave . . . ah . . . precipitately, if you ken my meaning?"

The mariner rubbed his hand. "I ken ye, sir! Come ye in a week, a month, or a twelfth-month, the little *Virgin*'ll be ready to slip 'er hawse on a moment's notice, keel'aul me else!"

As the pair went out, Mr. Paxton got up to follow, but Sir Guy gestured him to remain.

"Tarry, Ancient," he urged. "Quaff a glass with me before you retire. At your age, one does not require much sleep."

The philosopher smiled. "Ah, but at yours, one does."

The younger man grunted. "The way I feel right now, I shall never sleep again," he said, crossing to a low sideboard on which stood a flagon and goblets. Pouring two drinks, he set one before his companion, then flung himself into a chair and stared reflectively at his outthrust boots.

"I have been somewhat surprised," he commented, after a long pause, "to hear you cross swords with our holy man."

"Why should you be surprised, young man?"

Sir Guy shrugged. "I don't know. I suppose I took it for granted you were religious."

The old man chuckled. "But I am, sir! That is precisely why I *crossed swords*, as you put it, with Belcher."

"He's such a fool!" protested Spangler. "How can you put any stock in what he preaches?"

"Pshaw, sir, what you are doing is damning a whole doctrine because of its servants! Oh, I grant you this rubbish of a revengeful God and eternal hell-fire is impossible to swallow if one has intelligence, yet the fault lies, not in the concept, but in the misrepresentation of the orthodox teachings. It was a realization of that which drove me to a study of the ancient philosophies, and I found they all taught essentially the same thing: ergo, that there is a light in the center of man's being. Jesus called it: 'The light that lighteth every man that cometh into the world.' " The speaker sighed softly.

"Alas, in its passage through many tongues and many mouths, a truth gets badly mangled, yet the greatest tragedy is that people have always worshipped the *messenger*, rather than the *message*, which invariably is either misinterpreted or forgotten. This has been the case with Jesus of Nazareth, Mohammed, Confucius, and Gautama Siddhartha, the founder of Buddhism. These great teachers, or messengers, have been deified while their priceless teachings have all too often been ignored or twisted into unintelligible jargon."

Sir Guy pondered that in silence, while one by one the candles gutted out until at last the room was illumined only by the reddish embers in the hearth. Finally he pitched his empty goblet into the fire with a gesture of desperation.

"Never in my life have I given a confidence or sought advice of another," he said abruptly. "Yet, by my troth, Ancient, you have such a miraculous way of explaining the inexplicable, perchance you can help me now."

"Giving confidence is like giving blood," the old man said with a smile. "Though it may quiet the nerves, it also weakens."

Sir Guy shrugged. "Even the most experienced mariner summons a pilot in strange waters, and by the Mass, I concede these waters strange. Perchance I've already tarried overlong, for though I cannot be sure when I lost my reckoning, as Lymeburner would phrase it, we seem to have carried into the shoals."

"Neither shoals nor other such dangers appear to have troubled you before, young sir. Why should they now?"

"I swear I do not know! It is as though I had suddenly lost my sight! We had our course carefully plotted, and though we haven't deviated a whit, we appear . . . well . . . to be coming apart at the seams. We are no longer a group with a common objective; we seem like enemies! You are wise in the peculiar ways of mankind, Ancient—can you tell me what is wrong?"

"Ah, my son, doubts are more cruel than the worst of truths," said the other gently, "and of these, self-doubt is the most relentless. I can tell you nothing, for I am no wiser than you. But let us examine the problem together: To continue using your descriptive analogy—what *could* make a vessel leave its course without the knowledge of the steersman?"

Sir Guy deliberated a moment. "Why, naught but some object with a strong magnetic attraction placed sufficiently close to the compass to throw it out of true. Howbeit, the steersman should take note of such foreign bodies and . . ."

"Ah, yes, my friend, he *should!*" interrupted Mr. Paxton. "Yet in our particular case, the steersman has—temporarily, I trust—lost his sight."

Sir Guy glanced sideways. "You talk in riddles, old one!"

"Nay, rather in parables," chuckled the other. "Like the fictional steersman in our hypothesis, you seem blind to the fact that the singleness of purpose represented by a compass in our analogy has been sadly deviated by the most potent of all magnetic attractions, a woman."

Sir Guy straightened abruptly. "Ridiculous!" he snorted impatiently. "Why, we all agreed . . ." He sank back into his chair, frowning thoughtfully. "By God, I wonder . . . ?" he mused aloud. "I wonder!"

Mr. Paxton's smile was kindly. "Alas, young sir, you must indeed be blind if I need call your attention to the fact that the Lady Ellen is very, *very* beautiful."

Leaving Sir Guy staring into the fireplace, the old man quietly left the chamber.

13

IF WISE OLD PAXTON'S REVELATIONS failed to improve Sir Guy's insight, at least it did sharpen his outward perceptions. In the weeks that followed, he was surprised to discover how potently Ellen affected the others. He conceded as much to the venerable scholar.

"'Pon my soul, though I find it difficult to believe, I vow everyone of these fools has lost his senses over the haughty chit—that is, all save you and me! You are too old and I, praise God, have too much sense!"

Mr. Paxton laughed. "Verily then, you and I can remain friends because there will be no cause for jealousy between us—it being a case of the halt leading the blind."

Sir Guy frowned suspiciously, but the old man's face was bland, so he let it pass; he had no time to read hidden meanings into every facetious remark. Though the physical aspects of the journey—a dreary, exhausting and interminable pilgrimage by boat, wagon, and horseback that consumed the better part of six weeks—was in the hands of Count Nikita, Sir Guy kept a tight rein over the personnel, and personal jurisdiction over the broad strategy of their reckless enterprise.

Fortunately, they had relatively little trouble. Philip Tutweiller appeared to have grown adjusted to being in "protective custody," and though Ellen maintained a chilly reserve when in the presence of Sir Guy, she, too, seemed resigned to her fate. Two minor incidents were nipped in the bud before they could flower into major crises: the first sprang from Affable Jones's predilection for gambling; the other from Charity's inability to say no.

Only the quick wit and boldness of Sir Guy saved the jolly knave from a mob of angry Tatars when one of his favorite swindles was discovered. Sir Guy thereupon sternly forbade him even to gamble *honestly* for the duration of the journey. Affable wailed that such a prolonged abstinence would be fatal to his technique, but when he found Sir Guy adamant, the wily rascal made a private treaty with Sergeant Pistol. This was to the effect that they should *play* together—not *gamble*, of course! God forbid!—with Affable paying off when, and if, Pistol was able to discern any trickery; Affable, however, agreed to take no winnings even when he won, deeming the play a mere exercise to keep his fingers supple and his wits nimble.

Charity's delinquencies came closer to being serious, for two Tatar officers went at it with scimitars over her favors, and their adherents were joining the dispute when Count Nikita and Sir Guy charged into the fray. The Count settled the affair by promptly hanging both would-be lovers, while Sir Guy threatened Charity that on her next offense he would have the blacksmith rivet her into a chastity belt, of the kind used by ancient knights to secure the virtue of their wives during long separations.[7] But as he should have anticipated, instead of being intimidated, little Charity was merely fascinated by the description of the iron girdle (a species of feminine undergarment with which she was not familiar) and asked so many disconcerting questions about it that Sir Guy became embarrassed and had to shoo her out of his presence.

Due, indirectly, to this affair, Sir Guy stumbled onto something which offered food for thought. When he remarked to Count Nikita that the Tsar might resent the summary execution of two of his officers, the Count announced quite casually that the Tatar contingent were not soldiers of the Tsar, but a body of personal troops owing allegiance only to Count Nikita's uncle, one Akhmet, Governor of a Prince Dominion in far-off Crimea. These "Prince Dominions" were of an indigenous character, being a bastard cross between a regular province and an independent state; a sort of loosely woven political compromise, like the troublesome feudatories of the Middle Ages.

With the almost animal sense which always alerted him to the unusual, Sir Guy wondered why this revelation had not come earlier. It could mean anything, or nothing, like the snap of a twig in the stillness of the forest, yet Sir Guy seemed to recall that on the night of the sinking of the *Sea Sprite*, Nikita had referred to these bellicose barbarians as "the Governor's horse." True, the Count might have meant the Governor of Crimea, rather than Governor Karamsin of Dwina. Be that as it may, it was undeniable that Count Nikita had been acting somewhat peculiarly since their arrival in Muscovy.

Sir Guy was not prone to oversensitivity, and he knew that other things than premeditated treachery could occasion this conduct. He had also discovered that the volatile Russian temperament, so jolly and hilarious at times, could on occasion plummet to depths of depression unknown to an Englishman. So after due consideration, he decided the matter was not of sufficient importance to create an issue. Count Nikita was as deeply concerned with the venture, and as heavily implicated in the deception, as was Sir Guy himself. Perchance he had tempted Fate by placing himself in the power of a fellow-conspirator—a thing he had never done before—yet having thrust his head in the noose, the only logical course now was to see it through.

However, as the journey neared its end, he concentrated on a careful survey of the political situation in Moscow. This dealt not with the pedantic, quasi-legal mummery, as elucidated in schoolrooms, but with the actual sources of power, the political puppeteers and their shirttail relationships.

The Muscovites were only too willing to talk about their Grand Prince and his various satellites. Sir Guy, being a natural linguist like Count Nikita, had become quite proficient in the Muscovite tongue; a great deal more so than he let on. Hence the jovial soldiery enjoyed discoursing with him, while he carefully sorted, checked, and classified this flood of information in the pigeonholes of his mind. And though he refused to be distracted by the tales of fantastic cruelties perpetrated by Ivan IV, the further his investigations carried him into the machinations of this remarkable monarch, the less reassuring he found the situation.

It was soon manifest that if Ivan deserved the appellation of "the Terrible," he was not the fool he was ofttimes rumored to be. Instead, he was highly intelligent, though entirely self-educated, and one of the hardest-working men of his age. Unfortunately, the few individuals who got sufficiently close to this complex character for study did not survive long enough to record their findings.

However, in fairness it had to be admitted that the less pleasant facets of the Tsar's many-sided nature had all but obscured the others. This was especially so in the more civilized countries of the West, where Ivan's penchant for favoring the common people at the expense of the nobility was viewed with self-righteous revulsion. Nor could the gentle-born of the Western world stomach his contempt for human life; and such wombs of culture as Spain and France were appalled when he summarily tossed a double-dealing *boyar* to his hounds. Certainly no Western monarch would act so—unless, of course, the victim was a heretic or otherwise of no importance. Ivan, on the contrary, was unbiased; he had put out the eyes of an Italian architect who had built him St. Basil's Cathedral (so the architect could not surpass it later), had forced a noble to imbibe a lethal potion of scalding soup, and had strangled a bishop. If these minor discourtesies had been isolated examples, they might readily have been laughed off, but unfortunately, they were not. They were honest samples of his complete impartiality.

To sum it up: Ivan was a creature of impulse, a despot of ungovernable temper, and an unorthodox prince. In the manifold contradictions of his nature lay the greatest danger to Sir Guy and his scheme, for being absolutely unpredictable, the slightest slip in dealing with him was more than apt to prove fatal. Withal, Sir Guy was not unduly perturbed. What was needed, he decided, was a cat's paw with which to extract the chestnuts from the fire. He examined the records of those creatures reputedly closest to the imperial flame.

His investigation uncovered two possibilities—the Metropolitane, a species of super-archbishop who was spiritual head of the country, and the Metropolitane's chief political rival, the Grand Equerry. And when Sir Guy began to delve into the characters and machinations of these worthies, he felt on firmer ground. For despite their foreign trappings, semi-oriental customs and unpronounceable names, they were, essentially, as familiar as old friends.

These two typified what theologians pronounced the eternal struggle of the "good" angel over the "bad" angel, of virtue over vice, or of heaven over hell. Being a realist, Sir Guy knew it wasn't quite that simple, but for want of an apter phrase, he let it stand.

Now it is most important to understand that the Grand Prince (as the Muscovites affectionately termed Ivan) had a conflict in his nature, as have all men; but his status being what it was, free from the normal restraints imposed on lesser males, this duality was grossly magnified. Ivan could be the most pious of men—he had once threatened abdication to enter a monastery—and his concern for the welfare and morals of his people was clearly established; on the other hand, segments of his private life had been abominable, his cruelties infamous, and his sexual orgies such as to make such gay old roués as England's Henry VIII and France's Charles seem pillars of moral rectitude.

Captaining these teams of virtue and of vice stood the Metropolitane and the Grand Equerry. In a pictorial sense, Ivan was in the middle, with the Metropolitane tugging him (as much as any man dared "tug" Ivan the Terrible) one way, and the Grand Equerry luring him the other.

Of the two, from Sir Guy's point of view, the Metropolitane Sylvester was the most dangerous, both by reason of his exalted station (even the Tsar had to do him homage on occasion) and his uncompromising hatred of foreigners and all things foreign. And though it was a settled conviction of Sir Guy's that every man has his price, he was finally brought to concede that the Metropolitane's was not readily discernible. A former monk, he was not interested in gold, and, due either to extreme asceticism or advancing years, was declared impervious to women. Since this ruled out the two best-known mediums of exchange, such an unnatural character posed a difficult, if not insoluble, problem.

But in Boris Smolovitch, the Grand Equerry, Sir Guy found a bright rainbow of hope. This jolly lecher was to Ivan what in the English court would have been known as the "Master of the Back Stairs"; he pandered to the "human side" of the Emperor's nature. He was reputed to have scouts combing the hinterlands, and even neighboring states, in search of women to delight his rakish master.

The ghastly tragedy of the Grand Equerry's own life (according to the reports Sir Guy gathered) was that Fate was fast putting him on the same shelf the Metropolitane had chosen. In the Grand Equerry's case, however, virtue was anything but voluntary; in desperation, he had filled his own palace with the most toothsome nymphs his agents could scratch out of the country; he had even married (it was reputed) thirteen women from as many different points of the compass, in the vain hope that the sanctity of marriage, combined with the distance traveled, might lend the necessary enchantment. They had not. And whether the number thirteen was unlucky for him, or whether such a lifetime diet of sweets had finally surfeited his carnal appetites, could not be ascertained. Suffice to say, Boris Smolovitch was a troubled man.

But as a "troubled man" is likewise a vulnerable man, the Grand Equerry became of increasing interest to Sir Guy. It was necessary, of course, to investigate other than his libidinous propensities, for no mere panderer could have attained the eminence of Imperial Grand Equerry and one of the Tsar's chief counsellors. Fortunately, the maxim held true that a man liberal in one way is likely to be liberal in all ways, and Smolovitch, in addition to his playful moments, encouraged Ivan in his search for knowledge and had personally founded the first scientific library in Muscovy. He was interested in foreigners and foreign customs, and if his agents scoured the surrounding states for virgins, they also inveigled scholars and scientists to visit Muscovy.

Detractors charged that his mania for collecting scientists stemmed from his terror of approaching impotence, and in support of this libel pointed to the irrefutable fact that most of his "scientists" were physicians, alchemists, and soothsayers; and that while devastating epidemics raged rampant on the very outskirts of Moscow, the imported scientists remained luxuriously ensconced in the Grand Equerry's palace, seeking a philter powerful enough to renew the aged man's waning vigor.

Sir Guy gleefully resolved that on the first opportunity—nay, for such a prospect, he would create his own opportunity—he would cultivate the patronage of Boris Smolovitch, Grand Equerry and Counsellor of Ivan the Terrible!

When he summarized the gist of what he had learned for the Count, that noble was aghast.

"By the forked tail of my mother-in-law!" he marveled. "I cannot understand by what miracle you learned so much! Surely none of my compatriots would be so disloyal as to pass along such scurrilous tales of their liege lord!"

"Are my facts inaccurate?" Sir Guy asked.

Nikita burst into uproarious laughter. "I will admit nothing, lest an agent of the *Opritchnina* be hiding under my saddle. Even to think such thoughts is apt to be fatal. Just so long as I remain under the surveillance of my Prince . . ." He stopped abruptly, as if he had said too much.

The Englishman eyed him closely. "Ah—you have an alternative?" he probed.

The Count brushed the question roughly aside. "We chatter like old wives! Look, my friend, you would be better occupied grooming our wench for her reception than prying into the politics of my country!"

Sir Guy ignored the tone. He knew that boldness and bluster, however great, are naught but masks for fear, and his eyes had been opened to some extent by the wisdom of Mr. Paxton. He made a mental note to "pry" into the cause of Nikita's recurring surges of terror.

"You have a point," he said goodnaturedly. "I shall have a chat with her ladyship this evening."

They had broken their journey about midday in order to rest the horses and freshen the gear, for they were now only two days' travel from Moscow. Earlier in the week, a swift courier had been dispatched ahead to herald their coming, and a reply from the Grand Prince was expected at any moment.

It was an unusually clean little tavern, bustlingly operated by a temperamental host and two ample-bosomed daughters. The food was good, and when the gentle folk had rested, humors were revived. Thus when Sir Guy went up to Ellen's quarters after dinner, and paused to rap on her door, he heard her laughing merrily inside the chamber, where she was playing at cards with Charity.

Delighted at the prospect of finding her in such excellent spirits, he knocked, and at her cheery bidding, opened the door and stepped inside. But the smile vanished from Ellen's face as she said coldly: "Oh, it *is* you!"

Sir Guy bowed. "Circumstances are such that I must intrude." He eyed the other girl. "Charity . . ."

Charity hopped to her feet. "Syve yer wind, sir!" she caroled, "I knows w'en I ayant wanted! Yer pardon, m'lydy!" She curtsied and swished out of the room before Ellen could object.

Sir Guy saw to it that the door was safely shut, then returned to the table at which Ellen was seated. He stood silent for so long, she said tartly: "Well, why do you not sit down?"

"I had not received your permission, my lady."

Her eyes widened in astonishment, then she gave a harsh little laugh. "La! If you aren't the strangest creature! Since when have you waited for my permission on anything?" She answered her own question with a disdainful snort. "Well, good heavens, sir, if that is what is causing you to stand there so—you have it! Sit down, by all means!"

Smiling, Sir Guy dropped into the chair so recently vacated by Charity, and took one swift, all-encompassing glance at the woman across the table.

Although Ellen's expression was intended to be stern, she was not entirely successful. Too, she now seemed to have made a nice distinction between pride and mere haughtiness, and this new regal quality Sir Guy found quite becoming. And there was yet another quality, nebulous and subtle, that he sensed without being able to identify. The thought occurred to him that perchance this was the magnetism of which old Paxton had spoken. He looked more closely, and for the first time realized that the old philosopher's pronouncement had been no exaggeration. Ellen was very, very beautiful!

Though her spine was as straight as if it had never so much as touched the back of any chair, she had an easy informality of manner. This was enhanced by the low-cut velvet gown she wore with just the right touch of dishabille, and by the studied casualness with which her wine-red hair was piled atop her head. Yet what astonished him was not alone that she was beautiful, but that her beauty had a radiance that seemed to spread to the most commonplace things around her until the whole room, even its very atmosphere, appeared warm and lovely.

Contradictorily enough, its reaction on him was not warmth, but a vague, disquieting sense of loneliness. Irked by this, his tone was gruffer than intended.

"Since we are almost upon Moscow," he said, "I deemed it proper we should have a thorough understanding of our respective roles."

"A *rehearsal*, sir?"

To his everlasting embarrassment, he felt his ears tingle. But before he could frame a retort, Ellen burst into laughter.

"Great day in heaven, Sir Guy—I never thought to see the moment when *you* were capable of blushing!"

Not accustomed to being laughed at, Sir Guy smiled rather thinly.

"*Touché,* my lady! Not anticipating such bawdy wit from you, I was taken by surprise. No doubt your close association with Charity . . ."

She silenced him with a gesture. "Shame on you, Sir Knight!" she reproved. "That was cowardly! Perhaps my remark was facetious, yet you have no call to blame my mistakes on that unfortunate child! Indeed, though Charity's vocabulary is . . . well . . . startling at times, she has other qualities which we all—aye, even you, sir—could emulate to advantage. I regret some of the rest of us lack her pureness of heart!"

"Well, I'll be damned!" he exclaimed. "Peradventure I'd best fraternize with Charity, since her purity impressed you so, my lady!"

Ellen was too sure of herself to be baited. "God forbid, sir! I certainly do not recommend such a thing—for Charity's sake!" she retorted. "Howbeit, by what right do you chide me about the company I keep, when you maintain such baseborn scullions as those precious hell-twins, Jones and Pistol! *That* association is beyond all comprehension!"

Something of her mood transmitted itself to Sir Guy. Although they were fencing as always when they came together, the raw sense of antagonism was missing this time. Matching her humor, he relaxed and absently fingered the cards Charity had left on the table.

"Forgive any seeming slurs I may have cast at Charity," he said. "If my lips spoke them, my heart did not. I stand corrected, and willing to grant that I could learn much from her. Yet, by the same token, my lady, perchance that is why I maintain the two stout rogues you mentioned in such unflattering terms."

She made a moue of disgust. "What possible qualities could one discover in such scum?"

"That most priceless of all human traits, my lady, and the rarest—sincerity! If you had seen as much of the world's hypocrisy as I have, you, too, would value the absolute sincerity of Affable Jones and Sergeant Pistol, vulgar and gutter-tainted as it may be."

"Sincerity?" she gasped. "In those two? You jest, sir! Why, one is an admitted gambling cheat, and the other a practiced liar!"

"You do them an injustice," he protested, smiling. "They are both practiced liars!"

"Murderers, too!"

He laughed outright. "Aye, but only when necessary! Yet sincere withal, for as I understand the word, it means *without dissimulation or hypocrisy;* it has no social or moral connotation. They are, I might add, extremely loyal—a characteristic I prize above rubies!"

She looked at him with renewed interest. "If the question is not impertinent," she said after a thoughtful pause, "tell me how you gained such doglike devotion. I suppose you saved their lives, or something of the kind?"

Sir Guy shook his head. "My dear young lady, you have much to learn about human nature. Gratitude, *per se*, is found only in copybook maxims, and the one certain method of building up hidden resentments is to make another human being indebted to you; the measure of the resentment being in direct proportion to the value of the indebtedness."

"Heavens, you are cynical!"

"Realistic, rather. However, to answer your question—I did not save their lives; they saved mine. As a result, they regard me as their collective property."

"But if your unpleasant thesis was so, *you* would resent *them!*"

He grinned. "I did, for a brief time," he confessed. "Then I had an opportunity to . . . er . . . extricate them from an embarrassment. For the past several years we have see-sawed the account back and forth so often it has become commonplace." He chuckled aloud. "They are a precious pair, these hell-twins, as you term them. I will not go quite so far as you did with Charity, and credit them with unusual purity of heart. Yet when you referred to Affable and the sergeant as murderers, I wonder if that is quite accurate, other than in a strictly legal sense? Granted they will kill, it is more in the manner of a hound killing a rabbit, without hate or passion. Or, if I may be pardoned for mentioning it—as Charity sins while meaning only to be kind."

A faint tint suffused the girl's features, and she lowered her eyes in confusion.

"You have made your point, and very ably," she murmured. "Though to put your theories into general practice would bring on social chaos." She folded her hands primly in her lap, and when she looked at him again, it was as though a veil had been drawn over her eyes.

"We have digressed, I fear," she went on. "You came here to discuss our respective roles on entering Moscow."

That subject had suddenly lost its zest for Sir Guy. "Why, 'tis of no great importance," he said.

She arched her brows. "Not important, sir? What manner of merchant are you that carries a commodity halfway 'round the world to barter with some potentate, then on the eve of consummation says the details are 'of no great importance'?"

Her mood had reverted to its former causticity, and Sir Guy felt like a man recalled suddenly from a pleasant dream to do battle. He found it difficult to adjust himself to the abrupt shift in humor.

"I meant only that we could discuss the matter on another occasion."

Ellen appeared relentless. "You came here for that avowed purpose," she reminded him. "So if we settle it now, you will be spared the irritation of another visit."

He bowed to cover his chagrin. "As you wish." His long fingers riffled the cards. "You know, of course, that you are supposed to be Ellen Hastings, the twin sister of Mary."

"So you gave me to understand."

"The Tsar will be informed that your 'sister,' Mary, was scarred by smallpox, hence the substitution."

"Go on."

He spread his hands. "That's about it! We will, of course, make certain that on presentation your coiffure and gown are patterned after the miniature. The Count will handle the ceremonial details."

She made a grimace. "Is there to be a mock wedding, or will I merely be included in the parade of the *two thousand maidens?*"

His face darkened angrily. "You will be properly . . ." He stopped abruptly as a commotion broke out in the hallway.

He crossed the room in a bound and jerked open the door, where he discovered a strange-looking character locked in the lethal embrace of Sergeant Pistol.

"This 'ere Musky was a-listenin' at the door," the sergeant reported gloomily. "I 'opes ye didn't s'y some'at ye'd no want repeated?"

It was distinctly a question, and while waiting hopefully for answer, he poised the razor-edge of his poniard on the captive's jugular.

14

THE GAUNT Pistol had obviously surprised the spy as he squatted to peer through a crack in the panel, and had pounced upon his back. There the sergeant now clung, like a caricature of a medieval knight riding a dragon.

Nor would a living dragon have appeared much more incredible than the creature lashing and bucking under the sinewy sergeant. So grotesque and misshapen was he, it took Sir Guy a moment or two to realize he was human; a dwarf, albeit a very large one. His massive head was keg-shaped, straight-sided and flat-topped, with two gimlet holes for eyes, a plugged bung for a nose, and an ax indentation for a mouth. The weird, under-sized body did not seem to belong to the head; it was almost as though a drunken doll-maker had created an abortive mistake. The arms were so long the knuckles trailed the ground, in the manner of an ape's, and the legs were short and bowed. And instead of dimming these deformities with inconspicuous raiment, the dwarf was gaudily and expensively appareled in a fashion which accentuated the repulsiveness of Nature's mistake.

The spy had been struggling when Sir Guy opened the door, then bowing to the inevitable, he gave one more token buck and stood still. Sergeant Pistol readjusted his death-grip, pricked the skin directly over the captive's jugular to make a "seat" for the point of his blade, and awaited his master's nod.

Sir Guy appraised the dwarf with a jaundiced eye. Mercy, as such, was not a common attribute in the sixteenth century, being then regarded as evidence of moral weakness, and justice was too often a summary affair.

But if mercy was absent, curiosity was not. Before Pistol could jugulate his victim, Sir Guy called: "Hold! Find out who sent him here."

The sergeant ill concealed his impatience. "'Ell, m'lud, 'e carn't talk."

The knight snorted. "Obviously not while you have a hand clamped around his windpipe. Give him air!"

Pistol kept the point of his knife inserted just below the first layer of skin, but slackened his stranglehold perceptibly. The prisoner managed a faint gurgling noise, as if under water.

"Ease you, you knave, ease up!" growled Sir Guy. "If you throttle him you won't have any throat to cut!"

The threat of deprivation was more than Pistol could bear, so he let go his choking hold and immediately secured a fresh grip on the dwarf's matted hair.

"Now talk, damn ye!" he urged grimly.

The dwarf opened his mouth, wiggled his tongue a few times, in the fashion of a chicken drinking water, and swallowed—all without sound. Then with a calmness which under the circumstances was hair-raising, asked in French: "Certainly, my masters! What would you like me to talk about?"

Sir Guy was completely nonplused. The most he had expected was a partially intelligible babble from which he might glean a little information. Pistol was so taken aback, he leaned over the dwarf's shoulder to peer into his face—and in so doing, all but lost his balance.

"For the love of Allah!" snapped the dwarf. "If you insist on playing piggy-back, have the decency to sit still!"

Sir Guy could not have been more astonished had a saddle-horse invited him to share a bucket of oats, but he recovered quickly. Beckoning the sergeant to ride his charge into the room, he closed the door and resumed his interrogation.

"Who are you?" he demanded.

"I, monsieur, am no other than Yaroslaf Pojorski," said the dwarf, bowing so suddenly he spilled Sergeant Pistol over his head and onto the floor. "A pursuivant, my masters, of the"—he bowed again—"incomparable *Oprichnina!*"

Sergeant Pistol had been angrily climbing to his feet, but when he heard the dwarf's announcement, he sat back on the floor. Sir Guy tried to conceal his own perturbation, yet despite his self-control, he could feel the blood draining out of his cheeks. When Nikita had cautioned them about the long and insidious tentacles of the dreaded spy organization, Sir Guy had deemed it an exaggeration. To find himself with an agent on his hands was of sufficient import to give him pause. His discomfort must have been evident, for the spy chuckled.

"Truly you are in a quandary, my master!" he mocked. "You have seized the tiger by the tail."

The implied challenge decided Sir Guy. "Silence him!" he commanded Pistol.

As the sergeant reared willingly off the floor, Pojorski sidled out of reach and wagged a playful finger at him.

"Ah, monsieur, you English are so unimaginative!" he chortled to Sir Guy. "Are you not even curious to know what happened to the courier you so bravely dispatched to Moscow?"

A dead silence fell. Sir Guy stared hard into the smirking face.

"You're lying!" he growled.

The spy laughed. "Possibly! I have to do something to save my neck from the bungling carpentry of this slow-witted sheep-butcher! Nevertheless, it does make a difference *who* received your message to the Grand Prince, doesn't it?" He stopped smiling, and snapped at Pistol: "Stop pawing at me, you clumsy lout!"

The poor sergeant was by this time so confused and uncertain he permitted himself to be brushed aside like a pestiferous insect. He looked wistfully at Sir Guy for instructions, but for the first time in his years of faithful service, he saw his master wallowing in a veritable slough of indecision. Pistol backed aggrievedly onto a chair near the door and sat hopefully stropping his dagger on the leathery palm of his left hand.

Sir Guy was spared the necessity for an immediate decision by the distraction of footsteps in the hall, followed by a sharp rap on the door. Half expecting to have the room swarming with acid-tongued

Opritchnina dwarfs, he was reassured by the imperious voice of Count Nikita.

"What is wrong in there, my friend," demanded the Count. "Are you in trouble?"

Before replying, Sir Guy shot a quick glance at the spy. The latter stood with his head cocked, and Sir Guy imagined he could almost trace the course of the envoy's voice as it was sifted through a gigantic memory-file in the monstrous cranium. Apparently the voice was identified, for Pojorski's eyes brightened, and as quickly veiled.

Sir Guy grunted to himself, then gave Pistol the nod. "Draw the bolt!"

As Pistol turned to obey, Pojorski bobbed his head in the general direction of the hallway.

"Trust a viper sooner than that *boyar*, monsieur!" he warned in a confidential aside. "He is a Tatar!" Seeming to sense the Englishman's resistance to advice, he added: "Mark then, monsieur—at the propitious moment, he will suggest I be turned over to him for disposal."

"And why not?" snorted Sir Guy.

By that time, Sergeant Pistol had opened the door.

Count Nikita lunged into the chamber, sword in hand and following closely in his wake, like pinnaces towed behind a ship of war, appeared Affable Jones, Mr. Paxton, and Charity. The Reverend Belcher sidled in some time later.

At first the burly *boyar* did not see the dwarf, who had edged into the shadow of the table, so he glared about in bewilderment.

"A lackey reported he saw men fighting in the hallway!" he explained. "I wondered if ... *ah!*" His eyes had lighted suddenly on the spy. "By the seven sacred beards of my ancestors!" he shouted. "*Pojorski!*"

Pojorski strutted perkily into the center of the room and bowed to the Count.

"Ah, Nikita," he said in his purring sneer. "Welcome home again! I note"—he tipped his misshapen head toward the silent Ellen—"that your voyage was *not entirely* unsuccessful! Felicitations!"

The implications of this ambiguous statement were not lost upon his hearers. Count Nikita scowled bleakly, but said nothing.

Sir Guy grunted. "Plainly, you know this knave!" he told the Count. "Are you aware he is an agent of the *Opritchnina?*"

The big Muscovite flinched perceptibly. "I knew only that he was one of Ivan's torturers!"

"*One of* ... ?" shrilled the dwarf, stung to the quick. "You lie in your unspeakable beard, you treasonous Tatar! I was the *chief* torturer, and because of that I was a close confidant of my beloved Prince!" His temper dissipated as quickly as it had flared and he went on.

"Ah-h! I was the prime favorite until that accursed Turkish executioner was imported with his oriental repertoire." He sighed. "But Pojo will be redeemed!" he boasted. "One good coup, just *one*, and"—he leered at them slyly and clucked his tongue—"*methinks I have it now!*"

Nikita fingered his sword. "What do you hint at, you devil's offal?"

Pojorski hooted. "*Hint?* Why, you great slobbering musk-ox—when has Pojo ever stooped to *hint?* I do not hint! I boast, I sing, I shout!"

"Lor' lumme!" marveled Affable Jones, *sotto voce*. "I never seen anythin' like it!"

Miraculously enough, the dwarf understood him. He whirled with a flourish.

"Nor are you likely to, my unsavory friend!" he told the startled Mr. Jones. "I am unique."

Count Nikita pulled his beard, then turning to Sir Guy, drew him aside. "This is bad," he breathed heavily, "very bad! We must have no trouble here, for the ears of the *Opritchnina* are very acute. I will have my men take him away from the village and dispatch him." Nikita started to turn away, adding: "Leave the matter to me, my friend!"

This last, though spoken in a low tone, sent Pojorski into a spasm of merriment which served to remind Sir Guy, as was doubtless intended, of the spy's prophetic warning.

"Hold!" he said authoritatively. "This spy has hinted at too much and said too little to be dispatched so summarily!"

"Bah! That is but one of his tricks!" snarled the Count. "Already he has lived much too long!"

Pojorski hooted at him. "One of my *better* tricks, you mean!" he jeered. "And as to the question of my longevity, you imp of hell, I will wager not only that I shall outlive you, but that I will in addition have the ecstatic delight of disjointing you with a dull knife at the rate of one limb per diem, and feeding you piecemeal to the imperial hounds! How now—do you care to accept the wager?"

Nikita exchanged glances with Sir Guy, then spread his hands meaningfully. The dwarf noted all this with a smile.

"Come, my masters," he chortled. "Be not perplexed; the matter is not insoluble. Oh, I grant you may feel some slight hesitancy about releasing me without reservation, yet the answer is simplicity itself, ergo—*take me with you!* I am indispensable! My insight, hindsight, and foresight are jewels beyond price! I know everything and everybody—

and everybody knows Pojo! Where I am not loved, I am hated; where I am not admired, I am respected! I marvel you have proceeded this far without me!"

"Bah! If you know anything I do not," snarled Nikita, now in a fine temper, "I shall be surprised!"

Pojorski laughed at him. "Then prepare yourself, you unspeakable Tatar! May you fall dead with astonishment!" His beady little eyes took in his silent audience. "Attend, my lambs: no doubt you believe your confidential message to the Grand Prince reached his ears and no other's?" He crowed like a cock when he saw the expressions on their faces. "Possibly you are even so optimistic as to expect to be met by the Grand Prince's own guards and whisked safely into his palace? Ah—I see you do!"

Count Nikita's control snapped, and he made a lunge for the dwarf. Pojorski, however, apparently anticipating some such outburst, skipped nimbly under the table. Before the irate Muscovite could kick it aside, Sir Guy seized his arm.

"Hold, damn it!" commanded the Englishman. "Let's hear the rest of this!" He looked coldly at the spy. "Proceed! But lie at your peril!"

Pojorski grinned insolently. "Why should I lie when the truth is so much more effective, monsieur? No, no, I shall be candid: your trusted messenger from Dwina met with an *accident*. But his secret did not die with him!" His smile expanded. "No, no—it is safe! *It fell into the hands of our saintly Metropolitane!*"

Nikita was staggered by this information. "The *Metropolitane* . . . !"

The dwarf bowed. ". . . in whose service, or at least, in whose *pay*, this unworthy servant happens to be!"

But the Count was too shocked to heed this last piece of bad news. "And the Grand Prince . . . ?" he demanded.

"The Grand Prince—may his shadow never grow smaller—not only knows nothing of your coming," purred the dwarf, "*he is not even in Moscow!*"

The Count snarled, but without conviction. "By the forked tail of my mother-in-law, I say thou liest!"

Pojorski laughed again. "It was thy own mother, and thy mother's mother before her who had the *forked tails* and the cloven hooves to go with them, thou spawn of Shaitin! But enough . . ." He looked amusedly at Sir Guy. "Are not my reasons sufficient to prove my inestimable worth, monsieur?"

Sir Guy made up his mind. He nodded to Affable Jones and Sergeant Pistol. "Take him down to your quarters," he instructed them. "You'll get your orders later."

Nikita opened his mouth to object, but the expression on Sir Guy's face stopped him. The two guards moved forward to assume their duties, Affable Jones with eagerness, Pistol after the fashion of a hound approaching a bear that had pawed him badly.

Yaroslaf Pojorski, torturer extraordinary and pursuivant of the *Opritchnina,* viewed them with amused contempt, then as they ranged on either side of him, he made a mocking obeisance to Sir Guy.

"May the tiny globules of wisdom which Pojo gave you play upon your mind like gentle rain upon a garden. If the soil is fertile, you may be amazed at what will grow!"

On that note he stalked out of the room between his guards.

The silence which followed this exit was awkward. When Charity clapped her hands suddenly, everybody jumped.

"Glory be, weren't 'e adorable?" she cried. "Jes' like a cuddly little doll!"

"Charity!" sobbed Ellen. "Dear Lord, what a hideous, revolting creature!"

"A duplicate of Satan himself!" piped the Reverend Belcher. "Verily, it was a revelation!"

Old Mr. Paxton chuckled. "It was that, Parson—a revelation! Yet now that everyone has circumnavigated the problem, suppose we admit the truth."

"Truth?" raged the Count. "Any fool could see that the fiend lied every time he opened his crooked mouth!"

"A fool might see that," Paxton retorted, "but not a wise man." He smiled to take the sting out of his words. "You, Count, were wise enough to be shaken by his statements!"

"Bah! It was the possibilities that shook me, not that ridiculous tale!" Count Nikita attempted to glare down the old man. "Did you swallow that rubbish?"

The old scholar nodded. "In toto! I shall go further, Count, though I cannot share little Charity's evaluation, I do declare I consider our diminutive acquaintance one of the most honest men I have ever encountered!"

This statement was greeted with groans and exclamations of protest, as heretofore the venerable patriarch's opinions had been respected.

"Sirrah!" fumed Belcher, blundering into the breach. "What manner of Christian are you to call that murdering pagan abomination an honorable man?"

It was evident Mr. Paxton, too, had come to enjoy baiting the parson, for his eyes twinkled and he had some difficulty keeping his voice sober.

"Tut-tut, Reverend, it is hardly fair to insert so many queries into a single sentence," he chided. "And as for being a Christian—you leave me uncertain."

When he saw Belcher starting to inflate, he made a soft placating motion with his hand.

"Be that as it may, I said nothing about his being an *honorable* man; I said merely that he was an *honest* man."

"I presume you can distinguish a difference?" sneered Belcher.

Paxton chuckled. "Precisely! We are not concerned with Pojorski's honor, morals, cruelty, lack of beauty or allegiances. Our sole interest —if we are wise—is whether or not he told the truth!"

"On the very face of it, he lied," snorted Nikita. "He made up that tale out of necessity, in the hope of saving his life."

"We shall soon be able to see for ourselves whether he spoke truly or falsely," said the old man. "Meanwhile I, for one, believe you should explore the possibilities."

Sir Guy looked grimly at the Count. "Assuming, for the moment, that he did tell the truth, Niki—that Ivan has not received your message, and this high priest has—what then?"

Nikita took a thoughtful turn about the chamber. "It is nonsense, of course!" he scoffed. "But to answer your question—if it *were* true, our position would be extremely grave! Sylvester the Metropolitane is an inexorable man! It is impossible to foretell what might happen!"

"Cannot we avoid this unpleasant saint and seek the Tsar?" snapped Sir Guy.

"Muscovy is a huge place!" Nikita reminded the Englishman. "And Ivan trusts few men. When he leaves Moscow, only two men know exactly where he can be located. One of these is the Metropolitane!"

"And the Grand Equerry is the other?"

The Count stopped short in surprise. "How did you know that?"

"I don't; I'm merely asking," Sir Guy said.

The Count shrugged. "It is not so simple as that. No foreigner can enter the gates of Moscow without official permission and then must be escorted by troops, either the Grand Prince's or the Metropolitane's."

"Good Lord! You mean this priest has a private army?"

Count Nikita explained that as spiritual head of all Muscovy, the Metropolitane had his own ecclesiastic troop, known as the "Household Guards," a force which in number all but rivaled the Tsar's own personal troop. As acting head of the government during the absence of the Emperor, he was afforded sufficient additional troops to maintain order and, in the event of an emergency, defend the capital city of Moscow. Thus the Metropolitane's temporary and temporal power was absolute—with one exception: the Grand Equerry!

Ivan, of course, was cognizant of the Metropolitane's implacable hatred of the Grand Equerry, and with that shrewdness of mind which had made it possible for him to have survived the diabolical machinations of the *boyars* in his youth, he skillfully played one minister against the other. Knowing that the Metropolitane would deem it a spiritual obligation to remove from the face of the earth the sybaritic little Grand Equerry, Ivan had excepted from the Metropolitane's authority not only the Grand Equerry himself but his thirteen wives, his exquisite flock of black-eyed *houris*, with their necessary appendages, such as eunuchs and Nubians, as well as all the other servants, lackeys, and slaves who serviced his palatial seraglio. In addition, the Grand Equerry was permitted a "Household Guard" of his own for the actual protection of his palace, but these troops had no authority beyond bow-shot of the palace walls.

But what was gall-and-wormwood to the austere Metropolitane was the afterthought which Ivan had appended to his commandment, like the sting in a scorpion's tail, to the effect that, *under no circumstances* could the Grand Equerry's palace be entered by the Metropolitane, nor by any of his officers or guardsmen. And—cruelest of all!—the said palace was declared an asylum *in perpetuum*, an inviolate sanctuary where *any* fugitive, be his crime secular or ecclesiastical, could find shelter and security.

Sir Guy smiled grimly as Nikita concluded his explanation. "'Pon my soul, my respect for your Prince's acumen rises, for if that arrangement does not keep these rivals at each other's throats instead of his, nothing will," observed the Englishman. "Howbeit, you haven't told us why this ill-tempered Metropolitane should interfere with us. After all, we are here at the Emperor's own request . . ." He grinned, and added: "Well, more or less."

The Count frowned. "I thought I made that clear. Next to Boris Smolovitch himself, Sylvester has three great hates—*foreigners, women,* and *pleasure!* He believes himself ordained by the Almighty to see to it that Ivan is *protected* against all three. I warn you—we can expect short shrift if we fall into his clutches."

"H'mnn! As I understand it, this so-called guard of honor is to meet us here tomorrow or the next day," mused Sir Guy. "If this spy lied, Ivan's troops will escort us into Moscow in state, and everything will be lovely. *But*, if Pojorski told the truth . . . ?" He paused.

"Sylvester's minions will escort us to the Kremlin," Count Nikita finished for him. "Only the gods know what may happen then!"

The Englishman sniffed. "I prefer not to place such a burden on the gods," he said dryly. "We'll have to find a way to reach the Grand Equerry's sanctuary."

"I explained why that is impossible."

"Nothing is impossible to the desperate," Sir Guy said.

Count Nikita gave a snort of impatience. "Bah! We haggle like women!" he growled. "That wretch lied to save his worthless hide, and you were gullible enough to . . ." He paused as hard-ridden horses clattered noisily into the courtyard below, followed immediately by excited voices shrilly demanding the whereabouts of the Count.

There was something so urgent in the overtones of those harsh voices that all other considerations were forgotten. Nikita strode to the window and shouted down to have the officer in command await him there. But he was already too late, for even as he leaned out to bellow his orders, the officer in question stomped heavily into the room.

Although he made his report in a language unknown to most of those present, the names he mentioned made his meaning shockingly plain. *The Metropolitane's guardsmen were coming!*

15

FROM THE ALL-BUT-EXHAUSTED OFFICER, they learned that the Metropolitane's troops were less than an hour's ride away and coming in such strength that it would be utter folly to dispute the issue with arms. The alternatives were either submission, which would assuredly be disastrous, or flight which would probably prove fatal.

It goes without saying that Sir Guy chose flight, whereupon the Count suggested that he and Sir Guy take Ellen and try to win through to the Grand Equerry's palace, arguing that from that place they might be able to reach the Emperor and ultimately rescue the others. But Sir Guy flatly refused to abandon his companions, insisting they would stand or fall together.

Count Nikita had, by this time, realized the futility of argument once the Englishman had made up his mind, so he acquiesced, but reasoned that it would be senseless to encumber themselves with the prisoner Tutweiller. And, naturally, Yaroslaf Pojorski must be strangled immediately since, by his own admission, he was a spy in the pay of the Metropolitane.

But even in the matter of prisoners, Sir Guy was stubborn. Philip Tutweiller was protected by his oath to Ellen, and as for the dwarf, no doubt he would have some value as a hostage. Nikita countered with a telling argument when he pointed out that if Pojorski so much as suspected the truth about Ellen's imposture, it would be fatal to take him into the Grand Equerry's palace, even if they were lucky enough to reach it. He climaxed his contention by reminding them of Pojorski's boast that he would personally officiate at the Count's execution.

Sir Guy deliberated but a moment.

"The dwarf goes with us!" he decreed.

Count Nikita threw up his hands in surrender and hurried out to make the necessary arrangement for flight.

The moon had not yet risen when the little cavalcade slipped out of the tavern courtyard. Led by the landlord, who had been forced without explanation to accompany them as guide, they filed down a cow-trail, forded a swift-moving stream, and with firmer ground underfoot, struck across country towards the south. It was rugged going, for they avoided all roads, and the ancient trails and animal runs were often blocked by fallen trees and other such impediments.

The party numbered four-and-twenty, half of whom were a Tatar guard brought along to be sacrificed if pursuit became too hot. Philip Tutweiller had given his parole until the immediate danger was passed, and had had his sword returned to him. But Pojorski, trusted by none, rode with his hands tied to the saddle and a rope with a hangman's noose around his neck.

The dwarf had not protested this indignity, but had merely pointed out that if his horse fell, or was injured, he, Pojorski, would be quite unable to save himself. Howbeit, he was bluntly told he was fortunate to be alive to run that risk, and that in the event they were overtaken by the Metropolitane's soldiers, he would be the first casualty. For reasons of his own, Pojorski seemed to find this excruciatingly funny.

Within the hour, the sounds of gunfire could be heard faintly from the direction from which they had come, and shortly thereafter, on topping a hillock, they could plainly see a telltale red glow to the north. To their puzzled inquiries, Count Nikita explained the precaution he had taken, which for realistic ruthlessness, even Sir Guy Spangler had never surpassed.

It was this: the landlord had two pretty daughters (whom he had done his best to keep out of sight) so the Count had given orders to his rear-guard to have the wenches seized and garbed in some of the

English clothing Ellen and Charity had been forced to jettison in their flight. Thus, the Tatar rear-guard would defend the tavern as long as possible, and after they had been overpowered and slaughtered, the two buxom wenches so attractively garbed could then be counted on to occupy the Metropolitane's guardsmen for some time.

Not grasping the cold-blooded viciousness of the stratagem, Ellen asked what would happen to the two girls when it was discovered they were not the sought-after English women. Count Nikita told her they would doubtlessly be assaulted by most of the guardsmen—the almost inevitable Eastern consequence of defeat.

Ellen subsided in horror, while Sir Guy cursed under his breath.

Meanwhile, the landlord, realizing what the glow in the sky signified, had thrown himself out of the saddle and was beating his head on the ground, all the while emitting such wails of lamentation that the others feared he would arouse the entire countryside. Count Nikita sternly commanded him to desist, but when the distraught landlord merely increased the volume of his yowls, the Count barked an order to his Tatars. Two of them leapt from their saddles and seized the landlord by the arms.

A sallow moon had just nosed over the horizon, and though it was still too dark to see plainly, objects in entirety could be discerned. Sir Guy was staring at the outline of the bawling landlord, yet offered no comment when the Tatars seized him, presuming they meant to gag or restrain him. Not until he glimpsed the reflection of slashing steel did he have any notion of what the Count had intended. Then it was too late.

A scimitar whined through the air, and the landlord was stilled in mid-note!

Ellen screamed and Charity swore softly. The rest of the English party endured it in grim silence. Sir Guy waited until he had regained complete control of his own voice, then he said with deadly quiet: "Nikita—so long as I am in charge of this expedition, *don't you ever execute another man without my approval!* Do so, and as God's my witness, you shall have to settle with me!"

The Count jerked around belligerently, but after a brief look at Sir Guy, shrugged it off.

"Bah! You English are soft-hearted fools!" he sneered. "I will not quarrel over that carrion! Come, we must ride, else we shall accompany him to hell!" He prodded his jennet, and guided her down the slope.

Something dark, perchance like the rush of a spirit, moved across the heavens. Sir Guy glanced upward. Only a vulture wheeled there in ever-narrowing circles, to mark the spot where one obscure Muscovite peasant had laid aside his earthly burden.

The Englishman sighed, gave the rope an uncommonly gentle tug as a signal to Pojorski, and followed the others.

The Tatars were consummate horsemen, and they set a grueling pace. Sir Guy had no difficulty holding his own with the best of them, but most of his party, especially Charity and Belcher, suffered cruelly. Howbeit, with pursuit inevitable, there was scant time for sympathy.

Goaded by desperation, they rode all that night by the light of the moon, and all the following day under a broiling sun—wallowing through marshlands, fording streams and swimming rivers, threading now at a snail's pace through primeval forests, now galloping across table-flat stretches of prairie. A pall of weariness settled over man and beast, until even the indefatigable Sir Guy himself was saddle-sore. Then in late afternoon, when the very thought of death began to lose its terror, they rode out of a stand of pine onto the edge of a plateau overlooking an endless plain. There, by common if unspoken consent, they reined in, hardly daring to credit their own eyes.

For in the center of this vastness, like an enchanted island in an enchanted sea, rose the majestic domes and glittering towers of Moscow! To the Muscovites in the party, it signified the journey's end; safety and a long rest. But to the travel-worn English, viewing it for the first time as it lay shimmering ephemerally in the late afternoon sunlight, it appeared as a fairyland extravaganza, a chimerical mirage conjured up by some Oriental *djinn*.

Perchance little Charity best voiced the common reaction when she exclaimed in an awed whisper: "Glory be, it looks jes' like 'eaven!" She choked back a sob, then stared at Sir Guy with wide, startled eyes. "God 'elp me, sir, I 'as the stryngest feelin'; a feelin' that I'm a-comin' *'ome!*"

"Oh, Charity!" cried Ellen. "Don't say that!"

Charity turned her big eyes back to the far-off gilded towers. "I carn't 'elp it, m'lydy! D'y reckon it means I'm goin' to . . . to *die?*"

"On the contrary," Sir Guy assured her gently, "it doubtless means you are going to get a good night's rest."

Affable Jones sighed noisily. "All I arsk is to reach port before this damned nag busts me wide open at the seams!"

"Verily," bleated the Reverend, determined not to be outtalked, "I feel as the immortal Moses when he led his children . . ."

Sergeant Pistol drowned him out with a doleful snort. "Burn me, if ye can still *feel*, Parson, then I s'y we been goin' too slow."

Satisfied that just as long as they could bicker, they could survive, Sir Guy prodded his exhausted jennet over to where Count Nikita and the captain of the Tatars were appraising the situation. This time he evaluated the scene in its more practical aspects.

Until this magnificent panorama had unfolded, Muscovy had seemed, in comparison with other countries Sir Guy had visited, naught but a vast and primitive wilderness, barely in the lowest stages of civilization. Now this erroneous conception was dispelled, for here was the very heart of an incredible empire from which arteries stretched into the unknown reaches of the Orient, into India and other mysterious lands of the East.

The nucleus of all this grandeur was the fabulous citadel of Moscow, known as the Kremlin, and already centuries old. Roughly the shape of an isosceles triangle, with one side running parallel to the Moskva River, and its huge pyramidal walls of pink brick surrounded with battlements, it looked over the metropolis like a protective mastiff. Numerous convents, each resembling a beautiful little village in itself, clustered in an admiring circle around this acropolis. Then there were the palaces of the *boyars*, the mansions of the wealthy citizens, the shops of the artisans—the woolen drapers, goldsmiths, saddlers and the like. There was a profusion of bazaars and markets, and then, as the Count indicated with a knowing grin, another quarter where the female "merchants" wore rings in their mouths and dealt in a familiar commodity not ordinarily dispensed in the public gaze.

The great walls of Moscow were pierced by gates from which roads diverged in all directions, like endless spokes. And along these white and dusty thoroughfares crawled caravans and convoys, weary travelers, plodding mendicants and drooping pilgrims; nobles homeward bound from the chase, serfs straggling in from the broad grain fields to their hovels under the protection of the Kremlin's guns—for all Muscovy lived under the everlasting fear of the Eastern barbarians. The day was waning rapidly, and lowering black thunderheads building behind the gilded mosques warned the traveler to seek shelter.

Nikita's summary of their predicament was not encouraging. While it was most unlikely that any of the Metropolitane's guardsmen involved in the chase could yet have reached Moscow, it was highly probable that the sentries guarding the city gates had been forewarned to be on the alert in the event they had eluded the guardsmen.

Sir Guy interrupted to ask if it would be feasible to send word of their presence to the Grand Equerry, and beg his intercession. Count Nikita pointed out that the Grand Equerry was subordinate to the Metropolitane beyond the limits of his own palace, hence such a plea would have to be rejected. Yet by the same token, when the Metropolitane did learn of their escape from his trap, the only place in all of Moscow or its environs where they would have even a remote chance of survival was that selfsame palace of Master Smolovitch.

The Count warned the city gates would close one hour after sunset, regardless of how many stragglers clamored for admittance. If they did not get inside the city before the gates closed this night, they would not get in at all—save as prisoners of the Metropolitane—for the pursuing guardsmen could not be very far behind, and would certainly reach Moscow before morning.

Sir Guy chewed on his nether lip and scowled at the distant walls. He was aware that Nikita and the captain of the Tatars were discussing the situation in their own dialect, and while by this time Sir Guy had picked up enough of the Russian language to get by, he could just barely get the gist of this harangue. It was something to the effect that it might be wisest to circumvent Moscow altogether and flee south to Crimea where they could be sure of asylum in the Prince Dominion of Nikita's uncle, Akhmet.

He weighed the idea in his mind. On the surface, it appeared to be not only a sensible solution but the only possible solution. Yet, Sir Guy did not like it. Crimea was many, many leagues south of Moscow, and they had already journeyed too far from their point of entry to suit Sir Guy Spangler, for bitter experience had taught him that the deeper one trespassed into a foreign land, the more difficult it became to extricate oneself. Over and above that, he had a lurking, uncomfortable sense of apprehension which, if he could not explain, he knew better than to ignore.

Then, just as Count Nikita turned to propose the long southward trek, a daring scheme blossomed in the nimble brain of the Englishman.

"I have it!" he exulted, forestalling the Count's proposal. "By my troth, with any luck at all we'll break our fast at the Grand Equerry's board this night!"

Nikita seemed vaguely chagrined. "It will take more than luck, my friend!" he retorted grimly.

Sir Guy chuckled, then outlined his stratagem as best he could in the Muscovite tongue so that the captain of the Tatars could comprehend him. It was naught but an old Whitefriars artifice in a new setting—a brawl staged to distract attention from the real purpose. The Tatar guard would be divided into two groups, one under the captain, the other under the Count, with the English contingent disguised as Muscovites and intermingled with the others. Arrival at the gate would be timed within a few moments of the actual closing, so that traffic would be at its height. Then the two factions would contend for the privilege to enter first, and in the ensuing "fight," the fugitives might be swept through the gates unnoticed. Once inside, they could regroup and head directly for the Grand Equerry's palace and safety.

Nikita was not enthused, for he could envision too many obstacles to success, but the captain, Feodor, was enchanted with the scheme, and reminded the Count that he and his men had salvaged enough clothing to garb the English in native costumes.

In a few moments, the Tatar began passing out the costumes, and while the men dressed behind their horses, the two girls retired to the seclusion of the grove to change.

From the richness of his own garb, Sir Guy surmised it had come from the Count's personal wardrobe. It consisted of a long coatlike garment of gold silk studded with silver buttons, a shirt of scarlet silk, and a pair of flowing pantaloons of exquisite linen. His shoes were soft-soled and turned up at the toes in a graceful arc, and on his head he wore a rich cap of black sable, wrapped with white Colepecke and trimmed with pearls and precious stones. He was grudgingly pleased with the outfit, but when he turned to view the others, he could not help laughing aloud. Beneath the barbarous exterior of Captain Feodor there lurked a cultivated sense of humor, for the costumes he had allotted were ludicrously apt.

First, Sergeant Pistol brought chuckles from the English and howls of glee from the Muscovites when he came out from behind his horse in the costume of a eunuch. When the reason for this unseeming outburst was made known to him, he threatened to disrobe and stalk through the gates of Moscow stark naked.

Before he could carry out his threat, however, the Reverend Belcher made his debut, and was greeted with such a clamor of merriment that the sergeant's tragic plight was forgotten. For the waggish Captain Feodor had fitted out the angular man with the spotted yellow costume of a nobleman's buffoon! In the skin-tight hose, Belcher's knobby knees and spur-boned ankles gave him the look of an arthritic rooster. And the flame-colored jester's cap, fashioned like a cock's comb, with its tinkling little bells dangling around the funereal visage, supplied the final touch of the ridiculous. Peculiarly enough, the parson seemed to enjoy the attention.

Affable Jones made a hilarious monk, but by comparison, he merely elicited a few smiles. But when the girls reappeared, the smiles turned to gasps of admiration.

Ellen's habit was somewhat similar to that of the ancient Greeks, with a skirt so short it barely covered the thighs. Under it she wore loose-fitting breeches of silk, and over all this a sort of waistcoat, reaching to her knees, with spacious sleeves so long she could not thrust her hands out of them without taking several folds. Like Sir Guy's, Ellen's whole costume was richly studded with pearls and other gems. She had plaited her hair in two long braids, after the fashion of unmarried Muscovite maids, and the impact of her soft, white-skinned beauty was startling.

For some inexplicable reason, Sir Guy was infuriated at sight of her. He considered the garb lewd and suggestive, and entirely unsuited to an Englishwoman about to be presented to the Emperor. In an outburst of irritation, he said as much, adding that the least she could do was to "show a little decency and button the damned coat!"

To his mortification, and the secret delight of the others, Ellen flatly refused.

"You surprise me, my lord!" she retorted. "I was assured on competent authority that this is the standard costume of beautiful slaves being prepared for auction. As for your concern about my presentation to the Emperor, I might remind you the sole purpose of this present masquerade is to pass unnoticed through the gates of Moscow."

"Pass unnoticed!" raged Sir Guy. "God's death, you're enough to draw the eyes out of a camel! Unnoticed? Why, you stand out like a . . . like . . ." He fumbled for a simile sufficiently apt.

"A fairy princess, eh, m'lud?" offered Charity.

Ellen favored her with a sweet smile. "Bless you, Charity, my dear!" she said. "I rather feel it does something for me myself. And you, dear, —despite the boorish remarks of our lord and master—look like . . ."

Sir Guy was ready with his own metaphor this time. "Something that belongs in a harem!" he cut in brutally.

Charity clapped her hands in delight. "Oh thankee, sir, thankee! D'ye truly mean it, sir, or be ye jes' tryin' to jolly me?" She pirouetted as blithely as her aching body would permit and beamed at Ellen. "W'at think 'e, m'lydy?"

"Lord love you, Charity, I declare I think the remark of our ill-tempered slaver very apropos!" Ellen said with a malicious side-glance at the glowering Sir Guy. "For I understand that in Muscovy, a female can aspire to no loftier estate than to be the plaything of some arrogant male."

"Glory be, w'at fun!" applauded Charity.

Sir Guy Spangler knew when to beat a retreat. "Come on!" he snarled. "Those damned gates will close before we get there!"

16

As SIR GUY ruefully admitted later, it was this momentary ill-naturedness that saved Pojorski's life. For no sooner had he turned from his defeat at the hands of Ellen, than Count Nikita reopened the discussion of what to do with the spy. So more to assert his own authority than anything, Sir Guy flatly refused to allow the dwarf to be executed—at least until they reached the sanctuary of the Grand Equerry's palace. Most of Sir Guy's own party sided with the Count on the issue. But all this merely increased Sir Guy's truculence to a point where even the Count felt it wisest to drop the argument. None present could foresee what that decision was to mean.

Thus it came about that Pojorski—completely unruffled by the narrowness of his escape—was disguised as well as his abnormalities would permit, and stationed between Sergeant Pistol and Affable Jones.

Like a stream coursing down a hillside, they shortly merged with the main current of humanity funneling towards the narrow main gate. This dreary crawling mass soon dispelled their earlier illusion of an ethereal fairyland. Beggars speckled with open festers, starving waifs, exhausted horses, perfumed *boyars* and unwashed peasants commingled to exude a noxious effluvium that was strangling in its pungency. It soon became painfully obvious why the Muscovite serf was designated by the appellation of *smerdi,* which simply meant "smelling offensively."

The Tatars formed a protective ring around the company, slashing the serfs with their whips, and riding down those either too old or too slow to get clear of the vicious hooves of their jennets. Several times Ellen burst out in horrified indignation as the ruthless Tatars ground a screaming peasant underfoot, and finally she rode up beside the Count.

"Is there no way you can restrain these bestial butchers of yours?" she demanded.

Count Nikita stared at her in amazement. "I do not understand?" he said, puzzled. "Has one of the dogs insulted you? If so, I swear by the sacred bones of my father, I shall have his heart torn out and make an example . . ."

"I am not concerned with myself!" snapped Ellen. "It is the needless maiming of these unfortunate peasants!"

The Count laughed relievedly. "I thought for a moment something was wrong! *Phoof*—think nothing of these *smerdi,* madame; they have no feelings! They are less than the dogs."

Sir Guy overheard this, and regretted her humane effort, for he had long since learned the futility of interfering with the mores and customs of a foreign country. So he prodded his weary nag up beside her and unobtrusively edged her away from the Count.

For a while she did not seem to know he was riding at her side; she sat very straight in the saddle, her face pale with rage and her eyes squeezed tight as if to shut out both sight and sound of the misery around her. Sir Guy was as well pleased to be ignored. He thought it likely, in the perverse way of a woman, she would hold *him* responsible for the barbarity of the Tatars; possibly for the very poverty of the Muscovite peasant. Yet in spite of this, he felt better at her side. He assured himself he was there merely to restrain any future outbursts, and to see that she should suffer no harm if he could prevent it. And—although he would have cut out his own tongue before admitting it aloud—he was forced to concede to himself that the daring oriental costume accentuated her cool Anglo-Saxon beauty. It also lent a touch of Eastern mystery; a hint, perhaps, of unsuspected qualities heretofore dormant. Yet if it piqued his curiosity, it also disturbed him because it was something he did not understand.

But now there was no time for further introspection, for the gate loomed through the dusk just ahead.

Captain Feodor, with his allotted quota of men, had already reached the portals and was profanely demanding the right of way, when up dashed Count Nikita with his contingent and tried to jostle the Tatar captain aside. Feodor resisted. The Count knocked one of the "enemy" out of the saddle with his whip, which enraged the others. From that instant, everything was chaos.

Amid screaming peasants, cursing sentries, neighing horses, and snarling combatants, it was difficult to control their nags. Captain Feodor's cohorts, after the first setback, had formed a flying phalanx that drove his opponents back and behind the rest of the company, where they paused to beat, slash and curse each other in one deafening din. But always they edged the fight closer towards the gate.

This, of course, was the cue for the others. Ostensibly unable to prevent it, they allowed themselves to be jostled and herded through the gates, despite the bawling protests of the guards. Staying close to the center of the press, Sir Guy held the rein of Ellen's jennet, and skillfully guided her inside the walls.

To give the devils their due, the Tatars were natural actors, and they carried realism to dangerous lengths. But what was most important, the ruse was working.

Count Nikita passed through the gates backwards, fighting every inch of the way, yet making a great pretense of calling off his men. He was politic enough to toss a bag of gold to the angry sentries to assuage their injured dignities, then as they scrambled to retrieve it, he whirled his horse on its hind legs, jerked his head for Sir Guy and the rest to follow, and galloped up a side street.

Satisfied the others were all safely inside, Sir Guy followed the Count, still clinging to Ellen's jennet. After twisting and turning through a tangled labyrinth of dark and dirty streets, Count Nikita drew rein and waited for the others to come up with him.

"By the seven beards of my seven ancestors, we made it!" he exulted to Sir Guy. "My friend, that was a priceless stratagem! How Ivan will chuckle when he hears of it!"

Sir Guy smiled thinly. "The credit for its success goes to you," he said, "and to you, Captain." This last to Feodor. "You staged that brawl well." He glanced at the torn clothing and bloodied heads, and added: "Almost too well, I swear!"

The Tatar bowed in appreciation. "My lambs needed to lose a little blood," he said dryly. "It was getting too hot for them."

Sir Guy looked around at the rest of his little company. Ellen sat taut and angry, while Charity fair bubbled with relief. Young Philip Tutweiller, practically ostracized since his disgrace, was flushed with excitement, whereas the Reverend Belcher was pale and palsied with fear. Mr. Paxton, as was his wont, had borne the ordeal with characteristic calmness which in itself was a veritable armor against both weariness and terror. Then Sir Guy Spangler felt a sudden constriction of the heart as he looked for the others. . . .

Three of the party were missing: Affable Jones, Sergeant Pistol, and Yaroslaf Pojorski, agent of the *Opritchnina!*

Impatient questioning revealed that no one could recall whether the three absentees had won through the portals or not. Young Tutweiller was of the uncertain opinion that they had been brushed aside during the melee, yet one of the Muscovites thought he had seen the dwarf on the inside of the walls, and he had no recollection of the two Englishmen.

"Which would not surprise me," growled the Count. "That devil could wriggle out of hell!" He gave Sir Guy an I-told-you-so glance. "It was rank folly to have spared him."

"To hell with him!" snarled Sir Guy. "It's my men I'm concerned about! I'm not going on without them."

Count Nikita grew excited. "That would be madness! I tell you their case is hopeless! We cannot pass out through the gates to seek them, for the Metropolitane's guardsmen will soon be overtaking us."

"Damn it, they *may* have gotten through!"

The Count spread his hands. "It is possible! Yet that does not help them, since they speak hardly any Russian and have that fiend Pojorski with them. As you only too well know, he is in the pay of the Metropolitane, and will doubtless guide them into his web. And if, by a quirk of fate, they should have become separated from that monster, their situation is as bad, if not worse. Believe me, Moscow is a dangerous place to explore at night! No, no, we must go on! It is our only hope of survival!"

Sir Guy opened his mouth to tell the Count to "go and be damned," then his glance fell on Ellen, white-faced beside him, and he snapped it shut without speaking. Much as he would have preferred to lead a personal search for his two loyal henchmen, he owed a duty to those still in his charge.

"We are not going to abandon them; that is definite!" Sir Guy repeated. "You, Count, can lead us to the palace, while Feodor takes his squad in search of Jones and Pistol. Now get him started, else we'll all turn back!"

Count Nikita's eyes blazed resentfully at the Englishman's imperious tone, but he finally shrugged, and turning, barked instructions to the ferocious Tatar. Captain Feodor whirled his scimitar above his head, pirouetted his horse, and followed by his wild fellows, clattered off into the dusk. With a heavy sigh, the Count looked at the remaining group.

"I fear it was a mistake to send off our brave watchdogs," he said grimly. "For though our greatest danger is passed, we cannot consider ourselves safe until we reach the sanctuary of the palace. So, I beg you stay close together, for stragglers will be doomed." He glanced questioningly at Sir Guy.

"Lead on!" said Sir Guy.

He would have much preferred to have taken his station in the train, the most vulnerable position, or, as second choice of danger, in the van, but he was grimly determined to see that Ellen was protected, so he took his place midway in the little cavalcade. Count Nikita and his Muscovites headed the procession, while Tutweiller and Belcher brought up the rear.

The city was quiet; the hushed silence of a sepulchre. The party jogged for at least a mile through a densely populated area without seeing a living soul, although occasionally there was a vague movement amongst the shadows. The cloppety-clop of hooves and the slap and retch of harness leather had a ghostly sound. No one spoke for a long time until at last little Charity burst out painfully: "Lord 'elp us, 'ow much futher be 't?"

"Less than three *versts*," the Count assured her in his fractured English.

Charity groaned. "I should-a known better'n to arsk! Oh, me poor battered buttocks!"

The streets grew narrower, and when Sir Guy questioned this, Nikita explained that he was avoiding the main entrance to the palace in the event an ambuscade had been laid along that route. Instead, the Count told of a semi-secret gate that opened onto a small alleyway.

Before long, they swung into a narrow corridor-like thoroughfare that terminated at its opposite end in a high brick wall. Now that their eyes had become accustomed to the velvety darkness, they could plainly distinguish the small but stout ironbound door set in the wall directly ahead. To all save one it meant safety; for Ellen it was the end of everything.

Perhaps she heard Sir Guy's unconscious sigh of relief at sight of the haven, for she leaned towards him, and in a voice that fairly vibrated with feeling, said: "Sir Rogue, before the Lord God in heaven, I swear that from the instant we pass that portal, *I'll hate and loathe you until the day I die!*"

Something like a talon tightened on Sir Guy's midsection. Yet before he could frame a reply, there came a strangled cry of warning from the rear.

"Sir Guy! Sir Guy!" It was Philip Tutweiller's voice. "Horses coming up fast! The riders bear torches!"

"Perchance those pagan Tatars?" gabbled Belcher.

"Not with torches!" growled Sir Guy. He called the news ahead to the Count, ordering him to proceed at a gallop. Then: "Courage, comrades, courage!" he buoyed the others. "We have only a bow-shot's ride to safety! Forward! Forward! He who stumbles is lost!" Taking a good fresh grip on Ellen's reins, he prodded his jennet and plunged ahead.

The others followed pell-mell. Fate teased them a moment longer until it seemed certain they would reach the gate, then with safety almost literally within arm's length, a body of horsemen sprang out of concealment ahead and unhooded their lanterns.

"*Halt, in the name of the holy Metropolitane!*" thundered their commander.

Cursing, Count Nikita swung his horse around. "Back!" he shouted. "Back the way we came!"

Sir Guy yanked Ellen's jennet around. But it was pointless, for now the alleyway both ahead and behind was crowded with horsemen by the light of whose torches and lanterns the sacred banners of the Metropolitane were plainly visible.

Sir Guy crowded Ellen's jennet against the wall, then shielding her with his own horse and body, drew sword. But the Count reined up beside him and stayed his arm.

"Hold, my friend," he cautioned resignedly. "If anyone resists, we will all be incontinently slaughtered, for we are sorely outnumbered. It is better to bow to the inevitable and live to fight again, perhaps. I am not without influence, and even the Holy Father Sylvester will hesitate to harm the nephew of a Tatar prince."

Submission of any kind came hard to Sir Guy Spangler. "You were not so damned optimistic a short time ago!" he snapped.

The other shrugged. "I am a fatalist. What is to be, will be!"

Sir Guy glanced at Ellen, but her stare was cold and haughty.

"Do not concern yourself about me, sir!" she told him scornfully. "Think solely of yourself, as you always have!"

Those were the last words she spoke to him for a long, long time. A wedge of guardsmen drove between them, and after he had reluctantly surrendered his sword, he was unceremoniously hauled out of the saddle. What was happening to Ellen at that moment, he had no way of knowing.

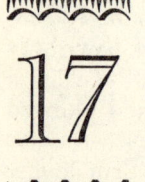

17

The Metropolitane's guardsmen operated with a cold efficiency that bespoke much practice. The captives were deftly cut into four groups; Ellen and Charity were whisked out of sight, the Tatars were herded off to one side as if they were so many cattle; and the Muscovites were separated from the English.

Disturbed as he was by the coup, Sir Guy had to concede that Count Nikita did all he could to alleviate their distress, vociferously protesting their detention every step of the way. Yet while the commandant of the guards treated him with respect, if not actual courtesy, it was plain that the officer had his orders. He seemed to know exactly how many foreigners there were in the party, and even to have complete information of their plans.

The explanation of this, manifestly, was Yaroslaf Pojorski, and Sir Guy roundly cursed himself for having spared the wretch's life, or for interfering when Nikita would have rid them of the blight.

Where the girls were taken, or what happened to the truculent Tatars, Sir Guy was unable to ascertain. He tried to communicate with the Count, but was prevented by the guards. Then, still kept apart, both the Muscovites and the Englishmen were driven across the city to what in the darkness appeared to be another gigantic castle, and herded into a tower honeycombed with small cells.

Once again the Count tried to assert his authority. He vehemently denounced the treatment they had received, and demanded to be conducted immediately into the presence of the Metropolitane. When he was assured the pious Sylvester could not be disturbed from his nightly prayers, Nikita insisted on being quartered with Sir Guy. This also was firmly refused: the English, being foreigners, could not be given the privileges accorded a *boyar,* since in the eyes of the Metropolitane they were spies and trespassers, therefore to be treated as criminals.

Thus finding himself blocked in every maneuver, Count Nikita suddenly raised his voice and bellowed across the intervening space to Sir Guy.

"Courage, comrade! Be of stout heart!" He knocked aside the restraining arms of the guardsmen who attempted to silence him. "I swear you will spend no more than one night in this viper pit!" At that point, the guards smothered his imprecations and hustled him out.

While appreciating the gesture, Sir Guy was not overoptimistic about the Count's power. He had already seen enough of Muscovy to realize that in this vast half-Oriental empire, an individual's influence hinged entirely on the whim of an extremely unpredictable tyrant. Then, too, Sir Guy Spangler was not accustomed to depend on another, so even before he had reached the tower, he had begun to lay the groundwork for an escape.

In similar predicaments, it had always been his practice to try and get himself put into a cell with someone either shrewd enough, ruthless enough, or active enough to be of some use to him. Now that Affable Jones and Sergeant Pistol were gone, of the present party the only one left who could conceivably be of any assistance was young Tutweiller, who, at least, was agile and daring. But whether the hard-headed gaoler suspected his intent, or whether long experience had taught this official never to lock two active men together, Sir Guy eventually found himself in a cell with the one man least able to afford him any physical help—the aged Mr. Paxton.

Sir Guy accepted this with a sigh. It could have been worse; he might have been locked up with the Reverend Belcher.

Their cell was like all cells; too small, clammy, ill ventilated and ill lighted, and pungent with the stench of soured urine. Sir Guy was too agitated to make even a cursory examination. He was vaguely aware that the old patriarch had crawled onto a wooden shelflike pallet, and that a rat had scampered across his soft-soled boots. Yet no rat could have gnawed at the nerve center of his diaphragm as savagely as his own imagination was doing. What had happened to Ellen, and, of course, Charity? All the grisly tales of mass rapine and ravishment that Count Nikita had recounted with such gusto came back now to haunt him. At the time of their telling, these stories had seemed almost humorous; ribald escapades involving strange and unidentified women. But now that his imagination made Ellen the very hub of these nightmarish visions, he felt suffocated. In truth, while too unfamiliar an emotion to be recognizable, Sir Guy Spangler was suffering his first pangs of conscience.

Back and forth across the cell he paced. The great iron door was solid, pierced with holes only slightly larger than a man's thumb. The walls were so thick—at least a fathom—that the tiny window seemed set at the distant end of a small tunnel. At first, Sir Guy could not even see the sky because of the lowering thunderhead, but after a short time the storm broke, and lightning intermittently illumined the tiny cubicle. It was by one of these flashes he saw his venerable cellmate stretched full length on his ledge, calmly contemplating the ceiling.

Inexplicably, this irritated Sir Guy out of all reason, for though he seldom permitted his emotions to get the better of him, when this did happen he could not tolerate calmness in another.

"Well, old one," he burst out in vexation. "I hope you've made your peace with your God because we'll doubtless be tortured to death ere morning! From what I have been told, these damned Moscovites make the Spanish Inquisitors seem like affectionate children!"

Mr. Paxton chuckled softly. "Alas, I fear that will depend on whether the zealous Sylvester is motivated by secular or ecclesiastical considerations. Let us hope it is the former, in which case we may be spared the exquisite anguish reserved for the heretic."

"By my troth, you are fortunate to be able to find humor in the situation!" the knight snapped, ill-temperedly. "This should certainly convince you of the fallacy of your much touted *mercy!*"

"Indeed? And pray how did you arrive at that remarkable conclusion?"

Sir Guy took another angry turn about the cell. "That accursed dwarf, how else! If I'd used common-sense, I would have cut his throat when we first caught him spying on us!"

Paxton sniffed. "I grant that would have been *common,* though I question the *sense* of it."

"God's death! We wouldn't be in this mess if it hadn't been for that twisted fiend!"

"Rather, let us say, we would not be in this situation if we had not set forth on an illicit enterprise with evil intent."

"Bah! You were willing enough to protect your investment in the first place," Sir Guy retorted bluntly. "The morality didn't seem to worry you then!"

The old man chuckled. "Young man, you are determined to justify what you are doing! Alas, whether I agree or disagree has no bearing on the rightness or wrongness of the enterprise. We are discussing facts, not morals. As for Pojorski, if perchance he was responsible for our arrest, he was merely doing his duty—more, I cannot help adding, than were we."

Sir Guy ground one fist in his other palm in an excess of bitterness. "A pox on your musty platitudes!" he raged. "You can play the ostrich and hide from reality if you will, but I'd give a sackful of gold to have that damned Pojorski in this cell for the next few minutes!"

This outburst was greeted by a shrill cackle from the other side of the iron door.

"By the seven heavens of Allah!" hooted a familiarly insolent voice. "Seldom can I earn my fee more pleasurably! Ho, gaoler! Open the door, you mangy scavenger! Open up, and let Pojo commune with his dear friends!"

Scarcely had this hated voice announced its presence when a bolt of lightning struck somewhere close by, and the ancient tower shuddered from the impact. Simultaneously came a clap of thunder that deadened the senses. The cell seemed to explode in a blinding flash, and, somehow concurrent with this elemental phenomenon, in the awesome fashion of a *djinn* in an Arabian folk-tale, Pojorski appeared.

Now Sir Guy Spangler was no more superstitious than others of his era, and certainly he did not believe in *djinns;* he knew that the dual arrival of the lightning and the Tsar's ex-torturer was pure happenstance. Nevertheless, there *was* a supernatural aura about the incident that was hair-raising. Pojorski appeared to evolve out of the lightning; nay, to be the very *cause* of it!

Dazed, Sir Guy backed against the wall. Meanwhile, a lumbering, heavy-set turnkey loomed in the background, holding a knobby cudgel in one hand, and in the other a torch which cast a nervous, jerky light about the cell.

In the aftermath of thunder and apparent miracle, the silence grew embarrassingly acute. Finally, the dwarf cackled so explosively the echoes went tumbling and frolicking along the prison corridors.

"By Shaitan, this is a chill homecoming!" he crowed. "Perchance you withhold your affections because of this monstrous goat?" He turned on the lowering, dullwitted gaoler, and snatching the flambeau out of his hand, thrust it into an iron sconce on the wall.

"Get out, you great stinking offal!" he screamed at the guard, making a sweeping gesture with his hands towards the door. "The very sight of you offends my gently bred companions! Begone, you mobile dungheap!"

Bewildered, the burly creature screwed up his face in the agony of unaccustomed concentration, then still failing to comprehend what he had done to merit the insults, he ambled bearlike out of the cell. When he slammed and locked the iron door behind him, Sir Guy thought he detected a flicker of uncertainty cross the dwarf's features. But if so, it was gone in an instant.

Pojorski broke into another chuckle. "On behalf of my master, I must apologize for your reception, my friends!" he remarked facetiously. "And for these accommodations!"

If the astounding arrival of the dwarf had somewhat paralyzed Sir Guy, the sound of the mocking voice jarred him back to reality with a rush.

"As God's my life, you won't escape me this time!" he roared, and made a dive for the leering visitor.

Astonishingly, Pojorski made no effort to elude him, nor to offer any defense. Mr. Paxton moved from his perch in a vain attempt at intervention, but Sir Guy, fairly exploding with bottled resentments, brushed him aside and closed his powerful hands around the dwarf's throat. The very pliancy of the neck muscles under his grasp maddened him further until, sinking his fingers in, he worried the spy as a terrier worries a rat.

Even then Pojorski did not struggle, while the Englishman shook him about like a limp rag doll. Eventually, however, he reached up and caught the knight's hands in his own.

Then occurred a phenomenon that smacked of necromancy even more than the *djinn*-like arrival. For without any apparent effort on the dwarf's part, the touch of his fingers on the back of Sir Guy's hands had the most disastrous effect. A sharp pain shot through his body from brain to groin; at the same time, all power was cut off from his own fingers, and with this paralysis came a sickening of the stomach. He sank heavily to his knees, but as his numbed fingers fell away from Pojorski's throat, he was aware the dwarf still maintained a grip on each of his hands—thumb in palm and the abnormally powerful middle fingers pressing the bones on the back of the hand.

Never before had Sir Guy Spangler found himself in such a position—on his knees and helpless before an opponent—and it did nothing to assuage his pride that the opponent in this case was a twisted cripple barely taller than his own chest. The pain was so excruciating, Sir Guy sank his teeth into his nether lip to stifle an involuntary cry, but just when he thought he could restrain himself no longer, Pojorski released him so abruptly he toppled over backwards.

"Ten thousand pardons, comrade!" the dwarf purred sympathetically. "By the golden beard of Allah, I swear that is not the handclasp with which I greet a cherished friend."

"My mistake was in not cutting your throat in the beginning!" grated Sir Guy. "If I had heeded Count Nikita . . ."

This time, the dwarf's surprise was genuine. "Do you still have faith in that renegade Tatar?" he marveled. "Your mistake, as you term it, was in heeding him at all! Even then, had you kept close to Pojo when we came through the gate, I might have spared you this!"

"As you did my two men, I suppose?"

"Precisely!"

Sir Guy scowled. "Are they alive and free?"

The dwarf chuckled. "Aye, they are alive, but not free," he conceded, and paused until he saw the hope fade from the knight's face, whereupon he burst into another peal of raucous laughter. "By Allah, I had to lock them in a wine-cellar because they hadn't been in my quarters a half-glass before the fat one cheated my servant out of every ruble he possessed, and he with the face of a saddened camel pawed the bodice off my housekeeper's daughter. So, though it pleasured me naught to incarcerate them, I dared not leave them at large!"

This graphic portrayal was so characteristic of Messers Jones and Pistol as to be circumstantial evidence of the strongest kind. Yet Sir Guy was not ready to admit as much to the dwarf.

"I wouldn't believe you under oath!" he grumbled. "What brings you here?"

The other chuckled again. "You say you won't believe me, then you ask a question! Well, no matter; Pojo is not oversensitive. My friend, I have been laboring in your service!" He shrugged. "I regret Allah has not blessed my efforts!"

" 'Pon my soul, you seem to have been successful enough!" Sir Guy said bitterly.

"Ah, you flatter me! No, Pojo's stars are not in conjunction—or whatever it is that brings the caress of fortune. I have tried to find out where my adored Prince is campaigning, but as this is a State secret, I can only learn it from Boris Smolovitch, the Grand Equerry. Before I communicate with him, I wanted to ascertain your condition and ... er ... state of mind."

Sir Guy stared in bewilderment at the grotesque little monster. The creature was so bland, so self-assured, so confident every absurdity he uttered was being accepted, it was incredible.

"Go on," prompted the Englishman.

Pojorski turned his palms upward. "Believe me, I would rather have spared you a meeting with the Metropolitane. Albeit, unless you aggravate him, I doubt it will be fatal—at least not at the moment. I shall do all in my power for you, and in the untoward event he calls for my professional services in effecting your disposal, I shall not forget the many little courtesies you extended to me during our journey together."

His hands still aching from his recent sample of the torturer's professional skill, Sir Guy winced involuntarily. He was satisfied the dwarf was quite mad, yet mad or sane, it was folly to push him too far.

"You spoke of business?" Sir Guy said, with somewhat less rancor in his voice.

Pojorski rubbed his hands and glanced suspiciously at the door. "E'en though the pious Sylvester pierces the eardrums of all his gaolers and personal servants so they cannot glean his secrets, he has others in his employ whose hearing is remarkably acute. Howbeit, you and I must come to terms, risk or no!"

The dwarf's tone became conspiratorial. "By means which I need not enter into at this time," he went on, "I am perfectly cognizant of the ingenious scheme you and the Tatar Nikita have hatched." He winked broadly. "That, my friend, is a priceless nugget of information!"

Sir Guy still maintained his cold silence. The spy seemed slightly disappointed, but covered it with a noisy laugh. "On the face of it," he went on, "the obvious course for me would be to lay this jewel at the feet of my master, since the very pinnacle of my ambition is to bask in his favor once more. Howbeit, I foresee only too well what would happen: that contemptible Turk who superseded me—the curses of Allah be upon him!—would be assigned the enviable chore of contriving a suitable demise for Nikita, and doubtless your good self, as well. I would have to content myself with minor conspirators like the old one here—no offense intended, Ancient!—or that caterwauling priest!"

"I own that seems a poor recompense for the risks you ran," jeered Sir Guy.

"My very thought!" agreed the dwarf. "I have also learned that the richest rewards are given for information which delights, rather than for that which enrages. A happy man is more generous than an angry one."

"A profound philosophy!" commented Mr. Paxton.

Pojorski nodded solemnly. "With this in mind, I have reasoned that it would be more profitable for Pojo not to disillusion my susceptible Prince, and scramble for the dregs of his rage, but instead, to assist you in your adventure."

Sir Guy felt a tendency to hold his breath. In any event, he held his tongue.

"In this I do not believe I am disloyal," continued the dwarf. "True, there may be some slight irregularity in the lovely creature's name or rank, but stripped of all such verbiage—and, I might add, gowns—her *real value* should be most evident. I am confident my Prince will be delighted!" He cocked his head to one side. "How now, my friend, you do not seem enchanted?"

"Salvage can be too expensive," Sir Guy said grimly.

Pojorski shrugged. "Phoof! My demands are excessively modest! I ask only this: that when you are presented to my exalted master, you will publicly acknowledge that solely through the efforts of the faithful Yaroslaf Pojorski were you enabled to bring your embassy to its fruitful conclusion. That, and no more!" Seeing the bitter cynicism on Sir Guy's face, he turned to Paxton.

"Speak true, Ancient—is that not little enough to ask?"

The old man smiled. "You are dealing with Sir Guy," he parried.

Spangler was too puzzled to reply immediately. If Pojorski had the power to effect the results outlined—a point Sir Guy doubted—his offer was too generous to make sense. On the other hand, it would be foolhardy to ignore him; obviously he must have some influence, else he could not have penetrated into this cell. Sir Guy decided to give him a little more rope.

"I could promise that much, certainly," he agreed. "Howbeit, you seem to have overlooked the Metropolitane."

"Hardly!" grunted the other. "Granted he is a difficult man with whom to do business, every man has a blind side. Under the circumstances, it seems best that Pojo arrange to get you out of this pigsty surreptitiously, although it will be impossible to effect a wholesale delivery at this time."

"You expect me to abandon my companions?"

The dwarf sighed. "Liver of Shaitan, you English are strange creatures!" he marveled, shaking his head. "I had the same difficulty restraining your two cut-purses when they wanted to attack the Metropolitane's whole force in an hysterical attempt to rescue you. I finally convinced them they could better serve you by remaining alive."

Mr. Paxton leaned forward. "Sir Guy, if there is any possibility of your getting out, for God's sake do not hesitate because of the rest of us! As our visitor told Pistol and Jones, you can doubtless be more effective alive and on the outside of this abominable hole."

Sir Guy set his jaw. "I'll not leave El . . ." he began, then hastily amended himself, ". . . the woman in here! If Sylvester learns of the purpose of her presence in Muscovy, he . . ."

"The Holy Sylvester is already cognizant of the purpose," interrupted Pojorski. "What he hasn't *yet* learned is that she is an impostor! When he finds that out, she is doomed!"

"And so are we!" finished Sir Guy. "I will not leave without her!"

The spy chewed on his nether lip. "My friend, with sufficient time, she, too, might be got out, but . . . *we . . . have . . . no . . . time!* I have used my influence to get you out immediately, hence we cannot delay. Remember—once the Metropolitane interrogates you, conviction will follow swiftly! That we must avoid at all costs. So, I beg you, be reasonable and . . ."

"You are wasting breath!" Sir Guy told him. "If I go, she goes!" Feeling Paxton's eyes on him, he added grimly: "Without her I have nothing with which to bargain!"

"But the question of time?" cried the dwarf desperately. "We must . . ." He stopped abruptly, and for the first time in their acquaintance, Sir Guy thought he detected a trace of fear on the ugly face. Yet for a moment or so longer, Sir Guy heard nothing. Then at last he caught the tramp of marching feet.

"Your *time*," observed Mr. Paxton sadly, "seems to have run out!"

The footsteps came to a stop outside the door and a key rattled in the ancient lock.

"Ho—you in there?" barked a voice. "Make ready! His Eminence, the Holy Metropolitane deigns to question you! On your feet!"

Yaroslaf Pojorski exhaled a long sigh. "Too late!" he muttered bitterly. "Too damned late!"

18

It seemed incongruous that before being arraigned, the English prisoners should first have been herded into a big room and furnished with clean white apparel, yet be given no water for their ablutions. Here, however, Sir Guy was relieved to find that all of his original company was accounted for—save Ellen and Charity, who, being females, were not permitted to profane the presence of the Holy Monk. Nor were Nikita and his entourage included in this audience.

Sir Guy wanted to question some of his companions about the possible fate of the girls, but all conversation was forbidden. The Metropolitane's personal guardsmen, conspicuous in uniforms marked by the Greek cross, hovered about to prevent any intercourse between the prisoners.

Somehow or other in the general confusion, Pojorski had vanished. Now that he was gone, leaving so many vital questions unanswered, Sir Guy regretted he had wasted the golden opportunity in pointless bickering.

Finally, arrayed in the plain but immaculate garments of supplicants, but with their hands and faces grimy, they were lined up and inspected by a pompous bubble-eyed major-domo. By dint of much poking and bawling, this ecclesiastic steward arranged them in a single file with Sir Guy at their head, then led them out of the chamber.

Under less straitened circumstances, Sir Guy would have been extremely interested in that march through the Metropolitane's palace. The place was a strange fusing of the stoic and the sybarite, with its cold bare cloisters crowded with lavishly garbed *boyars*. Even the vast antechamber was frigidly unadorned, but when they entered the audience chamber a moment later, they found the situation almost exactly reversed.

This great hall was of a magnificence to beggar description. Square in shape, it had a high vaulted ceiling roofed with gilt and interspersed with sacred murals. The walls were hung with huge tapestries of incalculable value, while the floor was a mosaic of semiprecious stones. The vast room was thronged with the hierarchy of the ecclesiastic government—archbishops, bishops, archdeacons, protopopes and priests, abbots and priors and lordly *boyars*. The clerical faction were distinguishable by their black cassocks, which, peculiarly, were all but hidden under an outer garment similar to that worn by the laity; but the secular nobles, seemingly chosen for their youth and beauty, were handsomely clad in long coats of white damask, with chains of gold which crossed on the breast and reached to their hips. On their heads they wore caps of lynx skin, and on their feet, white leather buskins. Each man had laid on his shoulder a silver ax, which he gripped with both hands as if about to deliver a stroke.

Yet imposing as these two groups might appear, they were only a backdrop for the figure on the dais. This dais was set against the wall opposite from the entrance doors and raised about three steps above the inlaid floor. On it was a chair the like of which Sir Guy had never seen before; certainly no Western monarch could boast of such a throne. At its corners were four pillars of vermilion gilt, of a diameter barely encompassable by both hands of a man, and approximately an ell-and-a-half in height. Atop each pillar was a silver eagle which held in its beak the corner of a brocaded canopy fashioned of cloth-of-gold. In this chair sat the spiritual father of all the Muscovites.

Though Sir Guy was not the type of man to respect prelates, much less venerate them, he could not help being impressed by the tall, emaciated figure crouched on this ornate throne. He must have been very, very old, and with his transparent parchment-like skin, a flowing waist-length beard, and silvery locks that broke about his shoulders, he seemed the very embodiment of an Old Testament prophet. His gaunt frame was clad in a simple white robe, with no ornamentation other than a small crucifix suspended from his throat by a slender black cord. On a pyramidal silver table nearby, as if he had just cast aside such earthly relics, lay a priceless crown and his scepter of office—a golden cross inlaid with diamonds. Thus the contrast between this holy man and his mundane surroundings was so pronounced, Sir Guy was put to mind of a single pearl of startling purity set in tinsel.

Yet if Sir Guy was impressed, he was anything but reassured. He found himself impaled by a pair of hypnotic eyes the color and coldness of an icicle. It was a terrifying sensation, for he seemed unable to free himself; he felt like a spitted animal convulsed on the tip of a lance. That stooped body, so frail one could distinguish the outline of the bones through the skin, housed the most powerful spirit Sir Guy Spangler had ever encountered. The experience shook him to the core.

Worst of all, he was at a loss to know how to cope with the situation. Heretofore, all the Princes of the Church with whom he had come in contact had been, in his phrasing, *practical* men, who could be influenced by the same mediums of exchange which influenced all the laity, from peasant to monarch. But now his intuition warned him he faced a saint so free of dissimulation and acquisitiveness that their very absence made him inhuman. Here, Sir Guy thought grimly, was the end result of virtue carried to the ultimate, whereby it became a vice. Here was the fanatic in power.

As soon as their warder had crossed the threshold of the great hall, he had begun saluting His Holiness in a loud voice, wishing him continued personal guidance from the Lord, a long life and everlasting wisdom. This harangue continued until he had brought his prisoners to within ten paces of the Metropolitane, whereupon he gestured them to their knees. The others knelt promptly enough, but Sir Guy, locked in ocular combat with the venerable holy man, was so tardy the officious steward had to tap him twice with a staff. Sir Guy had the sensation of being pried apart from this awesome judge, but it did break the spell, and for a moment he was almost grateful. But his gratitude did not last long, for as he bent his knee, his glance swept the haughty assemblage and, half hidden behind the cloaks of the *boyars*, lurked the one individual Sir Guy did not want to be reminded of at this time—Yaroslaf Pojorski.

Then of a sudden, Sir Guy had other troubles to concern him, for the trumpet-voiced steward began enumerating their alleged crimes with all the prejudicial vehemence of an Inquisitorial prosecutor.

Unfortunately, the bug-eyed steward conducted his harangue in the Greek language, so that though Sir Guy was able to extract the pith, he could not grasp the literal meaning of each word. These English devils had crossed the forbidden seas to trespass into Muscovy and to impose on the gracious benevolence of the Grand Prince Ivan. As if that wasn't sufficiently nefarious, they had brought with them a vile foreign wanton with the avowed intent to try to lure the Tsar from the rigorous paths of virtue which he always trod. They had defied all the laws of exclusion, they had violated this, and dishonored that....

As the peroration rose in crescendo, Sir Guy discovered he was holding his breath. Was the verbose fool holding back in an effort to heighten the suspense, or dare they hope?—*was it possible he did not yet know the true facts about Ellen's identity?*

Sir Guy's heart began to pound violently. He risked lifting his head to look about him for the diabolical little fiend who alone held the key to that question. He finally spied him skulking behind the skirts of a *boyar*. As their glances met, the dwarf had the temerity to wink.

One of the steward's assistants was already prodding Sir Guy in an effort to make him resume his supine position, but wearied of the turgid bombast of the prosecutor and stung by what he deemed the dwarf's insolence, Sir Guy pushed to his feet. This unprecedented action accomplished in ten seconds what the garrulous steward had failed to do in twenty minutes—it galvanized the assembly! The ax-bearing *boyars* advanced in a body.

Sir Guy was past caring. Brushing aside the sputtering prosecutor, he squared his shoulders and stared into the icy eyes of the Metropolitane.

"Your Eminence!" he said clearly, in ringing Latin. "I demand leave to speak before this tiresome monologist wearies your Holiness out of all patience!"

This heresy robbed the prosecutor of the power of speech. He stood gaping in tongueless wonder, as if expecting a bolt of wrath to flame down from the throne and obliterate them both. The *boyars,* too, paused in shocked surprise; fearful, perhaps, of heavenly intervention. Recovering, they started forward once more, only to halt rigid when the Holy Monk lifted a frail but imperious hand.

Then followed a moment of terrible silence; the sort of awesome quiet that settles as an executioner begins his stroke.

The venerable Metropolitane leaned forward. "You *demand?*" he echoed finally, in Latin.

It was a voice that sent a charge rippling up and down the nerve-centers of Sir Guy's spine, as if it had been so much chain-lightning. Not loud, not precisely strong-timbred, it had an armor-shattering power of penetration, a ventriloquistic quality that made one feel it could be as distinctly heard a league away as here in the very presence of this dread speaker.

"Aye, your Holiness, *I demand*—in fairness, in justice, and in reason! Buried in that tirade was just one syllable of truth: we came from England. The rest is a lie from beginning to end."

The holy man remained as immutable as though sculptured from marble. Sir Guy took a deep breath.

"We came," he thundered, "not as trespassers or interlopers, but as diplomatic envoys at the request of your own Grand Prince Ivan! As such, we claim—nay, your Eminence, we *demand,* the immunity and privileges such as a diplomatic mission makes requisite. These are the facts, your Holiness!" It was on the tip of Sir Guy's tongue to ask that Count Nikita be summoned to corroborate his statements, but he hesitated lest he implicate beyond redemption the one Muscovite who might conceivably help them. He bowed then to indicate he had said his say.

Either the ecclesiastic steward did not comprehend Latin too well, or else he was a trifle slow, for the Englishman had fully completed his caustic rebuttal before the former evinced his understanding. This came in the form of an emotional explosion. With a screech as of pain, he seized a silver ax from the hands of the nearest *boyar,* and before anyone could interfere, swung it in a hissing downward arc towards Sir Guy's skull!

Had Sir Guy not provoked the assault deliberately, it is hardly possible he could have survived. Anticipating some such outburst, he stepped nimbly aside so that the whistling blade rang on the marble floor. Before the berserk steward could again raise the weapon, Sir Guy stomped on the hardwood shaft. This counter-stroke knocked the weapon out of the assailant's hands and brought the butt crashing down on his instep. Yowling in hurt pride and body, the steward tried to claw out his jeweled dress scimitar.

Then the Metropolitane made an almost imperceptible motion with his finger and immediately two stout *boyars* seized the frenzied prosecutor.

Sir Guy had a strong impulse to smile. It was part of his standard *modus operandi,* when in a dangerous cul-de-sac, to set his enemies quarreling amongst themselves, and the past efficiency of this divide-and-conquer technique was evidenced by the very fact that he was still alive. It pleasured him that it should succeed again.

Heretofore, however, Sir Guy's experience, extensive as it had been, had not included Muscovites. Now, instead of castigating the steward for his conduct, the Metropolitane waited unmoved for him to speak. To the Englishman's astonishment, he found himself charged with full guilt while the steward, assuming the role of a martyr, claimed personal injuries and demanded indemnification!

With pontifical solemnity, the Metropolitane asked what the steward deemed his due. Sir Guy could hardly believe his ears when he heard this pop-eyed buffoon request a *trial by combat!*

Now trial by combat, an archaic variation of the age-old trial by ordeal, had been practiced in England for some time after the Conquest, but had long since fallen into disuse. A remnant of primitive culture, it was based on the medieval principle of the miraculous decision, so fell naturally into the hands of priests. It seemed inconceivable that now, in this modern sixteenth century, such an obsolete legal procedure could be taken seriously in a country that regarded itself as civilized.[8]

Yet, incredibly, the Metropolitane somberly nodded his head!

Sir Guy stared about him, as if to make sure he was still in the land of reality, yet what he saw hardly confirmed it; the setting was far too exotic to be genuine, and certainly the terrible adjudicator was more spirit than man. Even Sir Guy's fellow defendants, immaculate of garb and grimy of hide, resembled naught but two-dimensional caricatures—especially the Reverend Belcher, who kept his face squashed against the marble floor in terror until it appeared embedded, and whose rump arched ceilingward so ludicrously Sir Guy couldn't understand how the *boyars* could resist pricking him with a sword. Yet even Belcher was not as ridiculous as this pompous little ecclesiastic ass who now demanded the right to a trial by combat with Sir Guy Spangler, probably the most notorious duellist in all England!

Apparently cognizant of the fact that the Englishman understood both Greek and Latin, the Metropolitane spoke briefly to the steward in a strange tongue. The Metropolitane thereupon beckoned two *boyars* to step forward, and from their maneuvers, Sir Guy presumed they had been appointed to act as seconds to the combatants. This precious pair put their heads together, and after a lengthy harangue, in which they haggled and gesticulated like Syrians in a bazaar, they moved apart; one took his stance beside the steward, while the other ranged alongside the Englishman.

These positions taken, the Holy Monk judiciously appraised the principals before addressing them in his sepulchral voice.

"My children, I beg you to repent your impetuosity, to stifle your impatience and to apologize to each other. Will you do so?"

While this was, admittedly, pure ritual, nonetheless Sir Guy was astonished at the apparent eagerness of the bumptious little steward to get on with the fight, as he loudly spurned all compromise. The *boyar* acting for Sir Guy shrugged to indicate his complete indifference, a gesture which the second spent nearly ten noisy minutes to interpret.

A squared space for the contest was quickly formed before the dais with a proficiency that suggested this type of trial was not uncommon. Up to this point, no mention had been made of the mode of combat, but since in England and Western Europe the choice of weapons invariably lies with the challenged, Sir Guy assumed the custom was universal. To his surprise, he was informed that in Muscovy the choice lay, *not* with the challenged, but with the *challenger!* This was difficult to credit, yet when he tried to debate the issue, it was his second who became incredulous. Who, argued the latter, had a better right to select the weapons than the man who picked the fight? To give the choice to the challenged was ridiculous in the extreme! Suppose he chose a type of weapon with which the challenger was not familiar?

Trying hard to control his fast-waning temper, Sir Guy demanded to know what mode of battle had been chosen. Once again he began to doubt his own hearing when he was informed that the bellicose little steward had elected to settle the dispute with bare hands to a finish.

Sir Guy had difficulty restraining his elation, for no choice could have pleased him more. The sport of bare-knuckle fighting had lately come to England and Sir Guy had already proved himself adept at the brutal game.

He stood impatiently, watching the little steward flail his arms about, and waiting for his moment of sweet revenge. Then suddenly the steward made some comment about "Mustapha Boy, the champion of the Holy Church," and beckoned with his arm. Sir Guy started to smile, but the smile froze as there was a cleavage in the crowd opposite him and a great hairy monster literally bounced into the arena.

Aware of the Muscovite propensity for tossing men to maddened bears and other wild animals, Sir Guy's first reaction was that the creature must be some jungle beast imported from Africa; a species of giant primate, perhaps. It was several agonizing seconds before he realized the hideous apparition was human, or nearly so.

This Mustapha Boy was quite the biggest man Sir Guy had ever seen. Not in height—in fact, he was so disproportionate as to seem actually short—but in breadth he was as burly as a great gnarled oak. Sir Guy knew at a glance he could not possibly encircle the creature's body with his own arms. A scarlet turban suggested he was either a Turk or a Persian, though by what means the wrapping was made to stay upright on the cone-shaped skull was not immediately apparent. The brute was bald above the ears, but below that level a hirsute crop cascaded like a cape over the lower portion of his face to merge eventually with the shaggy pasture of his chest.

He was bared to the waist—that is, if one did not count the luxuriant fur supplied by a bountiful Nature—and the muscles lay on his arms and legs like tangled cordage. His legs were abnormally far apart, and his great webbed feet were also bare, save for a panel of hair on each instep.

As Sir Guy stared in fascination at this mobile nightmare, he heard his second explain that in the Muscovite version of a *trial by combat,* either the plaintiff or the defendant had the privilege of using a proxy to do the actual fighting. Mustapha Boy, the torturing Turk, was officiating in that capacity. Sir Guy had three choices under the law; he could personally fight the challenger; he could default, thereby conceding his "guilt"; or, as was customary in the majority of such cases, he could have one of his "fellow criminals," or anyone else for that matter, substitute for him. He must decide at once.

Sir Guy sighed bitterly. He had been "rigged" before; both the Spaniards and the Italians had, on various occasions, jockeyed him into a difficult spot, but Sir Guy was fast learning that those Western masters of trickery were rank amateurs by comparison with the wily Muscovite.

Now the Metropolitane announced the rules of the contest, to wit: no weapons were to be allowed, save those supplied by God, but these could be used at discretion. Interpreted freely, this meant biting, gouging, kicking, and other such primitive modes of mayhem were permissible. It was to a finish—in other words, to the death—unless the victor ordained otherwise. Did the Englishman comprehend?

The Englishman did!

The Metropolitane impaled Sir Guy on the tip of his steely glare.

"Dost thou refuse to meet the plaintiff?" he demanded. "Thus proving thy guilt?"

Sir Guy unconsciously flexed his hands, still stiff and sore from his late joust with the dwarf, but he shook his head.

No flicker of expression modified the frozen mask of the holy man as he went on in the same funereal tone.

"Hast thou anyone to fight for thee?"

Sir Guy shook his head, but before he could add more, a mocking voice shouted: *"Before God, he hath!"*

A faint arching of the snowy brows was all that hinted at the surprise of the venerable Sylvester, but Sir Guy was frankly startled. He jerked his head around, yet could see no likely champion in the press of haughty *boyars* and haughtier clerics. His first thought was of Nikita, yet the voice was not his. Then as he stared about in puzzlement, an avenue opened in the crowd and strutting down it came . . . *Yaroslaf Pojorski!*

If any single thing had been needed to lend the final touch of unreality to the scene, it was this unexpected resurrection of the dwarf. An instant before, Sir Guy had considered Mustapha Boy the most repulsive creature he had ever seen, but now, after one astounded glance at the dwarf, he had to rate the Turkish nightmare a poor second.

For Pojo had also stripped to the waist in preparation for the combat, and this accentuated the ghastly accident of Nature—the oversized head, the warped, humpbacked torso, and the long, tentacle-like arms. Watching him slither into the cleared square, one was reminded of a great venomous spider.

In the shocked silence occasioned by his unheralded entry, he stalked over to the dais and bowed low before the Metropolitane.

"The meanest of your Holiness' slaves dares to approach the sacred dust of your Holiness' feet to humbly petition a boon!" he wheedled, in a tone that suggested scant humbleness. "O patriarch of Metropolitanes, Holy Father of all Muscovy, Vicar of God upon earth, most beloved of Masters, hear this inferior person's plea: that he may have the privilege of enduring this trial by combat in the stead of the tall Englishman—a privilege ordained under a recent decree promulgated by our Exalted Grand Prince which permits true Muscovites to voluntarily substitute for foreigners manifestly incapable of securing a fair trial. Hear me, O holiest of Holy Fathers: Let me, Yaroslaf Pojorski, deal with this insolent Turkish infidel who has the effrontery to pose as the champion of the True Church!"

The stillness which followed this remarkable declamation showed the assemblage to be completely astounded. Sir Guy, however, suspecting it was but another sample of Muscovite chicanery, was about to reject the dwarf's offer when his glance turned upon Mustapha Boy.

To his amazement, that burly brawler seemed palsied with terror, after the fashion of an elephant faced with a bellicose mouse. Bewildered, Sir Guy hesitated. He recalled the ease with which this selfsame dwarf had handled the redoubtable Sergeant Pistol; he remembered, with good cause, the terrible power and fiendish skill that lay in those weird blood-stained hands.

"Wonderful! Wonderful!" burst out a handsome young *boyar*. "Let us add our prayers to the little beast's! Grant his boon, O Holy Father!" And a hundred voices echoed variants of this plea.

Though it galled the Englishman to consider accepting this act of dubious charity, he grimly kept his mouth shut. He was not yet convinced the whole performance wasn't a carefully staged trap.

One thing was obvious—neither the challenger nor his proxy was pleased.

The steward groaned loudly, slapped his forehead twice with each palm, then said: "Holiest of Holy Fathers, as thou represents the Almighty God on earth, do we so represent thee in this ordeal! Let us proceed! We place our trust in our Heavenly Father!"

Pojorski caught Sir Guy's eye, dropped him a surreptitious wink, then swung around to face his opponent.

But it soon became apparent that Mustapha Boy had a will of *his* own. He began jumping up and down like a mad dervish, then with a howl of "*Mashalla! Mashalla!*" he suddenly spat full in the steward's face. Before anyone could divine his intent, he pirouetted and fled the hall—his "*La Allah il Allah!*" echoing profanely through the marble cloisters.

The only sound in the Great Hall was that of a falling body. The challenger had fainted!

19

BACK IN THE CELL once more, Sir Guy paced the narrow confines between the window and the door.

Mr. Paxton, always a firm believer in the healing powers of complete relaxation, had resumed his horizontal position on the wooden pallet. But there was much of the tiger in Sir Guy Spangler, and patience during inactivity was not among his virtues.

"It just doesn't make sense!" he fumed, more to himself than to his venerable cellmate. "Why did that damned runt pretend to defend me?"

"*Pretend?*" echoed the old man. "I thought he was rather effective."

"Bah! That was staged! Common-sense should tell you that a monster like that bloody Turk, or whatever he was, wouldn't be terrorized by a stunted dwarf!"

"You have a point there," conceded the philosopher. "Being reasonably intelligent men, you and I both recognize the ridiculousness of the situation. Unfortunately—or, in this instance, fortunately—the big man himself was not so enlightened. To my not unbiased eye, he gave a very convincing demonstration of sheer terror."

"But, damn it, you haven't explained *why*," persisted Sir Guy.

"Alas, I do not know why. Let us say, rather, if a man throws me a rope when I am mired in quicksand, I will not quibble over his reasons for rescuing me."

Cursing under his breath, Sir Guy flung himself onto the empty pallet. It was futile to argue with the old man; though he never assumed the offensive, Mr. Paxton was impregnable, for he used knowledge as a sword and wisdom as armor.

With the darkness and rats had come a dank, marrow-pervading chill. Sir Guy's mind began to spin: he thought of Affable Jones and Sergeant Pistol. Were they still alive? What would become of them?

What of Ellen and Charity? These damned Muscovites, fumed Sir Guy, for all their pose as Christians, were Orientals at heart, with the Oriental's refined lusts.

Yet, Sir Guy was basically an optimist, and almost in spite of himself, he had a feeling that something would happen to better their plight. He still had hopes that Count Nikita would find some way of communicating with the Tsar before it was too late.

He must have fallen asleep, for next thing he knew he was being awakened by a discordant wailing, as if someone were being tortured further down the corridor. He sprang to his feet in the darkness, and groped towards the door, visible by reason of a faint light glowing eerily through the small holes in the iron panel. Mr. Paxton, likewise aroused, joined him.

The raucous yowling seemed to be drawing closer. Absolutely tuneless, it seemed to swell in volume, then fade away.

"Great God in heaven, what is it?" whispered Sir Guy. "It cannot be human!"

The old man chuckled. "I'm afraid it is. I strongly suspect it is the chanting of a monk, though I confess I never heard anything quite so inharmonious."

"*Inharmonious?* Hell, man, it's plain ghastly! It sets my teeth on edge!"

"Howbeit, I suggest you conceal your distaste," grunted the gaffer, "for unless I'm sorely mistaken, our nightingale is headed this way."

"May heaven spare . . ." began Sir Guy, then suddenly he gasped out: "My God—*did you hear that?*"

"What?"

"The words! *They are English!* Listen!"

Tense with excitement, both men pressed their ears to the holes in the door. For a moment or two, Sir Guy feared his senses had played him a trick, for the tuneless caterwauling was utterly incoherent. Then just as he was about to concede his mistake, the chanting swelled in volume and he plainly heard these words:

> *W'at-'o, Sir Guy, ye jolly rogue,*
> *Yer pals 'ave come fer ye to syve!*
> *Stretch out, stretch out, an' dead h'appear,*
> *Else dead ye'll be, ye quaint ol' dear!*

At this point the words trailed off into a senseless cacophony.

Sir Guy felt an unfamiliar constriction in his throat. "Did you hear what I did?" he asked, startled.

Old Paxton sighed windily. "I hesitate to confess it, lad!" he muttered. "Yet if you heard what . . . *Hark!* There it goes again!"

Scarce daring to breathe, lest they miss a syllable, they listened, and once again the blatant howls lapsed into Whitefriars English.

> *Ho, the ruddy Muskies grabbed Sir Guy,*
> *An' rammed 'im in a cell.*
> *The fools don't know Ol' Nick 'imself,*
> *Couldn't 'old Guy in 'ell!*

Sir Guy grabbed Paxton by the arm. "By my troth! It's Affable Jones!" he cried. "What the . . . Oh, Lord—he's off again!"

The sing-song chanting, considerably more earthy than celestial in flavor, had suddenly seemed almost beautiful to the ears of the two Englishmen.

> *'Ark, Sir Guy, fer God's syke, 'ark!*
> *Ye fail me now, we'll miss the mark!*
> *Lie down, pl'y dead, we'll get ye out!*
> *Myke one mistyke, we'll get the knout!*

Mr. Paxton drew Sir Guy away from the door. "I don't pretend to know what is going to happen," he whispered. "Yet Jones's meaning is obvious; he is attempting a rescue and wants you to simulate a corpse!"

Sir Guy agreed, and climbed onto his shelf, where he stretched out stiffly. "I've heard of men feigning death to fool animals in the jungle, or soldiers on the battlefield, but I doubt its practicality in a situation like this."

"With poor lighting and sufficient distraction, it just may be possible," said Paxton. "In any event, you have no choice but to try it." He gave Sir Guy an encouraging pat on the shoulder and returned to his station by the door.

As always in moments of extreme danger, Sir Guy was comparatively cool. But since on this occasion, the control was in the hands of another, he was unable to stop the pounding of his heart.

The "nightingale" was close outside the cell by now, and from the muffled footfalls, it was plain he was accompanied by others. Sir Guy strained to catch the other voices, hoping against hope to hear old Pistol's gloomy drawl, but all he recognized were the biting snarls of Yaroslaf Pojorski, who was profanely urging speed. Then as the company came to a halt just outside the cell, while the turnkey fumbled with the lock, Affable chanted his last warning.

> *Fer God's syke, marster, 'old yer wind,*
> *W'en ye sees me as a monk.*
> *Ye bust out larfin' now, me friend,*
> *We'll bloody-well be sunk!*

Then the door opened, and the procession marched into the cell.

It took all of Sir Guy Spangler's will-power to keep his eyes closed and hold his breath. From the sounds, he knew there must be at least four men in the company. Affable was chanting what sounded like a doleful orison, but the words, if lacking in spirituality, were anything but gloomy.

> *Marster, marster, flat on yer arse,*
> *Play along wi' our little farce.*
> *If we can all h'appear devout,*
> *Me'n the little bastard'll get ye out!*

The last-named personage so inelegantly described now made his presence known in no uncertain terms. He stormed across the flagging and poked Sir Guy in the ribs.

"By the blessed beards of my sainted ancestors, what goes on here?" he shouted in Latin. "You, old one—what has happened?"

Paxton replied: "Why, Master Pojorski, I am not prepared to say. As you can see, we had no light. Pray, tell me, what *has* happened?"

"What?" shrilled Pojorski, apparently in a fine rage. "The ungrateful knave is dead, that's what! Dead!" He loosed a wail as of intense pain. "Dead, just when my holy master turned him over to me!" He swung his head to address the gaoler.

"And you, son of an illegitimate camel! Have you poisoned him with the swill you feed to vultures?"

"Before God, he was alive when last I saw him," grumbled the gaoler.

"Curse you for a clod of dung, it is plain he's dead now!" The angle of the voice shifted. "Come, good Father, perchance it's not too late to absolve the sins of the flesh, e'en though his spirit has departed. Speak a prayer over him!"

There was a shuffling, then Affable was bending over Sir Guy.

"Alleluia! Alleluia!" he murmured with false piety. "I'd be a month o' Sundays recountin' yer sins o' the flesh, m'lud, but 'ark w'at I s'y: we be goin' to cart ye out fer dead. Meanw'ile, 'tis arrynged wi' the Musky h'envoy—I'll no mention 'is nyme—to get the wench out. So steady, m'lud! Easy does it! *Alleluia! Alleluia!*"

"That's enough! That's enough!" barked the dwarf officiously. "Pojo shall not be cheated of his prey! His Supreme Holiness promised I could question him, and question him I shall! *Take out the body!*"

This command touched off a bitter argument. The gaoler claimed that Pojorski's privilege was limited to questioning the prisoner in his cell; the dwarf screamed that his authority in all matters relating to State prisoners was unlimited.

The gaoler was no match for the razor-tongued dwarf, and as his counter-blasts became weaker, Pojorski's grew stronger. Finally, the gaoler must have surrendered, for rough hands seized Sir Guy and he was dragged across the flagging. It was all he could do to remain limp and take the bumps as they came. When he was beginning to doubt he could stand the punishment much longer, Pojorski snarled: "Pick him up, you crawling spawn of hell! What good to me is a carcass after it has mopped this festering cesspool! Lift him clear, I tell you!" Then as the men grudgingly hoisted Sir Guy off the stone floor, the dwarf again addressed the "monk."

[155]

"Speak a short prayer for the ancient, Father. Tell him something of the life to come!"

"Ya—in the salt mines!" jeered the gaoler, who, like all his kind, was hungry for someone to abuse.

Sir Guy risked a peek under his lids, and was just in time to see Affable Jones make a gesture that looked remarkably similar to a thumbing of the nose. Then the bogus monk extended his doubtful blessings to Mr. Paxton.

"Lor' love ye, Ancient, an' damn all Muskies!" he intoned. " 'Ow'm I doin'? Think ye I sound so angelic as the Archbishop of Canterbury?"

Mr. Paxton bowed with just the proper shade of humility. "Without intending any irreverence, lad, I must confess the archbishop's voice never sounded quite so welcome to these old ears of mine."

"Glory! Glory! Glory!" Affable chanted. " 'Tis plain I've found me true callin'! But to business: we also be gettin' the wench out tonight, an' we'll deliver 'er syfe to the Big Poo-bah! Then we'll dicker fer the rest o' ye! So keep a stiff upper lip, Ancient, an' s'y a prayer fer Father Jones!" He made what he meant to be a benedictory gesture, but what in truth resembled a small boy crossing his heart.

Hic, hoc, hokus-pokus! Toodle-oo!

And then Sir Guy was being toted down the corridor.

Everything went smoothly—everything, that is, save Sir Guy, who had never endured such a manhandling—until they came to a small gate in the wall which opened onto the river, and was used chiefly for the discreet removal of the corpses of political prisoners. Here the gaoler balked.

His change of heart at this particular juncture was understandable. When Pojorski had first challenged his dominion in the cell, the gaoler had been supported only by one very subwitted turnkey, and he was not fool enough to get into a brawl when the balance was even. Too, he was frankly afraid of this infamous dwarf, nor did he trust the strange monk who chanted in a tongue never before heard in this ecclesiastical prison.

However, now having reached the gate where he was buoyed by the presence of two armed sentries, he found the courage heretofore denied him. He refused either to open the gate or to permit them to otherwise remove the "corpse."

Pojorski cursed and screeched, and coined such obscenities as taxed the imagination—all to no avail. The louder he bawled, the firmer became the gaoler. To Sir Guy, it was torture of the most fiendish kind. Worse than the awful agony of uncertainty was the necessity to remain lifelessly inert on the damp flagging while this life-and-death argument was going on directly above him. Unable longer to stand the suspense, he gingerly raised one eyelid sufficiently to see what was going on.

It *looked* even worse than it *sounded*. The sentries were brawny devils, who carried their huge scimitar-like weapons bared and who, unlike the gaoler and his turnkey, were obviously alert and quick-witted. Pojorski might be Satan incarnate, and Affable Jones the world's greatest brawler, nevertheless it was plain they could not intimidate the gaoler and his armed henchman with their bare hands.

Pojorski himself was fast growing aware of the hopelessness of their situation, for a frantic note of desperation crept into his voice. He began to wheedle. This proved nigh fatal, for the gaoler promptly shifted his tactics from the defensive to the aggressive. Finally, he commanded his sentries to put Pojorski and the "monk" under arrest.

Sir Guy held his breath. Pojorski began to try bribery, as he backed away from the reach of the sentries.

Howbeit, there was no way of avoiding them. The turnkey had the wit to produce a cudgel and now blocked the retreat of the two would-be rescuers. The gaoler again thundered for the pair to be seized.

It seemed at this point as if the bright thread of Sir Guy Spangler's destiny was about to snap. Yet, when from under his shuttered lids he saw one of the sentries step over his inert body, he also recognized the shadow of opportunity coming within his grasp. He abruptly loosed a spine-numbing war-whoop, and seizing the sentry by the leg, rose so suddenly as to fling him on his face. The scimitar, as if guided by Fate, slid neatly along the flagging toward the nimble hand of Affable Jones.

The other sentry turned to repel this unexpected attack, but as he raised his sword, Affable Jones lopped off his head with one swinging swipe. The gaoler opened his mouth to scream for help, but the facile talons of the Tsar's ex-torturer terminated both his call and his career. Sir Guy, meanwhile, had put the tripped sentry out of his embarrassment.

There was a certain rude pathos in the plight of the cloddish turnkey. He had exhibited an understandable pride in having armed himself and taken his station blocking the passage. But his poor clouded brain couldn't function as rapidly as events, and he was gaping bewilderedly at the severed head of the sentry when the pseudo-monk ended his earthly tenure.

"Lor' lumme!" Affable observed genially. "Jes' w'en I feel like h'extendin' mesel', the fun's o'er!"

Sir Guy gave a grim snort. "The same old scamp, I swear!" he said

[157]

with rough affection. "'Pon my soul, you're a sight for sore eyes!" Then realizing the dwarf was standing beside him, and that he was doubtless chiefly responsible for the reckless attempt, Sir Guy included him in the greeting. "And you, too, Pojorski! By my troth, you conducted that boldly!"

The ex-torturer beamed. "Did I not tell you I was invaluable?" he said perkily.

"That you did," Sir Guy agreed. "Now what of the woman? You agreed to include her in the delivery!"

Pojorski nodded, and jerked his head towards the gate. "Pojo never lies! She is waiting down at the old convent by the bend in the river."

Affable corroborated this. "'Tis all arrynged," he assured Sir Guy. "The Count 'as bribed someone to bring 'er to the top o' the wall, w'ere Pistol is w'ytin' to lower 'er into the punt. 'E'll be 'arf cryzy if we don't get there soon. We be lyte a'ready, maybe too lyte, I own!"

Pojorski slashed the gaoler's belt, took the ring of keys, and after a few vain attempts, succeeded in opening the door. Sir Guy thought he had never smelled anything sweeter than that first gulp of outdoor air.

Pojo next hooded the sentries' lantern, then beckoning the others to follow, stepped onto a small, slimy landing, where a flat-bottomed skiff was secured. He hopped in and Sir Guy followed as nimbly as his aching body would permit. Meanwhile Affable disappeared, to reappear with the two scimitars under one arm, and the severed head of the late gaoler in the other.

"I want to show this to Pistol," he explained jovially. "Jes' the other day 'e argied ye couldn't lop off a noggin wi'out somethin' to steady it, because . . ."

Sir Guy's temper had reached the boiling point. "Throw that damn thing overboard and take an oar!" he snarled. "You can settle your silly arguments in some other fashion!"

Affable sighed, took one last affectionate look at his macabre prize before flipping it over his shoulder, whereupon it went bobbing grotesquely downstream.

With Affable at the oars, and Pojorski conning him from the bow, Sir Guy had naught to do but squat in the stern-sheets and stare about him. The huge stone fortification looked as endless as the Great Wall of China as it meandered along one bank of the river. Occasionally he could glimpse a castellated tower through the weird half-mist blanketing the scene.

It suddenly came to Sir Guy that he had not yet thanked the dwarf for his astounding performance before the Metropolitane. He quickly sought to make amends.

"In the general excitement, I haven't had an opportunity to thank you for taking my part in that mock trial," he called to Pojorski.

The latter turned in surprise. "Taking *your* part!" he scoffed. "Frankly, I never thought of you; I was anxious to get my hands on that infidel Turk! He eluded me again, but I swear I shall corner him anon! Did I not tell you how that Turkish dung-hill superseded me in the favor of my beloved Prince?"

Sir Guy whistled softly. "Good Lord! You mean this Mustapha Boy is Ivan's chief tor . . . er . . . executioner? Your rival?"

Pojorski nodded glumly as the boat slewed around the bend in the river. Then he cursed aloud: "May the putrid soul of that accursed gaoler roast ten thousand years for delaying us! There is no light! We are too late!"

Affable Jones stopped rowing and peered into the gloom ahead. "Geld me if it ain't so!" he groaned. "Pistol was to 'ave a light on the wall if all was well. This means 'e's dead, Lor' luv 'im, an' the bastard owed me two shillin's thruppence!"

Pojorski gestured Affable to head for the opposite shore. "Obviously our plan has been discovered!" he fumed. "Let us begone whilst we are able!"

Sir Guy was understandably reluctant to abandon the venture. "Can you be certain? May not . . ."

The dwarf spat in impatience. "It is too late, I tell you! Pistol was hoisted onto the wall before we came for you! Something has gone wrong! We dare not tarry longer, for I have left our horses with a nervous man who may not wait if trouble starts! No, we must race to the Grand Equerry's palace before we are caught."

Affable swung the boat and resumed his rowing. "Damme, I'm sorry about poor ol' Pistol!"

Sir Guy was not accustomed to being a mere passenger on an expedition of this kind, and now that Pojorski had in effect abdicated his command by counseling flight, he felt entitled to take control. The boat had almost reached the shore when he said sharply: "Affable—bring her about!"

It was a tone that Mr. Jones understood and respected, and his teeth gleamed whitely in a smile as he whipped the punt around. The dwarf started to object, but Sir Guy ordered him silent. However, when Spangler reached for the hooded lantern, Pojorski gave a startled bleat.

"*Don't show a light!*" he cried. "Every cannon on the walls will open up on us!"

"We'll chance it!" snapped Sir Guy, and unhooded the lantern thrice in quick succession.

Affable Jones had paused at the oars to watch; so drifting with the sluggish current, the three conspirators waited with baited breaths.

Nothing happened; neither cannon shot, nor answering signal. The ramparts remained as dark and inscrutable as the very night. Finally, Sir Guy sank into the stern-sheets with a weary sigh.

"Very well, Affable—lay a course for shore! I guess the only thing left is . . ." He started to his feet so suddenly he nearly overturned the boat.

"A light!" he cheered. "Praise God—*a light!*"

There it was, winking teasingly at them, right where the dwarf had said it should be—clear and welcome as an evening star!

Affable counted the flashes aloud. "*One . . . two . . . three!* 'E's alive, is Pistol!" He literally spun the boat on his keel and headed for the spot where they had seen the light. "W'at-'o! I'll get me two shillin's thruppence arter all!"

20

THE FLAT-BOTTOMED LITTLE SCOW fair skimmed along the surface under the powerful manipulation of Affable Jones, yet to Sir Guy it seemed as if they barely made headway against the current. He did not dare risk another exchange of signals.

But eventually they nosed against the wall, which at this point rose sheer from the river. Affable shipped his oars, and they worked their way along the wall, hand over hand, until they were directly under the spot where Sir Guy felt certain he had seen the light. He took a deep breath to steady his nerves, then softly whistled a familiar signal. Swift as an echo came an answering whistle, following immediately by the whispered growl of Sergeant Pistol.

"W'ere the bloody 'ell ye been? Me'n the wench 'as 'ad time to ryse a fambly!"

"Quiet!" Sir Guy silenced him. "Pistol! I take it then you have the girl?"

"Aye!" came the dour voice from above. "Trussed up like a ruddy fowl, she be! Myke ready to tyke on cargo, mates! I been 'earin sentries prowlin' close by!"

"Lower away!" ordered Sir Guy. "I believe we're directly under you! When we have Ellen safe, secure your end of the line to a merlon, or the like, and slide down. We'll guide you. Understand?"

"Aye, aye, sir! Stand by to receive boarders!" Then after much grunting and puffing: "Look out below! 'Ere comes the li'l white carcass!"

Sir Guy rose to his feet. "You two steady the boat!" he warned his companions.

Sir Guy tried to force his eyes to penetrate the darkness, but here, close to the wall, it was even more intense than it had been out in the stream. So he held his arms above his head, weaving them about like the antennae of an insect, groping for Ellen. Peculiarly enough, his customary calm had given way to a breath-taking excitement. He could hear Pistol grunting as he lowered his burden a few inches at a time. It seemed to take an interminably long time, and Sir Guy was about to snarl in impatience, when his searching hands encountered the girl's body.

"I've got her!" he called softly. "Lower away!"

"Burn me, I'm doin' the . . ." began Pistol in an aggrieved grumble, then of a sudden his voice soared into a roar of warning: "*Shove off! Fer Christ's syke, shove off! We're spotted!*"

Simultaneously, he let go his end of the rope!

Not yet braced to receive the full weight of the girl, Sir Guy was knocked off balance by the unexpected impact. For one terrible instant, he teetered on the gunwale, then, rather than risk injury to her, he threw himself headlong into the bottom of the boat, twisting in midair so that his body would cushion her fall.

As he crashed to the deck, his left elbow struck the thwart, sending a dizzying stab of pain through his entire body. He lay there stunned, with the breath knocked out of him, the girl lying limply atop him. Then he heard Pistol snarl an obscene imprecation at his pursuers, and an instant later the redoubtable sergeant hurled himself off the ramparts into the river. The splash all but inundated the little craft.

Affable Jones, with his characteristic disregard both for danger and the suitability of expression, adroitly shoved the boat clear and headed for the floundering Pistol, observing heartily: "First bath the bastard's 'ad since I've known 'im!"

Meanwhile, the ramparts seemed to have burst into life with shouting men and bobbing lanterns. Fortunately, the lights aided rather than betrayed the fugitives by intensifying the contrast between the now brightly illumined wall and the abysmal blackness of the river. A few cannon bellowed in defiance but without accuracy. However, a flight of arrows came uncomfortably close; one nailed the dwarf's flowing sleeve to the stem-head.

Guided by the beacon of Pistol's gurgled profanities—for having been a professional seaman at one stage of his mottled career, he naturally could *not* swim—the others drew alongside and, with hardly a pause, hauled him aboard. Despite his ducking, he sprang onto the thwart behind Affable Jones and grabbed one oar.

"Draw, damn it, draw!" he snarled at his rowing mate.

Sir Guy crawled into the sternsheets and pulled the girl close in front of him, so that his body served her as a shield. His injured arm felt broken, but he suspected it was just a severe bruise. While his two henchmen did their best to plane the little craft out of bow-shot, he bent over the girl.

"Are you all right, Ellen?"

She did not reply, but he felt her head bob. Sergeant Pistol explained her silence.

"She's gagged, that's w'at! The Count said the cove 'e'd bribed to sneak 'er out insisted, so she couldn't yelp an' betray 'im. I figgered 't was a good ideer, so I left 'er so."

"You damned scoundrel!" Sir Guy snapped ungratefully, then in a softer tone told the girl: "I'll release you at once!"

He tried to pick the knot, but in the darkness and the heaving craft, he found it impossible. Nor did he dare risk using a knife in the same circumstances.

"We'll have to wait until we get ashore, Ellen!" he apologized. "It will be only a little longer."

Once again she nodded her understanding, and when he drew her head against his shoulder in an effort to make her more comfortable, she did not resist. In this wise they crossed the river and, conned by Pojorski, worked into a small covelike anchorage where, the dwarf assured them, horses awaited them.

The instant the stem grated on the gravel, Pojorski leapt overboard and waded ashore in search of the nags. While Pistol steadied the boat, Sir Guy tried to lift out the girl, but his injured arm failed him, so he took the lantern instead and Affable scooped her off the bottom as if she were but a feather. Pistol then shoved the boat adrift so as to leave no trace of their landing.

By the time the others climbed onto the bank, Pojorski reappeared, followed by a confederate and a string of horses. He wanted them to mount at once but Sir Guy brushed the suggestion aside.

"Affable, put the Lady Ellen down beneath this tree, then hold the lantern so I can remove that damn gag!"

"By the mercy of Allah—do not uncover that light here!" Pojorski cried frantically. "You'll lead them to us, sure as death!"

"She has been tied up too damn long now," growled Sir Guy. "Affable, do as I tell you!" He took out a small poniard he had had the foresight to remove from the sentry he had silenced earlier, then knelt beside the girl. "Steady!" he encouraged her. "I'll have you free in a moment. Come, Affable, the light!"

Then, wonder of wonders, Affable Jones seemed peculiarly reluctant to obey. Pojorski further encouraged his insubordination.

"It's suicide, master!" protested the dwarf. "Here—let me cut her loose! I can see in the dark!"

Sir Guy's voice took on a terrible softness. "Jones! Unhood that light!"

It was a tone Mr. Jones knew better than to ignore. "Sobeit!" he sighed, and cautiously eased up on the hood. As the saffron fingers of light slipped their bonds, Sir Guy leaned over the girl.

"Now, Ellen . . ." he began, only to stop short in astonishment.

For the big eyes staring up at him in such hurt dismay belonged, not to Ellen, but to Charity.

There was an awkward silence, as the four men stared at the gagged girl. Affable, as usual, was the first to speak.

"I knowed it," he acknowledged, wagging his head. "I knowed it the minute I picked 'er up in me arms! Recognized the turn o' 'er . . . I mean, 'er curves!"

Sir Guy saw the big eyes well with tears, so cursing his own thoughtlessness, he severed first her arm bonds, then the gag. Charity flexed her numbed fingers, wiped her mouth with the back of a hand, then exhaled a long sigh.

"I'm awful sorry, m'lud!" she said wistfully. "I allus seem to pop up w'ere I ayant wanted, but, truly sir—'tweren't me fault!"

Sir Guy felt like a swine. "Good Lord, Charity, it isn't that you are not wanted!" he said earnestly. "It is just that we were expecting . . ." Realizing he was only making it worse, he trailed lamely to a stop.

"Oh, I understan's 'ow it is, sir! I knowed this 'ad to 'appen, fer w'en ye drew me 'ead against ye an' w'ispered in me ear, I knowed then ye mistook me fer Ellen. Believe me, m'lud, I'd o' let ye know the truth then, 'ad me tongue been loose, w'ich it weren't. I be sorry."

"Where is Ellen?" he asked her.

Charity spread her hands in hopelessness. "Lor' love 'er, sir, I do not know! The Count come to our cell an' said 'e was tryin' to fix it fer our hescape. 'E was 'avin trouble bribin' anyone to go agin ol' Silly-vester, or w'atever 'is nyme be. Then 'e tolt us 'e'd got a knave w'at would get us out, on'y the rascal insisted me an' Ellen be bound an' gagged in a sack, so if anythin' went wrong, 'e could just chuck us over the wall."

Sir Guy winced. "Did . . . did Ellen get . . . er . . . sacked, too?" he asked.

"W'y, as to that, I cannot s'y, m'lud!" replied Charity. "She seemed to mistrust the scoundrel. But me, not bein' afeared o' any man—beggin' allus yer ludship's pardon!—I offered to go first. I did." She gestured eloquently. "An' that's all I knows, sir!"

"Oh, well," Affable observed optimistically, "better an' 'arf loaf than none!"

"Aye!" Pistol concurred sourly. "One wooman be pretty much like another!"

"Hold your puling tongues!" rasped Sir Guy. He shot a quick, suspicious glance at Pojorski, but the latter's expression was one of puzzlement rather than guilt. He felt Charity's eyes searching his own, so he closed the lantern with a snap.

"To horse!" he ordered grimly. "We've work to do!"

In silence the company mounted, then without a light of any kind, they were piloted hastily through a labyrinth of pitted lanes and muddy bypaths by a jittery character who kept his features concealed as zealously as any Moslem *houri*. This dubious knave spake not one word himself, and insisted on absolute silence in the others. Whether or not he was an actual mute, Sir Guy had no way of knowing, but the creature did have a most fascinating gift of pantomime, for whenever the party came within the radius of a patch of light, he transmitted his limited instructions by eloquent gesticulations of his left hand.

Under these repressive conditions, Sir Guy had to stifle his concern as well as his temper. He was not yet sure whether he should bless Pojorski, or damn him; the dwarf seemed to warrant both. Sir Guy fairly itched to cross-examine him about the "mistake" in the identity of the rescued girl; it was, he felt, utterly ridiculous to accept it as an honest error.

In brief, Sir Guy Spangler was irritated with everything in general, which meant, of course, that he was irked with himself. Somehow, he seemed to have lost his old, sure touch. Being human, he looked outside himself to seek a reason; something, or somebody, to blame. He decided he hated Muscovy; certainly everything had gone awry almost from the moment of landing; he considered it the very homeplace of treachery and intrigue. And the person of Yaroslaf Pojorski, torturer extraordinary, confessed spy and assassin, seemed to epitomize the whole bloody country. Sir Guy took a silent vow that he would deliver the woman as soon as possible—assuming she was still alive—and hurry back to the West, where thieves and murderers were relatively understandable.

The guide's extreme nervousness eventually infected the others. However, he led them at long last to the same blind alleyway where, earlier, they had been seized by the Metropolitane's guardsmen. The instant they came within sight of the small gate in the wall of the Grand Equerry's palace, the guide raced away into the darkness.

It was now well past midnight, and though a few windows were illumined, the palace for the most part was darkened. The little company proceeded to the gate and dismounted, and since Pojorski was presumed to have made all the arrangements, Sir Guy waited for him to take the initiative at the gate. But for once the dwarf hesitated.

"We may encounter some minor difficulty at this point," he confessed blandly. "By a remarkable coincidence, Boris Smolovitch is not numbered among my more ardent admirers. In a word, we may not get in."

The Englishman was momentarily startled. "God's death!" he exploded. "This is one hell of a time to tell us that!"

The dwarf chuckled impishly. "Pojo never admits defeat!" he boasted, then striding up to the little gate, rapped briskly with the hilt of his poniard.

There was no reply.

Pojorski frowned and thumped again. "By the blind eye of my grandfather!" he muttered. "This is a pretty pass! If I pound louder, I will surely draw Sylvester's guardsmen, who always lurk in this vicinity."

"Me very own thought!" put in Affable Jones, who had suffered most from the enforced silence. "I'm surprised they weren't 'ere w'ytin' fer us! Lemme work on that lock! I've opened better doors 'an this one."

The dwarf shrugged. "As you will. Howbeit, I warn you they have a fat cannon loaded with rusty spikes and broken glass pointed at this gateway from the inside, in the event it is opened without authorization."

Affable backed hastily away.

Sir Guy shoved them both aside. "By my troth, I'm not going to stand here waiting for the Metropolitane's cutthroats!" he growled. "I'll have that door opened from the inside, or we'll stave it in from the out!" He rapped loudly.

The dwarf flinched. "May Allah protect us! You'll wake the neighborhood!"

Charity pointed to the palace windows shimmering with soft candlelight. "*Somebody's* up, m'lud."

After a few suspenseful moments, the gate was flung open suddenly and they were almost blinded by a flood of light. When their eyes adjusted, they discovered a cannon yawning at them, beside which stood a gunner with a linstock in his hand, and behind him, in turn, an officer and an armed guard.

Sir Guy was the first to recover from this reception. He bowed and contrived to show that he carried no weapon in his hands. Then he addressed the officer in Latin. Whether that worthy was ignorant of the international language or chose to pretend so, he shook his head vigorously and bawled something in a tongue that, to the English, sounded even harsher than Russian.

The gunner blew on his smouldering match to make ready.

Sir Guy had hoped to keep the dwarf out of sight until he had made his arrangements with the captain of the guard, but this obviously was the time for a change in plan. He beckoned Pojorski.

"Tell him we come in peace!" he instructed. "That we are envoys to the Grand Prince!"

However, when the dwarf stepped out of the shadows, the officer nearly had a convulsion. Drawing his saber, he charged around the gun and would have assaulted the ex-torturer had not the Englishman stepped between them.

Then ensued a bitter three-cornered argument, complicated by excited translations. The captain of the guard insisted that his master, the Grand Equerry, had given strict orders that Yaroslaf Pojorski was to be banned eternally from his palace; if caught within the grounds, he was to be treated as a trespasser. All communications from him were to be refused.

Sir Guy, on the other hand, maintained that the Grand Equerry's personal feeling for or against Yaroslaf Pojorski had no bearing on the issue; that the present communication came, not from the dwarf—who was present merely as an interpreter—but from himself, an envoy of the Queen of England.

But the captain had what even in that day was known as a "military mind"; a peculiar, small-calibered intelligence functioning in an unswerving rut, in the manner of a mouse running down a narrow pipe. He had been forbidden to receive any communications from one Yaroslaf Pojorski; no exceptions had been made as to whether said Pojorski was interpreting for another, or talking for himself. From this insular position, the captain would not budge. Logic, reason, threats, and bribes were all missiles deflected by the armor of his blind adherence to "duty."

Meanwhile, time passed. The party was half in, half out of the gate; Sir Guy had stepped inside, flanked by the stout-hearted Affable Jones, while Pistol remained outside, ready to duck if Sir Guy failed to block the obdurate officer. Then came that sound which they had been dreading—the clatter of approaching horses.

"Jesus wept!" groaned Sergeant Pistol.

Sir Guy stiffened, cast a quick glance over his shoulder, then turned back to the captain. "Tell him," he commanded the dwarf, "that this is a life-and-death matter of State! That he must summon the Grand Equerry and that I, personally, will assume full responsibility! Make him understand that the Metropolitane's men are coming! We're doomed if you fail!"

Pojorski did his best, but it wasn't good enough. The captain declared he could not admit them without a personal order from the Grand Equerry, and since the Grand Equerry was at this precise moment in his ladies' apartments, it would be fatal to disturb him.

"It will be fatal if you do not!" swore Sir Guy.

The captain shrugged. "Not to me," he said, through Pojorski. "Go now; I must close the gate! We do not want needless trouble with the Metropolitane's guardsmen!" He started to shoo them out as if they were chickens.

Charity, meantime, discerned the approaching horsemen.

"In the nyme o' 'eaven, w'y don't we go inside?" she hissed at Pistol.

"Wery simple," jeered the dour sergeant. "'E won't 'ave us, that's w'y! In fact, the stubborn bastard won't do nothin'!"

"Be ye afeered o' 'im?" marveled Charity. "*Be Sir Guy afeered o' 'im?*"

"See that cannon?" snarled Pistol impatiently. "It's loaded, that's w'at! Now 'old yer silly femyle tongue an' leave important matters to yer betters!"

Sir Guy held his ground until the gunner once more blew on his match, then realizing the position was untenable, he began to retreat. They might have a small chance if taken alive by the Metropolitane's troops; none at all if blown to bits by this cannon.

He had almost backed outside, and the captain was reaching for the gate to slam it shut, when an irate figure catapulted through, brushed Sir Guy aside, knocked the officer against the cannon muzzle and jerked the glowing linstock out of the astounded gunner's hand.

It took a moment or so for the assorted males to realize that the fury who had perpetrated this *coup de main* was none other than little Charity. She did not leave them long in doubt.

"Come inside an' close that ruddy gyte!" she screamed at her dazed companions. "I got a word to s'y to this contrary 'oreson!"

Sir Guy was the first to recover from surprise, in time to slam and bolt the gate almost in the very faces of the approaching horsemen.

Then the captain of the guard found his voice and bellowed at the gunner to "Fire!" But the gunner, no longer having the match in his possession, was unable to comply, and being a married man himself, knew better than to try to take it from a wrathful woman.

It was a new Charity, a Charity none of them had ever seen before!

It must be acknowledged the captain was a fearless man: he attempted to wrest the match from Charity. This was sheer folly! Having seized control, she had no intention of relinquishing it, so she lashed him over the face with the whiplike linstock until she had maneuvered him with his back against the cannon mouth. Deeming this an excellent place to retain him, Charity let up with her whip and took up with her tongue.

"Now ye listen to me, ye stubborn jackass!" she screeched in his face. "We want to talk wi' the big muck-puddle! Quick! *Unnerstan'!*" This was punctuated with a piercing shriek that seemed to stab the captain in his vitals. He howled for his squad to seize her, but the squad, whether paralyzed by this fiery Jezebel, or secretly enjoying his discomfiture, remained immobile.

"He cannot understand you, Charity!" Sir Guy said.

"Oh, 'e carn't, carn't 'e!" shrilled Charity, raising her voice an octave or so to make it audible above the clamor of the Metropolitane's minions outside. " 'E'll bloody well unnerstan' afore *I* get done wi' 'im, the dirty, low-lifed . . ." Thereupon she lapsed into a radiant efflux of Billingsgate English that was well-nigh lyrical. The Muscovite officer seemed to shrivel, and even Sergeant Pistol, no mean practitioner himself on occasion, blushed slightly at the imaginative obscenities.

And all the while, the holy Sylvester's pursuivants beyond the wall chorused their demand for the fugitives in the name of God and the Metropolitane.

This obstreperous outcry had roused up the relief guard, and it was with sinking hearts that the fugitives saw these fresh troopers come streaming across the courtyard on the double. Sir Guy made a half-hearted attempt to subdue the irate Charity, but when she shook him off and screeched even more loudly than before, he gave up.

Finally, having exhausted her repertoire, she turned to Pojorski.

"Now arsk the 'oreson will 'e do w'at we tells 'im!" she commanded.

The captain's reply was prompt: he ordered them all thrown through the gate into the waiting arms of their pursuers!

In the presence of so many reserves, resistance was futile, and as the soldiers surged forward to seize them, even Charity realized that she had failed. Screaming like a swooping hawk, she eluded the timorous grasp of two troopers, and sprang upon the captain of the guard. Together they rolled onto the flagging, but this time his howls triumphed over hers when she set her talons in his face.

So intent was Sir Guy on this fantastic bout, that he failed to note the arrival of yet another group of men. His first intimation that something exceptional had happened was when his own captors suddenly released him and jerked to attention. Surprised, Sir Guy turned his head. . . .

He needed no one to tell him then that he was staring at one of the three most powerful men in all Muscovy—the Grand Equerry to the Tsar!

21

THE EXTERIOR OF BORIS SMOLOVITCH would appear less distinguished than might be expected of an intimate and counsellor to the dread Ivan the Terrible. A short, rolypoly old man—he was then somewhere in his middle sixties—with sleepy, heavy-lidded blue eyes, a benign expression, and a curled beard startling in its whiteness, he resembled the popular conception of a sycophant much more than a shrewd and wily Minister of State. In his younger days he had served as ambassador to Persia, with the result that he adopted many of that nation's luxuriant customs and its mode of dress. Hence the lavish costume he now wore: a gorgeous *jubbah* of flame-colored velvet embroidered with solid gold thread and speckled with precious stones, all of which looked slightly ludicrous on his rotund little figure.

However, Sir Guy Spangler was far too seasoned a campaigner to be hoodwinked by such externals. Behind those lazy lids was a pair of eyes sharp enough to seize the essentials of a scene in one fleeting glimpse; behind that ingenuous expression, a cool intelligence quite detached from emotion. Boris Smolovitch, the Englishman decided, was a complex character more to be dreaded than the relatively singleminded Sylvester.

So, with all his senses alerted, Sir Guy bowed diplomatically, and in English, hissed *sotto voce* at Charity: *"For God's sake, girl, let be!"*

The desperate urgency of his voice got through to the infuriated girl, for she sheathed her claws at once and came to her feet. The captain of the guard, on seeing his master, sobbed out a broken little prayer and likewise staggered gamely erect, with the flourish of a man who means to do his duty if it kills him.

The stillness was portentous as the Grand Equerry waited for an explanation no one dared to give.

Charity, meanwhile, looked wonderingly about her. She saw the minister, of course, but failing to recognize his importance, gave him only a fleeting smile before turning back to her late antagonist. The sight of *him*, tottering dazedly on his heels, was more than she could bear, so she carried the feminine prerogative of the *last word* one step further; she got in the *last lick*. Before anyone could divine her intent, she moved forward and with all her might—which proved considerable —sank her left fist in the inviting mid-section of the captain of the guard. As that unfortunate snapped forward, in the fashion of a closing jackknife, Charity met his descending face with an upraised knee.

No sacrificial sheep ever dropped more limply than dropped now the captain of the guard before his master.

The Englishmen fully expected to be slaughtered where they stood, and when an instant later the Metropolitane's troops renewed their wolfish clamor outside the walls, they would have considered themselves fortunate in being permitted to walk out quietly and surrender themselves. But at this point, the Grand Equerry *laughed!*

It was a high-pitched girlish titter—more of a giggle than a laugh— yet for all that, it was the most potent expression of mirth any of that desperate little band had ever heard. Certainly it took them by surprise, but no more so than it did the gloomy-visaged Muscovites comprising the minister's own retinue. These cautious courtiers blinked a couple of times to be sure he was *really* laughing, not just clearing his exalted throat; then, convinced, the entire entourage burst into a series of minor guffaws. Eventually everyone present was chuckling to a greater or lesser degree—everyone, that is, but the captain of the guard. For the moment, *he* was incapable of expressing any emotion.

Charity looked wonderingly at Sir Guy, then tilted her head towards the Grand Equerry.

" 'Oo's the li'l rascal, m'lud?" she asked.

Sir Guy winced. "For the love of heaven, Charity . . ." he barked warningly, then caught his breath.

The Grand Equerry stopped laughing abruptly!

"What did the woman say?" he demanded in Latin.

All mirth went into an eclipse. Sir Guy stepped valiantly into the breech.

"Your Grace . . ." he began, then to his everlasting horror, found himself interrupted by the minister's own interpreter, who propounded a translation worse, if that were possible, than the original.

"Your Highness, Most Beneficent of Ministers, Noblest of Statesmen, and Fount of All the Wisdom of Muscovy—this brazen female (for such this unworthy servant assumes her to be) dares refer to thee as a diminutive rogue!"

The Grand Equerry pondered that, and while pondering, tugged absently on a curl of his snowy beard.

"Astounding!" he mused at long last. "By the Mass, that is a remarkable statement for a female!" He flicked his little button-like eyes towards the embarrassed Englishman.

"She *is* a female, is she not?" he inquired in Latin.

"Almost too much so, your Magnificence!" grimly conceded Sir Guy.

Charity had followed this exchange without comprehension, looking first at one and then the other as the conversation changed hands. Finally, she puckered her nose at Sir Guy.

"M'lud, I may be wantin' in manners, yet I been given to unnerstan' a real gent'man doesn't talk about a lydy be'ind 'er back!" she said tartly. "'Oo, I arsked ye, be this funny cove, an' w'at's 'e s'yin' about me?"

Sir Guy gave her a cold stare. "This *nobleman*," he told her in a tone calculated to convey far more than the actual words, "*is the Grand Equerry, the Chief Minister of Muscovy!*"

Charity's mouth flew open in amazement and she gaped at the venerable dignitary as if seeing him for the first time.

"Glory be!" she gasped after an anxious pause. "Ye mean—'*e's* wot we been tryin' to see!" She went into a spasm of laughter. "An' all the time I expected somethin' fierce! W'y, bless 'is li'l ol' 'eart, 'e's adorable!"

Sir Guy turned red and the interpreter turned white.

"What did she say?" reiterated the Grand Equerry.

"It was sound without meaning!" muttered the interpreter nervously.

"I shall be the judge of that!" said the Grand Equerry. "Translate!"

"Oh, Minister of Ministers, Kindest of Masters, Star of Intellect, Most Glorious Example of Manhood—this base creature barefacedly confesses that in thy glorious personage she expected to encounter a veritable monster of ferocity. Discovering otherwise, she apparently begs some unnamed deity to pass a benediction upon the small muscular organ which they term the *heart*, then adds that thou (as all others know) art worthy of adoration and worship."

"By Gemini," marveled the Grand Equerry. "This incredible creature must be a veritable wizard of words! I cannot recall ever having heard a language which afforded such a broad range of expression while at the same time preserving such a wealth of delicate nuances. Perchance we should adopt it as our diplomatic language! What tongue is it?"

The interpreter grimaced in horror. "Master! Master! Thou jests, surely! Why, sire, this English language has the abrasive quality of shagreen!"

"English!" cried the Grand Equerry. "Did you say . . . *English!*" He stared at Charity with renewed interest. "By the blessed St. Basil, if it is English, then she . . . she must be the pearl Ivan sent Nikita to England to bring back! What a prize!" He scanned the numbed little band of intruders. "Where is Count Nikita?" he demanded sharply.

"In the Metropolitane's dungeon," Sir Guy replied crisply, "where we too would be, sire, if this courageous young woman had not . . . er . . . overwhelmed your officer!"

"Lo! Then it is true—you are English?"

Sir Guy nodded. "We are, your Grace, and as such, we ask asylum until we can communicate with the Tsar!"

The minister brushed aside the request with a gesture of impatience and concentrated on Charity. While his guard tried to maintain a soldierly rigidity, and while the English tried to still their pounding hearts, the Grand Equerry waddled around the girl, appraising her as a judge of horseflesh might appraise a mare. Charity followed his circumambulation with puzzled eyes, but when he experimentally pinched a buttock, she gave him a hearty shove that toppled him into the trembling arms of his interpreter.

"'Ere, 'ere, ye li'l bastard!" she chided goodnaturedly. "'Oo ye be gettin' fresh wi'?"

The Grand Equerry was too astounded to recover his balance, so he remained in that semi-recumbent position and gasped: "She said . . . ?"

"Oh, Master, Master! May the Almighty God forgive me!" wailed the horrified interpreter. "The incredible hussy termed thee an illegitimate! Oh, sire, shall I summon the strangler?"

"No, I should say *not!*" cried the Grand Equerry in high glee. He then called for assistance, and three strong but anxious retainers set him vertical once more. "By Gemini, how I envy Ivan the taming of this . . . this . . . veritable nymph!" He suddenly became aware of the clamorous demands of the Metropolitane's guardsmen on the other side of the wall. His cherubic expression changed.

"Inform those rabid mongrels that these people are my honored guests, and that unless they scatter instantly and return to their fossilized master, I shall order this cannon emptied into their worthless entrails!"

As an officer sprang forward to do his bidding, the Grand Equerry addressed himself to Sir Guy.

"If you will follow us," he purred suavely, "my castellan will show you and your remarkable menage to quarters. In the morning, you may present your credentials. Until then, I bid you good night."

Sir Guy bowed, hardly daring to risk disturbing the precarious balance of their fortune. But Affable Jones, who knew sufficient Latin to absorb the gist of what had been said, was not so inhibited. He winked broadly at Charity.

"W'at-'o, gal, ye done it!" he whispered aside. "'E s'ys fer us to toddle along to the palace wi' 'im!"

"W'y, bless 'is cute 'eart!" Charity squealed delightedly, and before anyone could intercept her, she brushed through the circle of retainers, grabbed the startled minister by the elbow, and spun him around. Then linking her arm through his and giving it an impulsive little hug, she started tripping gaily with him towards the palace proper.

At this irreparable breach of protocol, Sir Guy and several Muscovite officers rushed upon Charity to drive her away from the sublime presence. Yet to their further incredulity, the Grand Equerry quickly recovered his equilibrium and motioned them away. So it was that in a stunned silence, both Englishmen and Muscovites witnessed a scene no one of them had ever seen before, or ever expected to see again—the Chief Minister to the Tsar of All the Russias being propelled into his own palace on the arm of a London street gamin!

On reaching the palace, the Grand Equerry adroitly disengaged himself from Charity's affectionate clutches, and vanished. The "guests" were then ushered into a small dining salon where food and drink were spread before them while their apartments were being made ready. It was then discovered that somewhere in the shuffle, Yaroslaf Pojorski had also disappeared.

Sir Guy's first reaction was the belief that it was a case of "good riddance to bad rubbish," but almost instantly he was ashamed of the thought. Cruel, self-seeking, and the very epitome of treachery though the little fiend might be, it was nonetheless true that Sir Guy and the others present owed him their freedom—if freedom, in fact, it was.

And that was precisely what troubled Sir Guy at the moment. The awe and trembling exhibited by the Grand Equerry's retinue clearly indicated that he could be a rip-snorting terror on occasion, and for all Sir Guy knew, his obvious good nature of the evening might well be dissipated before the dawn. Sir Guy spoke of this to Charity.

"There is no doubt your courageous, if unorthodox, assault on the captain of the guard saved the day for us," he told her. "And for that we are grateful. Yet it is a wonder we were not all slaughtered where we stood when you spoke of his Excellency as you did. Good heavens, child, don't you know better than to call a minister of state a . . . *a little bastard?*"

"Or a *rascal!*" put in Sergeant Pistol. " 'E's mebbe touchy!"

"Mebbe I be, too!" Charity retorted, tossing her head. "An' if 'e's so 'igh an' mighty, 'e better keep 'is paws off'n my backside! *It* ayant got nothin' to do wi' affairs o' state!"

Affable Jones chuckled heartily and gestured at her with a half-gnawed chicken leg.

"Plenty backsides not so well-rounded as your'n 'as been reckoned *affairs o' state,*" he contributed. "Howbeit, I agrees wi' 'is ludship, m'gal—ye weren't very subtle! Ye 'ad no call to knock 'im down; ye jus' don't knock down these Muskie ministers! An' Lor' luv a gallopin' goose—I like to died w'en ye 'ooked 'is wing an' started a-skippin' 'im along the path! It jus' ayant done, m'gal!"

" '*E* didn't seem to mind!" sniffed Charity.

" 'Ere now, don't get no big-'eaded ideers!" warned Pistol sourly. "Ye ayant no lydy, so don't try to get above yer stytion!"

The girl's eyes welled abruptly. "All right, all right—let be! I'm just a vulgar little Whitefriars slut! Ye don't need to rub my nose in it no more! I won't ferget again."

Sir Guy sighed softly. "Charity, my dear," he said kindly, "we are not trying to 'rub your nose' in anything. But there are certain tried-and-true rules of conduct, varying somewhat in different strata of society, beyond which it is not safe to trespass."

Her big eyes searched his face in wonder. "Ye mean, sir—'tis wrong to be kind an' jolly?" she asked.

"Well, no, not exactly," he countered, secretly wishing he had not brought up the matter in the first place. "But you see, Charity, it is all a question of degree. For example—it is never permissible, and particularly in the Eastern countries, to touch the person of a high dignitary, such as a minister of state!"

"H'especially fer a wooman!" Pistol expanded the point. " 'Is carcass be sycred! No wooman kin get near 'im!"

Charity's eyes bulged. "Well, I never!" she gasped, then looked to Sir Guy for confirmation. "Be that true, m'lud?"

Sir Guy nodded. "In the main, aye!" he agreed.

To the utter astonishment of the three males, Charity sank back in her chair and howled with laughter. Affable wagged his head.

" 'Ighsterical!" he observed.

"Balmy!" opined the sergeant.

After a moment or two, Charity brought herself under partial control, then punctuating her remarks with explosive giggles, she explained her merriment.

"Oh, glory! H'excuse me, m'lud! But I got to wonderin' w'at this cute li'l pot-bellied minister does wi' thirteen wives an' seven hundred an' thirty-two columbines if . . . no *wimmen* can *touch* 'is sycred person! Saints o' glory, somebody's wystin' somebody's time!" Charity collapsed into another paroxysm of mirth.

Sergeant Pistol gravely eyed Sir Guy. "Damme, sir, she's myde 'er point!" he conceded.

Further discussion of the problem was cut short by a lackey who came to escort them to their individual quarters.

For his own part, Sir Guy was glad enough to turn in. He could hardly recall when he had last enjoyed a good night's rest, and now it appeared that he was destined for an uninterrupted sleep. So when he was ushered into a large bedchamber and at long last found himself alone, he carefully bolted the door on the inside and stretched out on the bed, to relax a moment before disrobing.

In the wan light of a single candelabrum, the chamber appeared immense. The lush Persian rugs caressed the feet as the rich silken cushions seemed to caress the skin. The massive bed was so voluptuously inviting as to hint that mere sleep in it was a waste of time. And on the walls, tapestries of a distinctly erotic motif encouraged this intimation in less subtle terms.

Sir Guy's only response to all these stimuli was one of mild amusement. Their effect was to make him wonder about the character of this extraordinary little minister. This cherubic, effeminate old man hardly looked the part of either a wily courtier or a notorious lecher, much less a wise and far-seeing minister of state. This reflection suddenly reminded Sir Guy of Charity's earthy comment, and when he tried to conjure a mental picture of pudgy little Boris Smolovitch surrounded by hundreds of passionate black-eyed *houris,* he chuckled aloud.

"*Ah! I am gratified to find you in such excellent humor!*" remarked a purring voice from the shadows.

The Englishman's laughter died in mid-air as he jerked into a sitting position. Sensing danger, he shot a quick, suspicious glance at the door. The heavy bolt was still in place. When he turned his attention towards the source of the voice, his brain had difficulty accepting what his eyes reported.

A huge tapestry had parted in twain, revealing a secret passage.

In the mouth of this passage, unguarded and unattended, stood the Grand Equerry himself!

Mute with astonishment, Sir Guy watched the minister step calmly into the chamber. The quality of unreality was so persistent, Sir Guy wondered if, perhaps, the whole incident was but a dream. Though he was vaguely aware that the tapestry had fallen in place so perfectly that the woven satyr had resumed his eternal rape of the woven nymph as if they had never been interrupted, Sir Guy could not take his eyes off his incredible visitor. The latter waddled soundlessly across the ankle-deep carpet and carefully lowered his bulk into a sturdy chair on the opposite perimeter of the candlelight.

The minister seemed quite out of breath from the effort of transporting his portly frame. "You will be granted an official audience tomorrow," he pantingly informed the startled Englishman. "Yet my own curiosity is such that I desire to ask you some questions informally. I trust you have no serious objections?"

Sir Guy wondered if he had not detected an implied threat in that last sentence, which was more of a statement than a query. Nevertheless, he shook his head.

"None, your Magnificence!" he murmured, bowing as well as circumstances permitted. "I am not only honored, I am entirely at your service."

The minister sniffed in a way that could have meant anything, or nothing. Then he daubed his puggy nose with a perfumed handkerchief, and went on.

"Pojorski assured us we would find you amenable!" he said, punctuating his remark with one of those girlish giggles which the Englishman found so distracting. "I had the dog seized and turned over to my own torturer for interrogation. Would you believe it"—the minister slapped his fat thigh and burst into a shrill cackle—"even on the rack the little devil had the temerity to embarrass my torturer by criticizing his technique! By Gemini, I never witnessed a sight to equal it! Finally, my man became so nervous and upset, he burst into tears and refused to go on! We had to release Pojorski. However, strange as it may seem, he proved willing to talk without mechanical inducement."

Sir Guy wasn't quite sure whether to laugh or be angry at the mishandling of his self-appointed confrere.

"I should have assumed he would," he said carefully. "In view of the effort he made to get in here for that purpose."

The moon face registered surprise. "Did he so?" Another giggle. "It is true Pojorski raised that very point, but I did not believe him!

The joke is on me!" He lapsed into another spasm of merriment, then sobered swiftly. "For the sake of everyone concerned, I hope he told the whole truth. We shall soon find out." He leaned forward, the better to keep his eyes on the Englishman. "Now tell me in your own words exactly why you are here, and what has happened to you en route!"

Sir Guy hesitated as long as he dared. He was not fooled by the lisps and giggles, for it was patent that having survived so long in close proximity to the infamous Ivan the Terrible, Master Smolovitch must be a veritable fount of cunning. On the other hand, Sir Guy would have traded five years of his life to know precisely *what* Pojorski had told him. A man on the rack was not necessarily trustworthy, and the dwarf was at all times given to exaggeration. Yet now any variation in their respective statements was liable to prove fatal.

"I am impatient!" purred the Grand Equerry.

So Sir Guy began. He spoke with slow deliberation, taking his time on the unimportant phases so that he would have equal time to consider his words when skating verbally on thin ice. Without seeming to stare, he watched the minister's expression for any indicative symptoms.

He saw none; the moon-shaped face remained unvaryingly bland, almost naïve. Sir Guy picked his way to the end of his tale as gingerly as a barefoot man stepping over broken glass. At last he spread his hands in an eloquent gesture of resignation.

"You know the rest, sire!" he concluded quietly. "Assured you were a faithful friend and counsellor to the Emperor, and trusting that you would arrange for our safe passage to him, we risked everything in one desperate effort to claim asylum at your hands."

For a painfully long time, the Grand Equerry said nothing. He pursed his sensuous lips and tapped his fingernails together.

"H'mnn!" he grunted finally. "A most unprecedented recital! *But*."— he cocked his head and his eyes seemed to pin-point—"there is something *very* peculiar about your narration when compared with Pojorski's! Very peculiar, indeed!"

Sir Guy's heart skipped a beat, but he managed to keep his voice on an even keel.

"And that, Magnificence . . . ?"

"Lo and behold—your versions are *identical!*" lisped the minister, and went into a spasm of laughter.

Sir Guy forced a smile, but it was woefully thin.

"As you were talking," continued the Grand Equerry, sobering again, "an idea occurred to me. Sylvester, the Metropolitane, that is, is a high-handed old fool with the single-purposeness of a camel, and, unfortunately, he has as many agents in Moscow as I have. Hence, if I grant you an official audience and supply you with an escort in the hope of reaching Ivan's encampment, Sylvester will learn of it immediately and will send out sufficient force to seize you."

Seeing his plan commencing to crumble, Sir Guy grew desperate. "Your Eminence, it is absolutely imperative I see the Tsar. A brush with the Metropolitane's troops is a chance I must take!"

"Ah, possibly!" The minister smiled. "But it is not one *I* must take!"

The Englishman was too weary for diplomatic double-talk. "Do you refuse to assist us?" he demanded bluntly.

The other made a patting motion with both hands to signify a plea for patience.

"I have not said so. Yet if I did as you request, Sylvester, in addition to sending out his scurrilous minions in pursuit of you, would immediately place those of your party still in his clutches well out of reach." He chuckled contentedly. "It is extremely fortunate *we* have in our charge the prize Ivan so ardently desires. It gives us a decided advantage."

Sir Guy paled. "But you haven't, my lord!" he said grimly. "I thought I made that quite clear: *the Lady Ellen is still in the Metropolitane's prison!*"

The Grand Equerry gasped and sat up very straight. His eyes seemed about to pop out of his head.

"What!" he shrilled. "By the seven-tailed serpent of hell, do not lie to me! Who, then, is this female . . . ah . . . who accompanied you?"

Sir Guy had come to his feet. "She . . ." He was about to say *only a servant,* but realizing the implications of what that might mean to a *boyar* who had taken her into his palace as a guest, he amended his statement in mid-air, as it were. "Mistress Charity is her Excellency's lady-in-waiting."

"Is she—this one you refer to as Mistress Charity—is she well-born?"

Sir Guy up-palmed his hands with fine Italian guile. "Sire, you are a better judge of women than I!"

The Grand Equerry laughed abruptly, rubbing his chubby hands in glee. "Yes, yes, to be sure!" he chortled. "To be sure! To be sure! H'mnn!" He moistened his lips and stared thoughtfully at the ceiling. "By Gemini, that alters the situation, doesn't it? I mean—we cannot leave Ivan's pearl in the icy hands of that celibate shark! *Na-na!* Unthinkable!"

The Englishman began to breathe steadily once again. "Then you will give us the escort, your Nobility?"

Surprisingly, the minister wagged his head. "No, no! I should say not! I cannot afford to lose any men; the way Ivan is burning them up in his campaigns, it is difficult to keep a soldier able-bodied enough to stand erect. No, my wisest course will be to refuse you an official audience and have you and your party thrown into the dungeons. Yes, that is the only thing to do!"

Though Sir Guy's mouth flew open, he was too surprised to speak.

The minister went on: "Sylvester's spies will report my conduct to him, which will mollify his pique over my abruptness with his guardsmen this evening. He will then dispose of his prisoners at leisure." The minister beamed. "Delightfully simple, isn't it?"

Sir Guy did not trust himself to reply immediately. He toyed with the notion of setting his knife to this lecher's throat and extracting a promise of safe-conduct, but almost simultaneously reason gained the ascendancy and he cast the impulse aside. What was it old Paxton had said: *He goes best who goes gentlest?*

"Am I then to consider myself, not a guest, but a prisoner?" he asked steadily.

The Grand Equerry nodded. "That is correct," he said. "But . . . if you and your fellow conspirators were to *escape*, aided by a deserter from my guard who might wish to serve with the Emperor . . ." He giggled softly. "I say, *if* such a thing should happen, why, it is very likely neither I, *nor* Sylvester, would discover you had got away until Ivan himself rode in to claim his prize. Conceive our astonishment—especially Sylvester's."

The tides of Sir Guy's hopes had ebbed and flooded so often since the inception of this remarkable conversation, he refused to let it soar again.

"Do I understand, sir, you will aid us to escape?" he asked.

"Oh dear, *no!*" breathed the minister in mock horror. "Good heavens, man, I never take part in subterfuges! God forbid! No, no, you misunderstand! What I said was that *if*—mark you, I say *if!*—you were to approach the officer who will call before you have broken your fast in the morning, I would not be surprised at anything which may happen. I've suspected the treacherous dog for a long time."

Sir Guy managed a smile. "I shall submit to the inevitable and place myself in the hands of . . ."

"*Kismet!*" interrupted the minister. "I am a great believer in Kismet—with a little urging, of course."

"Of course," agreed Sir Guy. "In which case I shall not further burden your Grace's mind with my problem."

The Grand Equerry smiled and pulled himself to his feet. "Good night!" he purred. Once more the tireless satyr was given a brief respite as the tapestry parted to close quickly behind a satiated little old man who happened also to be the Chief Minister of Muscovy.

22

WHETHER DUE TO fatigue or the incredible visitation of the Grand Equerry, Sir Guy slept fitfully through a series of horrendous nightmares wherein he and the Chief Minister of Muscovy were pursued through celestial corridors by uncounted thousands of beauteous and over-ardent maidens, while following this amorous pack came Affable Jones, chanting ribald doggerels, and Sergeant Pistol accompanying him on a zither. This at-any-other-time-pleasant dream left him so exhausted, that when, shortly after the break of day, he was awakened by an officer of the Palace Guard, it took him some time to get his wits together.

To begin with, the officer was not at all what Sir Guy had expected. Instead of a shrewd, seasoned man-of-the-world, here was a callow youth barely out of his teens, with an overzealous stiffness of manner and a strained, humorless face. The "child," as Sir Guy silently dubbed him, sported a reddish pubescent-looking beard and a do-or-die expression that emphasized his adolescence.

After awakening Sir Guy, the officer stood at such rigid attention the Englishman wondered if he had suffered a sudden paralytic stroke. It became evident he was waiting to be "approached," so after downing a goblet of *aquavitae* which had been placed at his bedside, Sir Guy eyed him warily.

"Do you know when my audience will be granted?" he probed tentatively.

The "child" stared rigidly at a spot over the Englishman's head. "Sir, you are refused an audience!" He spoke as if reciting a well-rehearsed lesson. "Sir, it becomes my duty to arrest you! The guard awaits outside the door!"

Since he made no immediate move to call the guard, Sir Guy fished a little deeper.

"By my troth, this is unthinkable!" he cried with a fine show of indignation. "The Grand Prince will be infuriated at this outrage when it reaches his ears, as indeed it shall. As God's my life, I'll see to that!"

He looked a little closer at the tense features. "I swear you have the look of an honest man. Tell me—what is your name?"

"Stanislaus Ptucha, my lord!" reported the officer. "Sub-lieutenant in the Palace Guard of the Grand Equerry of . . ."

"Splendid!" cut in Sir Guy with enthusiasm. "Look you, Lieutenant, is there not some way . . . er . . . that is . . . of getting me out of here? The Emperor would not prove ungrateful, I vow! Nor would I!"

Lieutenant Ptucha kept his eyes fixed on infinity, but his skin had paled. "I can make the necessary arrangements, sir!"

The Englishman swung his legs out of bed. "By God, I admire a man of decision! What do we do now?"

"Dress and accompany me, sir!" intoned the officer.

The rest was so realistically carried out that Sir Guy began to lose confidence in the implied promises of the Grand Equerry. First, he was taken before a large gathering of *boyars* where in the presence of all he was officially "refused" an audience with the minister and denounced as a trespasser by a minor aide. After that, he, Affable Jones, and Sergeant Pistol were unceremoniously hauled through various parts of the palace for all to witness their degradation, then dropped into a cell which made the Metropolitane's hell-hole seem, by comparison, a favorite's boudoir.

As the cell door clanged shut behind them, Sergeant Pistol groaned. "Ye cert ye didn't jes' dream it larst night, sir?" he asked.

Sir Guy took no offense. He was beginning to wonder about that very possibility.

"W'at I admires about these Muskies," observed Affable, "is they never tips their 'and. Ye carn't imargine w'at's comin' next!"

"Ayant *that* the bloody trufe?" agreed Sergeant Pistol.

This particular statement proved prophetic as well as accurate, for what came next was one of the most appetizing and ample meals any of them had ever eaten. Later, as Affable lay belching in happy discomfort, he said: "See w'at I mean, Pistol?"

But the sergeant was too full for utterance.

Drugged with food, they contrived to sleep most of the day. As darkness filtered into the cell, more food and drink was brought them. Even the customarily ravenous Pistol could not down another bite, but he did cache the bottled refreshments in corners of the cell against a future emergency.

With so much time on their hands, it was inevitable that Sir Guy's thoughts should stray to his companions in the other prison across the city. He tried not to dwell on their plight, especially Ellen's; he needed his wits sharp and his nerves cool in the event an escape was being arranged. Yet he could not help but wonder if she was alive. Her death, he felt certain, would mean the death of them all.

He wondered, too, what had become of Count Nikita? Doubtless he had won his freedom; he must have, to have cooperated with Pojorski in the attempt to liberate Ellen and Charity. But why had he acquiesced in such a vicious scheme as the sacrificing of the tavern keeper's girls? Sir Guy shook his head; there was a cold-bloodedness about these Muscovites an Englishman could never hope to understand.

Thinking of Ellen automatically brought Charity into focus. He still felt guilty over his pique and ill-temper when he had discovered she was not Ellen during the escape, and his clumsy effort to correct that blunder had gone from bad to worse until he climaxed it with his subsequent reproach of her conduct with the Grand Equerry. And what now twisted the knife in his conscience was the undeniable fact that the Grand Equerry himself had not exhibited any sign of umbrage. He cursed softly and tried to crowd the whole matter out of his mind.

The darkness lengthened, then grew opaque. Still no one called for them. Finally, Pistol heaved a sigh.

"Think ye 'e'll show up, sir?" he asked without preamble.

"If you refer to the 'child,'" snorted Sir Guy, "it would be hard to say."

From the gloom across the cell came the bubbling chuckle of the irrepressible Jones.

"W'at's worryin' me, gents, is—supposin' the chee-ild does come to lead us astray, 'oo's to chynge the nipper's diapers, 'e's so tender in 'is years."

"Not I," laughed Sir Guy, glad of the diversion. "I'm a bachelor!"

"Me, too," grumbled Pistol dourly. "I ain't got no brats . . . well, none to speak of, as the sayin' is. It'll 'ave to be ye, Affable; ye bein' the on'y married man amongst us!"

Sir Guy whistled. "'Pon my soul, I didn't know you had ventured on the pikes of matrimony, Affable!"

"Aye, I got 'ooked onc't," Affable confessed blithely, "but got me a dee-vorce!"

"Oh, come now!" scoffed the knight. "Only the Parliament and the Queen can grant a divorce. And I feel reasonably certain, for all your dubious charm, you have scant influence at Whitehall!"

"True—every blessed word o' it!" conceded Affable. "Yet, if I ayant w'at ye might call pop'lar at White'all, I be a fair-'aired laddie in Whitefriars, an' that's w'ere I got me a dee-vorce!"

"By my troth, that's a new one on me!" Sir Guy said sarcastically. "I never even heard of a 'Whitefriars' divorce'! Pray what authority sanctions such a thing?"

"W'y the Bible, no less!" insisted Affable Jones. "W'en the bishop married us out o' it, 'e read some'at about 'lettin' no man put asunder' an' *'on'y death do us part!'* Ain't it so, m'lud?"

"Why, I own that is true, Affable! I take it your wife died, then?"

"On the contrary, the bitch 'opped off wi' a *courtesyman!*" acknowledged Affable, without regret. "So w'en I found out w'ere she was livin', I got me a dead cat an' called on her."

Sir Guy gasped. "*A dead cat?* You jest, surely?"

"No, sir. That pussy was dead, every last nine lives o' 'er! So I talked it o'er wi' me faithless spouse, an' 'er bein' h'agreeable, we got a Whitefriars' dee-vorce by puttin' the dead cat on the floor an' me bitch walkin' on one side o' the carcass w'ilest I walked on the other—that is to s'y *until death* (the cat's) *done us part!* That's w'at the Good Book s'ys, an' that's enough fer us! Proper clever, eh?" And Affable whooped with laughter.[9]

Their merriment was cut short by the arrival of the "child."

"Gentlemen!" he hissed melodramatically. " 'Tis time to fly!"

"Not until I collecks this bloody liquor, it ayant!" growled Sergeant Pistol, as he groped in the darkness for his recently hidden loot.

Lieutenant Ptucha appeared to be entirely alone, so when they were escorted into the dim-lit corridor, Sir Guy asked him where he had left Charity. The youngster paled at the very intimation that a woman should accompany them.

"In Muscovy, sir," he gasped, "we do not carry women on such escapades as this one."

"I don't give a whoop in hell what you do in Muscovy!" snapped Sir Guy. "I came in here with that young woman, and I'm not leaving without her!"

But Ptucha was equally adamant. The lieutenant swore that Charity was safely and circumspectly ensconced in her own quarters in the women's wing of the palace. He was quite emphatic that she could not be included in their break, since all arrangements had been made on the basis of their present number, four males.

In the end, a compromise was reached. Sir Guy agreed that Charity need not accompany them if he could have sufficient time to visit with her and explain the situation; Ptucha concurred in this provided Sir Guy would limit his visit to a maximum of five minutes. He also engaged to guide the Englishman to the girl's apartment.

So leaving Affable Jones and Sergeant Pistol in the now unlocked cell, Sir Guy followed his guide through the sleeping palace. He had no conception of the time, but he presumed it was well after midnight. They reached the so-called "female wing" without event, but at a turn in the great circular staircase leading to the second story, they were intercepted by a globular old eunuch.

Apparently the fat creature had been dozing on the stairs, for he appeared to rise out of the very carpet before them. The surprise was so complete, they had no opportunity to retreat. The lieutenant stood stock-still, but Sir Guy reached for the little dagger he had concealed in his sash. The eunuch read the meaning of the motion, for he held up his fat hands in a placating gesture.

"Peace be with you, master!" he said in bad Latin. "You have come to see the English female, I presume?"

"How did you know?" asked the lieutenant in an awed voice.

The old slave cackled again. He seemed a right jolly sort. "Ah, young master, you might call it a sixth sense, or almost anything you please. Is it not enough that I have waited half the night to conduct this tall Englishman to the maid's bedside without having to explain my mental processes?"

Sir Guy gave a grim nod. "Lead on!" he told the slave, who plucked a candle from a sconce on the wall, and padded silently ahead of them. The two men exchanged wondering glances, then Sir Guy shrugged and fell in behind the eunuch. After a moment's hesitation, Lieutenant Ptucha followed.

Eventually their guide stopped before a stout hardwood door of beautiful design, and from beneath the maze of cloth that comprised his swaddled garment, fished out a large key which he fitted into the slot. Never had Sir Guy heard a lock function so soundlessly. Shoving the door slightly ajar, the old slave withdrew his key and stepped back.

"The threshold to paradise—or so they tell me!" he chortled wickedly. "You are young and virile; how much time will you require, master?"

"Keep a civil tongue in your head!" the Englishman snarled at him. "And you, Lieutenant, keep your eye on him! Slit his throat at the first sign of treachery!" On that note, he jerked the candle out of the slave's hand, and stepped into the room.

He had not known quite what to expect, but what he did encounter shook him to the very marrow of his bones. It was a scene no detail of which he would ever forget.

Through a bank of triple windows along one side of the chamber streamed three rose-tinted shafts of moonlight which by some clever

[184]

artificial means—perhaps a slight angling of the panes—appeared to converge in one blazing, golden halo on the massive bed. Unlike English beds, which were posted and curtained, this huge couch was as open as a downy cushion. And in its exact center, spotlighted by all the glorious radiance of the moon's beams, little Charity lay, curled as gracefully as a kitten. She was asleep.

But her slumber was not the ordinary limp, wheezing collapse; rather she looked vitally alive, a tiny half-smile teasing one side of her generous mouth. Plainly her dreams were pleasant.

For some reason which he did not then—or ever, for that matter—understand, Sir Guy felt almost overwhelmed with embarrassment. Perchance it was a sense of intruding into the presence of a dream; perhaps . . . but this was not the time for speculation.

"*Charity!*" he cried sharply, almost defensively. "In God's name, *wake up!*"

She sat up with a start, fully awake now, her eyes rounded in wonder.

"*Sir Guy* . . . ?" she gasped. "Did ye walk out o' me dream?" Having seen enough outward manifestations of that dream to guess at its content, Sir Guy was a trifle nonplused. Yet when she moved over and gestured for him to sit down beside her, he forced himself to comply.

"Listen to me, Charity," he said grimly. "We're leaving in a couple of minutes, so you must heed what I tell you!"

She whipped around on the bed and started to rise, but he gently caught her arm and pushed her back on the bed.

"No, Charity—not you!" he told her. "It is no journey for a woman!"

She said: "*O-oh!*" with a world of expression in it, and settled back. "I ayant wanted, m'lud?"

"Let's not go into that again," he pleaded. "To be frank with you, I argued a long time with the man who is taking us away. He insisted it was far too dangerous a trip for you."

"'Ave I ever shrunk from danger, m'lud?"

"Would that I had a company of men of your kidney, Charity! I'd be unbeatable!"

"Ye be unbeatable wi'out me kidney, as ye calls it, though I thankee kindly fer the thought. Gi' me yer orders, an' though I'd ride by yer heel were the choice me own, I'll obey ye, sir!"

So he told her the whole story of his talk with the Grand Equerry, the double-talk which resulted in the appearance of Stanislaus Ptucha and the subsequent "arrest."

"I hate like the very devil to leave you, Charity!" he reiterated. "I hope you'll be safe here."

She sniffed. "I'll be safe enough, sir! W'at could 'appen?"

"Some of these men . . ." he began, then his voice trailed away as he realized the ridiculousness of what he was saying. Charity saw it, too, for she burst into laughter.

"Glory be, sir! There's naught could be done to me w'at ayant been done afore, save the slittin' o' me throat, w'ich God willin', won't 'appen!" At the sudden rush of color to his cheeks, she put a hand over her face and giggled heartily.

"Lor' love ye, Sir Guy, ye're jes' like all men!" she teased, her eyes laughing between the lattice of her fingers. "Willin' to pertect any woman against any man but 'imself!"

He contrived a grin, albeit a woeful one. "Charity, you're an undisciplined vixen!" he chided her, rising to his feet. "I should not have come!"

"Oh, say ye not so, m'lud!" she cried contritely. "If I've said some'at wrong, I beg yer forgiveness! Aye, I knows I jests w'en I should cry, m'lud, yet life be grim enough wi'out tears, an' sometimes a little laughter sort of brightens things a mite."

"You cover me with shame!" he said. He pulled himself together. "Keep smiling then until our return. Then we'll get Ellen and . . ." He bogged down again. Resolutely, he turned towards the door.

"Good night, Charity."

"*M'lud! Sir Guy!*"

He paused, then turned slowly.

"Yes, Charity?"

The smile on her lips was belied by the suspicious shimmer welling in her big eyes.

"M'lud, may I arsk one boon, in case we may never meet again?"

He forced a jocular laugh. "Why, don't talk like that, girl! We'll meet ere the week has run its course!"

"May God grant that's so, m'lud! Yet our little company has been scattered an' . . ." She swallowed, but kept her chin high. "It's such a little thing I'd beg from ye, sir?"

"Name it, Charity?" he said. "And if it's mine to give, by heaven, you shall have it and welcome."

"Certes, an' 'tis yours!" she whispered. "Would ye *kiss* me, sir?"

When he stood blinking in surprise, it was she who grew embarrassed. "Oh, it will mean naught to ye, m'lud!" she cried impulsively. "I knows me stytion, an' 'ow much gall I 'as to arsk a great knight like ye to stoop to sech a thing! Yet, base-born an' ignerant though

I be, I am a woman fer a' it! We none o' us knows w'at termorrow 'olds, and since we may not see each other again in this life, I'd thankee kindly, sir, fer jes' one kiss!"

He was suffused with a tenderness quite apart from desire. He stepped over to the edge of the bed and took her in his arms. She was strangely shy, as if this was a new thing, never before experienced—which, perchance, it was. With his nose, he pushed aside an unruly curl that had sprung between their faces, then her mouth hungrily sought his. He was astonished at the gentle flexibility of her lips; theirs was the clean, cool softness of dew-moist rose petals. Her bare arms entwined his shoulders, her fingers explored his neck and ears in a kind of wondering eagerness.

"Sir Guy! 'Tis time ... *Oh, sir, a thousand pardons!*"

Sir Guy released his hold and whirled in a rage he had difficulty controlling. But the sight of young Ptucha framed in the doorway, his mouth sagged open and his face flame-colored, brought the Englishman to his senses.

"Get out!" he managed shakily. "I'll be with you in a moment!"

The lieutenant was only too glad to escape and would have pulled the door closed, but Sir Guy caught and held it ajar. Then with his exit assured, he was about to turn again to Charity, when her voice stopped him.

"Please, sir, don't look back!" she pleaded. "Don't *ever* look back! Go now, I beg ye, an' wi' ye goes this prayer from the little Lunnon 'ore ye was kind to: May the dear Lord bless an' keep ye, an' bring ye that w'ich ye desire wi'out knowin' it!"

"God bless you, Charity!"

He did her bidding; he closed the door behind him without looking backward.

23

SIR GUY AND LIEUTENANT PTUCHA returned to the others in silence, and in silence the lieutenant led them through a maze of passageways and underground tunnels until at long last they found themselves in a small stable where in semi-darkness a peasant cart was being loaded with vegetables for the great markets just outside the walls of Moscow. The lieutenant then explained that they must submit to burial in the produce in order to pass safely through the city gates.

"I wish't to 'ell we could myke up our minds onc't an' fer all!" grumbled Sergeant Pistol. "On'y a couple d'ys ago, we risked our necks to get through them damn gytes t'other w'y!"

While Ptucha pulled a grimy peasant costume over his immaculate uniform—for he was to drive the vehicle—the three Englishmen burrowed into the cart and permitted themselves to be covered. A minor crisis developed at this point when Pistol discovered under what particular vegetable he was being interred; he all but refused to proceed and it required the full force of Sir Guy's dominance to subdue him.

"Worser'n anythin' else in this bloody world," he wailed plaintively, *"I 'ates turnips!"*

The journey proved so uneventful, Sir Guy was certain he could recognize the skillful touch of a master intriguer, and his respect for the wily old Grand Equerry rose accordingly. Peculiarly enough, young Ptucha did not seem aware how adroitly everything had been arranged in advance, for he suffered agonies of apprehension at every potentially dangerous point.

They remained buried in the turnips for less than three hours—during which time Sergeant Pistol complained more bitterly than he had since leaving England—following which they were exhumed at a small inn. Here, two hostlers awaited them with excellent Turkish horses, fully accoutered for the road. After a hasty toilet, they were in the saddle and riding hard to the westward, where Ivan IV was engaged in one phase of his perennial war with the Poles.

It was obvious that an agent of the Grand Equerry had preceded them, and a most remarkable procurator he was; for regardless of what time of the night or day they galloped into a *cursemay*, food, drink and fresh, magnificent steeds were invariably ready and waiting. Many times on that arduous journey did Sir Guy mutter a blessing for this unknown but efficient genius.

Howbeit, despite these well-greased facilities and a killing pace, the trip took slightly over three days. Impatient as he was, Sir Guy had to confess the time was not wasted, for not only did he garner much valuable information about Muscovy and the Muscovites in general, he gleaned some highly pertinent facts about two men, widely disparate in character and rank, whose shadows were already falling across his path—Stanislaus Ptucha, their guide, and that fantastic enigma Ivan IV, Tsar of All the Russias.

What Sir Guy learned about the former was largely by a sort of half-conscious absorption, for at the time he was not particularly interested. Yet if he had started the journey with a feeling of mild contempt for the stiff-necked young officer, he ended with a grudging, if puzzled, admiration.

To begin with, Stanislaus Ptucha was the antithesis of all Guy Spangler knew and believed in. He was young, even for his adolescent years, painfully naïve, and honest to a point of prudery.

He fairly burst with ideals—of loyalty, of *noblesse oblige,* of knight-errantry. To the Englishman's incredulity, the boy *was* deserting the ennui of the Grand Equerry's luxuriant sinecure to place his sword at the disposal of his Emperor! That kind of selfless patriotism was beyond Sir Guy's imagination.

And as rigidly honest men are often blinded by their own sincerity to a degree where they become the dupes of crafty schemers, so had young Ptucha become the unwitting tool of the wily old chief minister. Yet Ptucha was not blinded in his observation of others; and in their three days of close association, riding stirrup to stirrup, he offered the most balanced and impartial verbal portrait of the Emperor, Sir Guy had yet received.

Born about 1533, Ivan was three years old when his father, Basil III, died, and his mother, Helen Glinsky of Lithuania, was proclaimed Regent. She promptly took on a lover, a Prince Obolensky, who ruled in her name—a name she made accursed in her own right by acts of cruelty never before equaled in Muscovy. She soon became known by the *boyars* as "Helen the Terrible," and by the people, as "That Drinker of Blood!" The *boyars* eventually wearied of this diabolical pair, poisoned Helen and tossed her lover into a dungeon where presumably he starved to death.

The Shuisky family then connived to control the Regency, and their handling of the somber young Ivan was such as to warp his character still further. Kept in strict "protective custody," ill fed and poorly clad, he was permitted neither tutor nor honest friend. Yet by some strange whim of Fate, but certainly through no fault of the Shuiskys, he contrived to lay hands on a Bible and some history books. These he studied avidly.

Sensitive and imaginative, he had been heartbroken over the terrible cruelties perpetrated before his childish eyes; but from his reading, he came to realize that to seize power one had to be ruthless. So he searched through the Old Testament for texts dealing with authority and obedience to regal power.

It soon became manifest he learned well, for at thirteen years of age, he abruptly turned Andrei Shuisky, head of the offending clan, over to the executioner, and seized the reins in his own hands. He chose three relatively low-born churchmen for advisors, and for a while followed their counsels.

But the *boyars* intrigued, and unwittingly taught young Ivan another lesson—that he must look to the common people, not to the nobles, for support. This unorthodox precept was dramatized when he was about seventeen, when, after the burning of Moscow, the *boyars* attributed the conflagration to witchcraft and began to threaten Ivan. Once again the young monarch acted with decision; turning his soldiers on the *boyars*, he began a series of executions which won him his dual titles.

From infancy he had been a contradiction, and these paradoxical traits increased with age, until he oscillated between the opposite poles of virtue and vice. In adolescence he passed his time either in deeply religious worship or in violently licentious and riotous living. Later, while surpassing his evil mother in exaggerated forms of cruelty, he became at the same time distinguished for his exalted love of justice, and at his personal order he had compiled a body of equitable laws known as "The Book of Justice." The most intemperate of men, he abominated intemperance, and severely punished this degrading vice in both prince and serf. Despite his faulty childhood and lack of formal education, he was, at maturity, eminently learned and well advanced in his views on science, religion and politics. He made it possible for the lowest of his subjects to petition him direct. Conversely, one of his keenest pleasures was the old Russian sport of setting a savage bear on an unarmed peasant. But in his cruelties he was no snob; he kept in a little notebook a list of the *boyars* he slaughtered with his own hand. It was these lightning-like shifts in mood that kept his people in such an agonized welter of perpetual suspense.

"Lor' lumme!" marveled Affable Jones. "'Ow the ruddy 'ell does ye ken w'ether the tide o' 'is humor be *in* er *out*?"

Sir Guy shrugged. "Apparently there's no way of knowing, Affable. It's a chance one has to take."

"Ye're a gambler, Mister Jones!" sneered Pistol. "Ye dote on chawnces!"

"Not the w'y *I* gamble, I don't!" chortled Affable Jones.

Invaluable as was all this intelligence about the Emperor, the two most astounding tid-bits of information gleaned from Lieutenant Ptucha concerned two of Sir Guy's own accomplices—Pojorski and Count Nikita. For the dwarf, despite all his bombast and swagger, was naught but a *slave* belonging to the Emperor; and the Count, even though trusted with an embassy, was, in essence, a *hostage* to the Tsar!

At first, Sir Guy could not credit this news. "By my troth!" he protested. "This is incredible! Pojorski had such an influence that even Nikita was wary of him!"

"As well he might be!" Ptucha said grimly. "That insensate fiend is a blight, a curse, which I pray the Almighty will never let defile my path!"

"What happened to him? I heard the Grand Equerry had him racked!"

"His Excellency would have been better advised to have had him beheaded!" muttered the lieutenant. "It was whispered about the palace that he finally turned him over to the strangler. Howbeit, that is but gossip, for the Grand Equerry never lets his left hand know what his right is doing."

"But where did Pojorski come from?" persisted the Englishman.

Ptucha sniffed. "Nobody knows, not even Pojo himself. Legend has it he was captured as an infant in a raid on a caravan by Tatars, who were fascinated by his hideous shape. These barbarians taught him their most despicable forms of cruelty, then gave him to some Khan who furthered the hellish curriculum. He passed through many hands and many countries, so 'tis said, until the Sultan of Turkey presented him to our Grand Prince. By that time, Pojorski was as skilled in the merciless works of Shaitan as was possible for a living creature.

"Ivan, eventually wearied of his turgid grandiloquence, loaned him to the Grand Equerry, who being unable to tolerate him, passed him along to the Metropolitane as a barbed jest. Unfortunately, he has a most insidious talent for absorbing and collecting information which makes him more dangerous than an adder to have around. That doubtless is why Nikita shies away from him, as you say."

Sir Guy frowned. "You must be mistaken about the Count being a hostage!" he probed.

"Oh, that is common knowledge, sir!" insisted the lieutenant. "Nikita's Uncle Akhmet, Khan of Crimea, was one of the hereditary Tatar princes who had broken away from their allegiance to the Golden Horde to set up an independent sovereignty. Ivan crushed Akhmet many years ago, but it took a gigantic army to win that war and exacted a frightful toll. To consolidate the victory would have meant maintaining a full-scale army in Crimea, which was impractical, so Ivan and Akhmet reached a compromise: Akhmet's principality would become a Prince-Dominion in the greater Russian confederacy, with Akhmet as hereditary Governor. To insure his loyalty, if not obedience, his favorite nephew and successor, Count Nikita, was made a 'member' of Ivan's household—in fine, a *hostage*—to be indoctrinated into the Tsar's philosophy."

"The Count," remarked Sir Guy, "seems to have learned his lesson well."

Ptucha shrugged. "Time will tell."

Sir Guy searched the youthful features for some hint of his meaning, but finding none, asked bluntly: "You do not trust Count Nikita, Lieutenant?"

The officer reddened. "Sir! It is not for me to criticize a member of my Prince's household! Yet this I will say: he who trusts a Tatar may live to repent it. Truly hath a great sage observed: 'A Tatar puts on a civilized hat, coat, and breeches, then calls himself a Russian. Verily, thou mayest as well tie the wings of a goose to thy back and call thyself an angel!'"

By late afternoon of the third day, the four adventurers were within ten leagues of the Emperor's cantonment, and Sir Guy was all for pushing ahead without pause. But Lieutenant Ptucha argued against it, pointing out that they could not possibly reach their destination until well after midnight. He also told them about the marauding Cossacks and Tatars which Ivan turned loose at night, like packs of bandogs, who would slaughter any living thing they encountered in the darkness.

Convinced, finally, that to disregard the lieutenant's counsel would be tantamount to suicide, Sir Guy stifled his impatience and agreed to stop for the night at a small inn which Ptucha had listed on his "schedule." Mayhap Fate had a finger in the pie, for it was here they overtook the mysterious agent-procurator who had so efficiently expedited their passage.

They found this minor genius awaiting them in the common-room of the little *cursemay*, with mugs and well-filled flagons already set up around the board and a fat fowl turning on the spit. At sight of him, the saddle-weary travelers were rendered mute with astonishment, and none more so than Stanislaus Ptucha.

"By the sainted memory of my mother!" he gasped. "I would have sworn on the Blessed Cross that you were either dead, or buried in my Master's dungeon!"

"Phoof, that is naught but wishful thinking, my cherubic innocent!"

jeered the *agent*, who was none other than Pojorski the dwarf. "Old Boris Smolovitch is much too intelligent to let my talents wither in a cell. We soon reached an exquisite understanding, he and I!" He let his little pig-eyes dance towards the others. "Ah, by the seven glorious stages of Paradise, I declare it is a treat to see you, my comrades! I burn with good news for you!"

The very sight of the pernicious imp had revived the apprehensive ache in Sir Guy's diaphragm—an inexplicable portent that was growing chronic.

"And this news . . . ?" he prompted warily.

"Why, comrades, I have arranged an audience for us with my Supreme Master for high noon tomorrow!" he crowed, then gave the Englishman a significant look. "I trust you will not forget your pledge to credit *Pojo* with your presence, if not your very existence? It would grieve me to be deceived!"

"I shall not forget," Sir Guy assured him.

Cackling gleefully, the dwarf scrambled stiffly onto the settle and brandished his mug on high. "Gentlemen—a toast!" he cried. "By the grace of God, may we all survive this audience with our joints intact!"

Sir Guy felt a little chill play up his spine, but he laughed it off and seized a mug.

"In sooth, I'll drink to that right willing!"

Sergeant Pistol passed over a mug to snatch up the flagon. "Me, I'll drink to anythin'—yeah, even Pojo!"

24

THE ANXIOUS LITTLE COMPANY left the inn before cockcrow, and piloted now by Pojorski, who had already traversed the route, they made such excellent time that by mid-morning they topped a rise and sighted the Muscovite army arrayed before the walls of Kalie, a city momentarily occupied by the Poles.

By common consent, the quintette drew rein on the summit to survey the spectacular panorama. Even Sir Guy, jaded by martial experiences in many countries, had never witnessed a lustier sight. A gigantic prairie, well over a league in width and brilliantly carpeted with flowers, extended from the very knoll on which the watchers stood to the banks of a bonny river on whose shore the beleaguered city crouched at bay. Kalie's history was writ in her architecture, for the place had changed hands many times in the centuries of chronic warfare between Muscovite and Pole; the gorgeous minarets of its numerous mosques mingled with the gilded domes of Christian churches and the towers of innumerable palaces.

Anticipating a lengthy siege, the Muscovites had erected before the walls of Kalie, just beyond the range of the Polish cannon, a rival city of tents for sixty thousand men. Gay, vividly colored and emblazoned they were, and laid out in orderly streets, with numerous canvas churches, each with its own little plaza. In these squares stood herds of camels and great stacks of supplies captured from the Poles and their renegade Tatar allies. The pennant of each captain fluttered bravely over the striped booths until it seemed there must have been a flag for every trooper.

Across this vast meadow, little groups of soldiers moved like chessmen on a board. Most of these bands were mounted, for a Muscovite never walked where he could ride. One company rode Moorish barbs, everyone so black as to be indistinguishable from its fellow; another company galloped into view on Arabs so white they seemed to have been formed of virgin snow. There were companies mounted on tawny camels, and—to the incredulity of the watchers who had never seen the like—a small squad mounted on elephants.

Fascinated as he was, Sir Guy had no illusions as to what he was observing. At this distance it was glamorous: you could watch the tiny figures hurling themselves at the beleaguered walls without seeing the gushing blood and maimed bodies. You could hear the stirring blare of the trumpets, but not the screams of the dying. Those things Sir Guy knew, but young Ptucha drank it in through tear-starred eyes.

"Look at it, gentlemen!" he cried, his voice choked with emotion. "Dear God, how glorious! Oh, I could weep with shame when I think of the slothful months I wasted in that . . . that brothel!"

Affable Jones stood up in his stirrups to ease his tortured posterior.

"Lor' lumme!" he groaned. "I wot *I'd* like to waste some slothful months in a brothel, startin' as o' now!"

"Time in a brothel ayant never w'ysted!" muttered Sergeant Pistol.

Pojorski signaled that it was time to proceed, so they nudged their lathered jennets into motion and cantered down the incline, Sir Guy and the dwarf in the lead. But halfway down, the dwarf heaved a deep sigh, and as the Englishman had long since learned that these lusty exhalations were never without significance, he glanced sharply at his companion.

Pojorski grinned self-consciously. "By the dusty bones of my ancestors, I pray everything goes well!" he remarked.

Sir Guy sensed trouble. "Why should it not? You boasted you had arranged an audience with the Emperor."

The other grimaced. "True," he agreed. "I swear it! Howbeit, Ivan's chamberlain, a vainglorious peacock, is another who, due to his extreme jealousy, cannot be listed among my more ardent admirers."

"Forsooth, I'm beginning to wonder just who can be!" Spangler said coldly.

Pojorski ignored the jibe. "The ostentatious ass at first refused to convey my message to the Emperor, hence it became expedient to imply that the audience I requested was for the purpose of presenting the Lady Ellen."

Sir Guy drew rein so abruptly his jennet was jerked onto its hindlegs.

"Why, you damnable liar!" he thundered. "We may all be executed for this!"

Pojorski spread his hands. "It is possible," he conceded. "Yet I do not foresee anything quite so drastic. Oh, I grant you, Ivan may be slightly provoked . . ."

"*Slightly provoked?*" raged Sir Guy, visualizing his whole venture crumbling around his ears.

The dwarf chuckled. "Phoof, comrade, where is your sense of humor? We must take the bitter with the sweet. After all, I did not perjure myself in the strict sense of the word; I merely implied. Is it my fault if that chamberlain let his prejudice against me befog his wits?"

"It'll bloody well be your fault if we get fed to the lions!" growled Sergeant Pistol.

"W'at-'o, man! Ye got yer varmints mixed," put in Affable. "Dear ol' Ivy feeds 'is wictims to 'is '*ounds*, not lions."

"W'at in 'ell's the difference?" snarled Pistol. "Ye got a choice o' w'at eats yer?"

Sir Guy was shaken with anger. "The fault is entirely mine!" he grated at the dwarf through clenched teeth. "I should have cut your throat the first time I saw you!"

"You won't go back on your promise?" the dwarf asked blandly.

"If we live . . . no! But when this business is concluded, I have but one prayer, that I may never set eyes on you again!"

Haunted now with rekindled apprehensions, the weary travelers continued down to the floor of the valley where, amid open pits half-filled with the dead, great pyres of screaming wounded prisoners, and vulture-plucked carcasses dangling from trees, the glamor faded. This was war, meditated Sir Guy; the costumes might vary, the weapons differ slightly and the trumpets peal another note, yet men died much the same whether they called upon God or upon Allah. War meant one thing, and one thing only—*death!*

On the edge of the cantonment, they were challenged by a sentry who, on learning their identity, hastily sent for the chamberlain. This dignitary, a pompous breathless little man almost hidden in a coat of purple satin, rode up, flanked by a secretary and an interpreter. All three were mounted on magnificent white chargers caparisoned in silver. The Tsar's own Master of Horse followed, leading a score of riderless barbs, also spotlessly white.

On reaching a position about fourscore paces from the new arrivals, the entire company halted, whereupon the chamberlain and his two aides dismounted and advanced on foot. Sir Guy gestured for his companions to follow suit, then sprang to the ground, uncovered his head, and walked forward to meet the welcoming committee with as much dignity as his aching bones would permit.

The chamberlain was, manifestly, one of those snobs who make appraisals solely on the basis of externals. In his flushed, lined face, his little eyes looked like spent musket-balls stuck in a pumpkin. His gaze flicked over the visitors with the nervous gyrations of a wasp. Nevertheless, he had ridden forth to do a duty, and he did it. In the dreary voice of a pedant reciting a monotonous lesson, he spoke his piece, while the interpreter echoed it in mutilated French.

"Honored sirs! The Grand Seigneur, Tsar and Great Duke, Ivan the Fourth, conservator of All the Russias, Prince of Vladimir, Moscow, Novogorod, Tsar of Kazan, Tsar of Astrakan . . ." The chamberlain sucked in a fresh supply of wind and rattled on: "Lord and Great Duke of Novogorod in the Low Countries, Commander of all the North, Lord and Sovereign of many other Seigneuries, receives you, as great Ambassador from his most precious friend, Elizabeth, Queen of England!"

At this point, the chamberlain contrived to stop so abruptly it had the sound, which was doubtless intentional, of drastically minimizing the English Queen's domain. Then with a little sniff, he concluded: "His Sublime Highness grants you and the *gentlemen*"—by emphasis he twisted the knife in that one, too—"the favor to make your official entrance upon his own horses, and hath appointed me *Pristaff* to have a care of you and to furnish you with all things necessary during your sojourn in this encampment."

As he and Sir Guy vied to outdo each other in the depths of their bows, Affable Jones was heard to remark: "No bloody wonder 'e needs a secretary! 'E damn nigh *ski*-ed me to death! W'at's a *Pristaff?*"

"Could be Muskie fer *bastard,* I swear," snorted Pistol.

Fortunately, the interpreter was too fatigued from his windy oration to catch this lese majesty. Too, at this precise moment, the chamberlain was demanding the whereabouts of the "English princess."

Once again Pojorski tried to worm into the limelight by commencing an involved evasion, but Sir Guy brusquely cut him off. Without accusing the Metropolitane by name, he explained to the haughty chamberlain that he and his entourage had been seized and thrown into prison at the order of a "certain high-ranking Muscovite"; that he and the two English *gentlemen* (and Sir Guy larded this with his own emphasis) now accompanying him were the only ones to escape; that he would explain the details to the Grand Prince in person, and concluded with the prayer that his audience be expedited with all possible haste.

The chamberlain received all this with the glassy stare of a moneylender. He refused to carry any further communications to the Tsar on the grounds that he had been grievously deceived once by the Englishman's messenger—to wit, Pojorski—and he was not going to be embarrassed a second time. The agendum of the audience clearly specified the presence of the "English princess," hence . . . *no princess, no audience.*

Sir Guy tried all his wiles, to no avail. From this position the chamberlain would not budge, and when in desperation the Englishman threatened to ignore him and go direct to the Emperor without regard for official protocol, the outraged chamberlain bleated for the guard.

A nasty incident was in the making. Then, with a blaring of trumpets, jangle of harness and arms, and the lusty clamor of great hounds, around a corner of tents swept a magnificent galaxy of some two hundred cavaliers, arrayed as if for battle except that their heads were uncovered. And at the head of this gallant cavalcade, shining as resplendently as a diamond among lesser gems, rode Ivan, Tsar of Muscovy!

On sighting the little band of Englishmen, the whole glittering company set spurs to their mounts and charged at a full gallop. Sir Guy caught his breath, for it did not seem possible the gigantic warhorses could be brought to a standstill before they had trampled the handful of men in their path. Plainly the chamberlain and his flunkies held the same thought, for they scurried for cover squealing like terrified rats. Then almost at the seeming moment of impact, the great steeds dropped their haunches and, in a cloud of dust, slid to a quivering stop within a fathom's length of the visitors.

Neither Sir Guy nor—he was proud to note—any of his company had moved. When the Emperor's suite had halted, the chamberlain came strutting forward, but the jeers of the nobles drove him back until he stood sullen and disconsolate on the sidelines, awaiting from his Prince a summons which never came.

Forking a superb Turkish charger with all the natural grace of a centaur, Ivan the Fourth looked every inch the monarch. He was a handsome, virile man, tall, well-formed, with high, wide shoulders and a broad and powerful chest. His face with its beaked nose, high cheekbones, and biting eyes had a decidedly predatory cast, heightened by a faintly sinister expression. This was contradictorily modified by an enigmatical smile which played around the corners of his mouth. It was a highly intelligent and sensitive face.

His elegant costume was in keeping with his station. His muscular figure was sheathed in a long, ankle-length coat of scarlet-colored silk, sumptuously embroidered, and on his dark head he wore a tall conical cap, embellished with precious stones and surmounted by gilded plumes which flourished in the wind. A short sword and a poniard sparkled in his girdle. His warhorse was fittingly bejeweled and caparisoned.

So much was Sir Guy able to absorb before he bowed in obeisance. At a sharp command, he looked up to find the Emperor leaning out of his saddle, proffering his hand to be kissed.

This was a signal honor, and Sir Guy moved to comply when Lieutenant Ptucha, who had edged up beside him, hissed a warning: "For the love of God—*do not touch his hand with one of yours!*"

Sir Guy was about to accede to this warning, when of a sudden the characteristic perversity inherent in him surged to the surface. Had he not knelt before the proudest monarchs of the world—the Kings of France and Spain and, greatest of them all, England's Elizabeth? He had raised their royal hands to his lips with his own, and, certainly, he would pay this Muscovite potentate not a whit more homage than he would his own beloved sovereign!

With cool deliberation, he reached for the Tsar's hand, and firmly lifted it to his lips!

Even with bent head, he sensed the tension and glimpsed some of the nearest *boyars* start towards him, then out of his wary eye, he saw Ivan motion them away. Sir Guy stepped back and raised his eye to find the Emperor smiling at him. It was more than a friendly smile; it was the smile of an intrepid man capable of appreciating intrepidity in another. Ivan spoke briefly to an interpreter, who reiterated the welcome with none of the chamberlain's wearisome verbiage.

Sir Guy, matching this admirable brevity, replied in suitable terms, after which the interpreter explained that the Tsar and his suite had ridden forth with the intention of meeting the English embassy en route and personally conveying the "Ambassador" and the English "princess" into camp.

This was the moment Sir Guy had long dreaded, for the interpreter's statement, was, in effect, a question: *"Where is the princess?"*

Sir Guy paused. Across the screen of his mind flashed other moments when his life had seemed suspended by a hair—in Spain, in Venice, a certain night in Burgundy, in Panama—yet, somehow, none of those incidents had held quite the same exquisite suspense he felt now. These arrogant nobles, more virile and more violent than those who had clustered around the Metropolitane or even the Grand Equerry, seemed blood brothers to the dozen or so slavering hounds straining against silver leashes held by burly handlers. These savage beasts symbolized his plight, for a word, even a slight nod, from this despot was sufficient to send them speeding for his throat. Any fool could plainly see that this was a time for extreme caution and discretion, if not humility and deference.

But Guy Spangler was not "any fool." In daring to ignore convention by touching the Emperor's hand, he had measured the temper of his man. It would strain credulity to say that Sir Guy Spangler of England and Ivan, Tsar of All the Russias, were two of a kind, yet it soon became evident they shared at least one trait in common—courage, with the concomitant ability to recognize it. So, following his unvarying practice of boldly attacking when everything seemed lost, he assumed the offensive.

"Your Majesty!" he began boldly, yet without insolence. "In the name of my gracious and adored Sovereign, Elizabeth, Queen of England, of Scotland, of Ireland and of many other dominions beyond the distant seas—I most vigorously protest the treatment accorded Her Majesty's envoy and his previous charge, a lady of noble blood, upon their arrival in Moscow!"

He paused to appraise the results of this opening barrage. It was potent! The interpreter stumbled and stammered over his lines, and the hawkish, swarthy faces of the attending cavaliers turned black as thunderheads before a summer squall. Behind Sir Guy, young Ptucha muttered an emergency prayer. Yet the only change in the Emperor's expression was a slight pin-pointing of the eyes.

"This passeth all understanding!" he replied slowly. "You will explain." Again it was a statement, not a query; but to Sir Guy, it hinted the Emperor was a trifle nonplused.

"Willingly, sire," Sir Guy continued in the same cool vein. "For this embassy, which I have the undeserved honor to lead, came to Muscovy at the behest of your Highness, and we thus believed ourself your

Majesty's guests. It was therefore with dismay and incredulity we found our train ambushed and assaulted"—he hesitated as if reluctant to identify the guilty official, but in reality to intensify the already rapt attention of his audience—"well, *by Russian troops!*"

Having lighted the fuse, Sir Guy now tossed the bomb into the Emperor's lap.

"We escaped this first trap, only to fall into another, during which we were taken prisoner! Sire, it was unprecedented! The noble lady and her gentle companion, seized and manhandled by common soldiers as though they were criminals, and thrown in prison; the envoy of the Queen of England and his gentlemen, arriving in state as invited guests of your Majesty, mishandled and incarcerated in a foul dungeon! Sire, at the risk of life and limb, shot and pursued, I, and the two gentlemen who now accompany me, contrived to escape so that we might protest in person to your benevolent Majesty this insult to the Queen of England and this unparalleled affront to your Majesty's own authority—for we choose to believe your Majesty was totally unaware of the affair." Sir Guy bowed slightly, then played his high card.

"Meanwhile, sire, England's incomparable gift to your Majesty—the loveliest flower ever to be transplanted from that Garden of Eden— withers in a cold, dank dungeon in Moscow!"

Into the vacuum left by this blast hurtled the Emperor's question, in a voice which bespoke a rage as tenuously restrained as the hounds on their leashes.

"In God's name—*who was responsible for this outrage?*"

The Englishman bowed again. "Sire, it is not the prerogative of a visitor to criticize one of your Majesty's most exalted servants," he said smoothly. "I know only this: that I was informed the troops who ambushed us, slaughtered our brave guards, and eventually captured us, belonged to the Metropolitane of Muscovy; that my compatriots and I were dragged in the manner of common thieves before the Metropolitane; and that in my presence, this self-same Metropolitane sentenced . . ." He gagged over the words. "Sire! That delicate flower of English womanhood has been sentenced to . . . *to the salt mines!*"

The bomb Sir Guy had so adroitly lighted exploded with devastating effect! Screaming with rage, Ivan sprang out of his saddle with so much violence, Sir Guy thought he was coming for his throat. The great hounds thought so, too, for they surged forward with such ferocity, their handlers were dragged with them.

Suspecting his end had come, Sir Guy leaped nimbly back apace, and reached for his poniard—a gesture that caused added consternation. Several cavaliers spurred forward to protect their berserk Emperor, and Lieutenant Ptucha made a grab for Sir Guy's arm. This last maneuver prompted Affable Jones to let an ever-ready knife slide from his sleeve to his palm while he took measure of Ptucha's ribs.

Ivan the Terrible, however, soon demonstrated his wrath was not aimed at Sir Guy Spangler. One of the huge dogs, snarling and slavering, had the misfortune to come within his reach. He broke its neck with a single blow of a clubbed fist. Then whirling on a too helpful cavalier, Ivan jerked him out of the saddle and kicked him under the flashing hooves of his own charger. The cream of his frenzy thus skimmed, he began bawling a word or a name which the Englishman could not comprehend because the interpreter had wisely scuttled for cover.

Slightly awed by the holocaust he had ignited, Sir Guy wondered if this notorious despot was summoning a torturer to make a thorough job of it. Nor was his anxiety relieved entirely when a giant Cossack came galloping roughshod through the assembled horsemen—who, it was noted, hastily made way for him—threw himself out of the saddle and prostrated himself before the Emperor in what seemed to be one flowing motion. Yet his obeisance was so brief, he appeared to bounce off the ground, to stand stolidly awaiting orders. One sensed there was no conceivable command this burly brute would not obey.

Ivan began barking orders at him, then caught himself and glanced about. Sighting his interpreter hiding on the off-side of a horse, he beckoned him closer and directed him to translate his words for the benefit of the Englishman.

His words proved terse enough, and to the point. The Cossack—whose name was Jaghellon—was to ride immediately for Moscow, as fast as horseflesh could stand, and command Sylvester, the Metropolitane, "on pain of rousing the Grand Duke's displeasure" to release instantly all members of the English embassy, their servants, guards, or people. That accomplished, Jaghellon was to command the Metropolitane to come in person forthwith—or, if too infirm, to send a suitable proxy deputized to speak in his name—to explain this unparalleled incident.

In the midst of this, as if suddenly recalling a facet which had previously escaped his notice, the Tsar swung on the Englishman.

"Where," he demanded harshly, "was Count Nikita when this outrage was committed?"

"Sire, Count Nikita remained at my side until we were forcibly separated by our captors," Sir Guy reported. "It was due to the tireless efforts of the Count and his men that we escaped the first trap . . ."

"*Pss't! Pss't!* That is not so!" hissed Pojorski in an undertone. "It was I who . . ."

Sir Guy ignored him and went on with his statement. "The Count was seized with the rest of us, and, to the best of my knowledge, may still be in prison." This was more dramatic than accurate, Sir Guy conceded privately.

The Tsar turned back to the Cossack. "See to it the Count accompanies you on your return!" He withdrew a large ring from his finger and tossed it at the other as one might toss a bone to a savage dog. "This signet will afford you *carte blanche*. Now take your cubs and ride!"

Jaghellon snatched the jewel out of the air and gave a bow that was like a whiplash. Yet before he could mount, Sir Guy stepped forward.

"*Your Majesty!*"

Once again the reaction of the assemblage indicated how rashly he was violating all convention.

The Emperor merely cocked his head. "Yes?"

"May it please your Majesty, I ask one boon—that I may accompany Captain Jaghellon to Moscow! I am deeply concerned about the health of her ladyship!"

The Cossack scrutinized Sir Guy with an admixture of appraisal and disdain, but Ivan shook his head.

"Your desire is understandable and your courage admirable," he retorted with gruff kindliness, "yet there is no need for you to submit to further rigors after what you have been through. Jaghellon and his wolf pack ride like hell-fiends, killing more horses under them than are slain by the enemy. The English princess will be assured the best of care and treatment—Jaghellon knows me too well to fail in *that!*—and, meanwhile, there are many things about which I wish to question you." He turned back to the burly Cossack.

"Get you gone! *I shall expect you three days hence!*"

Jaghellon shot in the saddle, jerked his magnificent Arab onto its hindlegs in a wild salute, then wheeled to spur headlong through the company. The manner in which even the highest nobles scattered before him was a testament to his ruthlessness.

Sir Guy stared grimly after him. "*Three days!*" he mused under his breath. "'Tis impossible! Hard as we rode, it took us three days to cover the distance *one* way! He cannot make it!"

Young Ptucha was still standing at his elbow. "Sir, you do not know Jaghellon!" he whispered in an awed tone. "Neither God, man, nor Shaitan himself can stop Captain Jaghellon once Ivan has given him a command! He will obey!"

25

THE CHAMBERLAIN, whose tongue-torturing name Sir Guy never bothered to learn, sang a different tune once he realized how well the Englishman was regarded by the Tsar. In point of fact, he then became so extravagantly solicitous it took him the entire day to get the honored visitors ensconced in what he deemed *suitable* quarters. Sir Guy, whose sole aim in life at the moment was to lay his weary head upon a pillow, was kept awake until nearly midnight by the chamberlain's unctuous ministrations.

He fell asleep at once, to dream what started out to be a very optimistic dream—the successful culmination of their hazardous journey, i.e., the safe delivery of Ellen into the hands of Ivan. Unfortunately for him, the dream did not terminate at that juncture, like the happy ending of a fairy tale wherein the Maid and Prince stroll hand-in-hand into the sunset. Instead, he envisioned those powerful hands—which in the dream appeared as talons dripping blood—groping for Ellen. She broke away, leaving most of her gown in a grasping claw, and screamed for Sir Guy. He tried to rush to her aid, only to find himself firmly pinioned by the Reverend Belcher, Master Lymeburner, and most of the other investors, while from the sidelines, little Charity jeered and mocked him.

Meanwhile, the terrible chase continued until at last Ivan, by this time fair slavering at the mouth, closed his great talons on Ellen's bare white shoulder. She screamed and struggled like a white dove in the clutches of the hawk, but the talon remained....

Then Sir Guy awoke to find Lieutenant Ptucha shaking him by the shoulder.

"Merciful God, sir! Are you ill?" gasped the young officer. "Your frightful cursing and bellowing may well betray the whole scheme!"

Sir Guy sat up and squeezed his temples between his palms. "Betray *what* scheme?" he groaned. "What in hell are you talking about?"

"The attack! You said last night you wanted to witness it!"

[203]

Sir Guy moaned dismally. He had only a faint recollection of the previous evening during which Ptucha had babbled something about a new mode of assault, and Sir Guy had murmured a desire to see it more out of politeness than anything else. Howbeit, though still exhausted, he was glad enough to have been rescued from the agonizing nightmare, so he dressed as swiftly as he could and stepped outside where Affable, Pistol, and Pojorski awaited him. The dwarf was still incensed over Sir Guy's failure to give him full credit for the escape, but when the knight renewed his promise to do so at the first suitable opportunity, his resilient good humor returned.

It was still dark when they rode up the slope to a vantage ground which afforded a sweeping view of the entire panorama. Ptucha had thoughtfully provided food and drink, and so the quintette settled on the greensward to await the day.

The morning dawned serene and cloudless. The earliest light revealed an immense timbered tower on wheels being rolled towards the beleaguered city by the Muscovites. This terrible engine of destruction, taller than the very walls of Kalie, was topped by a sheltered platform mounted with numerous cannon; gunners with lighted matches were already stationed at their posts. Viewed from the summit of the hill, the grim machine, jerkily propelled by hundreds of men and horses, resembled the carcass of a wasp being dragged by a swarm of ants. Ptucha explained, in a reverent tone, how the great tower had been constructed secretly a couple of miles away behind a hill and moved up during the hours of darkness.

The first flaming tip of the sun touched off the carnage. A dozen cannon thundered simultaneously from the tower platform to spew their shot directly over the walls into the streets and dwellings of the city. While the bulk of the Muscovite army was drawn up in reserve, like spectators to the pageant, a dashing segment of favored nobles, with gay pennons streaming from their lance tips and trumpets pealing, surged forward in a direct assault upon the walls.

Sir Guy wondered why the many should remain while the few attacked; in his considered opinion, it showed poor judgment on the part of the Muscovite commander, but the others in his party were elated.

"W'at-'o!" cheered Affable Jones. "These Muskies gi' ye a show!"

Even the dour Pistol was impressed. "In sooth, they don't do things by 'arf, they don't!" he conceded.

Stanislaus Ptucha viewed the scene with a worshipful adoration usually reserved for sacred subjects.

"Praise God! Our glorious troops will carry the city before high noon!" he prophesied.

Hardly had he expressed this view, when the massive gates of the city rolled open and mounted divisions of Poles and renegade Tatars swept out, flanking the tower and the attacking Muscovites, and fell upon them with a shock that was utterly irresistible.

Then while this Polish division was slaughtering the encompassed Muscovites in the presence of the Tsar and his whole army, a smaller band of Polish sappers exploded a carefully prepared bomb under the tower. As the lofty structure crumpled in ruin, shedding men and cannon indiscriminately, the victorious Poles swept back into the city.

Of the five, Pojorski was the first to break the shocked silence.

"Comrades, I verily believe it might be advisable to keep out of my Royal Master's sight for the nonce. It is barely possible this incident may put him out of humor!"

"For onc't," breathed Sergeant Pistol, "I wot ye speak the trufe!"

It was potent advice: Ivan *was* "put out of humor." With his own hand, he disemboweled the commander responsible for making the assault without adequate supporting troops, and he caused to be executed the entire general staff. Contradictorily, instead of torturing the few Polish wounded who had fallen in the sally, as was his wont, he commanded they be afforded the best of treatment. Ivan well earned his appellation of "the Terrible," yet no man respected bravery and daring more than he.

So Sir Guy and his companions *laid low,* in the phrasing of Sergeant Pistol, but the following day, the siege being stalemated, they wandered about the cantonment. Nothing was seen of the Emperor or his suite, so it was assumed he was licking his wounds in seclusion. But late in the afternoon, the chamberlain panted up to Sir Guy and announced that the Emperor commanded them all to appear forthwith before him in a private audience.

It was then a hurried counting of noses revealed that Affable Jones was missing. A hasty search proved unavailing. Pistol finally confessed that he had last seen Affable (despite Sir Guy's strict ruling to the contrary) performing his gambling tricks before a group of Cossack officers. Pojorski wagged his head and insisted that by this time Affable would have had his throat cut. Lieutenant Ptucha sadly agreed with him; Muscovites were peculiarly sensitive to being cheated.

Sir Guy was concerned, but the chamberlain was distraught. He had been commanded to produce *five* guests, not four. He became so frenzied, Sir Guy finally promised to explain the situation to the Emperor.

The four were decorously outfitted in borrowed costumes and the chamberlain read them a little lecture on court etiquette. Under no circumstances were they to speak unless asked a question; never should they volunteer any remarks, and in all cases let His Highness choose the subject to be discussed. When this monologue was concluded, Pojo wrangled a fresh promise from Sir Guy to credit him with their existence, and Lieutenant Ptucha added some friendly advice.

"In God's name, sir," he pleaded, "do not be lulled by the Emperor's seeming tolerance! He is a stickler for the correct observance of official conventions! He never permits an intimacy, nor forgives a familiarity!"

Once more the chamberlain nervously examined them to make certain everything was as it should be, then with trepidation conducted them to the royal tent. It was so rare for Ivan to grant a private audience that the outer space was thronged with the curious (and in some cases, *envious*) *boyars*. In the wake of the by now officious chamberlain who cried everyone out of their path, they passed rows of armed guards, officials, generals, nobles, diplomats, and a myriad of other satellites until eventually they came to a small antechamber. Here they were halted by two hard-visaged pages who bluntly informed them they would have to wait because the Grand Prince was closeted with an unexpected visitor, and had issued strict orders that, under no circumstances, was he to be disturbed.

This explanation threw the chamberlain into a perfect foment of anxiety. His sole aim in life was to obey his Prince to the letter, yet the very Fates seemed in conspiracy to frustrate him. He had been commanded to produce *five* charges at *six* of the clock; it was now precisely six, and he had garnered only four, and in addition, was barred from the royal presence. His suffering was intense.

Howbeit, Sir Guy now had his own bone to gnaw on, for in addition to his deep personal concern over the disappearance of Affable Jones, the mention of the *unexpected visitor* had given him a nasty jolt. Ever since their arrival in this hostile land, the horrendous possibility of an agent of the *real* English Muscovy Company, or, worse, an emissary from Elizabeth, bobbing up to unmask him had hung over his head like a sword of Damocles. This *unexpected visitor*, now in close conference with the Tsar, could well be such a harbinger of disaster.

As they stood wallowing in apprehension, a sudden roar of laughter filtered through the curtained archway. The chamberlain shuddered in a kind of converse ecstasy. "That, by the grace of God, came from our immortal Prince!" he babbled. "Everything must be all right! He is happy!"

"Doubtless!" murmured Pojorski. "I have heard him laugh just exactly so when I performed some particularly exquisite bit of torture!"

"I fear that is true," sighed Lieutenant Ptucha. "There is a touch of cruelty in that merriment, may God forgive me for saying so!"

Another volley of belly-laughs ripped through the tapestries.

"One thing sure," Sergeant Pistol observed grimly, "'Is ruddy Ighness be either 'avin' 'imself an 'ell o' a *good* time, or 'e's givin' some poor bastard an 'ell o' a *bad* time!"

Further discussion was prevented by the appearance of an usher who beckoned them to their audience.

The chamberlain crossed himself, took a final dance around his charges to ascertain that all was perfection, then with a nod to the others stepped through the curtains. Sir Guy braced himself after the fashion of a man about to dive into icy water, and followed. The others crowded in behind him. Yet Sir Guy made only two steps into the sacrosanct chamber before he collided with the chamberlain who had paused in horror. After one swift glance at the tableau before them, Sir Guy, too, was similarly paralyzed.

On a raised dais at the far end of the lavish tent stood a table where a candelabrum lighted in bold relief the faces of the three men grouped around it. On one side of this table sat Ivan the Terrible, tapping the table absently with a small dagger while his blazing eyes watched with rapt attention the three half-shells being manipulated by a short, squat man, gaudily arrayed in the uniform of a Cossack officer, who sat directly across from him. An interpreter stood on the far side of the table, midway between the two principals, his apprehensive features lighted eerily from below.

"O-O-oh, Goddamighty . . . *no!*" breathed Pistol fervently.

To a stranger the scene might have suggested a famed military genius demonstrating for his monarch, by means of the fragments of shell, some highly involved tactical maneuver. But to the shocked little group frozen in the entryway, the *unexpected visitor* was no stranger.

Affable Jones had reached high to find a gullible victim!

Even as they stared in silent awe, Affable grinned across the table.

"Busk ye, yer Gryce, this be yer larst chance!" he chortled. "W'ich shell covers the pebble? Guess right, w'y, ye cuts me ruddy finger off, an' no 'ard feelin's, I trow! Guess wrong, an' I gets the 'ottest little baggage in yer 'arem! Right-o?"

The interpreter reddened, stammered, then bent forward for a closer look at the astounding character opposite his Prince.

"'Ottest *baggage?*" he echoed, puzzled. "I do not comprehend!"

Affable gave him a prodigious wink, and a sly dig in the ribs that all but knocked the breath out of him.

"'Ere, 'ere, don't josh me, pal! Ye knows w'at I means—*baggage* be a mopsy, minx, filly, bitch. . . ."

The dawn of understanding broke over the interpreter's features.

"Ah-ha! Yes, yes, I now comprehend!" He bowed to his royal master and gabbled swiftly in Russian.

The Emperor nodded affirmatively without for an instant permitting his gaze to stray from the shells. In profile, his face appeared more predatory than ever. Then while the newcomers held their breaths, he suddenly stabbed a finger at the middle shell!

Affable Jones appeared stricken, but only momentarily—then slowly, oh, so slowly, he lifted the middle shell and peered under it. There was no pebble!

"'Ard luck, yer Marjesty!" he chuckled. "Wrong ag'in!"

The interpreter—the only one of the trio who seemed *not* to be enjoying himself—translated this with understandable trepidation. But after a dark scowl of bewilderment, the Tsar guffawed lustily and leaned back in his chair.

"We must play again!" he said with a hard smile. "But for a head, not a mere finger. Would you gamble your head, Englishman?"

"Lor' love ye, chum," Affable began affably. "If the stakes be 'igh enough."

The Tsar laughed, then realizing his visitors were already in the room, he told the interpreter to see to it that "Sir Jones" received his "baggage," dismissed Affable with a friendly nod, and beckoned the others to approach.

Affable faced his compatriots with feigned surprise.

"Aye, come on in!" he hooted genially. "Me'n 'is nibs 'as been 'avin' an 'ell o' a time!"

It soon became evident why Ivan the Fourth was deemed one of the best informed men of his era, for his curiosity was insatiable. He inquired into every detail of their long journey, and his questions became so pertinent, Sir Guy began to suspect a snare. Yet having decided that honesty was the best policy—unless, of course, a lie would serve better—Sir Guy kept his tale as truthful as expediency permitted.

Fortunately, the Emperor was in great good humor, and in manner and voice he exuded more courtesy and charm than the Englishmen had thus far encountered in all Muscovy. It was difficult to remember that he had personally butchered several army commanders but a few hours past.

The comic relief to this audience was the effort of Pojorski to catch the attention of the Tsar. Not even when Sir Guy related the farcical details of the trial by combat did the Tsar deign to intimate that he had ever so much as heard of Yaroslaf Pojorski. Pojo was crushed.

When the interrogation, carried on through the interpreter, worked around to Ellen, Sir Guy entered upon the truly hazardous stage of his verbal journey. He had earlier prepared an elaborate fabrication to cover the exigency that the Tsar might discover, that the name of the woman brought him was not Lady *Mary*, but Lady *Ellen*. Howbeit, Fate again demonstrated that she was not yet ready to abandon Sir Guy Spangler, for as things turned out, Ivan never once spoke of the girl by name, invariably referring to her as "the princess."

Now, since the stars of his good fortune seemed propitious, Sir Guy decided to ride his luck to the limit. In a larger sense, he was duplicating the gamble of Affable Jones: his head for a high stake. He had already learned from both the dwarf and the chamberlain that Ivan seldom granted private audiences to visiting envoys, and then rarely more than once. Shrewdly surmising that the Tsar was the sort of man who would be more generous in a private audience than in public, Sir Guy took one of the wildest gambles of his career: He sought his reward before he delivered his goods!

By describing Ellen's charm, beauty, and desirability until he had the Emperor's eyes dancing with anticipation, Sir Guy switched his tactics so abruptly it had the effect of leaving his listener dangling by the ears.

"Sire!" he said then. "At nearly every stage of this long and arduous journey, men have commented not only on your Majesty's boundless generosity, but have openly speculated on what riches *I* hoped to gain from your Majesty because of the risks taken in this embassy. I hasten to assure your Majesty that I seek no reward!"

"God 'elp us!" groaned Pistol. " 'E's got a bat in 'is belfry!"

Sir Guy continued: "What my confreres and I have done, we did for our beloved Queen who, above all else, desires to cement a lasting friendship between England and Muscovy! Elizabeth—God care for her!—envisions a glorious tomorrow when the fabulous riches of Muscovy will be exchanged for the priceless products of English craftsmen!"

Ivan smiled politically. "All of Russia likewise awaits that happy day!" he lied in suave diplomacy.

Sir Guy made a magnificent bow. "Those words, sire, from your

Majesty's own lips are sufficient reward for a score of embassies! Would that I had a carrier dove to wing them straightway to my royal mistress, but failing that, I shall rush back to England and lay this golden message at her feet! 'Tis with abysmal regret that I will be unable to return to this enchanted paradise which is Muscovy and deliver to your Majesty my sovereign's happy reply. Unfortunately, the stupidity of an agent of mine in his dealings with your Majesty's servants has all but impoverished me!"

The Tsar's brows collided. Sir Guy appeared overwhelmed with embarrassment and began to stammer an apology.

"Sire! Ten thousand pardons for intruding the personal! That breach of good conduct was inexcusable! I cry your mercy!"

Ivan leaned forward, the puzzled frown darkening his expression. "To what did you have reference?" he asked.

"Oh, sire, I should not have mentioned it! I was carried away by my enthusiasm for Muscovy! I pray your Majesty's forgiveness."

"I prefer an explanation," retorted the Emperor. "You spoke of having been impoverished through the dealings between your agent and my servants. It is evident certain of my subjects have not been overscrupulous in their treatment of you and your entourage, and these will, I assure you, have occasion to regret their misconduct. If there are others who have dealt dishonestly with your agent, I insist on knowing of it!"

Sir Guy made a hurried gesture of protest. "Sire! I have unwittingly created a false impression. On my oath, I did not mean to impute dishonesty to your Majesty's servants, who, in this particular instance, were most zealous in the performance of their duties! No, sire, the fault was entirely ours—or, I should say, the fault of that blundering knave in whose hands I placed my fortune. What happened, sire, was this: In the first flush of our enthusiasm for your Majesty's incomparable domain, a few of us with faith in the future risked our all in seeking to hasten the goodwill by sending a cargo of English goods to Muscovy.

"Unfortunately, the master of the vessel was a better mariner than diplomat, for the fool had not the wit to ascertain the provisions of your Majesty's agreement with the English Muscovy Company. So in his gross ignorance, he sailed into a remote northern port of Muscovy, where, after disposing of his cargo and gleaning a few inconsequential odds and ends for ballast, he was about to depart when his ship was seized and—I confess justly—impounded by your Majesty's loyal servants!" Sir Guy spread his hands in an eloquent gesture of resignation.

"Thus, your Majesty can see that, though innocent of wrongful intent, technically the fault is our own. And were it not for the tragic fact that the loss spells disaster for several of my countrymen, all due to my personal eagerness to further the goodwill between our respective countries, I would have forced the affair out of my mind."

Ivan combed his beard reflectively. "What is the name of this vessel?" he inquired. "And where is she now."

Sir Guy sighed. "Her name, sire, is *The Dainty Virgin*—in honor of our Virgin Queen. As to her position: at last report, sire, she was impounded in a small bay near the village of *Slobitia* in the province of Dwina."

The Tsar sniffed. "Does your Virgin Queen know of the incident?"

The Englishman hazarded a rueful smile. "Sire! So desirous is Her Majesty of gaining your Majesty's esteem that were she to learn of it, and notwithstanding all the sacrifices I have made personally to atone for my agent's blunder, *Elizabeth would have my head!*"

The Tsar laughed heartily. "By my sword hilt, that sounds just like a woman!" He paused to pick a flea off the tip of his beard. While his audience waited with bated breaths, Ivan slowly and deliberately maneuvered the insect onto one thumb nail, then abruptly popped it with the other. He went about the operation methodically, demonstrating a skill which bespoke long practice, yet with an automatism, as his mind was on something else. At the flea's demise, Ivan again gave his attention to Sir Guy.

"Young man, you do not appear to me the type of visionary who would spurn this year's fruit for next year's blossoms," he observed. "Nonetheless, I shall accept you at your word and not impinge upon your honor by offering you the usual monetary emoluments."

He paused—it almost seemed as if to afford Sergeant Pistol time for an audible groan—then made a signal to a lackey who at once placed a small knee-desk bearing writing materials before him. As Ivan sent his quill scratching across the vellum, the interpreter melted a piece of scarlet wax over the candle, and when the monarch raised his quill with a flourish, the other deposited a glob of wax beside the signature. Sand and the impress of a signet concluded the ritual.

"This billet-doux," said the Tsar dryly, as the interpreter handed the document to the Englishman, "may in a slight degree offset the scurrilous treatment given you and your retinue heretofore, since it authorizes you to reclaim your vessel. And whereas it does *not* entitle you to engage in trade—which, obviously, would conflict with my concession to the other company—it does grant you the privilege of acquiring *any and all ballast*"—the little webs of crows'-feet deepened around the Emperor's eyes—"necessary for the *safety* of the return voyage to England." Ivan erased the half-smile. "If your Sovereign disapproves of this, I shall, of course, rescind the order!"

Sir Guy accepted the scroll and bowed in deep obeisance. "Sire! Your Majesty's boundless generosity and, dare I add, *understanding*, is a fitting testament to the incomparable magnanimity of the Russian spirit! It will insure your Majesty's fame, and the grandeur of Muscovy, being sown in the rich soil of that glorious little isle which is England, there to ripen into a rich harvest which both our people may share. Sire, I thank thee!

"And now, sire, I have but one debt left to repay—that of calling to your Majesty's notice the loyalty and devotion of two servants who risked their lives, over and above the normal call of duty, in your Majesty's service." He turned and indicated young Ptucha, who almost swooned in embarrassment. "Your Grace, Sub-Lieutenant Stanislaus Ptucha, abandoning a luxurious sinecure to seek glory in your Majesty's arms, guided us skillfully through the forces of your Majesty's . . . ah . . . may I say *less-enlightened* subjects, and saw us safely here."

Ivan nodded approvingly before turning to the flabbergasted chamberlain, who never in his hazardous career had witnessed such an audience. "I created several vacancies in the army yesterday," he remarked. "Find a suitable command for *Captain* Ptucha."

As young Ptucha prostrated himself in gratitude, and the chamberlain swore windily to obey, the Tsar eyed the Englishman. There was a noticeable glint of impatience in his glance, so Sir Guy came directly to the point.

"Sire, there is one other, without whose valiant assistance, remarkable skill, and nigh unparalleled personal devotion to your Grace, this humble envoy would not be standing here at this moment. This individual has refused all offers of reward, asking as his only boon that I mention to your Majesty his inimitable service. I refer, sire, to your Majesty's faithful servant . . . *Yaroslaf Pojorski!*"

The Tsar made a *thucking* noise with tongue and teeth as he impaled Pojorski with a jaundiced stare. The dwarf wriggled forward in the manner of a spanked and repentant puppy, and crouched before his Royal Master, figuratively wagging his tail. Ivan, meanwhile, reached under his beard and scratched the wattles of his neck.

"It is a novel experience for a prince to receive three supplicants in succession who ask for *nothing*," he rumbled finally, in a tone that brought a sudden chill of apprehension to his hearers. "Nonetheless, it remains the obligation of a just sovereign to see that exceptional service is always fittingly requited. In this instance, I have a heaven-sent opportunity to—if you will forgive an apt but threadbare platitude—'kill two birds with one stone!'" He emitted a sardonic chuckle that was markedly lacking in mirth.

"Yaroslaf Pojorski is a *slave,* a token of esteem given me by the Sultan of Turkey. Since I no longer have use for his peculiar talents, it is but just that I reward his inimitable devotion to my interests by finding him a master who will fully appreciate his qualities." He waved a royal hand towards the startled Sir Guy.

"You, young sir, by dint of your heart-tugging eulogy have relieved my perplexity. So—let it be known that here and now, I, Ivan of Muscovy, hereby renounce all right, title, and interest in the slave, Yaroslaf Pojorski, and command that ownership of said slave be legally transferred to your name, to have and to hold *in perpetuum,* as a living testament of my regard. In fine—he is now *yours!*"

Even Sergeant Pistol was rendered mute. Ivan the Terrible chose this moment to rise abruptly and stride out of the chamber.

Back in their own quarters, Sir Guy stalked restlessly up and down.

"W'at's eatin' ye, sir?" asked Affable Jones from a recumbent position on a couch. "Lor' lumme, sir, ye e'en got yer pay wi'out deliverin' yer prey!"

Sergeant Pistol concurred in this. "'Ell, yer 'Onor, ye not on'y got a doc-eement to grab the ship an' everythin' else w'at ayant nyled down, but ye got a remembrance . . ." He tipped his head towards a pallet in the corner where Pojorski sat staring dazedly at his toes. ". . . 'Im!"

Sir Guy cursed them roundly. "Stop it, you goosebrained gulls!" he thundered. "Haven't you the wit to see our plight is worse than at any time since leaving England?"

Affable sobered. "Oh, come now, master!" he protested. "W'y, ye 'ad 'im eatin' out o' yer 'and, ye did, I swear!"

Sir Guy snorted. "Aye, precisely as a mouse has a cat eating out of *its* hand! I tell you Ivan senses something is wrong! One slip and . . ." He ran a finger graphically across his throat.

26

It was now the third day, the day of Jaghellon's return.

From the moment of awakening, the three Englishmen and the dwarf had been haunted by premonitions of impending evil, enthralled in a common gloom. Not so Ptucha; he never descended from the clouds. He had heckled the methodical chamberlain until, to be rid of him, that unimaginative official assigned him to command a raiding party which had been ordered to set a ram against the great gates of the beleaguered city. Bursting with pride, this youngster hardly old enough to grow a beard had coaxed Sir Guy and his companions to trudge to the summit in the early morning, there to watch his bid for glory. And so, from the very vantage Ptucha himself had selected, they witnessed his cycle run its course.

Destiny might have expended him to better advantage; it was all so senseless. He led his little band of reckless volunteers through a curtain of arrows and shot; with less than a fourth surviving, he set up the unwieldy ram. When the Poles attempted to duplicate their previous sally against the ill-fated tower, Ptucha, with but six men left, prevented the gate's being opened by an ingenious wedge. Then, not having sufficient force to operate the mechanical bludgeon, he withdrew. Of the four who retreated with him, he alone limped up to his Prince to beg reinforcements.

The Tsar at first ordered out a seasoned veteran to finish the daring task so ably begun, but Captain Ptucha wept for a second chance. He got it. He was made a colonel. He was granted the privilege of kissing his Prince's hand. He was rewarded by a beautiful jennet from the Emperor's own stables.

While the little group on the summit watched with horrible fascination, the boy took his station at the head of his fresh troops. They saw him rise in his stirrups and lift a hand in salute—not to his master, but to three forlorn foreigners and a slave. One clear cold note of a trumpet pealed; the charge began. . . .

He rode to meet death with all the dash and color of an ancient knight at a tournament. To the stirring fanfare of trumpets, his jennet appeared to skim along the carpet of flowers in a headlong, eager plunge.

Death met him halfway. A cannon ball lifted him out of the saddle, in two parts. His clay fell to earth, to be trampled under the onrushing horses, but his spirit, like the loaves and the fishes in the parable, was divided amongst the multitude. A fragment lodged in the consciousness of at least one English adventurer.

[214]

"By the grace of the Almighty God!" breathed Sir Guy. "There died a *man!*"

Late that afternoon, Jaghellon returned.

The Cossack and his "wolf cubs" swept over the crest of the knoll just before sunset. For one alarming moment, they were silhouetted against the fiery disc of the sun, then down the slope they plunged, howling and brandishing their primitive weapons like a horde of raiding barbarians.

Eager for word of their compatriots, Sir Guy and his companions hurried forward to greet the party. But Jaghellon knew his master—Ivan would want to see his prizes before all others—so he stormed through the cantonment at full gallop, his charges herded in the center like stolen bullocks. Thus, in the confusion and waning light, the anxious Englishmen could see little. Sir Guy did spot Belcher—largely because the parson was being jounced so high above the saddle—and he thought he glimpsed young Tutweiller. But he saw neither Paxton, Nikita, nor the one in whom he was most vitally concerned, Ellen. It came to him, with a pang of conscience, that in the earlier excitement he had neglected to ask the Cossack to fetch Charity as well.

And if Jaghellon knew his master, his master, likewise, knew Jaghellon. Ivan, never doubting the redoubtable Cossack would return at the time decreed, had ordered the stage set for receiving the "English princess" in a style befitting the occasion. As the reception was to be held out of doors in a public square, it was to this place the three Englishmen went now in the wake of the Cossack.

Though no stranger to the ostentatious courts of western Europe, Sir Guy had to concede that this impromptu fete, set in a military encampment in a time of siege, had savage beauty. A portable throne had been erected before the entrance to the Emperor's great tent, under a striped awning of many-colored silk, and beside this jeweled and gilded seat stood a slim, tall-backed chair of alabastrine whiteness. From the foot of this royal dais, a snow white carpet reached invitingly to the "street," where waited now the fussy chamberlain and his assisting satellites.

On either side of this spotless pathway, like twin hedgerows of flowering plants, crowded the lordliest nobles of the land to the number of five rows deep. Behind these the various guards of honor were displayed as chessmen are arranged on a board, each guard colorfully identifiable by the standard of the noble who commanded. And surrounding the entire square was a veritable barricade of lances and staffs, topped by the pennons, flags, and banners of the entire army.

Sir Guy wormed to a place a few paces to the right of the dais, and a trifle closer to the white chair than to the imperial throne. Since he was deprived of an opportunity to coach Ellen in her lines, he hoped by this means to be able at least to prompt her. And as if to remind him of the precariousness of his plight, directly opposite him, on the far side of the dais, stood the Master of the Royal Hounds with three of his largest and most vicious beasts on silver leashes.

Sir Guy had barely taken his station when a distant trumpet call from the far end of the carpet announced that the "guests" had arrived. Immediately, two beautiful youths, with golden curls and golden trumpets, stepped onto the dais and poured forth trilling music as sweet as the first fair bird of spring. This heralded the Emperor.

Then was loosed such a cacophony of sound as no Englishman had ever heard. Against a background of exploding bombs, thundering cannon, shrilling trumpets and clashing cymbals, fully fourscore thousand masculine voices cheered and shouted in hysterical enthusiasm. The great hounds bayed in agony, and for once Sir Guy felt a common bond of sympathy with the evil brutes, for the all-encompassing clamor seemed to fill his very arteries. To the accompaniment of all this, Ivan the Fourth, Tsar of All the Russias, made his entry.

With a shrewd sense of the theatrical, his own costume was simple and unobtrusive; he had the look of a man who required no external pretensions to bolster himself. As he stepped from behind a tapestry onto the dais, his glance flickered over the scene. Brief as it was, Sir Guy felt it touch him in passing, and sent a tremor up his spine. Then the Tsar settled in his throne and nodded for the audience to begin.

As golden-haired pageboys pealed the signal, Sir Guy strained forward to get his first glimpse of Ellen and his friends. Yet it was not Ellen but Captain Jaghellon who came striding down that immaculate pathway, his great mud-covered boots profaning its whiteness.

Despite his disappointment, Sir Guy viewed the giant Cossack with interest. Although the veteran had been in camp but a matter of minutes, the whole army was buzzing with the miracle of his feat. To Moscow *and back* in three days! It was impossible, yet Jaghellon had done it! True, he was reputed to have ridden two horses to death, and foundered several others, and unless he had slept in the saddle at full gallop he had been without sleep since only the devil knew when. Yet Jaghellon now marched towards the throne as tirelessly and energetically as if he had just hopped out of bed.

Ivan nodded in reply to the Cossack's flamboyant salute, greeted him briefly and asked, as common courtesy demanded, after his trip.

Jaghellon's report, translated to him by an interpreter he had requested to stand by his side, was something Sir Guy would long remember. In keeping with the man's character, it was bluff, terse, impartial, and irreverent. Jaghellon made no mention of the trials and tribulations of the journey: the horses foundered, the Metropolitane's guardsmen hacked from their saddles when they disputed the way of this Juggernaut, the loss of his own "cubs." In his clipped growl, he stated merely that he had delivered his Prince's message to the Metropolitane in person, and that he had brought back all the prisoners of quality, save two—Count Nikita and the "English princess"!

As the Cossack bit off these last words, there was a terrible stillness. It seemed to Sir Guy, stunned as he was by the news, that not a man of the thousands assembled so much as breathed. In this awful quiet, the Tsar leaned forward and seared the courier with a stare that would have shriveled a less robust soul. The three words he spoke crackled like a whip.

"Where are they?"

Jaghellon, not one whit disturbed, shrugged his massive shoulders.

"Sire, Sylvester, the Metropolitane, could not answer that," he reported in a tone calculated to remind his master he was acting solely as a messenger. "Nor would his Holiness' health permit him to obey your Majesty's summons. In his place, sire, I brought a lesser holy man to speak for him." Jaghellon stepped abruptly to one side, revealing what his huge bulk had concealed, the Metropolitane's emissary—*the ecclesiastical steward!*

At sight of their old antagonist, the three Englishmen stiffened. This boded no good!

The ecclesiastical prosecutor, looking even more ludicrous than ever, came waddling down the carpet like an overstuffed gander. In one hand he carried a sizable scroll; in the other, a small letter, carefully sealed. Following him, about ten paces behind, came a red-turbaned little blackamoor leading a magnificent white mare.

After halting the prescribed distance from the throne to make his obeisance, the steward tucked the sealed epistle under his arm, opened the scroll and began trumpeting his florid address.

"Oh, King of Kings, Emperor of Emperors, as the firmament possesseth but one sun, the imperishable land of Muscovy worshipeth but one Tsar! This humblest of your Divine Majesty's devoted servants comes now in the stead of our Holy Metropolitane, the Shadow of God upon..."

The Tsar cut him off as abruptly as the fall of an ax. "Answer my question! *Where is the English princess?*"

The orator stopped with his mouth wide open. By nature loquacious, he could not believe anyone would prefer brevity. Yet, as there was no mistaking the Tsar's meaning, he reluctantly folded his scroll and attempted to answer the question.

As he explained it, a certain unnamed spy had informed that paragon of godliness, the Metropolitane, that the English female was naught but a *fille de joie* smuggled into Muscovy by a disciple of Satan to tempt the purity of that best-of-all-possible Princes, namely Ivan. Hence the pious Sylvester had ordered the English party taken into custody for the good of the adored Grand Prince.

It came to pass, however, that Count Nikita finally convinced the sainted Metropolitane that his information was erroneous, that the female in question was of royal blood, and as such should be housed in less stringent quarters until that most virtuous of princes should state his pleasure regarding her. To this reasoning, in the greatness of his understanding and devotion, the noble Metropolitane had acceded.

Ivan inched forward to the edge of his chair. "*Where . . . is . . . she?*" His voice had the rising crescendo of wind rustling through the trees before a squall.

"Why, sire, *where* she is, I do not know!" the prosecutor stammered, his bugging eyes blinking like signal lights. "When this rude Cossack hounded nigh to his death-couch that gentlest of godly deputies, I hied myself to the palace where Count Nikita was presumed to have quartered this female." (To a celibate such as the ecclesiastical steward, any woman, whether princess or peasant, was a "female.") "Neither the Count nor the female was to be found! A lackey informed me that Count Nikita had removed her to a—and, sire, I quote his exact words!—*'a more salubrious climate.'* "

Ivan sprang to his feet. In his towering rage, he seemed even larger than usual.

"Nikita removed her? In God's name, *why?*"

"Oh, Star of Muscovy, I have here the answer—for your eyes alone!" the emissary announced grandiosely, holding up the small sealed packet. "Count Nikita, no doubt anticipating your Blessed Majesty's natural concern, had left this message and this exquisite mare with instructions that they were—and again, I quote precisely, sire!—to be *delivered together to your Supreme Grace in person!*" He bowed low and proffered the document. "This lowly person, sire, has the unwarranted honor to lay these twin gifts at your Incomparable Majesty's feet!"

Ivan slammed back into his seat. "Read the message and be brief!" he commanded darkly. "I weary of this bombast!"

The steward beamed his pleasure, and by the eagerness with which his chubby fingers broke the seals, betrayed his intense curiosity. He beckoned the blackamoor to lead the white jennet closer so the Emperor could admire her splendid conformation. Then, edging in front of her, so as not to lose the full attention of his Prince, he tilted his head after the fashion of a cock about to crow, and began to read in a clear, sonorous voice that carried out to the multitude.

"To the Grand Seigneur, Tsar and Great Duke, Ivan the Fourth, of Muscovy! Greetings! My Lord, aware of the sole purpose for which your Majesty desires a wife, and knowing the treatment she will receive at your Majesty's hands, I have . . ." The steward's voice cracked abruptly and he came to a stammering halt. An expression of utter incredulity spread over his face.

Ivan had leaned forward so that his elbows rested on his knees. "Proceed!" he barked impatiently.

"Sire!" whimpered the emissary. "I believe your Majesty should first peruse . . ." He held out the document with a hand that plainly trembled.

"God in Heaven!" thundered the Tsar. "Must I repeat a command? *Read it!*"

The steward's tongue made a salivous circuit of his lips, and he began falteringly: *". . . I have taken the liberty of . . . of making a . . . a more practical substitution which I trust will meet with your Grace's approval, because by the time you receive this token of my esteem, I shall be beyond recall."* The reader closed his eyes a moment, as if in prayer, then stumbled on: *"Be that as it may, so satisfied am I . . . that . . . that . . ."* His hands fell to his sides and he stared piteously at the Emperor.

"Sire! Sire! I cannot go on!" he wailed.

Ivan turned and gestured the Master of Hounds to move forward with his drooling charges. Susceptible to the emotional tension, the savage dogs bayed eagerly and leaped against their leashes with such force their handler ploughed twin furrows with his heels. He managed to halt them about three paces from the terrified emissary. Then he glanced over his shoulder at the Emperor for further instructions.

Ivan clamped his chin between thumb and fingers. "If this bumbling fool stops once more before he concludes his reading," he commanded in a low tone that was far more ominous than his roars, *"loose the dogs!"*

To Sir Guy, it seemed that not one man of the thousands gathered—unless, perhaps, Jaghellon and Ivan himself—so much as breathed as slowly, oh, so very slowly, the emissary raised the paper.

"So satisfied am I," he read, *"that your Majesty will find in this wellbred mare a connubial partner . . . more in accordance with your Majesty's . . . character and wants, I . . . I have exchanged her for the English maid!"* [10] The reluctant reader once more let his hands fall limply. "Sire," he concluded, "it is signed *Nikita!"*

For a full moment, the Emperor never moved a muscle—nor, it might be added, did anyone else. Then, when the full implications of the outrageous insult finally penetrated his consciousness, Ivan went berserk.

Convulsed with fury, he staggered drunkenly to his feet. *"Set the dogs on him!"* he exploded.[11]

As the Master of the Hounds slipped the leashes, Sir Guy automatically started forward. He had no time to analyze his reasons. While he had no particular affection for the officious little steward who had so recently sought his life, the insensate cruelty revolted him. Howbeit, before he had completed a full step, Pojorski caught and held him in a grip of steel.

"For the love of Allah, stand back!" he warned.

Though horrible, it was soon over. The three beasts shot forward in a wedge-shaped phalanx, the middle hound slightly ahead of his mates. The steward staggered backwards and loosed just one long scream of terror before the teeth of the leading dog clamped about his throat. After that, the victim lost consciousness.

The little blackamoor was more fortunate. When he perceived what was coming, he swung himself into the saddle, using the silver reins as a monkey uses a vine, and pivoting the terrified mare on her haunches, sent her flying back along the once white carpet at a dead gallop.

Not until the hounds had completed their grisly chore did the Emperor resume his seat. Then he sank back and made a motion with his hand. The Master of the Hounds released his snarling charges and two flunkys came forward and cleared away the human debris as casually as if cleaning a table.

Ivan slumped back as if the violent paroxysm had exhausted him. His long fingers gripped the arms of his throne.

"Jaghellon!"

The Cossack, who through it all had remained as imperturbable as a statue, now strode to the center of the stage.

"Sire?"

The Tsar eyed him bleakly. "I ordered you to bring back Nikita and the English woman!" he said in a voice somewhat less than sane. "Where are they?"

"Sire! You commanded me to return on the *third* day," was the unruffled reply.

"Do you know the whereabouts of Nikita?"

"No, sire!"

Ivan spat in impatience. "May the devil seize you, Jaghellon! I know you better than that! You would have found *some* hint of his destination!"

The Cossack bowed. "A hint, sire, yes. I learned that the Count had engaged a caravan to travel south!"

Ivan started out of his chair. "To *Crimea?*"

"So it is rumored, sire! To the Prince Dominion of his uncle, Akhmet, the Governor!"

The Tsar leaned his head back, staring into the darkness overhead. "I see it now!" he mused. "I see it now!" He struck his fist on the arm of his chair and sprang up with a shout that set the dogs to clamoring again. "By God, I'll move the army south to crush him!" he foamed. "Hark ye all! We march tonight!"

The chamberlain came howling down the carpet. "Your Majesty! Your Majesty! If we raise the siege, these accursed Poles will overrun Moscow! We dare not move so much as a division, sire! Reconsider, I beg you!"

The frenzied monarch glared wildly, then sank into his seat. "True!" he growled. "True! Then I am to be robbed, insulted, and outraged by this miserable mongrel upstart who was little better than a slave in my household?"

"Oh, best of Kings!" cried the chamberlain. "Better lose a woman than an empire!"

"A pox on your platitudes, yet I own that is true," conceded the Emperor grudgingly. "*The Englishman!*" he added abruptly. "*Where is he?*"

Sir Guy unclamped the dwarf's restraining grip. "Right here, your Majesty!" he said clearly.

As he pushed through the nobles before him, he was conscious that Affable Jones and Sergeant Pistol were in his wake. He paused to order them back, then with a deliberately unhurried stride marched to a place before the enraged Emperor.

"Your Majesty summoned me?"

Ivan glowered as if attempting to beat down his resistance by the very heat of his gaze.

"You knew of this perfidy?" he accused.

"No, sire, I did *not!*"

The Tsar started up. "You dare defy me?" he challenged.

Sir Guy shook his head. "My lord, I *dare* tell only the truth! But defy you—no!"

"We shall see! We shall see!" muttered the tyrant, clawing his fingers through his beard. "We have ways of getting at the truth!"

"So I have seen!" Sir Guy said evenly. "Howbeit, sire, I might at this point call your Majesty's attention to the fact that I am a subject and a representative of the *Queen of England!* She is a jealous mistress, sire!"

The Tsar's eyes blazed, but he held his temper in check. "We shall see! We shall see!" he reiterated in a knowing chant that made the hair stand erect along the back of Sir Guy's neck.

Ivan turned to the Cossack. "Jaghellon! You are familiar with the gist of the Englishman's tale of three days agone! Did you discover anything to the contrary in Moscow?"

"Not as yet, sire!"

The Emperor appeared so disappointed by this intelligence, the Master of the Hounds relaxed, but he was alerted a moment later by the tone with which Ivan again spoke.

"If you did not know that Nikita had fled south with your charge," he barked at Sir Guy, "*why were you in such haste to wheedle your passport out of Muscovy?*"

For one sickening moment, Sir Guy found himself completely tonguetied. True, he had had a premonition the Tsar suspected *something*—he had told his companions as much the night of the private audience—but that Ivan should believe him an accomplice of Nikita nonplused him. He pulled himself together and characteristically sought the offensive.

"Your Majesty!" he said, as coldly as he dared. "In the name of England's Queen, whom I have the undeserved honor to represent, I protest this intimation! Had I knowledge of Count Nikita's perfidy before it was a *fait accompli*, I would have slain him with my own hand. Had I known it before this hour, I would have gone in pursuit!" He patted the sword at his side. "And that, your Majesty, is the privilege, nay, the *right*, I now ask of you!"

The Emperor pursed his thin lips reflectively. The fire of his eyes was dimmed by shuttered lids, and when next he spoke, his voice was dangerously soft.

"So? You would pursue Nikita . . . even out of Muscovy?"

Sir Guy did not see the trap in time to save himself. "To the ends of the earth, if necessary!" he said stoutly.

Ivan cackled like a money-changer. "Ah, I thought so!" he jeered. His manner underwent a remarkable metamorphosis. He sat bolt upright, his eyes aflame with their former madness.

"You take me for a fool!" he shrieked. "Nikita goes one way with the woman, you the other with credentials signed by me! I've had enough of this impertinence and treachery! Here—hand over that safe-conduct I granted you!"

Sir Guy kept his gaze steady, but he had thrust his head into the noose, and he knew it. Out of the corner of his eye, he saw the Master of Hounds fingering his leashes. His heart sank. This was no time to cavil. He reached his hand into his doublet, where, next to his heart, he kept his precious papers. He hesitated, wondering if there was some way out, something he could say, or do, that might forestall losing all that he had gained.

"Well . . ." growled the Tsar.

Sir Guy withdrew his hand and reluctantly proffered a parchment, but Ivan did not deign to touch it.

"Jaghellon, destroy that!" he barked.

The Cossack took the folded vellum from the Englishman with one hand, while with the other he seized a torch from a nearby trooper. He lighted one corner of the document and held it until the flames touched his fingers, whereupon he dropped it to the ground and crushed it with his heel.

"Now," rumbled the Tsar forebodingly, "you two have either betrayed me or failed me; one crime is as bad as the other! You, Sir Envoy, came to deliver to me a certain Englishwoman; therefore, you will neither be received in audience nor be permitted to leave my domain until you have accomplished your mission!"

Sir Guy paled. "Sire! What of my retinue?" he demanded. "Regardless of my guilt or innocence, they cannot be . . ."

The Prince cut him off with a curt gesture. "The ruling applies equally to them!" Then, before Sir Guy could frame an objection, Ivan shifted his rage onto the Cossack.

"As for you, Jaghellon, you were sent after the Englishwoman and Count Nikita! By returning without them, you deserted your post. You know the penalty for desertion?"

"Death!" said Jaghellon.

"I so sentence you, Captain Jaghellon!" pronounced the Tsar. He paused, but if he expected the Cossack to exhibit any reaction, he was sadly disappointed. "However," he went on, "execution shall be de-

[223]

layed until the twelfth month from this day. If before the expiration of this reprieve, you produce the Englishwoman and either Count Nikita or his head, you will be eligible for pardon. Do you comprehend?"

The Cossack nodded. "I do, sire!"

"Very well. Now since this Englishman is so eager to take up the chase," continued the Tsar, with a malicious sidelong glance at Sir Guy, "he and his compatriots shall accompany you. While not technically under arrest, I place them in your *protection,* since it would be fatal for them to wander about the country without credentials or authority. I thereby hold you responsible for them. Is that also clear?"

"It is, sire!"

"You shall be permitted one thousand men, two small cannon, and supplies for one week! You will leave at daybreak!"

"Thank you, sire!"

At this, an audible groan rose from the assembled officers. A white-bearded old general stepped out of line and dared to lift his voice in protest.

"Your Majesty! Your Majesty! Reconsider!" he pleaded. "Execute Captain Jaghellon if you see fit, sire, but for the love of the Almighty God, do not doom one thousand valiant soldiers! We cannot spare them, sire! As your Majesty well knows, I was on that campaign in Crimea. We marched with a brave army of ninety thousand men; we expended forty thousand in the subjugation!"

"Are you disputing my authority, Omansky?" shouted the Tsar.

The old soldier shook his bald head. "God forbid! I've followed you since you were seventeen, sire, and I hope to follow you until I die! But as a practical matter, sire, you demand the impossible! We can assume that Nikita has gone to his uncle in Crimea. No doubt Akhmet, knowing your Majesty is engaged in a death struggle with these accursed Poles, has chosen this dastardly affront to herald a rebellion. But, sire, the chances of Captain Jaghellon's overtaking Nikita before the latter reaches the protection of Akhmet are remote. He is going through hostile territory. A thousand men would be annihilated before they had traversed half the distance."

"That is Jaghellon's problem!" snarled the Tsar.

"And supplies, sire?"

"Jaghellon can live off the land!"

The old warrior heaved his shoulders. "Then, sire, I can only say—*God help Jaghellon!*"

27

THE TSAR HAD COMMANDED; Jaghellon obeyed. Even before the first gray heralding of daybreak, the luckless cavalcade began forming for its desperate enterprise.

Under different auspices, the Englishmen might have considered it a gay and colorful spectacle, with the great golden carpet of flowers, the battered ramparts of the ancient city in the background, the half-wild Cossacks cavorting their mounts in a kind of disciplined disorder.

Some of these desperadoes carried long lances from the tips of which fluttered brilliant pennons, and their strange trumpets had a ghastly sound, like the cry of a night-hunting heron. Occasionally, in an outburst of uncontrolled exuberance, one would toss his razor-edged scimitar spinning high into the air; then, at the risk of losing a hand, catch it before it could strike the ground. If a single one of the barbarous-looking horde was concerned with the hopelessness of the task assigned them, he concealed it as effectively as did the stony-faced Cossack who led them.

The Englishmen were somewhat less stoical. Sir Guy was grim and embittered; resentful of the Emperor, enraged at Nikita for his treachery, and infuriated with himself. Affable Jones and Sergeant Pistol, having enjoyed three days of comparative leisure, were as well pleased to escape the uneven disposition of the Tsar, but the others, already exhausted by their brutal journey from Moscow, were in pathetic condition. This was especially so of Horace Belcher, whose unpadded posterior had developed a painful boil from the pounding received in the saddle.

Young Tutweiller, too, had fared badly. He had lost weight from a case of flux brought on by prison fare, and in addition had worried himself into a near-collapse over the fate of Ellen.

Old Paxton had borne the severities much better than his younger and hardier companions. He had, to be sure, lost more flesh than he could afford, so that, as Affable Jones phrased it, he resembled an "unwrapped mummy." Yet, having maintained his characteristic calmness of spirit, and taken his rest when opportunity offered, having endured no consciousness of guilt nor gnawing of unrequited passion, he had expended much less energy and emotion than the others.

Their departure was without fanfare. The rest of the army, considering them doomed, made no demonstration, and of course the Tsar did not appear. The only official recognition came in a very unwelcome form just at dawn, when, as the company was mounting, the chamberlain fluttered up, followed by the Master of Hounds, who, in turn, was accompanied by a particularly vicious-looking hound which he had the utmost difficulty restraining.

The chamberlain, despite his bulk, kept skipping blithely ahead of the dog. He seemed to be searching for someone. Then he spotted Affable Jones, and with a bleat of triumph, headed for him. When Affable saw this entourage bearing down on him, he hastily vaulted into the saddle and would have galloped off if a mounted Cossack nearby had not grabbed his reins. Affable's curses drew the attention of Captain Jaghellon and Sir Guy, both of whom converged on the scene at almost the same time.

Meanwhile, the chamberlain had delivered a grandiloquent oration to Affable Jones which that happy warrior received with apprehension but no comprehension. He sighed with relief when Sir Guy rode up beside him.

"Hey-day, m'lud, w'at in the ruddy 'ell's this blighter yammerin' about?" he demanded, folding his chubby legs over his nag's neck to keep them out of reach of the hungry-looking hound.

When Sir Guy questioned the chamberlain, that dignitary stared in amazement. "Why, sir, I am but carrying out the orders of my liege lord in delivering to this . . ." The chamberlain looked suspiciously at the worried Mr. Jones, then with a sniff, continued: ". . . this *gentleman* the lovely treasure he won from my master!"

When this was translated to Affable, he grinned from ear to ear. "Why, damme, that puts a different complexion in the sky!" he chortled. "W'ere is me little darlin'?"

The chamberlain's arm swept in a glorious gesture. "Here!" he said proudly, and pointed to the drooling hound.

"An 'ound *dog!*" Affable gasped.

The chamberlain corrected him. "A hound *bitch*, sir. Little Olga!"

On hearing her name, Little Olga stood on her hind legs, which put her red-flecked eyes on a level with Affable's own, mounted though he was. Either this, or the awful realization of what had happened, nearly unbalanced him. At the same time Sir Guy and Sergeant Pistol caught the drift, and their howls of merriment sent the big hound berserk.

"All right!" wailed Affable. "I been gulled before this! Ye've all 'ad yer bloody joke, so tyke 'er aw'y afore she chews a leg off'n me!"

Here a difficulty arose, for take her back the chamberlain could not. Disposing of the Emperor's property was an involved procedure, not to be lightly undertaken. Whether he wanted her or not, Mr. Jones was now the proud possessor of Olga, one of the finest, and meanest, hounds in the imperial kennels. To all this, Jaghellon agreed.

"You must cherish her!" warned the Cossack.

"Cherish 'er?" howled Affable. "I got about as much use fer an 'ound bitch as I 'ave fer another neck!"

"You'll need another neck if you refuse her now!" cautioned Sir Guy.

Sergeant Pistol gave one of his rare chuckles. "Oh, come now, me lad—we've all got our crosses. Sir Guy's got 'is Pojo, ol' Ivy's got 'is white mare, an' ye've got yer little Olga—God love 'er!"

Whatever else might be said about Olga, she was not lacking in intelligence. When the Master of Hounds, his eyes abrim with maudlin tears, put his arms around her neck and explained in voluble terms that henceforth she was to be the sole property of the vulgar little fat man seated on the horse, Olga seemed to understand. The hard gleam with which she had been regarding Affable began to soften until her eyes had the melting look of a love-sick sheep.

"As God's m'life, myke 'im stop fillin' 'er full o' that rot!" Affable pleaded frantically when he caught the drift. "The bitch now looks like she's plottin' to rype me, no less!"

Being assured that henceforth Olga would love, honor, and obey her new master, the chamberlain and the Master of Hounds retired to the sidelines, the latter sniffing and daubing his nose with his sleeve. Jaghellon cantered to the head of the column, and a moment later, the trumpeter pealed the signal. Olga took one last forlorn look at her ex-handler, then loosing a farewell yowl, she dutifully took her station just abaft Affable's left stirrup.

The procession swung into motion.

Those next five months were to Sir Guy Spangler what fire is to steel, and the valley of the Volga was the crucible. To an Englishman, accustomed to the compactness and varied scenery of his "tight little isle," the vastness and sameness of the Russias seemed incredible. Sir Guy began to feel a bit like a Moses lost in the Wilderness.

Through it all he nursed his hatred of Nikita as guardedly as a desert traveler cherishes his last drop of water, for it was the solitary flame which kept him going. Once, as he lay at night in the sand, watching the dance of the stars, the thought that Ellen might have conspired with Nikita to take her away burst into his haunted mind as clearly as if a viper had sprung from its coil and bitten him. Sir Guy ruthlessly beat the notion out of all recognition, but the venom it left in his mind startled him.

Almost from the start it became manifest why Jaghellon and his Cossacks were known as the "wolf pack," for with them the *law of the wild* prevailed. After the first niggardly week's supply of food was exhausted, the raids became an almost daily affair, and as food and fodder for a thousand mounted and hungry men would have impoverished many of the larger towns, to say nothing of the miserable villages, many resisted. Hungry men are desperate men; fire and the sword were commonplace. And almost nightly the screams and wails of women in a raided village haunted the Englishmen.

Yet one of the raids supplied humor of a kind. The scouts who had marked this village for their prey reported it as too small to offer serious resistance, so the assault was made in force and in daylight. But as the first of the raiders swept into the village, their horses suddenly went berserk, screaming, leaping into the air and rolling on the ground as if bewitched. Jaghellon himself was unseated, and Sir Guy voluntarily sprang out of his saddle when his nag went to her knees.

A hasty examination revealed the cause—*bees!* Countless thousands of them swarmed over the attackers, both man and beast. Swords were frantically exchanged for cloaks and other garments to beat off the diminutive warriors while a retreat was in progress. Finally, defeated, swollen and sore, the hungry Cossacks made a wide detour around the village and headed for the next one, many leagues away. A short time later they chanced upon a little shepherd lad, and from him learned that their rout had been no happenstance, but a deliberate strategy of the inhabitants, who maintained the bees for the purpose of incensing them against intruders.[12]

Sir Guy half expected the angry Cossacks would slaughter the hapless lad, but again he underestimated the Muscovite sense of humor. Once they discovered the incident had been a cunningly premeditated scheme, they roared with delight and admiration and loaded the terrified and incredulous shepherd boy with gifts—mostly loot they had pillaged up to the time—sufficient to insure his entire future. After this unexpected philanthropy they rode on, hooting and laughing at each other, and vying to see which had been most roughly handled by their winged victors.

Olga lightened many an otherwise drab moment. She had, willy-nilly, become the property of a certain portly Englishman, and her inbred duty was to protect him, whether he appreciated it or not. This she did with a typical Muscovite singleness of purpose. She was a huge tawny beast, whose back, when she stood squarely on her four feet, was slightly higher than her master's navel. When she reared onto her hind legs, she was forced to look down upon him.

Unfortunately, nearly all of Olga's ideas conflicted with her master's. The very pinnacle of her delight was to plant her forefeet on his shoulders and lick his face. This exhibition of canine ardor sent the others into convulsions of laughter, which seemed to encourage the big hound. And, need it be said, Affable drew scant sympathy from his companions.

"W'at the 'ell are ye bellyachin' about?" hooted Pistol. "Ye got h'exackly w'at ye arsked fer—the lovin'est dove in the covey!"

In this wise, with fire, sword, and rapine on one hand, and an occasional laugh, a coarse jest or two, and death on the other, they shoved deeper and deeper into the hostile wilderness. If they laid a scar across the land, they themselves did not come off unscathed. Man has no precision gauge with which to measure the ultimate results to the individual of exposure to intense hardships, to bestiality, and the constant expectation of sudden death. Some became brutalized and depraved; others, perhaps the majority, grow calloused and indifferent; a very few seem elevated to a state of exaltation. But, inevitably, all are marked in one fashion or another, for as tempering alters the outward appearance as well as the internal composition of steel, so, too, is man affected. And Sir Guy Spangler was no exception to the rule.

If he could not truthfully be said to have *aged* in the passage of months, he most certainly *matured*. In his case the distinction was patent. His finely chiseled features grew firmer without growing coarser. Wind and privation had accomplished some of this, as had a self-imposed continency; the balance came from an undefined inner source. The faint curlicues of mockery which heretofore had haunted the corners of his mouth disappeared. It was not so much that the expression of the mouth became harder as that it became stronger. His gait, too, underwent a subtle change. The bounce, the suggestion of swagger, gave way to a solid, hard-heeled stride. It was as if he weighed more, whereas in actuality he had lost weight. This gauntness was, in his case, becoming.

Sir Guy assured himself that his sole object was to recover Ellen—to kill Nikita was, of course, a requisite part of that accomplishment—and deliver her to the Tsar. That, and that alone! Yet though he would admit nothing more, sometimes of a night, when the roistering Cossacks were having their way with captive women and the pitiful cries made sleep impossible, he would be racked by the unbearable thought that such a frightful thing might be happening to Ellen.

Never before had mere *thoughts* had the intense virulence of a toothache as they had now. Even the passing notion that Ellen might have fallen in love with Nikita knifed him so hard he was nauseated; a transient mental picture of her in Nikita's arms made him unapproachable for days.

He pondered the wisdom of discussing this phenomenon with Master Paxton, but finally decided against it. It may be he dreaded the old man's analysis; perchance he half consciously sensed a truth that would have been quite obvious to a man less stubborn.

Though Count Nikita had enjoyed a full week's headstart through a region sympathetic to his uncle and himself, he not only did not gain on his avengers, but slowly, very slowly, they gained on him.

As the pack closed, he began to behave like a man in a small boat beset by sharks. He jettisoned cargo; he baited hooks and traps. He dropped the sick and aged among his entourage and these, on falling into the toils of the Cossacks, were persuaded to talk with astonishing fluency. The Count, as the pursuers had surmised, was heading for Crimea and Akhmet; in fact, Akhmet was presumed to be advancing to meet his favorite nephew. Yes, the English wench was alive and in good health, though a sullen piece of baggage she was! Had the Count violated her? It was possible—who could tell? And since the Count was going to wed her anon, what mattered it if he bedded her now? Perhaps it was Kismet!

Kismet or no, Count Nikita was not destined to reach Astrakhan. A hundred odd leagues short of it, and a half day's hard riding from the ancient fortress of Budeüa, Jaghellon's wolves caught sight of him. Only by sacrificing most of his company in a hopeless rear-guard action was he enabled to escape with Ellen and a handful of retainers. Now that the pack had scented the kill, they slaughtered the rear-guard with hardly a pause, and lustily giving tongue, chased the Count and his precious hostage to the very gates of the fortress. They were literally snapping at his heels as he and the remnants of his followers scuttled behind the ancient walls.

Sir Guy offered up a grim little prayer of thanksgiving. After two and twenty hellish weeks of pursuit, he had at long last treed his quarry. Best of all, Ellen was within hailing distance, and safe! It remained only to kill Nikita and recover her.

Captain Jaghellon was noncommittal. While he could not accurately be described as pessimistic, since that word connotes a form of emotion —and Jaghellon never permitted such weakness—he certainly took a dim view of the situation. Budeüa would be a tough nut to crack. This venerable stronghold had withstood the assault of Timur the Lame (he whose terrible name has come down to us contracted to Tamerlane) and his Mongol horde in the fourteenth century, and it was still stout. Jaghellon intended to reconnoiter in the morning.

That was the best Sir Guy could wring out of him.

28

Though doubtless he would have been reluctant to admit it, Sir Guy had developed a grudging respect for the gruff warrior whom Fate had made both gaoler and ally. It was a peculiar relationship; neither quite trusted the other, which is to say neither understood the other. In almost every conceivable way they were antithetical. And while Jaghellon on the surface seemed the very epitome of his breed, little differences stood out. He could, for instance, execute a man (or a woman, too) without exhibiting a trace of so-called human feeling; yet he killed solely because a soldier's profession is killing. He never interfered with the traditional customs of pillage and rapine; he could stride past a group of his barbarians violating a screaming woman without a flicker of expression, yet it was noticed that he himself never took a woman, willing or otherwise. Sir Guy had come to regard the burly Cossack as something less than human, so that it was with complete surprise he inadvertently learned Jaghellon had a wife and seven children in a little village whose unpronounceable name lent it a sort of unreality.

The travelers had left the dreary plains country for a region of primeval forests and rolling hills. Here the tip of a mountain range had nosed its way into the river so that it lay cradled in an arm-crook of the mighty Volga, which flowed caressingly on three sides. On this verdant spot stood the historic fortress of Budeüa, its white crenellated walls gallantly squired by little minaret-shaped towers, whose golden cupolas glittered in the early sunlight. Conceived originally by a feudal baron whose purpose was to levy tribute on all traffic plying the river, it had become more than a mere monument to that avarice; it was a testament to a poetic sense of beauty.

But to the two grim-faced adventurers who appraised it now, it was less a work of art than a tactical problem, and with the eyes of soldiers, they considered not its beauty but its strength. Jaghellon stared so long with neither a word nor a change of expression, that Sir Guy finally burst out: "Well—what do you make of it?"

Slowly, and without heroics, the Cossack analyzed the situation. If not actually impregnable, Budeüa was too stout to be stormed successfully by a band of weary men who were without either food or the crudest of siege implements. In fact, Jaghellon conceded, with the force at his command it would be extremely difficult to maintain a siege.

"It is pointless to discuss a siege," Spangler said. "If Nikita were to pass a courier through our lines, his uncle could have an army here from the south within a month!"

Jaghellon came as close to laughing as he ever did. "You need no longer worry about that: Nikita dispatched such a courier last night. *Akhmet's army will be here within the fortnight!*"

Sir Guy gaped in amazement. "You let a courier get through?"

"I am not a fish," retorted the Cossack. "The courier who tried to go by land, I caught; the one who went by boat got away. This much we learned: Akhmet's army will come, not from the south, but from the *north* where already five thousand troops are stationed to guard against a surprise assault by the Tsar." Jaghellon shrugged. "Nikita missed that army, and so, thanks be to God, did we."

Sir Guy whistled. "Then by the same token they straddle our return route!"

"Obviously. It is not Nikita who is trapped. We are."

"What do you propose to do?"

"Storm the place! Fortunately the Count does not know how miserable a force I have!"

"But damn it, you just conceded that was impossible," argued the Englishman.

Jaghellon wagged his head. "Not impossible—*improbable!*" he grunted with Slavic fatalism. "I cannot leave without taking or killing Nikita. Those are my orders!"

"Oh, the hell with Nikita!" fumed Sir Guy. "The main consideration is the *girl!*"

The Cossack growled his retort without heat. "I am responsible only to my Prince."

Sir Guy was worn and exhausted, and unfamiliar emotions had played havoc with his usually impervious nerves. In his present frame of mind, an open break might well have occurred between him and the Cossack if at that particular moment Pojorski, accompanied by Mr. Paxton, Sergeant Pistol, and Affable Jones—and, of course, the inevitable Olga—had not appeared on the scene. Jaghellon nodded curtly and stalked off down the hill.

"I 'opes we didn't spoil a jolly bit o' 'omicide, yer Gryce?" chortled Affable.

"Seems we did, though!" opined Sergeant Pistol.

"Mind your own God-damned business!" Sir Guy snarled, so vehemently that Olga was moved to hover closer to her adored master.

Sir Guy's mood having been so adequately demonstrated, three of the four arrivals had the wit to hold their tongues. The exception was the dwarf.

"By the liver of Shaitan, this will be a tough nut to crack!" he observed, waving a hand in the general direction of the fortress. Sir

Guy ignored him, so after a pause, Pojorski went on: "If we could but get inside, it would be simple."

Sergeant Pistol made a derisive noise with his mouth. "W'at the ruddy 'ell d'ye know 'bout it?"

Pojo turned on him angrily. "More than any camelfaced Englishman! I spent three happy weeks in that place!"

"Torturin' someone, no doubt," jibed Affable Jones. "That's all it tykes to myke ye 'appy."

"True!" retorted the dwarf. "It was after the last rebellion, and, I might add, I wish *you two* had been among the victims!" He held up his hands for inspection. "With these very thumbs, I blinded one hundred and seven rebels, strangled three and thirty, and . . ."

Sir Guy's roar of anger silenced him. "Begone! All of you! Damn it, I came up here to think, not to listen to the braying of jackasses!" As they jumped to obey, he motioned Paxton to remain seated. "Not you, Ancient!" he growled. "I'd like a word with you."

When the banished trio had taken Olga and their bickering out of hearing, Sir Guy told the old philosopher about the courier, and the bitter fact that Akhmet's army was between them and Moscow. He also summarized what Jaghellon proposed to do. During this recounting the old man listened, not with the stolid stoicism of the Cossack, but with a great and kindly patience which, to Sir Guy, was almost as galling.

"Well, that's all of it! What do you think?"

"*You* tell *me*," urged Paxton, smiling. "I am not in command."

Sir Guy sniffed. "Neither am I—as that hammerheaded Cossack reminded me!"

"I am not so sure of that," said the old man. "Captain Jaghellon is a brave and fearless soldier, but methinks he has the warrior's scorn for the power of imagination, a faculty he lacks, but which you do not."

"It's going to take more than imagination to storm that damned fort!"

Paxton smiled. "Yes, it is going to take honesty."

"What are you talking about? Who's been dishonest?"

"*You*, Sir Guy!"

Sir Guy started up in rage, then sank back. "To whom have I been dishonest?"

"Yourself!"

"Prove it!"

"Very well. Why are you so determined to get Ellen away from Count Nikita?"

"To deliver her to Ivan, of course!"

"You are *certain* of that, eh?" probed Paxton. "Certain of it, knowing in your heart that with Nikita she would assuredly fare better than at the bloodied hands of Ivan the Terrible? At least Nikita desired her enough to risk his life!"

Sir Guy went deathly pale. "How she fares has nothing to do with it!" he roared. "This is a strictly business proposition!"

Mr. Paxton made a gesture of resignation. "I have proven my point, sir."

In a surge of fury, Sir Guy reached over and gripped the old man's shoulder.

"You dare accuse me of lying!"

Paxton was not perturbed. "Not *you*, Sir Guy—your *tongue!*" he said quietly. "Your heart spoke true when it jerked the very blood out of your face at the thought of another man possessing Ellen; when it made your hands tremble, and your temper snap. Those manifestations, my son, are hardly indicative of a 'strictly business proposition,' as you phrased it! Your words are of no importance, for the unlying truth is not revealed in *what* you say, but *how* you say it!" He sighed again. "Alas, there is just one thing that puzzles me."

"You have gone this far, you may as well get it all out of your system!"

"Aye, I suppose that is so. Well, it is just this: why you, who have the keenest intelligence and sharpest wits of the whole company, should fail to see what the rest of us have known for months!"

"And that is . . . ?"

The old man smiled gently. *"That you, Sir Guy, are desperately and uncontrollably in love with Ellen!"*

Sir Guy sat staring at the old man, yet not seeing him. The latter remained where he was a little longer, then slowly pushed to his feet.

"Charity told me something like that!" stammered Spangler, half to himself.

"Charity would feel it first," murmured Paxton. He turned away. "I think it best I leave."

But of a sudden, Sir Guy Spangler was afraid to be alone. "Don't go!" he pleaded. "What you've told me cannot be! It *cannot!* Why, man, I could not turn a woman I loved over to that insensate beast Ivan!"

Mr. Paxton chuckled. "I did not expect you would, if she were recovered from Nikita."

Sir Guy was completely befuddled. "But what of the deal we made?" he cried. "Why, the whole success of the venture, our very lives, in fact, depend on Ellen's going to Ivan!"

The old man sighed gently and shrugged his shoulders. "I am not arguing the matter with you, my boy; you have the entire conflict within yourself!"

The clear, icy summons of a trumpet brought them back to the present. Sir Guy sprang to his feet. Below, in a clearing just out of bow-shot of the walls, Jaghellon was marshaling his wolf pack.

"The fool!" groaned Sir Guy. "He's going to try to carry the place by storm!"

"*Stop him!*" commanded the ancient in an imperative tone he had never before used in the other's hearing. "Whether he fails or succeeds, for *you* all will be lost! *You will never get Ellen out of there alive . . . by force!*"

Sir Guy felt suddenly overwhelmed by something akin to panic. "There is no other way!"

Paxton seized him by the arm and they started running down the hill. "There is, there is!" panted the older man. "There is *imagination*—the most potent force in the world! Use it, man, use it!" He fell back exhausted.

Sir Guy plunged on down the slope. *Stop Jaghellon!* Possibly he might be stopped by the blade of a sword, yet that would be to use force. *You will never get Ellen out of there alive . . . by force!*

Then how? Oh, God, *how*?

What happened to Sir Guy Spangler in those next few moments was more than a mere passage through the forest. Man, it is said, never changes. This may be technically true, yet at various stages in this brief passage we know as "life," he undergoes an inner metamorphosis—call it change, maturity, development, or what you will—as marked, if not as manifest, as when an insect larva becomes a pupa, or a tadpole a frog. Thus, though in a physical and geographical sense Sir Guy Spangler simply plunged down a wooded slope on the banks of the Volga, in the vaster imponderable scheme of things his real experience was incomparably more significant, for he passed through a trackless valley wherein he came to grips with man's worst enemy—himself! There, in that darkness, and after a terrible travail, he triumphed by resolving the schism which had all but ruined him. He made his peace with himself by a very simple confession: his love for Ellen.

And so, if he did not have the solution to the problem by the time he reached the company, he had something of equal, if not greater, importance—repossession of his reasoning faculties.

As he pounded up, Jaghellon had just completed an inspection of the improvised ram he had devised for battering in the gates of

Budeüa. This ingenious implement was merely a long straight tree trunk suspended on ropes between two lines of horses. The working-end of this hardwood shaft had been adzed to a sharp point and capped with a steel casque, such as Jaghellon was wearing on his own head.

This was the first time Sir Guy had ever seen the implacable Cossack in armor; heretofore Jaghellon had scorned such defensive protection. He nodded briefly to the Englishman, then turned to mount his champing war-horse.

As yet Sir Guy had no plan, but he did have an objective—to get Ellen out safely. This, on the surface, was not original; it was the purpose for which he had come. But now, in some mysterious fashion, it seemed entirely new and fresh, and Jaghellon, instead of being an ally in the endeavor, had perversely become an obstacle. So if Sir Guy had no tactics laid down, his over-all strategy was to play the game as old Paxton had suggested: to meet brute strength with intellect.

He bellowed for Pojorski to bring up his own charger, then walked over to the Cossack.

"So that dog Nikita rejected your ultimatum, eh, Captain?" he commented, not questioningly, but rather in the tone of a man making conversation.

Jaghellon grunted disdainfully. "I sent no ultimatum! It would be a waste of time!"

The Englishman feigned astonishment. "Really? I gathered from the remark you made a little while ago, about Nikita not knowing the miserable extent of your force, you meant to capitalize on that ignorance." He paused, then when he saw the black brows begin to knit, added with a shrug: "Howbeit, if he already knows, I presume we might as well commit suicide. Ah . . . here's my horse!"

Sir Guy mounted, then sat staring at the distant gate as Jaghellon figuratively sniffed at the bait. Behind him his men began cavorting restlessly. He waited until the Englishman was in the saddle before speaking.

"What do you mean—*capitalize on that ignorance?*"

"Why, obviously the governor and other elders of Budeüa won't long harbor Nikita once they are convinced it is hopeless! Only a fool throws his life away to no purpose!"

Jaghellon felt the barb, for he flinched and started a verbal lunge, but curiosity brought him up short.

"Bah! You spew words without meaning!" he growled, yet his tone implied an invitation to continue.

Sir Guy grinned disarmingly. "Methinks you jest, Captain! Why, I'll wager that in your various campaigns you've gulled a score of commanders far wilier than either that hot-blooded Tatar or the provincial oaf who governs this molehill!" He chuckled aloud. " 'Pon my soul, an old fox like you should be able to concoct a ruse that would make Budeüa deliver you Nikita all trussed up like a fowl!"

Jaghellon's slant eyes narrowed to mere slits. "All things are possible . . . with time," he mused, almost as if to himself. "But the dog has only to hold out two weeks!"

"Ah, true!" pressed the other. "Yet *Nikita* does not know that, for he cannot be certain his courier passed our lines."

The pupils of the Cossack appeared between shuttered lids, like the lowering mouths of two small cannon.

"Speak your mind!" he snapped, with the soldier's contempt for diplomacy. "When do *you* suggest we attack?"

"As I see it, Captain," Sir Guy said agreeably, "the problem is not *when* to attack, but *how!*"

"*How?* Bah! The direct, head-on attack is the surest!"

"That," said Sir Guy, smiling, "is the principle held to by the bulls in Spain. The matador holds a contrary opinion. Statistics clearly prove which of the two most frequently survives the encounters."

Jaghellon fairly squirmed in the saddle. "God grant me patience! We gossip like old wives!" he roared angrily, and it was, perhaps, the first time Sir Guy had discerned an emotional response in the bluff warrior. "Is it that you are afraid to go, Englishman?"

Sir Guy kept his head and met the jibe with a bland grin. "On the contrary, my bull-headed comrade," he retorted without malice, "it is just that I am not afraid not to go! My concern is to recover the woman, not exhibit my eagerness to die like a soldier. By my troth, I can do that later!" He laughed heartily. "And the later the better, say I! Be that cowardice, *mon capitaine?*"

Jaghellon's barklike guffaw took Sir Guy by surprise. "Englishman, you called me a *fox* when you desired me to perpetrate some trickery, then a *bull* when I would not!"

"A figure of speech," murmured Sir Guy, unable to guess which direction the Cossack was taking.

"Yet truer than you intended, no doubt!" rumbled the Cossack. "Now I am just an ignorant soldier, and therefore had no knowledge of the mortality rate of bulls in Spain, but in Muscovy, and particularly in the service of my Prince—who perhaps I should inform you, dislikes cunning and trickery, *bulls* enjoy a longer, safer life than the clever *foxes.*" He snorted contemptuously. "Hence, I am content to be a bull."

Despite all his good resolves, Sir Guy could feel his temper slipping.

"Very well!" he said irritably. "Since we scorn the use of brains, let's proceed to beat them out against the damned fort and get it over with!"

Strangely enough, the rugged veteran wagged his head. "No, not yet! Since you prefer figures of speech, I will put it this way, the bull has listened to the fox insinuate that it is not necessary to butt down the barn door to get the grain; that there is a safe and easy way to get the farmer to open it willingly. Now *that* is a trick this old bull wants to learn!" His laugh was brutal in its mockery. "So, Sir *Fox*, for one week, and *one week only*, my gentle lambkins and I will rest on this hillside and watch *you* perform the miracle!"

Sir Guy was taken full aback. "Now, just a moment, Captain! I did not . . ." he began, but the other silenced him ruthlessly.

"No more!" he commanded. "I do not take kindly to interference, and, by God, you have interfered too much already! To learn *why* is the chief reason I have decided on a week's delay! There is something going on here which I do not yet comprehend. Possibly the fox has the same objective for getting into the barn as the bull has, but before I take that risk, I mean to make certain! So—you have just seven days in which to secure Nikita and the woman by guile. After that . . ." His words seemed to hang suspended, like the stroke of an ax stopped in mid-air.

Not trusting his own voice, Sir Guy merely bowed in agreement.

29

The second dawn, like the first, found Sir Guy atop the high ground facing the fortress, waiting for an opportunity to continue his study of the living map. But this time he was entirely alone.

By arousing Jaghellon's suspicions about his motives, he had immeasurably increased the danger to his companions and himself. Nor had he any illusions about his compatriots. Belcher would turn against him the instant he suspected Sir Guy wanted Ellen for himself, rather than to use as a medium of barter for the ship. Tutweiller, already lovesick over the girl, would consider him a personal rival. Old Paxton would never betray him, but the venerable philosopher could offer no tangible assistance. Pojo, obviously, was utterly unpredictable. Of course, there were always those two faithful spaniels, Affable Jones and Sergeant Pistol, loyally ready to cut any throat their beloved master should specify, but at the moment the circumstances called for something more than cheerful assassination.

Having cleared up the confusion of his own emotions by admitting his love for Ellen, he carefully shelved that love—insofar as it is ever possible to shelve such a flame—so that it would not becloud his thinking. It was a settled fact, hence there was no point in stewing about it. Precisely what Ellen might have to say about this newly discovered ardor was another problem that could be faced in the future.

Now, as the pale light spread over the scene, first colorless, then budding into iridescence, the fortress looked more impregnable than ever. Try as he would to marshal his wits and evolve a plan, certain salient points loomed so large as to obliterate all else. He set them up in his mind, as targets to be shot down one by one.

Budeüa was too strong to be stormed!
There was not sufficient time to maintain a siege!
Their retreat was already cut off by a force outnumbering them at least ten to one!
They had nothing, neither threat nor prize, to offer Nikita by way of a compromise, let alone to induce him to surrender his stolen treasure and his own life.

These facts were irrefutable.

He rummaged through his memory and reviewed the various romantic stratagems he had utilized in the past in other daredevil enterprises, in Spain, France, and Italy, but these were countries of romance, and the actors had danced to his pipes. But here, in the cold face of Slavic realism, such schemes had a hollow, almost childish ring and evaporated like dreams.

By mid-morning he gave up the struggle and tramped down to the encampment. The instant he passed within the lines, he sensed a change of attitude in the Cossacks. He doubted that Jaghellon had discussed their difference with his men, but primitive peoples have a kind of clairvoyance which ofttimes makes them aware of things hidden from those supposedly more "highly civilized." Affable Jones and Sergeant Pistol sensed the altered mood, for they dogged his footsteps unbidden, as Olga dogged theirs, with a stiff-legged protective truculence.

In a moment of desperation Sir Guy dispatched his servant—a stalwart Kalmuck whom Jaghellon had assigned him—to the fortress under a flag of truce, with a request to Nikita to meet with him on neutral ground and discuss prevention of needless slaughter and the sack of Budeüa. The emissary had barely left before Sir Guy regretted the impulse, and when he returned, Sir Guy had even more cause for self-recrimination.

The Kalmuck staggered into Guy's tent, supported by Jones and Pistol. His eyes had been gouged out of his head at Nikita's order, but before fainting, he managed to gasp out the gist of the Count's reply, to wit: the Count considered the request that he leave his sanctuary as childish, the threat to sack Budeüa as ridiculous. Howbeit, if the Englishman still desired to converse, and had the courage to ride alone within hailing distance of the main gate of the fortress, the Count would tear himself away from the charming company of his beautiful betrothed, and appear himself on the ramparts of the southwest tower this same afternoon at precisely four of the clock.

Sick with fury, Sir Guy waved his men away with their tragic burden. He decided he had best face Jaghellon and concede his error before the commander heard about it from another source. As he started across the camp towards the Cossack's booth, Affable, Pistol, and Olga appeared as if by magic and fell in behind him. He ignored that at first, but within sight of his destination, he stopped and forbade them to accompany him further. They made no comment, yet when he strode on, they continued at his heels. He whirled in a temper.

"Didn't you hear my order?" he roared.

The two knaves exchanged bewildered glances. "Mister Pistol," Affable asked politely, "can ye 'ear anythin'? I be stone deef!"

To which the solemn sergeant wagged his head. "Nary a bloody sound, Mister Jones," he rejoined. "I be e'en deefer'n a stone!"

Olga bared her fangs and contributed a warning growl.

Conscious that the commander's sentries were taking it all in, Sir Guy muttered dire threats to be executed privately in the immediate future, then still dogged by his unwelcome attendants, stomped into the presence of the redoubtable Jaghellon. There he told his tale without adornment.

He anticipated an explosion, but the Cossack heard him out with a calmness that bordered on indifference. The result, Jaghellon insisted, was precisely what should have been expected of a Tatar. The flag of truce? Bah, that was effeminate nonsense!

When the Englishman expressed concern for the poor Kalmuck who had been mutilated, that, too, Jaghellon shrugged aside. You could not hope to send a spy into a fortress and have him allowed to see it. When you lived by the sword, you died by the sword. It was nothing to worry about.

"By God, it may be *nothing* to you!" Sir Guy burst out bitterly. "But if I accomplish naught else when I see Nikita, I'll have the satisfaction of telling him what I think of his cowardly act!"

Jaghellon's eyes widened a hair's width. "See him?" he grunted. "Are you mad enough to walk into his trap?"

"I have no fear of Count Nikita!"

The Cossack loosed what was intended for a laugh, but which, as Affable Jones aptly described it, sounded like the bark of a seal.

"And I called you a *fox*? Bah, a sheep has more sense!"

"You afforded me a week!" Sir Guy reminded him coldly.

Jaghellon snorted. "Because I overestimated you! Howbeit, if you get within bow-shot of that tower, Nikita will shorten your week." He wagged his head. "Well, if you must go, I have a suit of full armor I can lend you."

"Thank you! I need no armor to face a coward!"

Jaghellon shrugged. "Englishman, you are a fool! We will bury you tonight, and attack at dawn!" He turned his back to indicate in his subtle fashion that the interview was over.

As the appointed time drew nigh, Spangler made what few arrangements he deemed necessary. The first was to give a pouch of gold, sufficient to assure a peasant against want for two normal lifetimes, to the suffering Kalmuck. But this very act of charity, which he unconsciously expected to lighten his burden, merely increased it. Gold, he realized, cannot purchase a pair of eyes!

On his way back to his quarters, he pondered the wisdom of writing a note to Ellen, but decided against it. To tell her at this late date that he regretted what he had done to her would be as futile as offering the gold to the blind man. He wondered, bitterly, if blindness was as terrible as this sudden ability to *see*.

It was now time to leave for his rendezvous, so he hurried into his tent to pick up his sword. To his amazement, he found a fine suit of chainmail spread out on his couch, and an instant later, discovered Affable Jones and Sergeant Pistol standing on either side of the entrance.

"May a murrain seize you two!" he roared. "I told you I would wear no armor! Now get the hell out of my sight! The next time either of you disobeys me, I'll have you . . ."

Affable heaved the sigh of a foundered mare. "Tsk-tsk, I feared 't would be necessary, Mister Pistol!"

The sergeant sadly concurred. "Do yer dooty, Mister Jones!"

Before the angry knight knew what was happening, he was spun off-balance, a cloak was dropped over his head, then while Pistol's bony arms encircled his neck, Affable pinioned his legs and flipped him upside down. Thereupon, in much the same rudely efficient fashion a sheep is sheared, they disrobed him.

"Pink 'ided, ayant 'e?" marveled the dour Pistol.

"Ne'er mind 'is 'ide!" panted Affable. "Pass me 'em steel pants afore 'e tosses me off!"

In this wise, Sir Guy Spangler, sometime Knight of the Garter, was arrayed in a suit of chainmail next his bare hide and, over that, his regular garb. Not until the last button was buttoned and the last point tied did his self-appointed valets permit him to rise.

By that time, Sir Guy's rage had passed its zenith, hence when he rose to his full stature and the flexible links of the armor caught and pulled on the hairs of his chest, the ridiculousness of the situation hit him so that he exploded into involuntary laughter.

"'Pon my soul, the very least you insubordinate bastards might have done was put a linen shirt under this accursed chainmail!" he stormed. "Oh, don't think because I'm laughing you're forgiven. By the gods, I'll have the hides flayed off you for this unpardonable effrontery!"

Affable Jones, with an arm carefully draped over Olga's broad back, appeared suitably humble. "I cryves yer Gryce's bloody fergiveness!" he whined. "Yet, as I ayant been pyd fer me fythful services, I 'as to perteck me inwestment."

"'E took the wery words out o' me mouth!" murmured Pistol.

Sir Guy hesitated. He had refused armor because he didn't want Count Nikita to get the notion he was afraid of him, but as it was now almost four of the clock, there was no time to change, especially since it required assistance to unbuckle the chainmail. Then there was another factor which he would not have conceded to these smug knaves—which was that the armor fitted so snugly it was not discernible under his outer clothing. So he seized his sword and glowered darkly at the smirking pair.

"I shall deal with you two when I return!" he assured them as he stalked out.

Jaghellon had ordered out a mounted escort of a hundred picked warriors, although he himself did not appear. These bearded centaurs followed Sir Guy in the manner of a pack of the beasts after which they were named, until he reached the broad clearing in front of the fortress. Then he commanded them to remain behind the fringe of trees, while he himself rode on.

It was a lonely ride. This open area between the forest and the main gate was in length about twice the distance of a bowshot, and surfaced with a fine gravel of such whiteness it seemed phosphorescent in the brilliant sunlight. While Sir Guy had no sense of physical fear, he did feel somewhat like a very small boat adrift on a very large sea. He kept a tight rein on his big black charger to control its nervousness, and an even tighter rein upon himself.

Like the rest of Budeüa (excepting, of course, its occupants) the main gate was a thing of beauty; even the great bronze studs in the oiled timbers had been arranged to form a design. On either side of the gate—nay, they were an integral part of it—were graceful minaret-shaped towers. In the turret of one stood a herald with a golden trumpet.

As Sir Guy held his lively mount to a normal walk, he tried to spot Count Nikita among the people lining the ramparts. But the sun was in his eyes, hence they appeared as so many brightly outlined silhouettes. It came to him, with something of a jolt, that doubtless Nikita had set the appointment for late afternoon with this very thing in mind.

Sir Guy had made some calculations of his own, and he had determined in advance to go but halfway across the clearing. This would bring him just barely within bow-shot, which was a risk to be sure, but if Nikita attempted anything so treacherous as a sally in the hope of capturing him, he would have an even chance of making the woods. As this possibility occurred to him, he felt almost grateful for the "wolf pack" skulking among the trees.

When, at last, he reached the halfway mark he had set for himself, he halted. The herald sent one thin cold note into the air. Sir Guy's charger began to prance first one way, then the other, the big hooves drumming musically on the hard-packed gravel.

And then Count Nikita appeared.

Though his features were in shadow, there was no mistaking him. Even at that distance, his prominent nose and truculent stance set him apart from the others as plainly as a hawk among barnyard fowl. He shouted something, and while the reverberations of his voice reached the Englishman, the words were unintelligible.

Sir Guy dropped his reins and made a trumpet of his hands. "Speak louder!" he bellowed. "Or come out and talk like a man!"

Nikita heaved his shoulders, made a pantomimic gesture that the request was impossible, then beckoned the Englishman to draw closer.

"Fer God's syke, *nay!*" called a voice which, had it not been so heavily larded with the flavor of Whitefriars, Sir Guy might have accepted as the cry of his own reason. He glanced over his shoulder to see Sergeant Pistol and Affable Jones, mounted and flanked by the inevitable Olga, lined up with the Cossacks.

Sir Guy gave them a curt nod; it was sound advice. He had fulfilled his part of the bargain, and if Nikita was too cowardly to come within hailing distance now, the onus would be on him.

So thought Guy Spangler, until he turned back to the gate and saw *Ellen!*

There was even less chance of mistaking her than there had been of mistaking Nikita, for the sunshine cast a radiant wine-colored halo around her matchless hair. She had, apparently, burst onto the balcony unbidden, for she seemed to be struggling with two soldiers, while Nikita stood, gesturing them to remove her.

Sir Guy felt the tides of his rage begin to flood. He tried hard to keep reason afloat, but his whole body began to tremble and small red flecks drifted across his vision. As he stared, Ellen broke from her captors, and leaning over the rail, called to him.

At that, Sir Guy threw discretion to the winds, and sank his spurs. The big black charger soared into a gallop, the great hooves drowning out the warning bellows from behind.

He had covered more than half the remaining distance to the gate before he saw that Ellen was trying frantically to motion him away. When this realization hit him he drew reins so sharply the war-horse went back on his haunches. As he slid to a stop, Ellen's cry came clearly.

"Flee, Guy, flee! It is a trap! For the love of God, flee!"

It was an unfortunate choice of words, for, to Sir Guy Spangler, the very suggestion of flight was offensive. But as this was no time to quibble, he jerked his steed onto his hindlegs and paused to shout: "Courage, Ellen! I'll be back!"

That was the most effective speech Sir Guy ever made, for it saved his life. In delaying his retreat to deliver it, he kept his heavy charger facing the gate. Thus the cannon ball, so perfidiously fired from a port in the tower, caught the horse in the bowels instead of taking the rider in the spine, as intended. At the impact, the horse was hurled onto its back before Sir Guy could fight clear of the saddle. Man and beast went down in a dusty tangle!

Fortunately the poor brute was killed outright, otherwise Sir Guy would have been crushed in its struggles. As it was, his left leg was pinned under the inert mass. But even this was not an unmixed blessing, for seeing the cannon had failed to complete the treachery, a shower of arrows attempted a *coup de grace,* which was foiled by the protective bulk of the dead beast.

Bitterly cursing his own culpability, Sir Guy huddled into the lee of his horse, which by this time had begun to resemble a gruesome pincushion, and wondered what the outcome would be. It was a paradoxical situation, for though as chief actor he held the center of the stage, he could take no active part in the play.

Unable to reach him with arrows, the Budeüaians decided on a sally to seize him. This was the thing Sir Guy dreaded above all else, so as he saw the ponderous gates begin to open, he rose up on one elbow to free his sword. This move, his first since the crash, brought a yelp from Affable Jones.

"'E's alive! Lor' lumme, 'e's alive!"

Glancing back, Sir Guy saw the whole cavalcade break the cover of the woods, and with Affable and Pistol in the lead, sweep forward with undisciplined fury. He smiled thinly, a sudden tickling irritating his throat. What a pair! What an incomparably precious pair of loyal, faithful, true-blue, thieving cutthroats! But though glorious, theirs was a hopeless charge, for they had three times the distance to cover as had the enemy—thanks to Sir Guy's own stupidity.

He turned his head.

This way the view was grimmer. About a score of Tatars, unhampered by armor and mounted on small swift ponies, were heading for him at full gallop. As things stood now, they could either kill or capture him and get safely back into the fortress before his own men could possibly overtake them. Sir Guy decided they would have to kill him if they wanted him, and having made this decision, he set about to make himself as expensive as possible.

Held down by the dead horse, there was not a great deal he could do. A petard would have been the thing, in which case he could wait until the whole vicious drove of them got sufficiently close to escort them all to hell in one flaming finale. With only his sword, he could collect but a pittance of his self-evaluation. Nevertheless, he slipped the weapon out of sight and feigned unconsciousness. As his ear touched the ground, the thunder of hooves was magnified to earthquaking proportions.

Lying there inert, with the drumming of approaching doom in his ears, it was inevitable he should contemplate the end. He was not afraid to die; he was merely irked that it should have been in such a senseless effort. He had a sense of embarrassment, rather than terror; a feeling of regret instead of rage. Then the Tatar ponies pounded to a stop above him, and he had other things to think about.

As has been emphasized before in this chronicle, Sir Guy Spangler was an opportunist; one of those rare souls who *can* change horses in the middle of a stream. Though he had planned to cut down the first Tatar to blunder within range, when from under nearly closed lids he saw two of the enemy loop ropes around the legs of the dead horse, he stayed his arm. Thus he remained motionless while they hauled the equine corpse off his leg. But when, following this, two of the Tatars—so sure of themselves they had not bothered to unsheathe their scimitars—reached down to seize him, he buzzed into action like an angry hornet.

He had no illusion about the outcome; he knew it was futile, but it salved his hurt pride to increase the price upon himself. A moment before, he had hoped to collect but one miserable Tatar; he now had two and was working on a third when, with howls of rage, the whole band started to circle him preliminary to hacking him to pieces. Sir Guy got his third Tatar and a bad scalp wound simultaneously. He decided now that if he got one more Tatar, he'd be extremely lucky. He tried to pick his victim. . . .

It was at this precise point that Sir Guy received a visitation from an angel.

He was reaching a state where angels might well have been expected, but this was a very unorthodox angel, though nonetheless welcome. She was deep-chested and massive, with the finely pointed ears usually accredited to fiends, and great slavering jaws with molars the thickness of a man's finger. She had four legs and her name was Olga, but as she soared out of the blue to lift the nearest Tatar out of the saddle, Guy Spangler was certain he had never seen a lovelier sample of the Creator's handiwork!

The unexpected precipitation of Olga caused consternation among the Tatars and panic among their ponies. Even to Sir Guy, dazed as he was, it seemed incredible that one hound bitch could create such an infernal din. Whether hamstringing a screaming pony, or ripping the throat out of a Tatar, Olga never stopped her scalp-tingling snarls. And while in the awful pandemonium it was impossible to keep an accurate score, in the few moments left to them, Sir Guy added two more kills and one probable to his earlier total of three, and he credited the big hound with at least one more than that. Then the wolf pack closed in, and the game was over.

Only one solitary, riderless pony survived that treacherous sally to dash wildly back to safety behind the walls of Budeüa.

Sergeant Pistol leaned down and put an arm around Sir Guy to lift him up behind his saddle, but Sir Guy made him pause a moment while he looked up at the tower. Ellen had been taken away, but Count Nikita remained crouched above the parapet.

"Nikita!" challenged Sir Guy. "Here and now, before God and this company, I take solemn oath never to give up until I have paid you for this day's perfidy! Henceforth, there shall be neither truce nor quarter between us!"

The Count hooted mockingly, then hurtled his guttural retort.

"You have demonstrated what I long suspected!" he bawled for all to hear. *"You want the woman for yourself!* Hence I shall take immediate steps to put her beyond your reach! I now invite you to come to this clearing two days hence and you shall be a witness, legal or otherwise, to the wedding which shall take place where I stand! That, before God, is *my* reply!"

Sir Guy stood numbed. Pistol gave him a tentative tug.

"We'd best go, sir, afore the bastards reload that cannon."

With a nod, Sir Guy hauled himself up behind the gaunt rider. A moment later, a hail of arrows speeded them on their way. Nor did they pause until they dashed into the cool shadows of the woods, where, to the Englishman's dismay, they found Captain Jaghellon coldly surveying the scene.

Sir Guy greeted him with mixed emotions. He wondered if the inscrutable Cossack had heard Nikita's accusation; if he had, Sir Guy's plight might well be as precarious as it had been just before the blessed arrival of Olga. He made a mental note to reward her in some caninely satisfactory fashion, then shoving aside the flap of scalp as if it had been an unruly lock of hair, he approached the commander.

"You were quite right in your estimate of the Count, Captain," he conceded.

Jaghellon poured no salt into the wound. "I was wrong in my estimate of you, Englishman," he said with a simplicity that was moving. "You are a magnificent fighter! Tell me—are you ready to release me from my promise so we can storm the place?"

Sir Guy caught his breath and searched the swarthy slant-eyed face for some hidden meaning, but could find none.

"Have you any reason to believe we could succeed, Captain?"

The Cossack shook his head. "None!"

"I'll take the balance of my week," Sir Guy said doggedly and turned away.

He saw Affable Jones across the grove, standing beside his horse, his head against the saddle. Fearing his faithful henchman might have been wounded in the sortie, Sir Guy stumbled over to him as rapidly as his bruised leg and aching head would permit.

"Affable!" he called as he drew nigh. "Are you all right, man?"

Affable turned, and to Sir Guy's amazement, tears coursed down his chubby cheeks.

"By my troth, you *are* wounded!" Sir Guy said solicitously.

But Affable mutely shook his head, and pointed to the ground where lay the great tawny body of Olga, slashed by scimitars and studded with arrows.

"Oh, my God, I am sorry," breathed Sir Guy, and was never more sincere.

Affable's chin checkered, and he wiped his nose with the back of his hand in a strangled sniffle. A new flood of tears welled over.

"She pawsed aw'y in me wery arms, sir!" he sobbed wretchedly. "Licked me fyce an' died, like a byby! Damme, she was the on'y femyle I could ever trust!"

30

For the third successive day, Sir Guy Spangler awaited the dawn on the little hillock overlooking the historic fortress. This time, it was without eagerness. The sun would mark the arrival of another day, and Sir Guy would willingly have traded his soul for the privilege of halting the march of time, since one more sunup would herald Ellen's wedding.

With the throbbing wound in his head it was difficult to concentrate, so he let his mind drift. This, experience had taught him, left the door open for inspiration. Other things entered, too; silly little notions and inconsequential recollections frolicked unrestrainedly in and out of his consciousness: Affable wagering his finger for what he expected was a woman and getting a hound! (At that, it had turned out to be an excellent bargain—bless the memory of Olga!) Charity playfully shoving the Chief Minister of Muscovy off his feet! Poor little Charity! What had become of her? Pojorski, with his maudlin memories of torturing expeditions with Ivan the Terrible! How much of that was so? True, they had never caught the dwarf in a direct lie, yet his tales were utterly fantastic. And his wild yarn about executing rebels in this very fortress! Doubtless he would know the very chamber where Ellen . . .

Doubtless he would know . . . !

Sir Guy leaped to his feet and stood trembling, while his eyes scanned the fortifications as if seeing them for the first time. Then orienting himself with the sun and the river, he fairly plunged down the hillside.

Sergeant Pistol and Affable Jones intercepted him just as he entered the encampment. They were in grim mood. Jaghellon, they told him, had put his wolves to constructing siege machines.

"Excellent!" cried Sir Guy. "It will keep them occupied. Where's Pojo?"

"Pojo?" echoed Affable bewilderedly.

"That's what I said! *Pojo*—Pojorski, the dwarf, the torturer, the slave! Where is he?"

"God knows!" muttered Pistol.

"Then you'd better pray the Lord for guidance," snapped Sir Guy, "for I want him—*quick!*"

Affable Jones looked at Sergeant Pistol, and Sergeant Pistol looked at Affable Jones. They burst out laughing simultaneously.

"'E's *back!*" crowed Affable. "Sir Guy's 'is bloody h'arrogant, cocky, pig-'eaded self h'again!" And off they scurried in search of the dwarf.

However, when they shoved into Sir Guy's tent, complete with Pojo, some fifteen minutes later, they didn't quite know what to think of their master. They found that worthy knight seated cross-legged on the floor, sewing a variegated collection of leaves and twigs onto his sole change of clothing. As if that wasn't sufficiently startling, Sir Guy had apparently mopped the dirt floor with the once-beautiful garment. When he looked up to greet them with a diabolical grin, they saw his face was daubed with stain.

"God 'elp us!" gasped Pistol. "'E's balmy in the crumpet!"

"Aye, 'tis plyne 'e's slipped 'is moorin'!" agreed Affable. He turned to the dwarf. "'Ere, Pojo—'op over an' arsk Cap'n Jug'ead to step this w'y!"

Sir Guy stopped that. "Hold your tongues!" he barked with all his old-time self-assurance. "You've been a blacksmith, I understand?" he said to Affable Jones.

"Only w'ilest in prison, yer Honor!" the stout man conceded modestly.

"I'm quite certain that was sufficient for our purpose," the knight observed dryly. "Now here's what I want you to make for me...." And he gave the sometime blacksmith an order that had him blinking in surprise. Before Affable could ask the inevitable "why," Sir Guy was snapping an equally astonishing list of requirements to the dour sergeant.

"'Ow'll I get all them things?" wailed the latter.

"Precisely as you've acquired everything else you ever owned—by *theft.*"

"*Jesu!* It'll go 'ard if Jug'ead catches me!"

Sir Guy snorted. "Not half as hard as it will if you fail to have those chores completed before sunset! And that goes for *both* of you!"

"What do I do, master?" chimed in Pojorski.

"You go with me!"

Affable glowered resentfully at the dwarf. "Ayant 'e the lucky one?"

Sergeant Pistol squinted at Sir Guy, then at the weird masquerade. "I doubts it, Mister Jones!" he said with a shake of his head. "I 'as me a feelin' 'twill be syfer 'ere, wi' on'y these gentle Cossack bastards to worry h'about!"

"Truer words you never spoke!" Sir Guy said, rising. "Be here at six of the clock! If Pojo and I are not back by midnight, we won't be back at all—in which case you can report it to Captain Jaghellon. Otherwise, keep your mouths shut! Now get out!"

At slightly after five of the clock that afternoon, Sergeant Pistol ducked into Sir Guy's tent and deposited the last of his loot under the couch, after the fashion of a squirrel stowing nuts in a hollow stump. That accomplished, he heaved a mighty sigh and stepped outside to relax. Never before in his not uneventful career as burglar, bandit and cat-man had he ever put in such a nerve-racking day. It was one thing to purloin what Fate set out before you, but quite another to steal specified items from a list. Honesty was almost preferable to that!

He had barely seated himself under a shade tree, where he could watch the solitary entrance to the tent, when Affable Jones appeared, staggering under a load of weird, unheard-of implements. Affable dumped the results of his labors inside the tent, then joined his companion under the tree. He, too, was exhausted.

"Lor' love a gallopin' goose!" he groaned. "I'd 'ate to be 'onest an' 'ave to work like that every d'y!"

Pistol shrugged. "Thievin' ain't all beer-an'-skittles, me man!" he grunted. "The responserwiliby be nerve-rackin'! 'At's w'y I'm here! Nobody kin get in the tent wi'out I see 'im fust, so if anybody comes a-snoopin' fer certain h'odds an' h'ends w'at m'y be missed, w'y, we can jes' fyde aw'y."

"*Ye* can jes' fyde aw'y, Mister Pistol, if it pleases ye!" snapped Affable, with a fine show of righteousness. "*I* been h'open an' h'above board the livelong d'y!"

"A rare h'occysion!" sniffed Pistol. "A very rare h'occysion!"

This schism over morals did not last long. "W'at d'ye myke o' it?" asked Affable Jones.

Pistol examined the matter on both sides. "Nuthin'!" he conceded after a judicial pause.

Six of the clock came . . . and went!

Affable sighed. "'E's been done in!" he sorrowed. "I've been h'abandoned! First 'twas li'l Olga, an' now 'tis Sir Guy!" He sniffled. "I've got nuthin', that's w'at!"

"W'y, ye still got me, ol' frien'!" said Pistol in an aggrieved tone.

But Affable was not to be deprived of his misery. "Ye're the syme as nuthin', Mister Pistol!"

It was at this opportune moment that the dwarf appeared. He was heading for the tent when Affable hailed him.

"W'ere's Sir Guy?"

Pojo looked surprised. "In the tent, of course!" he said with that tinge of arrogance the two denizens of Whitefriars found so offensive.

"'E's not!" growled Pistol curtly.

Pojorski paused, looking from one to the other. "You lie!" he snapped. "I say he *is* in the tent!"

The sergeant started to rise belligerently, but Affable put out a restraining arm.

"'Old one moment, Mister Pistol!" he purred sweetly. "Permit me to 'andle this." He solemnly eyed the dwarf. "Master Pojorski, ye've myde a wery, wery serious charge. There's but one honorable w'y to settle it!"

"And that, obviously, is to look in the tent!" snorted the dwarf.

"Not so fast, not . . . so . . . fast, me good man!" cautioned Affable. "Ye've left a wound w'at'll tyke time to 'eal!"

"Well, maybe *I* was injured by what Pistol said!" reasoned Pojo.

Affable nodded sagely. "I've tyken that into consideration also! Now a true gent would settle the dispute by a little wager."

"That is quite agreeable to me!" said the dwarf.

"Be it?" marveled Mr. Jones, perking up. "W'at-'o! 'Ow much be ye prepared to wager, me short-arsed li'l frien'?"

In answer, Pojo reached into his tunic and jerked out a pouch of gold that almost sucked the eyes out of the two Englishmen.

"All o' it?" gasped Affable incredulously.

"'Ere, 'ere!" yelped Pistol. "I want a piece o' that!"

"Do not fight over it," snickered Pojo. "There's more where that came from." Whereupon he produced a companion pouch of equal magnitude.

The two knaves nigh swooned with joy. Though it taxed their resources to the utmost, the wagers were soon arranged, after which the trio, with Pojo sandwiched in the middle, marched up to the tent. Sergeant Pistol was so elated, he shed his customary air of gloom as with a lordly flourish he threw back the tent flaps.

"Now tyke a good look!" he jeered at the dwarf. "W'at d'ye see?"

"Two of the most gullible fools in Muscovy!" came a familiar voice from the tent's interior.

Pistol went rigid for an instant, then bent so sharply to peer into the tent, his back cracked like a broken board. When he saw Sir Guy seated calmly on the couch, he closed his eyes.

"Gulled!" he moaned. "Oh, *no!* I'm ruin't!"

"That may be truer than you realize, Sergeant," said Sir Guy, laughing. "Come in! I've sent for Paxton and . . . Ah, here they are! Come in, gentlemen!" He made room on the couch as Paxton, Belcher, and Tutweiller filed in.

As they silently seated themselves, Sir Guy appraised each man in turn, re-evaluating them in the light of the dangerous venture he had in mind. Of late—in fact, almost since leaving the Tsar's cantonment—the last-named pair had avoided him. It had been subtly done, without open hostility, yet with a noticeable air of disapproval. This evening, however, there was a decided grimness in their attitude. Sir Guy was satisfied he knew the reason for it: the virus of Nikita's accusation was spreading.

He began to wish he had not invited them to the conference, but it was too late now for regrets. Signaling Pojo to close the tent flaps, he prepared the ground for his reckless scheme. First, he summarized, their plight was perilous in the extreme; if they failed to recover Ellen, they'd not be permitted to leave Muscovy, to say nothing of recovering their ship and cargo. That they knew already, what they did not know was that the Governor of Crimea had an army of five thousand men flanking them which cut off any retreat; that Jaghellon had conceded he could not successfully storm the fort, yet refused to leave without making the attempt; that nothing short of a miracle could possibly save them.

"Sounds like the simplest thing 'ud be to cut our ruddy throats, an' 'ave done," mumbled Sergeant Pistol, still brooding over his financial disaster.

"Verily, we could demand succor from the Almighty!" Belcher proposed.

"Damme, seems ye been *demandin'* e'er since we left England!" Affable told him. "Yet things get worser'n worse! Methinks yer bloody screechin' be irkin' the Lord!"

Paxton smiled. "A profound observation, Affable!" he chuckled, then turned to Sir Guy. "In this enlightened era, sir, miracles are rare."

"Only God can bring a miracle to pass!" cried the parson.

Affable snorted. "Olga done a damn good imitation yesterday!"

Sir Guy brought them back to a point of order. "Gentlemen, we digress. I summoned you here to ask for volunteers to help perform the necessary miracle!"

There was a startled pause, broken finally by Paxton. "Which is, sir . . . ?"

"*Going into the fortress and capturing Ellen and Nikita!*"

They stared in bewilderment. "But you just told us it could not be stormed!" cried Philip Tutweiller.

"True!" conceded Sir Guy.

"Nor are we doves that can fly over walls!" said the parson.

Sir Guy smiled. "*That,* I'll most certainly grant you!"

Affable Jones had stiffened. In something akin to panic, he looked at Sergeant Pistol, only to find that worthy staring back at him with a tortured expression of dawning apprehension.

"Glory be!" gasped Affable. "Them stunted shovels 'e 'ad me forge— w'at 'e tolt me was Christmas presents fer Pojo's children . . . ! God 'elp us, I get it! *'E means to dig under the walls!*"

"H'impossible!" snorted Pistol. "I've seen coves w'at dug out o' prisons, but none w'at dug *in!*"

"Nonetheless, my astute compatriots, that is precisely the plan," said Sir Guy. "And I demonstrated its feasibility by digging into this tent from the rear just now."

"Ayant *that* the ruddy trufe!" groaned Pistol.

He was ignored. "Who volunteers to follow me into Budeüa?" Sir Guy demanded.

The Reverend Belcher paled. "Let us not be unduly precipitate!"

Pistol jeered. "Parson, ye're allus pratin' about the glories o' 'eaven, so this be yer chawnce to slide in. Now I knows w'y 'is nibs 'ad me steal 'arp strings! We'll need 'em w'en we become eye'n'gels!"

"It will be a long, cold day before you become an angel, Sergeant," remarked Sir Guy. "Howbeit, you are partially correct. That fine gut is for garroting anyone who interferes with our progress. Come now— who volunteers? Remember, though, I want no man to come against his will!"

"I," cried Belcher, pointing a bony finger skyward, "am a man of the cloth!"

Sir Guy cut him off. "Who is next?"

Tutweiller made a sound of disgust. "For my part, I rue the day I ever became enmeshed in your toils, Sir Guy. But having come this far, I'll see it through. Count me in!"

"Thank you, Philip! That makes one!"

"'Old, sir!" yelped Affable indignantly. "'E mykes number *two!* Naturally, I be first!"

[253]

"The 'ell ye s'y!" snarled Sergeant Pistol. "*I* be first! 'Oo's cut the most throats I arsk—me or ye?"

"By Allah's beard, *I* have!" Pojo broke in. "Hence my right to be considered the *first* volunteer!"

"What eager pit-dogs!" laughed Sir Guy. "But do not fight about it; you'll all have a bellyful of throat-cutting before we return from this picnic, that I promise." He shrugged. "I guess that does it."

"Your pardon, Sir Guy," interposed Mr. Paxton. "Have I not the right of refusal?"

"I took that for granted," said Sir Guy, a trifle embarrassed.

The old man chuckled. "Manifestly, neither age nor temperament inclines me to digging under castle walls and strangling men with harp strings," he conceded with a touch of irony. "Yet it ill becomes a man to profit by the risks of another, hence I volunteer to serve in any capacity you deem me fitted."

"Excellent!" approved Sir Guy. "I swear no monarch ever had a more polished diplomat, nor general, a more adroit emissary. You shall be my ambassador, Ancient! At the hour of midnight, you shall awaken Jaghellon and inform him of the venture."

Belcher burst out: "Why not tell him in advance? He would give us more men and lessen the risk to us!"

"Us, 'e s'ys!" snorted Affable Jones, and made a derisive noise which had the sound of a flute blown under water.

"It is not quantity I need; it is quality," snapped Sir Guy, turning again to Paxton. "Suggest to Jaghellon, in such a way he will think it is his own idea, that he be prepared to march at daybreak. We should be back by then."

"Do you plan to emulate the Trojans?" inquired the old man. "I mean—open the gates and let the Cossacks charge in?"

Sir Guy shook his head. "No. If I opened the gates, I fear the Budeüaians would charge *out!* To speak true, I suspect they outnumber us. Hence Jaghellon would be well advised to beat a quick retreat once the objective is obtained."

"He may hang you for desertion," Belcher said.

"He won't if I have Ellen."

"Yes, but if you do not have her?" persisted the parson.

Sir Guy smiled thinly. "Why, in that event, your Reverence—we won't come back!" He rose and displayed the weird collection his two henchmen had garnered. "Come, my merry moles, prepare for burrowing!"

Philip Tutweiller viewed the array, then chose a slim dagger, honed on both edges, a short-handled tool that was to pass for a spade, and a length of harp string fitted at the ends with wooden grips.

"'S'death, the simile of the moles is apt," he said bitterly, distributing the gear about his person, "for five blinder creatures never crawled the face of God's green earth!"

31

By the third hour of night, the quintette crawled to the edge of a fringe of underbrush and thus came in sight of the spot selected earlier by Sir Guy and Pojorski. To the casual observer—and to some not so casual, of which Tutweiller was one—Sir Guy had chosen not only the worst possible night for the chore, but the most unsuitable site. A full moon rendered the entire countryside visible for miles. As if this weren't sufficiently suicidal, the chosen spot was almost directly under a guard-tower, where now, in the motionless air, they could hear the sentries joking as they met at the end of their round. Then, at this particular spot, the wall dipped so that its foundation was almost level with the beach; even if they survived long enough to burrow beneath the surface, the seepage of the water might well drown them.

To all these objections, Sir Guy retorted merely that anyone who didn't like it was at perfect liberty to retire. Then, warning Affable Jones to awaken him the instant the moon dipped out of sight, he stretched out on the sandy ground and went to sleep.

It seemed he had barely closed his eyes when they prodded him back to consciousness. The moon had sunk behind the ramparts, and with its disappearance, the shrewdness of Sir Guy became evident, for the spot he had selected was now hidden in a glob of shadow which, in the surrounding brightness, seemed opaque. So, stripped to the waists, their bodies rendered nearly invisible by a sooty concoction, they slithered out of hiding and snaked into the pool of darkness.

Now it was noticed that above them the sentries on meeting were less alert than when tramping alone, and if the soil was wet with seepage, it was also easy to work. Sir Guy himself started the digging close under the wall.

Each man knew his allotted part, so the only word spoken for a long time was a profound observation made by Sergeant Pistol when they passed the halfway point and started angling upward.

"I on'y 'opes to God we don't come up under no privy."

They did not; they bored out of the ground behind a stable. Here they paused to wipe the sand and mud from their bodies, and apply a coat of grease which made them slippery as eels. It only remained to trade their shovels for knives and garrotes, and they were ready.

"Burn me, I feel like a bloody fox in an 'en-'ouse!" muttered Sergeant Pistol.

Sir Guy pointed upward, where, high above them, a sentry marched slowly along the ramparts, pike sloped across his shoulder, his tall, graceful casque glinting in the starlight.

"Those are hawks, not hens!" he warned grimly. "One blunder, one slip, one sneeze . . . we're done for!"

They had no hard-and-fast plan, for the obvious reason that they could not know what lay ahead, but even Sir Guy had to admit (to himself alone, to be sure) that the whole scheme looked a hundredfold more foolhardy within the walls than it had without. Howbeit, to the credit of all, now that they were committed, no complaint was made.

Sir Guy had ordained that Affable Jones guard their exit—an order which drew forth a torrent of objections from that genial scoundrel. It was a woman's work, he argued. But because he had the nimblest wit of the four, he was sternly told that it was that station or none.

Sir Guy naturally would take the lead, piloted by the dwarf, who had by this time convinced him that he really knew the plan of the castle. Pistol and Tutweiller were to follow, maintaining a distance, necessarily flexible, which would at all times enable them to keep the leading pair in sight. This was insurance against surprise, for if Sir Guy and Pojo were seized by a small group, the two "shadows" could succor them; if they were overwhelmed or killed by a large force, Pistol and Tutweiller could fade gracefully back into the shadows and escape.

As Affable had done, Pistol balked, preferring to fight in the van with his master, not "skulk in the rear wi' a lovelorn ninny." And the "lovelorn ninny," in his turn, drew Sir Guy out of hearing of the others and propounded a question which set the hair a-tingling along that bold gentleman's nape.

"Sir Guy," Philip said, keeping his taut voice keyed low, "though I have a feeling none of us will survive this mad venture, I want you to tell me one thing true: if a merciful God should permit us to rescue

Ellen from this Tatar devil—*do you intend turning her over to the Tsar?*"

Sir Guy hesitated but an instant. "No, I do not!" he said.

The younger man exhaled a relieved sigh. "Had you answered affirmatively, I should have killed you here and now!" he said between his teeth. "If we succeed, then it boils down to just you and me!"

"That's a stream we can ford when we come to it!" Spangler snapped. "Meanwhile, may I remind you there are a few trifling difficulties ahead?"

"Aye," agreed Philip. "And while we fight in a common cause, you'll not find me wanting! The rest can wait!" And he turned away.

There was some slight indecision as to whether it was advisable to strangle the stable-boy whose raucous snores tortured the silent night. Pojo pleaded for the privilege, but Sir Guy decided the snores—which had the sound of a lost lamb baa-ing for its dam—were advantageous, for you could shoe a horse in the vicinity without risk of being heard. Affable was cautioned that if the snores ceased, he should seek the cause.

Then the quartette started.

There was little difficulty traversing the outer wards, for with the dawn still an hour away, the place was almost deserted. The "almost" was brought about by a soldier who had stepped behind a hedge for a short nap. Sergeant Pistol, who stumbled onto him, deftly made the nap everlasting.

Ostensibly, there were only two ways of reaching the castle proper from the outer wards. One, by a steep staircase from the inner gate, was at all times heavily guarded, for it led to the state apartments and was used only by privileged persons. The other was a winding road used by troops and the common people. To attempt either of these entrances would be the rankest folly.

Howbeit, Pojo, in the course of his professional duties, had once passed into the castle through an ancient sally-port, connected with both the state chambers and the dungeons. To the best of the dwarf's recollection, this semi-secret egress was but loosely guarded by a pair of sentries stationed on the outside. When the four adventurers finally reached this point, after a circuitous crawl, they discovered that Pojo was only partly right: the sentries *were on the inside!*

Sick with disappointment, they backed off to consider.

Pojo, smarting under some pungent asides by the redoubtable sergeant, suggested that he attempt to bluff the guards into opening the gate, but Sir Guy, remembering all too well the last time Pojo had tried to bluff his way through a gate, rejected the proposal. The guards would doubtless summon a superior, and discovery would follow inevitably.

Pistol, never completely able to forget his earlier profession, wanted to *jimmy* the gate, but this, too, was turned down. Tutweiller felt they might do better at the big gate used by the troops.

"That we might, lover-boy," sneered the sergeant, "if we 'ad a ruddy h'army!"

Philip's angry retort was cut off by Sir Guy. "'Pon my soul, you've given me an idea, Pistol!" he mused thoughtfully.

"Reckoned ye'd see h'it me w'y!" Pistol grinned. "'Oo's got a likely jimmy?"

"Alas, that's not the question," said Sir Guy. "Who's the best *lover-boy?*"

Sergeant Pistol was taken aback, but not downed. "W'y, since ye arsk so plyne, I'll not let modesty . . ."

"You and Philip ease over to the gate," Sir Guy silenced him. "Pojo and I will bring the guards out!"

"But . . . but . . . 'ow . . . ?"

"Do what you're told!" snapped Sir Guy. "Leave *thinking* and *love-making* to your betters! Just remember—if a guard cries out, we're finished!"

Puzzled, and a trifle irked, Sergeant Pistol and Tutweiller crawled back and took up their station beside the gate. They could hear the sentries talking and laughing inside.

"There's times," Pistol muttered darkly, half to himself, "w'en I get bloody well fed up wi' . . . *Mother o' God! 'Oo's that?*"

The electrifying sound came from an opaque stain of shadow, about fifteen paces further along the wall—plainly the titter of a titillated woman! This was followed by a sharp warning from a man, after which he could be heard whispering *sotto voce* in the most intimate terms. If the actual words were unintelligible to the startled Englishmen, since they were spoken in the Tatar tongue, their *meaning* was universal—especially to Sergeant Pistol.

The "female" squealed softly in delight!

"Be that really Sir Guy an' Pojo?" marveled Pistol.

The humorless Philip kept his eyes on the gate wicket. The gate was opening!

Curiosity did for the guards what the old adage claims it did for the cat. Since the greatest danger lay in the discovery of the corpses, these had to be concealed before the four could proceed. Thus the defunct guards were neatly laid out in the deepest shadow, and the intruders entered the castle proper. Between the dungeons and the third floor, they encountered only one sleepy servant. Pistol wanted him, but Pojo got to him first. There was no outcry.

But all this took time, and time was running thin. When Sir Guy reached the third landing where, according to their information, Ellen and Nikita had quarters at opposite ends of the wing, he waited for the others to come up.

"We divide forces here," he told them grimly. "Pistol, you and Philip go get Ellen. Don't let her delay for clothes or anything else! The whole damn castle will be alive within the hour, and we've got a long way yet to go."

"An' ye, sir?"

"Pojo and I will see that Count Nikita troubles us no more," Sir Guy promised. "But don't wait up for us. We'll cover your retreat if possible." He looked at young Tutweiller, whose every sinew was taut. "Good luck, Philip!" He offered his hand.

The younger man looked startled, then gripped the outthrust hand. "Damn it, sir!" he whispered hoarsely. "For the first time since leaving England, I can honestly say the same to you, sir!"

Sir Guy watched them disappear around a bend in the corridor, then he turned slowly to his twisted companion. He was suddenly, for no apparent reason, overwhelmed with depression. Old and jaded, he felt, a fit companion for a torturer. He wondered how Ellen was going to appreciate the effort, even if it succeeded; she would doubtless think there was very little to choose between Count Nikita, Tsar Ivan, and Guy Spangler!

Pojo beckoned him; he had opened a door. With a heart full of misery and bitterness, Sir Guy sidled inside the chamber and flattened himself against the wall to permit his eyes to adjust to the darkness. As he stood thus, he considered his *modus operandi*, and decided the harp string would be too swift, too merciful. He hated Nikita, and felt that nothing short of having the devil's neck snap under his fingers would alleviate his consuming enmity. So when the vague outline of the bed became distinguishable, he shoved the garrote aside and cat-walked across the room.

The bed was empty.

With every nerve keyed to the highest pitch, this disappointment was almost more than Sir Guy could bear. He pawed all over the counterpane, even under the bed. The only thing he learned was that the bed was faintly warm, as if someone had lately lain in it.

"Curse the luck!" he fumed aloud, sitting on the edge of the deserted bed. "Where in hell *could* he have gone?"

To his surprise, the dwarf burst into soft laughter. "By Allah, I had

[259]

a feeling I'd been in this chamber before!" he crowed. "Now I recall—this used to be the old noble's private chamber, before I strangled him! If memory serves me, there's a private passage which leads to the room where your princess . . ."

Sir Guy was on his feet in an instant. "Great God! If Nikita is down there . . ." The very thought numbed him.

"If he is, Pistol and Philip are in trouble!" muttered Pojorski.

"Take me there at once!"

Pojo fumbled in the darkness a few moments, then found an opening in the wainscoting. Handing Sir Guy one end of his strangling cord, while he himself retained the other end, he plunged into the intense blackness. Clinging to the wooden grip, Sir Guy followed him.

The passage had a musty smell, faintly reminiscent of a burial vault, and as Sir Guy felt his way along, he noted the walls were rough and unfinished, the floors covered with a double-thickness of carpeting which deadened the sound of their footsteps. After what seemed an interminable time, he caught the muffled murmur of voices, and, muted though they were, he recognized first the dour growl of Sergeant Pistol and, an instant later, the startled cry of Ellen! Goaded by apprehension, he lunged forward, only to stumble against the stumpy figure of the dwarf, who had stopped short.

"It sounds as if our friends are trapped!" Pojo whispered.

"I'll soon fix that!" vowed Sir Guy. "Where's the entry?"

"There are *two* entrances, master, from this passage. One comes out at the head of the bed, the other at the foot. I am not certain which would be the best for our purpose."

"We'll use both!" growled Sir Guy. "Show me the nearest, then you take the other!"

Pojo, whose ears seemed able to hear through solid stone, was listening. "It shall be as you say," he agreed, after a pause. "If you will count fifty from the instant I leave you, I can make my entry simultaneous with yours."

"All right, all right!" rumbled Sir Guy. "Where is this opening?"

Pojo tugged the gut thread that joined them, and they advanced about ten paces, whereupon the dwarf stopped, placed a warning finger across Sir Guy's lips, then reaching up, uncovered a tiny peephole about eye-level. As the Englishman put his eye to the hole, Pojorski scurried away.

The sight that met Sir Guy's gaze drove all thought of counting out of his mind. To the left, just inside a door which probably led into the hall stood Pistol and Philip Tutweiller, disarmed and pinioned in the hands of four soldiers. To the right and so close to Sir Guy that he could hear her labored breathing, stood Ellen, proud, defiant, and horrified. In between, and almost directly opposite the peephole, was a massive poster-bed, its drapes drawn back; on that bed, propped up on one elbow, in all his native arrogance, lounged Count Nikita.

". . . either of them!" Ellen was concluding. "No power on earth can force me to submit!"

"And if I spare them?" Nikita drawled, with an arching of one brow.

"Nay, my lady . . . in God's name, *don't!*" cried young Tutweiller, lurching in the grip of his burly captors. "I'd rather endure a thousand . . ." His head bobbed like a cork on rough water when one of the guards knocked him silent.

"If I spare them . . . ?" repeated Nikita.

When she did not immediately reply, he made a perceptible signal with one hand. Instantly, a poniard was placed against Tutweiller's throat. The Count did not repeat his question, but his brows lifted quizzically.

Ellen read his meaning. "I . . . promise . . . that, if you so insist . . . knowing how I loathe you for the beast you are . . . I promise that I will submit to this wedding!"

Nikita threw back his head and laughed heartily. Ellen covered her face with her hands.

Peculiarly enough, Sir Guy's attention turned from Ellen to a crease in the drapery directly behind Nikita's head. Twice it moved, and once he thought he glimpsed a familiar talon, but the claw jerked back, as if dreading premature discovery.

Sir Guy Spangler pushed open the panel, and strode boldly into the chamber.

"Fortunately, my lady," he said with a coolness that was breathtaking in itself, "you may save your submission for someone more worthy than this rabid jackal!"

Every eye in the chamber automatically whipped around to stare at this incredible visitation. Sergeant Pistol's description of the incident, if admittedly exaggerated, probably gives a truer version than any formal recounting.

"Right out o' the bloody wall 'e popped, did Sir Guy, breathin' fire an' brimstone, an' the image o' ol' Nick 'isself! I tyke oath them damn Tatars stared so 'ard ye could 'ear their eyeballs a-bangin' aroun' inside their 'eads wi' the sound o' cannon balls rollin' across a ship's deck!"

"Do not move, any of you—at your peril!" commanded Sir Guy in a tone that implied he had an army at his back.

Yet if his voice exuded confidence, it was but an illusion, for the draperies failed to part again. He was suddenly jolted by the fear that what he thought he had seen was naught but a figment of his imagination. If so, he had doomed them all! But where *was* Pojo? Sir Guy had staged his bluff on the strength of the dwarf's support. If that failed, he had merely walked into a trap himself.

Nikita barked an order for his soldiers to cut the prisoners' throats and assist him; then reaching for his own poniard, he started to rise. At that blessed moment, the draperies parted and a noose, bespeaking a practiced hand, coiled through the opening to drop neatly over Nikita's head. His startled yelp of panic was sealed in his throat.

"Don't kill him . . . yet!" warned Sir Guy sharply. Then bounding across the chamber, he jerked the poniard out of the hand of the soldier who held it to Tutweiller's throat, and felled the knave with a blow from the hilt. Meanwhile, Sergeant Pistol, no mean opportunist himself, seized upon the moment of indecision to do a bit of felling of his own. He began laying about him with such happy disregard, he very nearly strangled Philip Tutweiller before discovering his mistake.

With his henchmen so thoroughly in command, Sir Guy turned his attention to the pair on the bed. They made a grotesque tableau. Pojo sat cross-legged on a silken bolster, his deformed body made more repulsive by the overlayer of black grease. On his face was the most diabolical smile Sir Guy had ever seen. Between his knees, contorted out of recognition, and seemingly already separated from the writhing body, was the head of Count Nikita.

"Damn you!" roared Sir Guy. "I told you not to kill him!"

"I haven't, master, I haven't!" leered the dwarf. "I'm just letting him peep into hell. Oh, when I'm in practice, I can let them get one foot through the Everlasting Gate, then haul them back for more fun! How Ivan loved that! Watch me, master. . . ." He began to twist the harp string, but Sir Guy made him stop.

"Turn him loose! I intend to settle with him personally!"

It was like depriving a child of a favorite toy to induce Pojo to release the Count. Three times he started to comply, three times his wrist flicked again as if impelled by a force stronger than his will. On each relapse, Nikita dropped back into the very shadow of death. But finally, when Sir Guy threatened to cut Pojo's throat as well, the little fiend reluctantly withdrew his noose.

"Ah, you are a cruel, hard man, master!" he complained. "You never permit me any innocent pleasures!"

"I pay my own debts," Sir Guy said, starting for the bed. Up to this point, Ellen had made no sound; she had remained pressed against the wall, her white face and staring eyes giving her the appearance of one dead. But as Sir Guy neared the bed, she broke out of her trance of horror.

"*No!*" she cried. "*Don't!*"

Sir Guy paused, but he did not turn. Other than a glance to make sure she was unharmed, he had deliberately avoided looking at her.

Sergeant Pistol had one of his rare flashes of good humor.

"W'y bless ye, m'lydy, Sir Guy on'y means to cut the bastard's throat!" he assured her genially.

Ellen was taut as a fiddle-string. "Don't murder him, Sir Guy!" Her words held a note of warning.

Sir Guy's determination held. "*Murder?* You deem it murder to stamp out this venomous spider? I but consummate my sworn oath that there would be no quarter between us!"

"Did you come here just for that purpose?" she demanded.

He spun around on his heel to stare at her. As he feared, the impact of her loveliness distracted him. It had been over six months since he had last seen her at such close range, and the change was marked. She, too, showed the impress of the harrowing experiences she had been through, but in a manner most attractive. For it is one of life's inexplicable anomalies, as Sir Guy had long noted, that pretty women who lead sheltered lives, carefully protected from vicissitudes and reality, almost invariably develop a tight-lipped primness, a pettish intolerance, which with the passing years precludes a true beauty. Whatever else this ordeal had done for Ellen, she had escaped that fate, for she was even more beautiful now than Sir Guy had pictured her in his mind. The tendency towards haughtiness had given way to dignity; she had matured without aging. Even drawn and fatigued as she was, her perfectly sculptured features were illuminated by the splendid character shining through. It was with extreme difficulty he broke the spell.

"You know damn well we didn't!" he said angrily. "We came to get you out of his rotten clutches! So enough talk. I'll soon release you from any promises you have made to him, and take you away."

The blood came flooding into her cheeks. "Sir Guy, so help me—if you kill him, I'll not go with you!" she cried. "Merciful God in heaven, have I become some filthy Circe that changes men into beasts? Leave the wretch be and let us go!"

He was incredulous. "Are you asking me to leave him *free?*" A thought struck him that was as bitter as wormwood. "Can it be that you gave your promise of submission willingly?"

She recoiled under the imputation, but her eyes blazed with the old fire.

"Sir Guy! That was contemptible! Yet it is no affair of yours whether I did or not! But mark this—if you expect me to accompany you out of here so you can peddle me to the Tsar, you will let that man live!"

"Sir Guy doesn't intend to turn you . . ." began Philip, but Sir Guy roared him down.

"*Silence!* By my troth, we cannot shilly-shally here debating the whims of fickle females! Pistol, you and Tutweiller start out with her ladyship immediately. . . ."

Ellen's feminine instincts rebelled. "I must have time to dress!"

"Wouldn't ye know!" snorted Pistol, once again his cynical self.

"You'll go as you are!" Sir Guy told her angrily. "If I'm to spare this Tatar swine, by God you'll obey me!"

"Do I have your promise not to harm him?"

"Aye, damn it! Aye! Now get going, you three!"

"But you, sir?" asked Tutweiller.

"Why, since her Highness is so solicitous of this viper," sneered Sir Guy, "there's naught I can do but remain to truss him up comfortable! Pojo and I will follow when we're through here. Now, for God's sake, speed your way! It won't be long before the castle will awake!"

He felt Ellen's eyes staring at him, so in self-defense, he turned his back.

32

AT THE MOUTH OF THE TUNNEL, Affable Jones waited with the calmness of a bridegroom at a wedding. Not that Affable bubbled with energy; it had been charged with some justice that he would probably fall asleep on his way to the gallows. But to be left alone, while Sir Guy and Pistol went off to high adventure, was more than he could stomach. Patience was not his cardinal virtue.

For the first half-glass after their departure, he crouched in the hole itself, popping his head out like a groundhog at every alien sound. When that bored him, he took to lying on his back and counting the strides of the sentries directly above him. This mollified him for a time because there were few things he liked better than to relax and watch someone else work.

Up to this point, the snoring of the stable-boy had settled into an off-stage drone. However, when the snores ceased abruptly, Affable took out his harp string and crawled into the stable to investigate the cause. The boy, a scrawny hare-lipped fellow, his face speckled with wens and warts, had just lighted a candle as Affable sidled into his cuddy. Mr. Jones was about to pounce, when he became conscious of two factors which stayed his hand: first, the dull-witted lout seemed blissfully unaware that his visitor was an enemy, and second, on the table which held the candle sat a pair of crude but usable *dice!* This nostalgic touch warmed the cockles of Affable's heart.

He sat down.

After the caterwauling snores, it was a trifle anticlimactic to discover his host was a deaf-and-dumb mute, but with dice in the offing, Affable was without prejudice. By elaborate gesticulations, he pantomimed his willingness to indulge in a friendly game of chance. The simple-headed youth not only agreed, he foolishly permitted the light-fingered Mr. Jones the first throw!

The outcome was not without a certain rude pathos. Precisely what happened, or, more accurately, *how* it happened, Affable was never quite able to comprehend, for when, considerably later, a trumpet blast jerked him back to reality, the stupid youth had won everything the Englishman had about his tubby person save his pants and harp string. Doubtless, the trumpet alone saved those. On the golden note, the mute signified he had work to do.

"Aye, plague take it, an' so 'ave I!" grumbled Affable, taking out his garrote.

However, professional ethics, no doubt seasoned with curiosity, would not permit him to slay a fellow-gambler in cold blood—at least, not until he had learned his tricks—so he contented himself by gently knocking the mute on the head, binding him securely, and purloining the miraculous dice. After that, he slipped below.

To his horror, he found the vanguard of dawn had already driven back the darkness, leaving the whole scene suffused in a baleful gray half-light. His first thought was that the others had made their escape without him, but as he opened the stable door with the intention of examining the tunnel, four ghostly forms flitted out of the dim shadows and into the stable.

"Lor' love ye!" gasped Affable, on recognizing them. "I ayant 'ad a moment's peace since ye left." He spotted Ellen. "Yer servant, m'lydy."

Ellen managed a brief: "Thank you, Affable. It is good to see you, too!"

During this exchange, Philip Tutweiller had been peering through a chink in the timbers. He now beckoned the others and grimly pointed to a small swivel-gun mounted above the spot where the tunnel coursed under the wall. A sergeant and two gunners were stationed in the watch-tower beside the facile little cannon.

"S'death, sir! We can't outrun the sting of that wasp!" Philip said.

Sir Guy pursed his lips in thought. Though reluctant to concede it, he had not spotted the gun in his preliminary reconnoitering.

"H'mnn!" he grunted noncommittally.

"Why don't you say it?" cried Ellen. "That I delayed you until daylight spoiled your plan!"

"Nay, my lady!" protested Philip. "The fault was mine!"

"Mebbe we could duck into the hole, an' wait there till dark?" suggested Pistol.

But Affable Jones—no doubt visualizing the potential of what he could do with the dice if they were all locked up for twelve hours—argued they would be more comfortable to spend the day in the stable. To his bitter disappointment, Sir Guy vetoed the notion.

"The bodies of the guards are certain to be discovered at any moment now," he reasoned. "Nikita will be found, and released, and then not a flea will be safe in Budeüa."

"W'ich was w'y I wanted to cut 'is ruddy throat!" growled Pistol, with a reproachful glance at Ellen.

She turned on him angrily. "Don't you ever tire of cutting throats and killing people?"

Pistol was surprised. "W'y, no, m'lydy!" he said honestly.

In an attempt to strike a more cheerful note, Affable inquired: "W'at 'appened to the runt?"

Sir Guy shrugged. "Poor Pojo!" he said, not without regret. "As we were making our getaway, he whispered he'd forgotten something and ran back. By the time we had discovered he had not caught up with us, it was too late to go back in search of him."

"'E'll doubtless betray us," opined Affable.

"You have no grounds for that!" Sir Guy said sharply.

"Well, by God, *I* 'ave!" hissed Pistol. "*Look!*"

The others manned all the available cracks in the door and looked! None was immune to a pounding of the heart. For down the alley came Yaroslaf Pojorski in full flight, a trio of scimitar-brandishing soldiery a few jumps behind him, and the whole followed by a locust swarm of yowling urchins and yapping mongrels. The dwarf had never looked more grotesque. Because he was hugging a bundle to his chest, his arms were not swinging, so that he gave the impression of covering the ground in a series of giant hops, like a huge toad.

"May a murrain seize him!" groaned Tutweiller. "He's leading them right to us!"

"Truer words was ne'er spoke!" grated Pistol.

Howbeit, this charge was an exaggeration; Pojo was heading, not for the stable, but for the tunnel—approximately ten paces away. Like a hare with the hounds at heel, he made a running dive and popped down the hole, head first.

The pursuing soldiers, not anticipating any such haven, were slightly nonplused, but not for long. They stood staring at the hole a moment, then one of them handed his scimitar to a companion, placed a dagger between his teeth, and started to crawl into the tunnel in pursuit. By now, the sentries on the ramparts were gazing down in puzzlement.

The tenacious soldier who had wriggled into the hole got as far as his knees before pausing. A moment later, his feet wig-wagged, which his fellows interpreted as a signal of success, for they each grabbed a leg and hauled him out.

Ellen gave a sob and drew away. Affable exhaled a weary sigh. "*Jesu!* 'At's w'at I calls losin' yer 'ead!" he whispered.

While the two soldiers gaped unbelievingly at the body of their late companion, the Tatar sergeant proved himself a man of decision. He dispatched one gunner on the run, obviously to round up a superior officer, and ordered the other gunner to keep the swivel-gun on the *outside* of the wall. These arrangements made, he himself hurried down to the yawning orifice and, scimitar in hand, loudly demanded the dwarf disgorge himself—an order which Pojo understandably rejected.

"Well, this does it!" remarked Affable, with all the bonhomie he could muster. "Pistol, ol' pal, ye kin forget the three shillin' thruppence ye owes me."

"I already 'ad," said Pistol.

But Sir Guy Spangler's fame had been built around just such moments as this, when the last few grains of time's sand seemed about to run out.

"Steady, my hearts—we can still make it!" he told them. "You lads take those three Tatars! Watch the officer; he apparently has some sense! Ellen, you go into the tunnel first—but be very sure to call to that damned dwarf and make him understand it is you. He's dagger-happy!"

"But it's suicide!" protested Tutweiller. "That gunner has his weapon aimed at the other end of our passage!"

"I'll take care of him myself!"

"Other soldiers are coming!" cried Philip, pointing towards a spot about a hundred yards down the ramparts where a squad of archers was moving on the double.

"Damn it, do what I tell you!" stormed Sir Guy, and turned to his two henchmen. "See that Ellen gets back to *England!*" he told them grimly. "Talk it over with old Paxton, and be guided by his advice. He's got the only brain in the party! Now, to your . . ."

A startled ejaculation from Affable Jones made him turn—in time to see Philip Tutweiller, scimitar in hand, dart out of the stable and head for the tower door left ajar by the Tatar sergeant. Even as they stared, he ducked into the tower and slammed and bolted the door from the inside.

The Tatar sergeant, sensing his intent, bellowed to the gunner above the Tatar equivalent of *"Look out!"* This order the gunner obeyed literally. He was bent far over the embrasure, his eyes doubtless focused on the outer end of the tunnel, his rump elevated invitingly, when Philip dashed onto the ramparts. It was not the sort of invitation the young Englishman could resist. It took but one well-directed kick to boost the gunner over the wall into eternity.

"Plague take it, I 'opes he don't plug our 'ole!" was the comment made, obviously by Sergeant Pistol.

Sir Guy had been momentarily distracted by Tutweiller's independent action, but as he saw that young man swerve the light cannon around and send a hail of small shot into the onrushing soldiers, he pulled himself together.

"The fool, the courageous fool!" he growled. "Come on, lads! Have at it!"

Since the Tatar sergeant and the two soldiers were staring blankly at the drama overhead, they were caught like sitting ducks. Under the circumstances, Ellen made no plea for mercy. That chore over, Sir Guy thrust his head into the mouth of the tunnel.

"Pojo! We're coming down!" he warned. "Put your knife away!"

"Very good, master!" came a smothered call from below.

Sir Guy backed out and motioned Ellen down, but she refused.

"You shall go first!" she cried bitterly. "I'm sated with masculine heroics! Since poor Philip has seen fit to throw his life away, I see no reason why you should endeavor to outdo him! Oh, men are such fools!"

Furious, Sir Guy dove down the hole, and an instant later heard Ellen crawling along behind him. He took his spite out on Pojo, cursing him for not moving faster, and in due time they debouched into the glaring sunshine. One quick upward glance showed that Philip had reloaded the gun and was presently holding another squad of pikemen at bay. But it could not last because a company of archers were advancing along the ramparts from the other direction.

Sir Guy set his jaw, and when Ellen crawled out, he caught her arm and held her until Affable and Pistol had their feet on the ground. Then he shoved her roughly into their arms.

"Take the woman and run for it!" he commanded.

"But w'at . . . ?" began Affable, only to be silenced by a fury he had never experienced before from his master.

"God damn you . . . go!" Sir Guy roared so savagely they lifted Ellen into the air between them and scuttled for the protection of the woods. She, in turn, tried to call something to Sir Guy, but he ignored her. Beckoning Pojo to follow, he moved to a spot directly under the gun.

"Philip! Philip, you fool!"

"Go away!" Tutweiller shouted down. "Make it whilst you can!"

"We can all make it!" Sir Guy yelled back. "Hang over the wall and drop! Pojo and I will break your fall!"

"Is . . . is Ellen safe?"

"Aye, that she is!"

"The Tatars will seize the gun and turn it onto us!"

"Empty it into them, then spike it!" Sir Guy ordered.

Philip hesitated, then a sudden forward movement of the pikemen decided him. He dropped the match to the touch-hole and the gun spewed a charge which wrought havoc in the Tatar ranks. As they re-formed to rush him, Philip pried the gun off its base and with a shout of warning, toppled it over the wall.

"Splendid!" cheered Sir Guy. "Now hang, then drop . . ."

Sir Guy tried to estimate where Philip would land. He was not so optimistic as he tried to sound, for the wall was doubtless much higher than it appeared. Be that as it may, even broken bones were preferable to the unspeakable fate that would await him if taken alive. He shaded his eyes with his hands and watched the young man crawl out between the merlons.

He almost made it. Yet as he rose above the embrasure, preparatory to backing over the rim, an archer placed a shaft squarely between his shoulder blades. Philip gave one involuntary cry and toppled backward. . . .

Even then, Sir Guy would have tried to break his fall, had not Pojo, recognizing the futility, shoved him roughly aside. Philip landed flat on his back, driving the arrow through his chest. When the others reached him, he was dead.

Pojo tugged Sir Guy's sleeve. "Come, master!" he pleaded. "God knows you can do him no service now, and the next shaft may be marked for you! Come!"

Sir Guy nodded. He paused to close Philip's eyelids. The dwarf retrieved his bundle, and together they fled through a hail of arrows to the safety of the woods.

33

For the first time in his life, Sir Guy Spangler was guilty of plain unvarnished cowardice; he was afraid to face Ellen after what had happened to Philip Tutweiller. This lack of courage stemmed from a confusion of emotional reactions, some of which he recognized and few of which were characteristic. Mainly, he dreaded lest she say something under the sudden impact of grief, which would close the doors forever on his own almost hopeless love. It may be that he was a trifle jealous of Philip; possibly even a little envious of a passion that asked nothing but the opportunity to die for the one adored. Of course that was romantic imbecility—Sir Guy admitted as much—yet it was the stuff from which heroes were made. Somehow, in his tangle of thoughts, Sir Guy had forgotten that it was he himself who had planned to do the very deed which had cost Philip his life.

Worst of all, Sir Guy was unsure of himself. After months of yearning for a glimpse of Ellen, now that she was within reach he avoided looking at her. Fortunately, the moment of reckoning was temporarily forestalled, for he had barely overtaken the trio when a scouting party of Cossacks swept out of the forest, scooped them onto wiry ponies, and galloped back to camp, where a very stern commander awaited them.

There was no doubt, as someone had forewarned, but that Jaghellon would have summarily executed them had they come back empty-handed. To state that he was raging, or even angry, would attribute to him an emotional mechanism of which no evidence was displayed, yet to describe him as *pleased* would be even more far-fetched.

When the four men and the girl were hurried into the presence of the Cossack commander, Jaghellon touched each with his slant-eyed gaze.

"Where," he demanded, "is the other?"

Sir Guy, assuming the question referred to Tutweiller, said quietly, "He gave his life that we might live."

Jaghellon blew a snort of impatience. "I speak of Count Nikita!" he growled. "What happened to *him?*"

Sir Guy colored angrily. "Nothing happened to him!" he retorted. "But something will happen to us if we sit here gossiping like old wives, while Akhmet marches down from the north and, no doubt, the Budeüaians prepare for a..."

"Did you kill Nikita?" Jaghellon cut in.

"No, damn it, I did not!" shouted Sir Guy. "I recovered the woman, which is a hell of a lot more then *you* accomplished or expected to accomplish! God's death, can't you be satisfied with that?"

"No!" said Jaghellon.

Sir Guy was furious enough to spring at the Cossack's throat. He had maintained a degree of calmness throughout the grim ordeal at the castle, but now reaction was setting in and his temper fast slipping out of control. Before he could commit so tragic an error, however, Mr. Paxton glided into the breach.

"Far be it from me to interfere, Captain," he apologized to Jaghellon. "But in the interests of harmony, may I point out that your exalted monarch is not the sort of prince to cut off his nose to spite his face."

Jaghellon scowled, not in anger, but in puzzlement. "What is this talk of noses?" he demanded gruffly.

Paxton smiled his kindly smile. "An English axiom, my Captain, which points out the futility of ruining what you can have for something you have not. In other words, while the Emperor would doubtless desire Nikita dead, of the two, he would rather have the girl—since, obviously, he cannot have both."

"Why *obviously?*"

Paxton stopped smiling. "Sir! Nikita is protected by a fortress! It was a miracle my adroit young compatriot rescued the girl! You must not demand the impossible!"

Jaghellon clawed the black wire of his beard with stumpy fingers. "Old one, I do not demand; I obey!" he rumbled. "My Prince said—'Jaghellon, do not come back without Nikita, *dead or alive,* and the woman!' I obey!"

Ellen moved closer to enter her plea. "Captain, it is my responsibility the Count is alive. Sir Guy wanted to dispatch him, but I forbade it!"

The big Cossack's surprise was genuine. "You *forbade* it!" he marveled. "*You,* a female?" He burst into rude laughter.

Ellen, face aflame, retreated in confusion as Sir Guy came charging to her rescue.

"By my troth, we've had enough of this!" he swore. "Do you refuse to leave, now that we have the girl?"

"We remain until Nikita is dead," said the Cossack bluntly.

"Very well! Stay and be damned to you! I'm leaving with my party!"

Jaghellon shook his head. "No one leaves!" he growled. He must have made a signal unseen by the English, for suddenly Sir Guy and his two chief henchmen were seized from behind. Jaghellon then leaned forward and considered Sir Guy. When he spoke, there was a trace of genuine regret in his voice.

"You are one very brave warrior, Englishman, but sorely without discipline. Yet that is to be expected of a race of males who take their orders from women, contrary to the laws of nature which, as every sane person knows, ordained the male should dominate." He shook his head, then his tone became crisp as he addressed the guards holding the trio.

"Take them away! Kill them if they make any trouble!"

Sir Guy was so enraged he might well have brought on his end then and there, if old Paxton had not appealed to his reason. Yet, it was Pojorski, not Paxton, who resolved the issue.

"Oh, Captain of Captains!" cried the dwarf, running forward and prostrating himself before the commander. "If it is only the death of that perfidious son of an illegitimate camel which troubles you, I, Yaroslaf Pojorski, will undertake to see he no longer stands in your light, nor ruffles the soft, angelic disposition of our anointed Master!"

If it did naught else, this vainglorious boast lightened the tense atmosphere. The assembled Cossacks guffawed lustily, and the corners of Jaghellon's mouth were suspected of quivering.

"I would pay well to see that," he grunted dryly.

"Would you so?" the dwarf shot back so quickly Jaghellon was taken unawares. "How much, my Captain?"

"A hundred rubles, by my beard!" growled the Cossack, adding grimly: "That is, if you succeed. Your heart if you fail! Agreed?"

"A sucker deal!" Affable said aside to Sergeant Pistol. "Jug'ead ayant got no 'undred rubles!"

"That mykes it even," grunted Pistol. "Because Pojo ayant got no 'eart!"

Meanwhile the dwarf pondered these terms for a moment or two, ignoring the jibes and ribald advice thrown at him by the crowd. Finally he shrugged his hunched shoulders.

"A hard bargain, Magnificence!" he conceded hesitantly. "Yet, I may as well die for a sheep as a lamb. In fairness, will you make it *two* hundred rubles if the deed is accomplished before the sun sets this evening?"

"Ho! Ho!" roared the assembled Cossacks. "By Shaitan, grant him that, Captain! We will take up a purse between us if the miracle happens, for pretty entertainment it will be!"

Jaghellon smiled, or, more accurately, he bared his yellow teeth. "Two hundred rubles it shall be!" he agreed. "But, mark you—we must have indisputable evidence Nikita is dead!"

Pojo's expression was an admixture of guilt and disappointment. "Oh, great Captain! Won't you take my sworn word for it?" he cried aggrievedly.

"No! No!" howled the assembly. "Words are composed of wind! We must have proof!"

"Or your heart!" concluded Jaghellon.

Pojo sighed, and appeared to bow. What he did, actually, was pick up his bundle, which he quickly unwrapped.

The only sound was a faint, strangled cry from Ellen, followed by a diabolical chortle from the dwarf.

"By the Grace of Allah, I made it, Magnificence!" he cackled as ecstatically as a laying hen. "There is the head of the treacherous hound, and the sun has not yet sunk! Where, my Captain, are my two hundred rubles?"

Pistol groaned audibly. However, his disgust was not engendered by the gruesome trophy, but by what he deemed his own stupidity.

"The tricky bastard! So that's w'at 'e went back fer, eh? W'y in 'ell didn't *I* think o' that?"

Jaghellon gave two orders without a change of expression.

"Release the Englishmen! Break camp immediately!"

In a remarkably short space of time, all was ready. All heavy equipment had been destroyed, as the company would have to be extremely mobile to slip through the advancing Tatar horde which, Jaghellon estimated, was only about five days away. He was just swinging into the saddle to lead the departure, when three of his scouts galloped in from an outpost with the staggering intelligence that Akhmet's army, rather than five thousand men, numbered slightly more than *twelve* thousand, and was spread out in a vast arc on three sides of Jaghellon's company. Instead of being five days to the north, this avenging horde was less than eight and forty hours away!

" 'Tis times like this," sighed Sergeant Pistol, "I wisht me mither 'ad never married!"

Affable looked at him in surprise. "Did she?" he asked ingenuously.

To everyone's astonishment, Jaghellon summoned the Englishmen to a council of war. His explanation of this action was that since they had but a negligible hope of surviving, it was meet they have a say in the dying. He made two exceptions: he ruled out Belcher as an irresponsible fanatic, and he banned Ellen on the grounds that as a man and a Cossack, he needed no advice from a female.

"Now 'e arsks us!" jeered Affable. " 'Tis the syme as pushin' a man off'n a church spire, then s'yin', 'Beggin' yer pardon, sir, does ye knows a nice soft plyce to land?' "

Save for such asides, the Englishmen had little to say. Some of the young Cossack officers proffered suggestions, which, though varying in degree, shared a common basis—a vainglorious willingness for riding to their deaths. Jaghellon, who better than any man present knew what could be expected, said nothing.

For his part, Sir Guy had had a bellyful of heroism and the valor of death. He was, at the moment, more interested in life. However, if it was his fate to get into trouble, it was his forte to get out of it. So he held his peace until the conference was stalemated between the faction who wanted to hack their way through the enemy lines in small groups, and the others who cried for a glorious head-on charge. Then he had his say.

"Gentlemen, in England we have a saying to the effect that he who fights and runs away will live to fight another day!"

"Are you a woman, or a coward?" jeered an arrogant young Cossack.

Sir Guy managed a smile. "A coward," he conceded.

Jaghellon's eyes had narrowed. "I would that I had an army of just such cowards!" he growled. "But where would you run, Englishman? The enemy is on three sides!"

"Captain, the answer is obvious—the *fourth* side!"

"That leads south!"

"I am without directional prejudice," said Sir Guy.

The officers raised a truculent outcry, but Jaghellon silenced them with a clap of thunder the old gods would have envied. Then he impaled the Englishman with a pointed stare.

"You have a sharp tongue," he rumbled. "Let us see if your wits are as keen. Speak, for it is plain you have given the matter some thought."

Sir Guy had, and he was prepared. He unrolled a crude map he had sketched of the country.

"We can follow the Volga to the Caspian Sea," he explained, tracing the route on the map.

"But we would then be in Akhmet's country!" protested the Cossacks in chorus.

"True," granted Sir Guy. "But at the moment, Akhmet is in yours!"

That stilled them for the nonce, so he went on: "On reaching the Caspian, we could veer towards the Sea of Azov."

Since most of his audience had been born on inland farms, he might have been discussing planets for all they knew of such remote places. But Jaghellon was better informed.

"That means we would have to cross Persia," he mused. "There is some doubt about the reception we would receive from the Khan."

"Perhaps. Yet there's none about the reception we would receive from Akhmet."

"By the liver of Shaitan, what is all this chatter about seas and Persia?" cried a bellicose young officer, eager to demonstrate both his valor and his ignorance. "Is not one Muscovite as good as ten Tatars?"

"Alive or dead?" Sir Guy asked quickly, and the ensuing laughter brought the youngster to his feet, scimitar in hand. Jaghellon wilted him with a glance, then turned back to the Englishman.

"So—you have us at the Sea of Azov," he growled, glaring at the map with the violent concentration of an unlettered man. "From there . . . whence?"

"You can follow the valley of the Don to Moscow," said Sir Guy.

Captain Jaghellon reared back and stared at him broodingly. "H'mnn! Has the fox another trick in mind?" he demanded.

Sir Guy could feel the blood warming his cheeks. "What do you mean?" he asked sharply.

"Perhaps something, perhaps nothing," grunted the Cossack. "Yet it is passing strange that when describing our route *south*, you used the word *we*, but in outlining the route *north* to Moscow, then *we* suddenly became *you!*"

"Pshaw! 'Twas but a slip of the tongue!"

"No doubt!" Jaghellon rose to his feet and solemnly considered his officers as they waited tensely for the decision which would mean glory and death, or flight and life.

"We ride south!" decreed Captain Jaghellon.

And so it was south they rode—for dusty days that stretched into sun-parched weeks. The ranks of the Cossacks had thinned: disease and the sword had buried nearly a third of the original thousand in the wound they themselves had reopened along the oft-bloodied banks of the Volga. Yet though each of them was a human being—a creature born of woman, who loved and laughed and wept—with the exception of Jaghellon, they remained to the little band of English but a faceless horde, a wolf pack only to be dreaded. To the foreigners, the loss of

Philip Tutweiller seemed to have left a greater void than had the death of three hundred Cossacks.

It had affected Sir Guy even more than the others. Alive, young Philip had seemed a nonentity, and to have considered him a competitor in the lists of love would, insofar as Sir Guy was concerned, have been ridiculous. Dead, he had become a formidable rival. And because Sir Guy had charged himself with the guilt of Philip's death, he assumed others, and Ellen in particular, likewise held him responsible. He saw to it he was never alone with her.

This was not difficult, for Jaghellon was seeing to the same thing. What suspicion lurked behind those obsidian eyes, none knew but he. However, soon after leaving Budeüa, he captured two old women and placed Ellen in their care. These venerable crones kept their faces covered and tried to force Ellen to do likewise. This she refused to do until they reached the borders of Persia, where it became mandatory.

34

As long as they journeyed southward, Sir Guy managed to avoid coming to grips with his emotions in regard to Ellen.

However, when at the mouth of the Don they turned their faces northward, the necessity for a decision was immediate. Every stride of their weary horses carried them that much closer to Moscow, to Ivan the Terrible, and to the inevitable. Time, like the sand in the glass, was running out.

Jaghellon, too, watched the passing days with increasing grimness. His year of grace was nearing its end, and as he candidly admitted, if he was delayed by so much as a day, Ivan would have his life. So the savage sun never caught the company at rest; they started before the dawn, and stopped only when darkness made it impossible to hold the trail.

All the wealth Sir Guy had in the world now reposed in one small pouch about his person. Unless he secured the liberation of *The Dainty Virgin* and saw her safely back to England, he was ruined. Then there was the trust the investors had placed in him when he agreed to manage the affair, whether they themselves were fools or worse altered his obligation no whit. And certainly, any further tampering with the Tsar's precarious disposition would not only doom the venture, it would in all likelihood doom all the English now in Muscovy.

Reduced to essentials, he had but two choices: he either presented Ellen to the Tsar of Muscovy and fulfilled his pledge to the *Companie of Merchant-Adventurers,* or he did not, and took the consequences. All the rhetoric and verbiage in the world could not becloud those bald facts.

Under the weight of inner conflicts, he grew increasingly morose. He no longer teased and jested with Affable and Pistol, nor baited the Reverend Belcher. He found the calmness of Paxton wearisome, the bluff directness of Captain Jaghellon offensive. He erected a shell about himself, and, turtle-fashion, pulled back into it.

Autumn had set in, and if the days along the Don were still warm, the night chill presaged winter. That coolness had a like effect on Sir Guy's feelings. The feverish gnawing was quieted and he felt, somehow, cleaner, saner, more mature. He took to dozing in the saddle during the heat of the day, partly to discourage conversation, but chiefly to permit himself the luxury of sweet loneliness in the stillness of night. At such times he would lie in his sheepskin saddle blanket and watch the gods of the ancients carouse about the heavens, but occasionally he would steal away from the bivouac so he could be free of the stench of sweat and leather to dream of what might have been.

On one such flight, he encountered Ellen.

It was a dream, of course; he knew that. She appeared standing, wraithlike, on a little promontory overlooking the river, her face turned towards the moon which, symbolically, was on the wane. He stopped short on sight of her, uncertain whether to advance or retreat, but even as he hesitated, she turned her head and saw him. Since she exhibited no sign of distress, he continued towards her.

Of the two, he was, perchance, the more embarrassed. He knew not what to say, nor how to commence saying it. She gave him no help. In turning, she had put her back to the pale source of light, hence her features were but soft and gentle shadows. Nevertheless, he retained an indelible impression of every precious detail.

Unlike dreams he had had of similar character, this scene took place in no empty vacuum of silence. The whole setting vibrated with a kind of abandoned ecstasy. A strange exotic bird protested their alien presence, yet its distressed song was pleasingly muted. The wind frolicked through trees whose leaves, growing stiff with their autumnal senility, rustled with the gayety of aged dancers. And as background music composed especially for the occasion, the mighty Don hummed a haunting overture as it marched around the bed. Thus even Nature contributed to the theme of Time's inevitable flow. A line from a new play he had seen, shortly before leaving London, popped into his mind:

*"Come what come may,
Time and the hour run through the roughest day."*

Hence, struck with an awareness of the value of each fleeting instant as he never had been before, he went directly to her. As usual, he counted on his ready wit to prompt his nimble tongue. Alas, this was not Sir Guy, the wily rogue; this was a great fumbling boy in love!

The next thing he knew she was in his arms!

Albeit oft in dreams he had envisioned this heady culmination, yet now, incredibly, he felt strange and awkward, as if he had never before performed this rite. Yet, in the finest sense, that was the truth, he had not! The thousand and one women who had passed through his arms were of hardly more consequence than partners at a dance; they had left undisturbed the deeper emotions. It was these emotions he was now meeting for the first time.

Still, he could not have bungled *too* badly, for she seemed quite content in his arms. And if she displayed no great ardor or passion, he, contrary to his wont, was entirely satisfied with her soft passivity.

When she finally drew away, a tiny kerchief fluttered to the ground. He retrieved it, and straightening, found her staring out over the river.

"I had no idea you felt that way about me, Guy!" she murmured.

"Nor I that . . . that you did, Ellen!"

She looked up at him with eyes that shimmered. "Not even I knew that!" she whispered. Then she took his hand and they returned to camp in silence.

Before separating, he kissed her once again, and that was all.

As was his wont, he wakened a few moments before trumpet call to luxuriate in recaptured fragments of his dreams, for if he did not imprison them immediately, they too often escaped during the day. So he had dreamed he walked and talked with Ellen? He smiled ruefully. Kissed her twice, and nothing more! Truly a schoolboy's dream, that! Yet, peculiarly enough, he felt better than he had on any morning since leaving England. Perchance, if a dream had such a salutary effect on him, he should take the bull by the horns and talk with her in the flesh. Doubtless she would excoriate him with a tongue-lashing, but that was to be expected. He confessed he . . .

The jarring blare of the trumpet shattered his reverie and simultaneously the whole camp came alive. Sir Guy threw off his blanket and rose. As he did so, something white fluttered to the ground. He retrieved it with fingers suddenly a-tremble—a wispy square of Flanders lace.

Then it . . . it had *not* been *just a dream!* The implications dazzled him.

He afterwards doubted he could have borne the dragging hours of that day had not Ellen managed a shy and surreptitious smile. That was better evidence than even the handkerchief, and wiped away the last lingering doubts as to the validity of their meeting. Somehow he survived the day, but the moment the camp was quieted for the night, he slipped out to what seemed the most logical place for a rendezvous.

Ellen did not come, but a rainstorm did, so after a miserable wait, he gave up and returned to his sodden blankets.

But the following night, his luck was better. He found her in a little dell walled on three sides by forest, with the river making a great magic window. This time he was under no delusions about its being a dream. This time, too, Ellen returned his kiss, as if, perhaps, she also had been looking forward to it. Then they sank onto the lush carpet of aromatic leaves, not to make love, but to discuss the future.

He summarized the situation for her much as he had for himself. "God knows I'm responsible for the ghastly mess," he concluded, "but perhaps it is not too late to rectify it."

She was staring at him with that wide-eyed wonderment peculiar to people who suddenly discover one another.

"It wasn't really your fault, Guy," she protested. "Things were in a frightful tangle."

"*Were* in a tangle?" he said with a bitter laugh. "What do you call *this?*"

Ellen laughed, but without bitterness. "I hardly know! Pojo would insist it was Kismet."

"Don't mention that creature in the same breath with yourself!"

"Why not? Oh, I grant you he's a veritable fiend at times, yet I must confess my debt to the little scamp!" She sighed softly. "Aye, I've learned some galling truths on this journey."

"'Pon my soul, I'm sorry!"

"Don't be—for that!" she said quickly, reaching over to touch his face. "The truth never hurt anyone, Guy."

He changed the subject. "We must come to some conclusion," he said grimly. "I'm sure of only one thing—I am not turning you over to the Tsar!"

For a time she sat quiet. He grew restless.

"Didn't you hear me, Ellen?"

She nodded. "Of course I heard you, my darling! I just wanted time to lock up those words in my heart, so that in the days to come I can find comfort in them when I'm alone."

"But, damn it, you're not going to be alone! I mean exactly what I say: *you're not going to Ivan!*"

She leaned over and kissed him, but when he tried to take her in his arms, she held him off.

"Wait, dearest, wait!" she pleaded. "We have to talk this out. I can't think sanely when I'm in your arms, and if we ever needed sanity, it is now."

"I'd rather be insane about you," he said, grinning.

"Idiot!" she scolded, but her eyes were misty. "Dear God, I'll never understand by what strange quirk of destiny you, I, and the others were enmeshed in this trap, yet it is so. We can no more escape than . . . than . . ." As she groped for an apt allusion, she saw an insect struggling in a spider web on a bush nearby, "than that poor fly!" she concluded.

Sir Guy smiled confidently, and reaching out, slashed the web with his finger. The liberated insect fell to the ground.

"There! You see, it can be done!" he chuckled. "That fly . . ."

"Ah, but look . . ." interrupted Ellen.

The fly had fallen onto a large leaf, where it stood trying to clear its wings and feet. As the two stared, the spider appeared. The fly saw him, and tried to escape, but its tiny feet were mired in the mysterious adhesive of the web. It made only a few futile jumps before the spider closed in.

Ellen shuddered. "God help us! If there ever was an evil omen, that was it!"

"Nonsense!" Guy growled. "I'll find a way!"

The demise of the fly had shaken her, she crept into his arms. "No, dearest, no! We haven't a chance to escape. And it isn't just you and me; there are all the others dependent on you."

"Avaricious vultures! To hell with them!"

"But you can't dismiss them that way, Guy! We, too, have our spiders: Ivan, and more immediate and dangerous . . . Jaghellon!"

"To hell with them, too!" But this time he smiled, albeit a bit ruefully.

Ellen continued to shake her head. "We can't fight against the inevitable, my darling! Tell me in so many words that you love me!"

"*Words,* you say? My God, haven't you heard my heart pounding out its message: *I love you?* Haven't you seen my eyes blazing their vow: *I love you?* Hasn't every step I've taken, every gesture of my hands, the very way I've sat in the saddle told you that—*I love you?* Can you believe my kisses lied when they trembled: *I love you?* And now, my lady, you ask for *words!*"

She had closed her eyes in a shivering ecstasy, and now, lying across his breast, she nodded.

"I know, I know!" she breathed. "But, oh, my darling, tell me! Tell me!"

"I love you, my Ellen!"

She turned in his arms and snuggled her face against his neck. "I wanted you to say that, dearest, before I said what I'm going to say. Listen . . . we are only a few days from . . . well . . . from Moscow; we both know what that means, so let us say no more about it. Parting will be hard, and in the years to come, we shall both have many regrets. So let us meet tomorrow evening and pretend that this single night is all the tomorrows compressed into one; let us live our whole life in that brief span and with the dawn say farewell forever!"

He bent over her. "Are you serious, Ellen?"

"I'd hardly jest now, sweetheart! Do you agree?"

Incredibly, he shook his head. "No, by God! I won't quit in that fashion! An experience so unbelievably beautiful to be followed by an act of despicable cowardice? Great God above, Ellen, you can't realize what you ask! I'd loathe myself even more than I do now!"

"Then do it for me, my darling!"

"Damned if I will—even for you, my dear!" he said grimly. "Before I have the faintest right to such a glimpse of paradise, I must in some measure unscramble this sordid mess I've brought about!"

"But, Guy dear—we agreed that is impossible!"

"*You* agreed, not I," he reminded her. "For my part I . . . *My God!*"

She jerked into a sitting position. "Guy! What's wrong?" she cried.

"Nothing's wrong! You've just given me an idea!" He grabbed her roughly by the shoulders and peered into her starlit eyes. "Ellen . . . *will you marry me?*"

Her eyes widened. "*Marry you?* Have you lost your senses?"

"On the contrary, I've found them!" He was too impatient to wait her further argument. "We can get Belcher to perform the ceremony, and Paxton and Affable can be our witnesses!"

She smiled whimsically. "Bless my soul! Has Sir Guy Spangler, the notorious rake, become so moral he requires a wedding to . . ."

"I'm deadly serious, Ellen!" he said, shaking her. "Not even the Tsar can marry you if you are already wedded!"

"Alas, he has already married one widow," she said nervously. "I'm quite certain he would have no compunctions about marrying another."

"That's a chance I'm willing to take!"

She started to object, then changed in mid-sentence. "Why not? Why should I try to fool myself any longer! I want you, and if I cannot have you . . ." She threw her arms around his neck. "Yes, Guy, yes! I leave everything in your hands!"

The following night when the camp had stilled, the conspirators, without Pojo but with the startled Belcher in tow, crept off into the woods. Safely out of earshot, they settled down on the banks of the river and Sir Guy announced his determination to marry Ellen and defy the Tsar.

Only Belcher opposed the plan. He insisted on a strictly business proposition, already agreed upon, and contended that to keep the woman from the Tsar would spell disaster to all the investors.

"The true Christian spirit, I declare!" commented Affable.

"'E's got a p'int," said Pistol. "If that thievin' Bendix don't get 'is share o' the loot, 'oo's to set the parson up in the business o' syving souls?"

Sir Guy said nothing, leaving it to Mr. Paxton to argue with the clergyman. This the old gentleman did in scholarly fashion, but Belcher flatly refused to perform the ceremony.

This impasse brought on an awkward silence, until Affable Jones, who had taken up a position almost directly behind the parson, now leaned forward.

"'Ow was that ag'in, Belch?"

The Reverend sat stiffly erect. "I have stated unequivocally that I will not marry these . . ." he began stridently, then suddenly stopped with a convulsive jerk. His eyes had grown round with fear.

"'Ow was that ag'in, yer Reverence?" Affable inquired with such an expression of exaggerated innocence, Sir Guy could hardly keep his own face straight.

"I . . . I . . . I . . . !" stuttered the parson, as if in time with his bobbing Adam's apple.

Ellen would have gone to his side, if Sir Guy had not restrained her. "What is it, Mr. Belcher?" she cried solicitously. "Are you ill?"

"'Ell no, ma'am, 'e ayant ill! 'E's jes' 'avin' an 'eavenly rever-lashun—ayant ye, Belch, ol' boy?" Affable said cheerfully, trying to keep his blade firmly against the parson's squirming ribs and at the same time out of Ellen's sight. "These gen-u-ine rev-er-lashuns 'urt bad if misunderstood. Ye don't misunderstan' this one, does ye, Belchy darlin'?" He emphasized his verbal point with a steel point.

"Nay! Nay!" choked the parson hastily. "Verily, certain truths hath been revealed! Mine eyes are opened!"

"Damme, that's the proper gospel!" chuckled Affable. "Now get yer mouth opened, an' stop actin' like an ass betwixt two bundles o' 'ay. Let's 'ave at the weddin'!"

Thus it came about that in a wild and primeval dell on the banks of the river Don in Muscovy, the notorious Sir Guy Spangler, the "greatest rogue in England," and a lovely woman known only as Lady Ellen were joined in holy wedlock by a dubious clergyman with a knife against his after-ribs. As legal witnesses were two very illegal knaves, and a kindly wise man.

When it was over, the gentle Paxton bade the clergyman and the two witnesses to come away with him and leave the two lovers to themselves. But as they rose to go, Affable was seized by a paroxysm of mirth that doubled him as in pain. It was some time before they could learn the cause of the convulsion.

"Oh-ho-ho! I jes' recomembered Sir Guy's 'oly oath!" he howled, bracing his jiggling carcass against a tree. "Oh, Lord, 'tis killin' me!" Another spasm hit him.

"What in hell are you talking about?" snapped Sir Guy.

"W'at ye 'ad me'n Pistol witness!" caroled Affable. "W'en ye swore ye'd ne'er touch, ner fondle, fer purposes o' rermantic or . . ."

"'Tis the bloody trufe!" agreed Pistol gloomily. "Reckon that sort o' spoils the weddin'!"

"You dog!" growled Sir Guy, embarrassed. "You have too damn good a memory!"

Ellen smiled with perfect calm. "On the contrary, my dear *husband*, his memory is atrocious! Affable, you great scamp, have you forgotten the proviso your master had the foresight to insert, to wit that what you said was so only—*unless the Lady Ellen herself should beseech it otherwise?*"

Affable sobered instantly. "W'y, I own that's true, m'lydy!"

Ellen smiled up at Sir Guy. "I'm *beseeching* now, my lord," she whispered.

As Sir Guy reached to take her into his arms, Paxton firmly collared his loquacious companions and started for the path. But ere he had taken a dozen steps, the bushes parted and a squad of Cossacks strode into the clearing, headed by the last man any of them wanted to see at this particular time . . .

Jaghellon!

[283]

Sir Guy shoved Ellen behind him and reached for his sword in motions that were almost instinctive. Affable, too, was motivated by a somewhat similar protective compulsion, though his took a slightly different form. He stepped behind Belcher, and with the tip of his ready blade reminded that untrustworthy cleric of the imminence of sudden death. In the deep shadows, these twin moves were hardly perceptible. Yet the tension was so taut it would have taken but a word or a gesture to have brought on a general massacre. In this supercharged atmosphere, Ellen's carefully modulated voice rang like a bell.

"Oh!" she cried relievedly in Russian. "Thank God it is only Captain Jaghellon and his men!"

The burly Cossack said nothing, but some of the stiff-legged truculence seemed to go out of his stance. Sir Guy, ever alert to subtle nuances of manner, caught this, and was guided accordingly.

"Why, so it is!" he agreed with what heartiness he could muster. "By my troth, I thought we'd been surprised by an enemy!"

"What are you doing here?" Jaghellon demanded of Sir Guy.

The Englishman hesitated, uncertain as to just how long the Cossacks had remained in the bushes.

"I often meet with my countrymen to talk things over in our mother tongue. What business is that of yours?"

Jaghellon appeared slightly taken aback. "This woman," he growled, "is the Emperor's property! She has no right to be . . ."

Sir Guy came close to exploding at this, but Ellen herself jumped into the fray.

"I beg your pardon, Captain Jaghellon!" she said (in a voice which Affable described later as being so cold "it sent a chill down me spine till an icicle 'ung off'n the butt end o' me like a tyle!"), "I am *not* the Emperor's *property* nor, might I remind you, am I yours! As for my rights, they are those of any Englishwoman on a diplomatic mission to a foreign state. You will kindly remember that, save as you command this expedition, you have no authority over me! Do I make myself understood, sir?"

Paxton attempted to ease the tension. "My countrywomen are spirited creatures, Captain," he said gently, "yet I own in this particular instance, her ladyship has justice and reason on her side." His soft tone, despite his words, seemed to imply that his sympathies lay with the Cossack.

Jaghellon, glowering like a confused bull, jerked his head in the direction of the bivouac.

"You will return to camp!" he growled with slow deliberation. "Nor will you meet again in this fashion!"

"You have no right . . ." began Ellen haughtily, but this time it was Jaghellon who cut her short.

"Enough! A moment past, you told me your rights; now I will tell you *mine!* I am under sentence of death unless before the wane of this moon, I lay at the feet of my Prince two objects; the head of Count Nikita and *you!* To accomplish this, I have lost many brave men and endured much, hence I am in no mood to haggle with you about rights and courtesies, nor to jeopardize my success. Make no mistake about that!"

Once again old Paxton cushioned the blows. "Oh, come now, Captain!" he chided softly. "Has anyone challenged your excellent leadership?"

Jaghellon grunted. "When a fox is about, the wise farmer locks up the hens *before* they are stolen, not afterwards. Go to camp!"

As Sir Guy moved towards Ellen, Jaghellon caught his arm. Paxton quickly stepped to her side and led her away. Affable and Pistol appeared to have developed an ardent infatuation for the Reverend Belcher, for they went off arm in arm. The Cossacks followed, until at last only Sir Guy and Jaghellon remained in the dell. The former, not trusting himself to speak, held his silence. The captain, on the other hand, seemed to be searching in his own mind for words.

"Englishmen," he rumbled finally, "you and I have forded many dangerous rivers together this past year. If we have never been friends, we have not been enemies. Until we recovered this woman, we seemed to share a common objective. That was good. But slowly that situation has changed. I do not know why. Nor do I know what strange thoughts are lurking in your mind, but heed this—at the least sign of treachery, *I shall put every man of you to the sword!* For it is either your life or mine!"

35

Here then was the notorious Sir Guy Spangler, famed among the court ladies of Whitehall and Versailles as a perennial bachelor and romantic rake, married at long last to a woman whose real name he did not even know —only to be separated from his bride within minutes after the ceremony.

Sir Guy found nothing droll about the circumstances, and it required all his self-control to keep from defying Jaghellon to do his worst. But the cold-blooded little guardian angel of reason triumphed over a natural hot-headedness, so Sir Guy stalked off to lick his wounds and try to view the problem objectively.

The waning moon was both calendar and barometer. When it was gone, so was Ellen, so was life itself unless Sir Guy could find a loophole. Naturally, his first thought was flight, but when he asked himself the obvious question—flight to where?—he was whipped. *The Dainty Virgin* lay hundreds of leagues to the north, if in truth she was still afloat. With only weary horses and no supplies—not to mention some six hundred hard-riding Cossacks always at his side—it was impossible.

He considered telling Jaghellon of his marriage, but the instant he gave that notion form, he saw the folly of it. Jaghellon would simply lop off his head rather than let the Tsar know that the Englishman had foxed him right under his nose. Sir Guy conceded grimly that Jaghellon would be a fool if he didn't.

The following day, he looked for Ellen, only to discover that Jaghellon had her riding almost directly behind him in the van, carefully shepherded by a group of junior officers, none of whom was friendly to the Englishman. Sir Guy had worried, too, about the possibility that the unpredictable Belcher might take it into his head to blurt out the truth to the Cossack commander. But the parson was afforded no opportunity for betrayal, Affable and Pistol chaperoned him with such sedulous concern. Then to Sir Guy's intense disgust, he discovered that Pojorski was tagging him with equal assiduity.

This tended to confirm what Sir Guy had long suspected, that Pojo was less an ally than a spy. In his first flush of resentment, he was minded to yank the dwarf into the shelter of the trees and cut his throat—a legal right he had, since the scoundrel was his slave. Instead, after a futile half-day of hide-and-seek, he suddenly shoved his property out of earshot of the others and demanded to know what he was up to.

For the first time in their acquaintance, Pojo appeared embarrassed. "I . . . I hardly know how to say it, master!" he stammered at last.

"Say *what?*"

The dwarf stared at the tip of his boots. "Master, I have tried to serve you well and faithfully. You know that! True, you have never called for my professional skills, nor permitted me to exercise them for amusement. Nevertheless, as Allah will testify . . ."

"For God's sake, come to the point!" snapped Sir Guy impatiently.

The dwarf shuddered. "It is just this, master—within three days, we will bask in the glory of my sublime Prince. Then you will reap your just reward, and go to your own land across the seas. I, as your slave, must go with you."

"God forbid!"

"Affable and Pistol have told me about this England, which—though I can scarce credit it—is ruled by a *female!* They have only a few torturers, and those are surly brutes without finesse or a sense of humor. Nobody tortures for the sheer sport of the thing. Are these things true, master?"

Sir Guy was puzzled. "What in the hell are you driving at, Pojo!" he demanded.

"I don't want to go to such an unfriendly and inhospitable land!" sobbed the dwarf.

"Ha! That can easily be arranged!" snorted the Englishman.

Pojo looked up with shining, eager eyes. "Then you will hear my scheme to accomplish this, master?" he asked unbelievingly.

"I'll listen to anything to accomplish it!"

"Excellent! Excellent! May Allah fill your harem with the very fruits of paradise!" Pojo was beside himself with excitement. "This is my plan: Ivan must be rife with anticipation to see whether Jaghellon makes it in his allotted time. It is my thought, you and Allah willing—not to mention Jaghellon—that I speed on ahead as fast as horseflesh can stand, with the head of Nikita and the information that this luscious maid will soon warm his couch!"

Sir Guy clenched his teeth. "You can ride to tell the devil to warm up hell for us, as far as I'm concerned. But methinks you'll not get Jaghellon to agree."

Pojo sniffed. "I can outsmart that great ox," he boasted. "Tomorrow night you must cross the river. If the ferry is not prepared to handle such a company, a delay might well follow, and a delay would be fatal to the Cossack. He will welcome an emissary who can smooth the way."

Something clicked in Sir Guy's brain, something too vague and nebulous to be called an idea.

"Do you want me to suggest it to the captain?" he asked.

Pojo frantically shook his head. "By the liver of Shaitan, *no!*" he cried. "You can assist by *objecting*, master! Say you refuse to permit me to leave! (Only do not be *too* vehement!) Argue against letting the Tsar know we are near. Then Jaghellon will insist I go! Agreed, master?"

"Agreed!"

By what legerdemain Pojo accomplished it, Sir Guy never learned, but accomplish it he did. Then, like a small boy leaving home on his first vacation, he was eager to get started. Arguing that he would save one whole day by reaching the ferry-crossing at dawn, he made such a pest of himself that even Jaghellon was anxious to be rid of him. The one thing to which Jaghellon would not agree was that Pojo carry Nikita's head.

"I was commanded to return two objects," the big Cossack reiterated doggedly. "That skull is *one* of them. I will obey!"

Pojo was disappointed, but not dismayed. When he had obtained one of the fastest horses in the company and made what other preparations he deemed necessary, he scurried up to the little company of grim-faced Englishmen, made a tearful speech, and insisted on kissing their hands.

All submitted with a modicum of good grace, save Affable, who while offering his right hand to be kissed, held his nose with his left, and Pistol who refused to submit either hand.

"The viper ayant gettin' 'is fangs that close to me 'ide," he growled.

The dwarf wagged a warning finger at him. "Pojo shall remember!" he assured the dour Pistol, then, with a wave, he was gone.

"I have a peculiar feeling we shall never see him again," mused Mr. Paxton.

Sir Guy grunted. "I hope to God you're right!"

The following day dawned grim and threatening. There was some talk among the Cossacks of laying over until the weather cleared, but Jaghellon wouldn't hear of it. By pushing hard all day without pause, even for a midday meal, they might with luck cross the river this night.

By noon, the sky was dark as night. They reached the crossing late in the afternoon, only to find that a great herd of bawling cattle had preceded them. Sir Guy estimated there must have been close to a thousand head in the drove—gaunt, leggy beasts with long spreading horns and very little meat. Sensitive in their primitive fashion to the nuances of the weather, they milled about in wide-eyed panic, to the anxiety of their drovers and the terror of the villagers in the little settlement nearby.

Having no liking for the longhorns, the Cossacks made a detour around the herd, and cantered up to the ferry landing. Here they encountered more difficulty, for the drovers were demanding the ferryman get the herd over to the other side of the river before the storm broke, and the ferryman insisted he wouldn't risk his barge in this weather if St. Peter offered him the keys of heaven.

When Jaghellon roughly attempted to commandeer the ferry, the drovers turned on him in fury, then drew back in terror on learning his identity. The ferryman was composed of sterner stuff; he maintained that it would be suicidal to crowd the little craft, which at best could not carry over a score of men and horses, and risk getting capsized in a squall. He salted his argument with good sense. Men he could carry in an emergency, for they could be induced to stand still, but even a clap of thunder terrified horses or cattle, and sent them lunging in concert. The ferryman concluded his reasoning by explaining that four years ago he had bowed to pleading, and attempted to take a noble party across. The horses had gone wild, overturning the craft, and the nobleman had lost a wife, and the ferryman had lost not only his boat, but a son as well. No! Ten thousand times *no!*

As a final resort, Jaghellon produced his Tsar's signet, which gave him *carte blanche*, but the ferryman was ready for such a maneuver, and countered with a parchment bearing the Tsar's own signature, giving him full majesty over his aquatic conveyance. Since his was the only means of crossing the Don within two days' travel in either direction, his ferry was deemed of military importance and his judgment supreme. They must wait.

When he saw the ferry, Sir Guy could understand the man's reluctance to venture out into a storm with it loaded with either horses or cattle. It was a clumsy raftlike contrivance, with a huge single sail squarely amidships, and monstrous sweeps for a half dozen men. In calm placid weather, its dominant virtue was its great size, but in a blow it would be at the mercy of wind and current. And as the point of crossing was made at a sharp bend, where the river was over a league in width and the current swift, this danger was magnified. Plainly it was the better part of valor to wait out the storm.

Spangler tramped around the unhappy bivouac. He hoped for a glimpse, at least, of Ellen; it was still difficult for him to believe she was his wife, yet the realization sent the blood racing through his arteries.

Unable to find her, he trudged down to the ferry landing to inquire if Pojorski had succeeded in crossing earlier in the day. The ferryman admitted that when he came to his boat that morning he had found the dwarf seated cross-legged on the landing. Startled, for he was satisfied only an emissary of Shaitan could be so ugly, he had taken the dwarf across the river so precipitately he had neglected to collect for the passage. At that, concluded the ferryman, crossing himself, he had probably got off cheaply. Was the creature, he asked, actually a fiend?

Sir Guy grunted. "If he isn't, he'll do until the real thing comes along!"

To which the ferryman nodded and crossed himself again.

Just then a clap of thunder jarred the very ground on which Spangler stood, and set the cattle bawling in terror. In that moment of elemental travail, an idea was born, and he hurried off to locate his confreres.

He found Affable and Pistol arguing whether it was safest to bed down under a big tree during a violent storm, or out in the open, and old Paxton pleading with them to do one or the other before it became too thick to see.

"The safest place for us is the other side of the river," Spangler told them. "We'll cross over."

"'Ow'd ye get the bloody ferryman to chynge 'is mind?" asked Pistol.

"I haven't. That's Affable's chore!"

Affable pursed his lips. "Oh-ho! 'Ere we goes ag'in!" he sighed. "W'at's the rest o' it, m'lud?"

"Why, only that since you have the greatest powers of persuasion, Affable, you will take our pious but erratic parson in tow and take possession of the ferry. Try not to use any more force than is absolutely necessary. I doubt anyone will dispute you in this weather, but be ready to cast off your moorings on an instant's notice."

For once Mr. Jones was mute; he could only nod. Sergeant Pistol, seeing Sir Guy turning his gaze towards him, braced himself. When his master didn't speak immediately, Pistol couldn't stand the suspense.

"An' w'at cute little trick 'a ye got reserved fer me, yer Gryce?" he asked gloomily. "Mebbe steal the river, or some'at light chore?"

Sir Guy didn't smile. "Pistol, you've proven yourself a peerless thief, hence I'm assigning you to a task that will be the apex of your career." He hesitated a moment, then went on grimly: "I want you to steal the Lady Ellen from under Jaghellon's nose!"

Affable exhaled windily. "An' I thought *my* job was tough!"

"W'y, curse me, sir!" Pistol assured Sir Guy. "W'en ye wraps it up in flowers like that, I'll steal 'is bloody nose if ye s'y the word!"

"If it ayant too ruddy h'impertinent, m'lud," Affable inquired with thinly veiled sarcasm, "w'at's our ol' pal Jug'ead agoin' to be doin' w'ilest we uns be cheerily puntin' up an' down this purty li'l stream?"

Sir Guy set his jaw. "The captain," he said slowly, "will, God favoring us, be doing his level best to keep clear of the horns and hooves of rampaging cattle!"

Mr. Paxton whistled softly, but Pistol failed to comprehend. "Burn me, sir, ayant that wishful thinkin'? W'at'll myke the ugly beasties rampage?"

"*I* will!" promised Sir Guy. To forestall any further questioning, he turned to the old man. "Will you undertake to secure the horses? We will require six, but it would be advisable to have a spare."

"After the assignments you have given Affable and Pistol, horse-stealing sounds ridiculously simple," said the old man with a smile. "Howbeit, have you considered what happens when we get across the river?"

"Ye mean *if*, not *w'en*, don't ye, gaffer?" snorted Affable.

36

RIDING THROUGH THE DRIVING RAIN and darkness a few moments later, Sir Guy began to wonder if he was not losing his old sure touch. The storm was his strongest ally, yet treacherous withal, and utterly undisciplined. A bolt of lightning, an extra loud clap of thunder, might terrorize the cattle before the stage was set. When Sir Guy considered this possibility, and his vivid imagination conjured a picture of Ellen being trapped by the bellowing herd, he suffered an emotion akin to common panic.

He made his way out of the bivouac without being challenged. Since his own clothing had long since worn out, he was dressed in Cossack garb, and in the downpour there was nothing to distinguish him from several hundred others. The few sentries who were stationed about the camp remained huddled in the lee of convenient trees.

His most difficult task was maintaining a slow and steady pace, for the very foundation of the scheme was timing—time for Affable to secure the ferry, for the indomitable sergeant to crawl past the headquarters' guards and get close enough to Ellen to slash her tent, dispatch any interfering attendants, and snatch her to safety—all between the first cry of alarm and the moment when the grinding hooves destroyed everything in their mad path. Perhaps it had been folly to have entrusted the aged Paxton with such a lively chore as stealing a half dozen horses. Yet there had been no alternative.

He came at last to the herd, huddled with their backs to the wind. The nervous herdsmen sat slumped in their saddles, spaced around the cattle like widely separated fence-posts. The Englishman could not see them until he was within arm's reach, and it was a ghostly sensation to come upon one in the darkness.

Reaching the destination he had chosen earlier, he dismounted and checked over his saddle. He tightened the girth, loosened his sword in its scabbard, then readied the single petard he had been able to pilfer. He would have preferred to have had two or three of these little bombs, but it had taken all his cunning to get this one. That done, he heaved himself into the saddle. One more check on his direction, and he was ready.

With the point of his sword, he prodded and poked at the flanks of the cattle nearest him. The brutes kicked viciously, and, that failing to stop their tormentor, started burrowing into the herd. After a few minutes of this, when he had them nervous and irritated, he offered up a grim little prayer and touched off his petard.

For an unbearable moment, there was some doubt as to whether the terror-stricken brutes would charge or flee. Then, howling like a banshee, Sir Guy drove his frightened horse full into the tail of the herd. The terrified bullocks tried to climb over those ahead. Panic swept the herd like lightning playing along their horns, and, in the manner of a bursting dike, the whole milling, seething mass cascaded into motion.

Yet this was child's play compared to the rest of the task. A herd of terrorized cattle was not like an arrow, which, when properly nocked and aimed, soars in a premeditated flight; no one could foresee with any degree of precision which way this crazed and bawling flood would go. It was not inconceivable that with sufficient distraction up ahead, they might turn and charge the ferry itself—an appalling thought! But, loosing his boots in the stirrups, so that if his horse went down he would have a fighting chance for survival, Sir Guy rode like mad towards the front, circling on the outside to keep the herd between himself and the river. It was fortunate he did, for several times the panicked beasts tried to change direction to escape running over the sentries' fires ahead. Each time, he managed to turn the leaders back.

That night Nature's very savagery was eclipsed. The ground shuddered under the drumming thunder of hooves, and the awesome rattle of horns and hocks was indescribable. Sir Guy went through the various stages of fear, from anxiety for others to pure terror for himself. Then suddenly all dread left him and he felt only a kind of wild exaltation. One with his horse, he was a centaur guiding the devil's herd; the frantic bawling took on a rhythm marked by the overtones of thunder; the lightning was hell's own flambeau! Then the whole avalanche crashed in among the terrified Cossacks, and this phase of the operation was over. Sir Guy turned his horse towards the ferry.

He almost lost his way in the confusion, but after a nerve-racking gallop, discovered the perilous craft right before him. His arrival was timely, for Affable and Pistol, aided by old Paxton, were trying to hold off the irate ferryman and a mob of Muscovites. Sir Guy, swooping out of the storm like an angry Valkyrie, threw them into a momentary panic. And the instant Sir Guy's horse got his front feet aboard, Affable slashed the mooring lines. The storm and the current did the rest. The unwieldy craft shot out from shore and was swallowed in the storm.

Sir Guy found the other horses tethered securely to the mast, so he tied his own amongst them, and clawed his way aft towards the others. En route, he stumbled upon Ellen.

She was on her knees, and without speaking, she drew him down beside her. There was no need of words; so much more could be expressed with arms and lips. This ritual over for the moment, he joined the others. Here again a handclasp, a clap on the shoulder, a pressure of the arm expressed a camaraderie no words could ever quite convey.

Then Sir Guy gave his attention to the next phase of his gamble. His plight was that of the fox loosed a few jumps ahead of the hounds; with not more than a day's start, he and his companions had to maintain that lead half the length of Muscovy. Even if by a miracle they succeeded, there was no assurance the "gate" would still be open.

Then he looked at Ellen, and the odds seemed inconsequential.

Instead of fighting the current, Sir Guy utilized it. True, he made his landing approximately two leagues further down stream than he would have preferred, but he was grateful to have made it at all. Sleep, of course, was unthought of, so after getting the horses ashore, and chopping the boat beyond peradventure of salvage, they mounted and headed into the storm. The tension and excitement had drained them of any desire for conversation, so they rode in a close-knit huddle, silent, yet grateful in the knowledge each other was present.

Before the night was over, the storm had blown itself out, and with the dawn the sun came up smug and warm. When the night chill had dissipated, Sir Guy led them into a little grove where they could command a view of the road, yet not themselves be seen. Here he called a halt.

"You'll have to tighten your belts," he told them grimly. "We dare not risk foraging for food this close to the river."

Everybody save Ellen looked properly glum, whereupon Affable rose to his stubby legs, made a grandiose bow, and from under his swathed garments, produced a chuck of beef.

"M'lud!" he began sonorously. "On be'arf of me dull-witted companions, I persent ye wi' this sma' token o' . . ."

Pistol jumped up in a temper and stamped his feet like an angry child. "There ye go ag'in!" he raged. Unwrapping his saddle-roll, he yanked out two legs of mutton and slammed them on the ground. "There, an' m'y ye choke on 'em, Mr. Jones!"

Mr. Paxton said: "I can sympathize with you, Sergeant, for I, too, thought I was being very original and provident when I . . . ah . . . garnered this minor contribution." And he laid two loaves of bread and a round cheese beside the sergeant's mutton.

"Verily, the Lord will provide!" said the parson, and hauled forth a skin of wine.

"Let us eat and drink," blandly suggested Belcher. "For tomorrow we shall die—doubtless!"

Old Paxton burst into laughter. "Didn't I tell you Brother Belcher was human?" he chuckled.

"One swallow don't make no summer," Pistol said grudgingly.

"Mebbe not," grunted Affable, reaching for the wine, "but one swallow'll sure 'elp!"

Sir Guy was suddenly overwhelmed with an emotion he could not explain. His throat seemed to swell, and his eyes misted. Here was the kind of fellowship the old gods used to boast of! Had ever a man had such true comrades, able to laugh and jest, with Death surrounding them? Even Belcher seemed for once an integral part of the company.

Ellen, feeling his reaction, reached over and squeezed his hand in understanding.

"God bless you all, my merry rogues!" she said, smiling. "Unfortunately, I have naught to contribute."

Affable lowered the wine-skin and made her a curtsy. "M'lydy, 'tis more h'important to feast the eyes than the belly! An' ye be a feast fer any eye."

Sir Guy's mood passed, and with a chuckle, he rescued the wine from Affable.

"Eat up, my hearties!" he told them. "God knows when we'll eat again!"

"Aye," muttered Pistol.

"Aye!" chortled Affable. "W'ere do we go from 'ere, m'lud?"

"North!" said Sir Guy.

Affable tore off sufficient meat to stuff both cheeks, then continued: "H'excellent, Magnificence! But if I might make so bold as to arsk, m'lud, 'ow does ye h'expect to eat an' sleep w'en ye carn't e'en go into one of these 'ere *cursemes* wi'out a royal safe-conduct?"

"I confess that is a technical point which has given me some concern," agreed Mr. Paxton.

Sir Guy glanced sideways at Ellen. "And you, my dear? Are you worried?"

She smiled. "I have the utmost confidence in my husband, sirrah!"

Affable said behind his hand to Pistol: "W'y don't ye 'ave such confowince in me, ye dog?"

Sir Guy reached into his doublet, and withdrawing a parchment, laid it beside the remains of the wine.

"My contribution," he said, smiling.

Affable was pop-eyed. "Lor' love a gallopin' goose!" he squealed. "'Tis the Tsar's own pass!"

"H'impossible!" growled Pistol. "Wi' these own eyes, I saw 'is ludship gi' it to Jug'ead!"

"What you saw," cut in Sir Guy, "was me handing the captain young Ptucha's commission. He had left it in my care. So, if we can keep ahead of the Tsar's couriers, we just may reach *The Dainty Virgin*—God willing!"

Affable staggered erect. "I be ready, sir! I 'ope there's a w'y aroun' Moscow, fer I 'ave no h'affwection fer 'is ruddy 'Oliness."

"There is," Sir Guy assured him. "We can veer . . ."

"But you wouldn't by-pass Moscow and leave Charity!" cried Ellen.

Sir Guy bit his lip. "For the love of God, be reasonable, my dear!" he pleaded. "It will delay us dangerously! Furthermore, it has been over a year since we left her in the Grand Equerry's palace! A lot can happen in twelve months!"

"All the more reason why we should try to rescue poor Charity!" insisted Ellen. "I am not ungrateful for all the sacrifices you men have made in my behalf, yet I am no more worthy of your concern than Charity! I shall not pass Moscow until I have learned what has happened to her! *That* is final!"

Sir Guy shrugged resignedly. "Very well, my dear!" he growled. "Since by your own admission you only learn the hard way, we'll take you so that, next time, perhaps you will trust our judgment."

It was shortly after noon of the third day when they reached the city's gates—obviously an inopportune time, for as traffic was light, the guards on duty had too much leisure to devote to them. They accepted Sir Guy's passport, but insisted on sending for an agent of the *Opritchnina*. At this the little party quailed, expecting another horror comparable to Pojorski, the only example of the *Opritchnina* they had heretofore encountered.

However, the agent proved to be a courteous if somewhat lynx-eyed young man, who interrogated them closely on their past movements and future plans. Fortunately, the company had agreed amongst themselves that Sir Guy would be the only one, ostensibly, who could speak the Russian tongue, and this saved considerable embarrassment. Then, just when all their troubles seemed to be over, the agent calmly picked up the precious passport and announced they would have to come down to police headquarters to recover it before they would be permitted to leave Moscow.

Sir Guy protested this seizure as vehemently as he dared, but when the agent began to grow truculent, he desisted. When they were again in the saddle, he bitterly cursed his luck.

"A pox on Moscow!" he fumed. "I knew no good would come of this! We are the same as in prison!"

Ellen had paled, but said nothing. Affable, however, started rolling his eyes and whistling in such exaggerated fashion, Sir Guy finally burst out in irritation.

"Well, what are you leering about, you oaf?"

Affable tried to look pained, but his eyes twinkled with mirth.

"Lor' love ye, m'lud, I was wonderin' w'at was troublin' yer?"

"Troubling me? God's death! By the time we recover that passport, Jaghellon will have us laid by the heels!"

"Want to bet?"

Sir Guy reined in sharply. "What do you mean? Out with it, knave!"

"Out wi' it, it is, sir!" chortled Affable briskly, and reaching into his coat, pulled out the Tsar's document. " 'Ere she be, m'lud!"

Ellen stared in amazement. "How in heaven's name did you get hold of it, Affable?" she cried.

Mr. Jones chuckled. "W'y, to speak true, m'lydy, 'twasn't strictly in 'eaven's nyme I done it! Sleight o' 'and, ye mout call it!"

"Plain thievery!" cried Belcher. "Thou shalt not steal, sayeth the Lord!"

"Thou shalt not 'ang—if ye carn 'elp it, sayeth Affable Jones," said Affable Jones.

Sir Guy pocketed the safe-conduct. "Thank you, Affable," he grunted, and spurred to the fore.

During the balance of the ride, Sir Guy and his henchmen tried, as subtly as possible, to prepare Ellen for the probable fate of the little London bawd. Finally they arrived at the fateful gate through which they had previously entered the palace, and all dismounted.

Warning the others to stand clear, Sir Guy braced himself to face either the cannon, or, worse, the irate young officer he had encountered on their former visit, then knocked on the portal.

It was promptly opened by a courteous old soldier who bade them enter before he even asked their business. Caught unaware by this welcome, Sir Guy requested to be taken before the Grand Equerry. The ancient was all apologies; unfortunately, he explained, his Worship was not in Moscow at present, but was expected momentarily, for he was escorting the Grand Prince.

Ellen interposed. "Ask about Charity, Guy. He may know if she is alive!"

Sir Guy put the question, but the aged sentry explained that he had but recently come to the palace, and was therefore unacquainted with its distaff history. However, he suggested the Grand Equerry's wife could doubtless give them what information they desired.

Sir Guy winced. "It's hardly a subject to discuss with a *wife!*" he said aside to the others.

Ellen sniffed. "You underestimate wives, my dear! Husbands fool them a whole lot less than some of them think! Tell him we shall see the . . . the whatever they call her."

"Mebbe the *Grand Aquarium!*" offered Affable Jones.

Sir Guy was grimly determined to teach Ellen such a lesson she would, in the future, respect his judgment. So he passed on the request to the sentry. A page was dispatched to notify Madame Smolovitch of their arrival and their request for an audience.

But Sir Guy was puzzled. The place seemed strangely quiet, subdued. Of course, the Grand Equerry doubtless carried most of his convivial companions with him when he traveled. Yet compared to their former visit, the palace seemed deserted. They wandered through great marble halls until at last the little page announced that Madame Smolovitch would greet them immediately in the audience chamber. Then he disappeared.

Ellen looked around the room admiringly. "I think you men exaggerated about this place," she said reprovingly. "I think it is rather nice!"

"You ayant seen the dungeons . . . *yet,* m'lydy!" warned Affable. "We'd best myke this brief. If Smolly's bringin' Ivan 'ere, there's other plyces I'd ruther be."

Sir Guy snorted. "I'd about as soon face Ivan as ask a man's wife if she knows where a little . . . er . . . well, another woman is!"

"Coward!" jeered Ellen. "*I* shall ask her!" Her eyes twinkled mischievously. "As one wife to another!"

Sir Guy found no humor in the situation. "No, no, Ellen! You keep out of this!" he cautioned grimly. "Men can handle these matters much better than . . ."

"*Glory be!*" screamed a familiar voice. "*At last! At last! Oh, God luv ye all!*"

And there was Charity running towards them!

37

THEY ALL GAPED IN ASTONISHMENT. She was heavier in body, and softer in face, but otherwise the same old irrepressible Charity. She smothered Ellen in her arms, hugged and kissed her, then flew suddenly at Sir Guy before he knew what she was about, and planted a noisy buss on his mouth. Whirling like a dervish, she pecked Mr. Paxton on the cheek, tweaked Affable's nose, chucked Pistol under the chin, and remembered Belcher with a dig in the ribs.

"Saints o' glory!" she shrilled. "I've dreamed o' this moment every night since we parted! Sit down an' tell me every blessed thing w'at's 'appened!"

Sir Guy winced, and glanced at Ellen. But when he found his wife staring at the buxom blonde in a kind of hypnotic fascination, he took the bull by the horns himself.

"Hark, Charity, can you get us out of here gracefully before . . . before Madame Smolovitch comes in? You see, we came in search of you, and not knowing just how to go about it, Ellen insisted on asking the Grand Equerry's wife."

"We was all set against it, naturally!" put in Affable.

"You can understand it will be rather embarrassing to meet her with . . . well, I mean, under the circumstances," added Sir Guy.

Charity looked a trifle startled herself. "Ye mean . . . h'embarrassin' because o' me, sir?" she asked.

Sir Guy nodded. "Does she know about . . . you?"

"Some'at," Charity conceded.

"W'at's the ol' bitch like, Charity, m'gal?" asked Affable.

"A reg'ler fire-eater!" warned Charity, rolling her eyes. "A dragon bitch, myke no mistyke!"

Pistol groaned. "Let's get out o' 'ere!"

Sir Guy heartily concurred, but as he turned to speak to Ellen, he found she had grabbed Charity by the shoulders and was looking her in the eye.

"Charity! Who *is* Madame Smolovitch?" she demanded. "Is she . . . ?"

Charity lowered her lids in mock humbleness. "Why, to speak true, m'lydy . . . *I* be!"

Sir Guy whistled in wonderment, and even Mr. Paxton registered surprise. But Affable Jones failed to comprehend.

"Ye be . . . *w'at?*"

"W'y, ye pot-bellied lout—*I be Madame Smolovitch!*" shrieked Charity, and went into another hurricane of laughter.

Affable pretended to faint into a convenient chair, but when Charity with her old-time rowdiness emptied a vase of water over him, he hastily revived. Then as they began to inundate her with questions, she bade them follow and she would lead them to her *secret*.

"For God's sake, make it brief!" warned Sir Guy. "Every minute of delay tightens the noose."

"Brings the 'ounds closer, ye mean!" amended Affable. "Recomember Ivy's comin' an' 'e don't 'ave no lapdogs!"

Anxious and apprehensive, they followed Charity up the great circular staircase to the second floor, thence, to Sir Guy's embarrassment, into the very chamber where he had formerly spent the night. As Charity opened the door, he glimpsed the tapestries still covering the walls.

He stopped short as a thin wail poured out of the chamber. Pistol spun around, prepared for flight.

"God syve me britches!" he yelped. "W'at was *that?*"

This was followed by an even louder shriek from Ellen as she darted into the room and dropped on her knees beside the bed, where, in the center of a priceless counterpane, lay a tiny red-headed infant who peered at them in a wonder only slightly less than their own.

"'Oo's responsible?" gasped Affable, with the normal apprehensiveness of the human tomcat.

Sir Guy kicked him on the shins, and Ellen gave him a glance which, in his own words, sunburned his eyeballs, but Charity took no offense.

"Itchy!" she laughed.

"Carn't s'y as I am," said Affable, puzzled.

"*Itchy!*" repeated Charity, laughing. "Oh, that's me pet nyme for me 'usband, Mister Smolovitch! 'E's a perfeck dear, 'e is! So kind an' considerate, an' cryzy about Guy!"

"About *who?*" gasped Ellen.

Charity giggled. "*Guy* . . . the byby!"

"*Oh, my God!*" choked Sir Guy, his face stinging with the rush of blood.

Ellen tried to look stern, but burst into uncontrollable laughter. Affable was busily counting the months on his fingers. Charity quickly stopped his calculations when she went on gaily: "'Is full nyme be Guy Ivan Affable Boris Paxton Dimitri Pistol Smolovitch!"

Affable threw up his hands in resignation. "Damme, at least I be third on the list o' suspects!" he remarked.

Charity hit him a belt alongside the mouth that sounded like the report of a cannon, and knocked him halfway across the room. But when he stopped rolling, she was smiling as cheerily as before.

"Ye shouldn't s'y sech things, Mister Jones!" she chided. "I'll 'ave ye know I be a respeckable wedded wooman. Matter o' fact, if ye'd got 'ere a couple of weeks earlier, ye'd 'ave been in time fer the weddin'!"

Ellen and Sir Guy exchanged glances. He tried to hide a smile, but Ellen could only wag her head.

"Charity," she said ruefully, "you defeat me!"

"'Cause the weddin' was so far from the beddin', m'lydy?"

Ellen colored. "I have no right to . . ." she began apologetically, but Charity stopped her with a laugh.

"Glory be, I'm right proud to tell ye all about it, m'lydy! Ye see, right arter ye folks left, I felt sorry fer poor Itchy, and was nice to 'im. W'en I started to pooch out, 'e talked o' marryin' me, but I tolt 'im *no*. 'Nay, Itchy,' I s'ys, 'I'll not play second-strumpet to no three thousand columbines!' 'Ye won't 'ave to, me liddle Jar-oddy' ('e allus calls me 'is *liddle Jar-oddy*), 'there's naught but thirty-seven!' 'e s'ys."

"Practically a ruddy pauper!" snorted Pistol. "*On'y thirty-seven!*"

"Itchy allus wanted a son," Charity continued, ignoring the interruption, "an' w'en wee Guy was borned, 'e was beside 'imself wi' joy. But w'en I tolt 'im I was tykin' the little bastard back to England, 'e wept like a chee-ild!"

"Charity!" murmured Ellen. "You shouldn't refer to that adorable little angel in such . . . a . . . well, such terms!"

"But 'e *was* a li'l bastard, m'lydy! Cutest I e'er seen! Anyw'y, Itchy coaxed an' pleaded wi' me to wed up wi' 'im. 'Not until ye get rid o' them columbines.' An' that part took time. There jes' ayant no market fer columbines in summer, so I let 'im fatten 'em up for the autumn auctions. They was some purty stuff, though a mite 'eavy fer English tyste, an' they went fer a song. I was almost sorry fer poor Itchy, but 'e seemed satisfied to be jest a fambly man!" Charity beamed. "We be very 'appy, m'lydy!"

Ellen hugged her impulsively. "I'm so glad for you, darling!" she cried.

"Me'n Itchy be lookin' forward to yer weddin' wit' Ivy!" Charity said. She seemed oblivious of the sudden tension her words brought on, for she continued blithely: "Ivy's a card, so 'e is! A bit 'asty-tempered, but 'e carn be tryned. 'E tried to get fresh wi' me, so I slapped his fyce...."

"The Tsar's fyce?" choked Pistol.

Charity bobbed her head. "Aye, a lusty clout it were! Glory be, was 'e mad! Myde all manner o' threats, 'e did! *'I could 'ave yer 'ead fer that!'* 'e tolt me. *'Aye!'* s'ys I. 'Mebbe ye kin, Mister Terrible, but, by God, that's *all* ye kin 'ave o' me!' sy's I. 'I be a respeckable wedded wooman,' I s'ys, 'an' if ye wants to come into my 'ome, ye'll ack like a gent, er go out on yer butt end!' I tolt him stryte!"

Mr. Paxton sighed. "Well, I believe I can assert without fear of contradiction that I have heard about everything!"

Ellen sank onto the edge of the bed. "Charity," she said slowly, "I cannot marry Ivan!"

Charity's eyes grew large. "'Oly Mother—w'y carn't ye, ma'am?"

"Because ... because ... six nights ago I was wedded to Sir Guy Spangler!"

Charity's scream of delight set the baby to caterwauling and the hounds in the kennels outside to baying.

"God luv ye both!" shrieked Charity, bussing them a second time. "I'm so glad fer ye, m'lydy! Lord knows, I wanted 'im meself, but 'e'd 'ave none o' the likes o' me! W'at a lover 'e mus' be! *Mmnnn!*"

Sir Guy and Ellen received this in understandable silence. But Affable was not inhibited.

"'Er lydyship wouldn't know," he chortled. "Not 'avin' 'ad a chance."

"An' married six d'ys? Oh, w'at a bloody shyme!" cried Charity, all sympathy. "We'll soon fix that! Ye'll 'ave yer 'oneymoon right 'ere! Itchy an' Ivy'll be 'ome in a few hours, an' though Ivy'll be disappointed, 'e'll tyke it...."

Sir Guy took over. "Charity, please listen to me!" he said firmly. "Ellen and I deeply appreciate your thoughtfulness, but had we dreamed of your situation, much as we love you, we'd not have come."

Charity's eyes filled. "Ye mean, sir, ye'd 'ave gone aw'y wi'out ..."

"Only because we wouldn't want to involve you in trouble," he cut her off. "We are fleeing for our lives from Ivan's Cossacks. Not knowing you were married, we came to take you with us."

"*Never!*" cried Charity. "What would I be back in England?"

"Alive!" breathed Affable grimly.

Charity paid no attention to him. "In England, I'd be naught but a

[301]

dirty little street 'arlot, kicked 'ere an' there, to dance me tune at the end o' a rope, else rot aw'y!"

"Wouldst rather live in sin in this pagan hell-hole?" demanded Belcher.

"I ayant in *sin,* ye brayin' ass!" retorted Charity. "I be as good as any woman in Muscovy! I got me an 'ome, a faithful 'usband, an' a son! W'at more could a girl arsk o' life?"

"*Nothing!*" said Ellen, giving the assorted males a look which sealed their lips. "You have everything that counts, and I only hope that some day Guy and I can boast of as much. But now we must get out of Moscow. . . ."

"Bloody small chance!" growled Affable. "We run the gantlet onc't tod'y!"

Since Charity didn't comprehend the allusion, Ellen told her briefly of their trials and tribulations. Charity listened wide-eyed, then offered to hide them until she could discuss the matter with her "Itchy." But Sir Guy wouldn't hear of it.

"Absolutely not!" he said with finality. "You have won your own place here in Moscow, and we're not going to spoil it. You just don't realize how serious this is, Charity."

"I'm wonderin' if ye do, sir!" she retorted grimly. "Ye carn't jes walk out o' Moscow like ye kin Lunnon Town!"

Pistol sniffed. "Mebbe they'll cart us out, feet fust!"

Affable laughed. "Under turnips, no doubt!"

Sir Guy snapped his fingers. "Capital! By my troth, my hearts, you've given me an idea!"

"If it's to do wi' turnips, yer Gryce, I'd ruther gi' Ivan's 'ounds a cyse o' indigestion!" said Pistol.

"We'll rent a wagon and get hauled out," schemed Sir Guy. "If we did it once, we can do it again."

"What if we encounter Mister Terrible?" queried old Paxton with a gentle smile.

" 'Ell, 'e carn't get 'ere so soon," scoffed Pistol. "It'll tyke 'im . . ."

" 'E's due 'ere fer dinner this evenin'!" Charity told them. "Ye'd better let me 'ide ye an' . . ."

"No!" said Sir Guy. "As for Ivan—why, it is always safer to charge than retreat. We'll pass through his lines if necessary."

" 'E'd pass through the jaws an' belly o' a lion, 'e would!" admired Affable Jones.

"Charity, where can I engage a wagon?" Guy asked. "Something large enough to carry us all."

Charity pouted thoughtfully. "I think I knows," she said after a pause. "Wyte 'ere a moment!" She hurried out of the room.

There was an awkward silence when she was gone. Ellen picked up wee Guy and stared at him in wonder. Belcher discovered the lascivious tapestries and stomped closer to focus his eyes.

"Well, I s'y!" exclaimed Affable delightedly. "W'at 'ave we 'ere?"

"A bloomin' Garden o' Eve!" yelped Pistol. "Pitchers o' 'eaven!"

"It is absolutely incredible!" said Sir Guy. "Imagine our little Charity the wife of the first minister of Muscovy, and slapping the Tsar and threatening to boot him out of her home!"

Old Paxton smiled. "I'm not so certain it doesn't make sense," he reasoned. "Charity would have delighted the old gods, for where now most women depend on virtue to shield them, Charity wears an impenetrable armor of absolute sincerity. With it, she can even face up to the formidable Ivan the Terrible!"

"*Mister Terrible,* she called him!" appended Sir Guy, wincing.

Ellen burst into laughter. "Guy, dearest, what was your remark about *men handling these matters better than . . . ?*"

"All right! All right!" growled Sir Guy. "I know when I'm beaten!"

The subject was hastily dropped as Charity burst into the room.

"Everythin's arrynged!" she announced gaily. "Me coach'll be at the door real soon."

"*Your* coach?" growled Sir Guy. "But I told you . . ."

Charity interrupted with a pitying smile. "M'lud, ye're a wedded man now, so yer d'ys o' givin' all the h'orders be o'er!"

"Bravo!" laughed Ellen.

"But seriously, sir, there jes' ayant no plyce in Moscow w'ere ye can rent wagons wi'out h'embarrassin' questions."

"I don't want to put you in jeopardy," Guy insisted.

Charity smiled again. "'Ave I ever fyled ye yet, sir?" When he started to praise her, she silenced him with a gesture. "Then 'old yer tongue, m'lud, an' let me 'ave me w'y this larst time." Dismissing the subject, she beamed on Ellen who was holding little Guy.

"Ayant 'e an innercent wee thing, m'lydy?" she murmured lovingly.

"Bless him, he is that," agreed Ellen. "But . . ." She hesitated, then went on: "Charity my dear, I do not wish to interfere, but these . . . er . . . these pictures are hardly suitable for a child in its formative years."

Charity turned and frowned at the tapestries. "W'y, w'at's wrong wi' 'em, m'lydy?" she asked finally. "I thought 'em rather pretty!"

Ellen winced, and Sir Guy hid a smile. "Well, to speak plainly,"

Ellen said, her face flushing, "they might put some wrong ideas into the tender mind of a young child."

"Oh?" Charity stared at them speculatively, turning her head first one way, then the other. At last she nodded.

"Aye, I sees w'at ye mean, m'lydy!"

A husky Kalmuck thrust his head into the chamber to announce that "Madame's coach" was ready.

The coach was a crude affair, better suited to the hauling of logs than passengers, but it did have four wheels which rolled. That, as Sir Guy politely insisted, was all that counted. The body was a boxlike structure, covered with a canopy and curtains obviously borrowed from a poster-bed. This ponderous conveyance was drawn, or, more accurately, *dragged,* by a four-horse team guided by a postilion. The convenience notably lacking was any form of springs.

This latter fact Sir Guy and his cohorts discovered the hard way; all, that is, save Ellen who, in the garb of a female servant and holding Charity's baby on her lap, sat primly on a silken cushion which modified the spine-shattering jolts. But the men lay flat on their backs on the unrelieved floor-boards, and in addition to their other sufferings were covered with a great stinking, half-cured polar bear-skin which, if it shielded them from stray glances, also nauseated, sweated, and smothered them at the same time.

Charity fair bubbled with excitement as they trundled down the long avenue in front of the Kremlin.

"Glory be, m'lydy!" she cried, beaming happily at Ellen. "D'ye e'er think ye'd be ridin' down the streets o' Moscow wi' Guy on yer lap?"

"You mean with her heel on Guy's neck, don't you, Charity?" came a strangled voice from beneath the bear-skin.

Ellen smiled. "A lot of things have happened that I never expected," she said, tapping the "lump" under her foot.

They reached the gate without incident; the same gate through which Sir Guy and his company had entered but a few hours earlier. Here a very young and very impolitic sentry insisted that he must search the conveyance before he could permit it to pass out of the city. At this, Sir Guy and his fellow-fugitives thought the game was over, but an instant later, with a snort like the pop of a champagne cork, Charity went into verbal action.

"'Ark, ye snivelin' illegitimate offspring o' a pox-ridden camel—*d'ye know 'oo I be?*"

The sentry did not, but his education was soon brought up to date when an officer, awakened from his nap by Charity's screeches, came dashing out of the guardhouse.

"Mother of God!" he thundered at the confused sentry. "Don't you know better than to interfere with the beautiful wife of our illustrious Grand Equerry?"

"But . . . but . . ."

"Silence!" thundered the officer. "Madame," he purred at Charity, "permit me in person to open the gates for you!"

Charity smiled her permission, and as the officer scuttled to comply, she winked at Ellen.

"Ne'er forget, m'lydy," she remarked *sotto voce,* "any myle can be 'andled if ye tykes the proper h'approach."

"You've almost convinced me," giggled Ellen, stabbing Sir Guy's head with her heel.

As the gates slammed behind them, Charity sighed. "O'ny a league more, then we parts," she murmured dreamily. "Let's 'ave no tears, fer we each o' us got w'at we want."

"W'at I want be fresh air!" sputtered Affable from beneath the rug. "Ayant we far enough past that damn gate to come up fer a snort?"

Though calm enough, Charity's voice held a slight edge when she replied: "Aye, ye're far 'nough past the gyte, Mr. Jones, but unless ye're anxious to meet me 'usband an' Mr. Ivan Terrible in the next two minutes, ye'd better keep yer noggin down!"

"Oh, dear heaven!" gasped Ellen. "This is the end!"

And that seemed to be the case, for a turn in the road had brought them face to face with the Tsar and his retinue. Riding stirrup to stirrup with Ivan the Terrible was Boris Smolovitch, the Grand Equerry.

When Ellen whispered this devastating news to her husband, he said grimly, "Courage, my love! If you keep cool they may not even notice us!"

The postilion was swerving the team out of the main rut. "It is barely possible . . ." Ellen began when she was drowned out by a frantic screech from Charity.

"*Itchy!*" she bawled. "*It . . . CHEE!* That's my 'usband!" she added gratuitously.

"Well, that did it!" sighed Affable. "Start prayin', Belchy darlin'!"

"But not too loud," warned Ellen, "because the gentleman in question is headed this way!"

The Grand Equerry rode up alongside the coach, beamed on little Guy, the baby, touched Ellen briefly with his eyes, then leaned over to kiss his wife.

"Mine liddle Jar-oddy!" he whispered affectionately.

"Itchy, m'lover!" yelped Charity ecstatically, then added: "I got so bloody 'ungry fer a sight o' ye, I brung little Guy to meet ye! But go 'long wi' Ivy, an' we'll follow."

The minister paused for another sidelong glance at Ellen.

"Itchy!" said Charity warningly. "Go 'long wi' ye!"

The Grand Equerry sighed. "Liddle Jar-oddy, I have bad news for you," he said slowly. "Your English friends are"—the suspenseful pause was almost unbearable—"*dead!*"

Charity's voice was almost relieved. "*Dead?*"

The minister nodded. "Captain Jaghellon arrived two days ago with the news," he told her. "They were on a ferry that overturned in the storm."

"'Ow did Ivy tyke it?"

"Hard," conceded the Grand Equerry. "Very hard. He had Jaghellon executed. He ordered torture, but when he turned the chore over to Pojorski, the dwarf, the scoundrel bungled: he killed Jaghellon almost instantly—with a harp string, of all things! Ivan suspected collusion, and banned him forever as executioner." He sighed heavily. "I know this will upset you, my cherub, yet unfortunately, I cannot come with you now. . . ."

"Oh, that's all right, Itchy!" Charity interrupted hastily. "If ye don't mind, I'll ride a way into the country wi' me grief an' try to shake off the memories w'at 'aunt me! I'll see ye 'n Ivy at supper!"

"Excellent!" approved the First Minister of Muscovy. He leaned forward to kiss her once again, and as he straightened was heard to say: "By the way, Jar-oddy, you might advise your *memory* with the big feet to pull them back into the carriage before Ivan notices them. Good-bye!"

Leaving a paralyzed little group of Britons, he rejoined his Prince. And in this wise Ivan IV, Tsar of All the Russias, and Boris Smolovitch, his Grand Equerry, pass out of this chronicle and into the mists and myths of history.

EPILOGUE or
Author's Addendum:

. . . and so endeth our tale, for when a man and a maid achieve their hearts' desire, and have naught but a fair wind and fair tide ahead, there's insufficient wool from which to spin out a yarn. In any event, no journal or other record exists of that northern trek of Sir Guy and Lady Spangler, nor of their long voyage home. Yet though all this happened nigh four hundred years ago, my affection for this lusty little company was such that curiosity impelled me to try and learn what ultimately became of them. The results of this research were somewhat spotty, yet it warmed my heart to know that . . . dear old Paxton was knighted for a scientific treatise he wrote on Slavic languages (though I own to wishing he had written a journal of his adventures instead); that Sergeant Pistol, according to the parish records of Winchester, married a widow of uncertain age but *not* uncertain fortune; that Affable Jones remained (insofar as official records reveal) a Whitefriars divorcé and established a very lucrative sporting club in London; that Master Lymeburner distinguished himself in the immortal sea battle when the Spanish Armada tried to attack England; and that Horace Belcher (Affable's "darlin' Belch") not only got his vicarage, but, miraculously enough, ultimately became a *bishop*.

Being unable to gain access to the archives of the Kremlin, I cannot be specific about Charity. Howbeit, in Hakluyt is the account of an English merchant who penetrated into Muscovy by way of Persia in the year 1617, and while his report does not identify Charity by name, it refers to a remarkable old woman then residing in Moscow who spoke Russian with a "Whitefriars accent," had thirteen stalwart sons, all with English-given names, and was adored by everyone. To my mind, this could only have been our little Charity.

As for Sir Guy and Lady Ellen—the records, if cold, are illuminating. That the venture was a financial as well as a romantic success is self-evident, for in 1580, Sir Guy purchased a great manor house in Surrey. A contemporary memoir has it that when Elizabeth heard the details of the escapade, she scolded Sir Guy in public and kissed him in private, for as Francis Drake, Magnus Carter,* and other lusty adventurers of the period early discovered, Elizabeth had a delightful sense of humor and a forgiving nature—just so long as she profited thereby. And in Sir Guy's case, it is obvious she was not unduly displeased, for two years after his return to England, he was elevated to a peerage. He and Ellen lived to ripe old ages, and had twelve sons. This is, admittedly, one less than Charity, but then Charity had a running start on Ellen.

FINIS

* See *Magnus the Magnificent* for details of this fabulous rover and adventurer.

HISTORICAL NOTES

While it is not my intention to append a bibliography, nor to substantiate every statement in a work of fiction, nevertheless, certain facts are so extremely interesting, the more-than-casual reader may wish to explore them further. For this reason, these brief notes are added.

Page 11. [1] In 1553, a British vessel seeking a northern passage to China and India landed on the coast of the White Sea, and thus Russia was *discovered* by the English peoples. A commercial treaty was soon consummated, and a *Companie for Trading with Muscovy, Persia, and Northern Lands* was formed; this was commonly known as the "English Muscovy Company" or just the "Russia Company." It was, of course, a rigid monopoly, and when Elizabeth came to the throne, she cut herself a piece of the cake.

Page 29. [2] The "Mary Hastings" incident is true—basically, that is, for in studying six *authentic* histories of Russia, I find six variations of the story. One, for instance, claims the Hastings girl, though flattered by the Tsar's offer, refused to leave England; another version declares she became Ivan's sixth wife, but complicated things by falling in love with the Tsar's emissary, Nikita Romanov, which understandably caused considerable excitement in Moscow. There is also a painting existent which portrays Ivan and Nikita playing a chess game to decide which of them would have Mary.

Page 59. [3] It is, apparently, impossible for the so-called Western mind to comprehend either the Russian character or the Russian temperament, hence Ivan IV heads the popular list of Slavic "villains." Whether he was a whit more cruel or more vicious than other monarchs of his era is, to my mind, a moot question, and I have tried to be as unbiased and objective as careful research would permit. And while I have certainly not glorified him, I have been kinder than most of the popular histories. The incidents of the scalding soup and the slaying of his own son are, reputedly, true.

Page 69. [4] This *Parade of the Virgins* is a persistent legend, although I cannot vouch for its authenticity. It may have been apocryphal, or mere wishful thinking on the part of the early historians.

Page 75. [5] This enforced isolation of Russia four centuries ago may well have supplied the groundwork for her attitudes and suspicions of today. In any event, whether we like it or not, the existence of the political barrier at that time is irrefutable.

Page 98. [6] The facts about the *Oprichnina* are as I have them in the story. It would appear that the Russian penchant for secret police organizations has a historic basis, doubtless from necessity.

Page 104. [7] The "Chastity Belt" should require no explanation for the modern reader. It belonged to the days "when knighthood was in flower"; when chivalrous knights fared forth in search of romance and adventure, but took this precaution to insure that during the knight's indefinite absence, his wife didn't find romance and adventure at home. And while this contrivance tantalizes our imagination, the old-time knight doubtless reasoned that if he could ride about the countryside in the hot sun, buckled up in steel armor, his wife could certainly tolerate being riveted by the local blacksmith into well-ventilated wrought-iron "panties."

Page 147. [8] An actual *Trial by Combat* was experienced by Master Henri Lane in Moscow, in the year 1560, following a controversy with a certain Sheray Costromitskey (whose name I borrowed). Master Lane, not feeling up to the contest, provided a brawny Englishman named Robert Best to substitute for him, whereupon Costromitskey's "champion" refused to fight.

Page 183. [9] I uncovered this droll method of divorce in a venerable book about London. It was delightfully uncomplicated—for everyone save the poor cat—and rigidly adhered to the letter of the law, if not the spirit.

Page 220. [10] The episode of *The White Mare* was lifted right out of history. Sigismond Augustus, King of the Poles, was feeling his oats when, about 1560, Ivan of Muscovy made proposals to Augustus' sister Catherine, so instead of sister Catherine, he sent the White Mare, with a sarcastic message, much as I have it.

Page 220. [11] When Ivan was but eighteen, he fed his first victim to the hounds; one of his three self-appointed guardians, sparing the other two "in his great clemency," as the old historian explained. Since he was almost always accompanied by his hounds, this summary mode of solving problems expedited matters considerably.

Page 228. [12] Fantastic as it may sound, this incident of the angry bees protecting a village is sworn to by Adam Alearius, an early traveler into Muscovy.